Worship Sacraments
We Celebrate, We Praise

Second Edition

Mary Kathleen Glavich, S.N.D.
Loretta Pastva, S.N.D.

General Editor: Loretta Pastva, S.N.D.

Now this is the message that we have heard from him and proclaim to you: God is light, and in him there is no darkness at all. But if we walk in the light as he is in the light, then we have fellowship with one another, and the blood of his Son Jesus cleanses us from all sin.
—1 John 1:5, 7

Benziger Publishing Company
Woodland Hills, California

Consultant
The Reverend Ronald A. Pachence, Ph.D.
Associate Professor Practical Theology
Director, Institute for Christian
Ministries, University of San Diego.

Nihil Obstat
Reverend Paul J. Sciarrotta, S.T.L.
Censor Deputatus

Imprimatur
The Most Reverend Anthony M. Pilla, D.D., M.A.
Bishop of Cleveland
Given at Cleveland, Ohio, on 3 February 1991

The nihil obstat and imprimatur are official declarations that a book or pamphlet is free of doctrinal or moral error. No implication is contained therein that those who have granted the nihil obstat and imprimatur agree with the contents, opinions, or statements expressed.

Scripture passages are taken from *The New American Bible with Revised New Testament,* copyright © 1988 by the Confraternity of Christian Doctrine, Washington, D.C. All rights reserved.

Excerpts from *Vatican Council II, The Conciliar and Post Conciliar Documents,* Austin Flannery, O.P., ed., reprinted with permission of Costello Publishing Co., Inc., Northport, NY 11768. Excerpts from the English translation of the *Roman Missal* © 1973, ICEL. All rights reserved.

Revision Editor
Ronald A. Pachence, Ph.D.

Copyright © 1992 by the Glencoe Division of Macmillan/McGraw-Hill School Publishing Company. All rights reserved. Except as permitted under the United States Copyright Act, no part of this publication may be reproduced or distributed in any form or by any means, or stored in a database or retrieval system, without the prior written permission of the publisher.

Printed in the United States of America.

Send all inquiries to:
BENZIGER PUBLISHING COMPANY
21600 Oxnard Street, Suite 500
Woodland Hills, California 91367

Second Edition

ISBN 0-02-655837-8 (Student's Edition)
ISBN 0-02-655838-6 (Teacher's Annotated Edition)

6 7 8 9 10 11 12 13   003   05 04 03 02 01 00

Cover Art: *Supper at Emmaus* by Caravaggio:
Reproduced by courtesy of the Trustees,
The National Gallery, London

Contents

Recognizing God's Presence

Chapter

1	Seeing the Face of God	6
2	Emmanuel—God with Us in Jesus	34
3	Jesus Lives On in the Church	62

Celebrating God's Presence in the Sacraments

Chapter

4	Signs and Symbols: Language of the Heart	88
5	Sacraments and Christian Worship	110
6	Sacraments of Initiation	132
7	The Table of Unity	162
8	Sacraments of Vocation	192
9	Our Need for Healing	222
10	Sacraments of Healing	250

Living in God's Presence Now and Forever

Chapter

11	Cycles of Time in the Worship of the Church	280
12	Taking Time to Praise God	308
13	Mary and the Saints: Roadsigns from the Past	334
14	Our Passage from Time to Eternity	360
15	Our Final Destiny	390
	Index	412

Acknowledgments

The authors wish to thank Sister Mary Joell Overman, S.N.D., Superior General, Rome; Sister Rita Mary Harwood, S.N.D., Provincial Superior of the Sisters of Notre Dame, Chardon, Ohio; and Sister Margaret Mary McGovern, S.N.D., Assistant Superintendent, Education, Diocese of Cleveland, Eastern Region, who supported and encouraged the writing of the *Light of the World* series.

Humble gratitude is also due to all who in any way helped to create the *Light of the World* series: parents, teachers, co-workers, students, and friends. The following deserve special mention for their assistance in planning, organizing, testing, or critiquing the series: Notre Dame Sisters Mary Dolores Abood, Ann Baron, Karla Bognar, Mary Brady, Mary Catherine Caine, Virginia Marie Callen, Deborah Carlin, Naomi Cervenka, Reean Coyne, Mary Dowling, Patricia Mary Ferrara, Dorothy Fuchs, Kathleen Glavich, Margaret Mary Gorman, Jacquelyn Gusdane, Margaret Harig, Joanmarie Harks, Nathan Hess, Sally Huston, Christa Jacobs, Joanne Kepler, Owen Kleinhenz, Mary Jean Korejwo, Elizabeth Marie Kreager, Leanne Laney, William David Latiano, Aimee Levy, Ann McFadden, Inez McHugh, Louismarie Nudo, Donna Marie Paluf, Helen Mary Peter, Nancy Powell, Eileen Marie Quinlan, Patricia Rickard, Mark Daniel Roscoe, Kathleen Ruddy, Kathleen Scully, Dolores Stanko, Melannie Svoboda, Mary Louise Trivison, Donna Marie Wilhelm, Laura Wingert; Dr. Jean Alvarez, Ms. Mary Anderson; Ms. Meg Bracken; Sister Mary Kay Cmolik, O.F.M.; Mr. Robert Dilonardo, Rev. Mark DiNardo, Ms. Linda Ferrando, Mr. Michael Homza, Sister Kathleen King, H.H.M., Ms. Patricia Lange, Mr. James Marmion, Mr. Peter Meler, Rev. Herman P. Moman, Rev. Guy Noonan, T.O.R., Ms. Christine Smetana, and Ms. Karen Sorace.

The following high schools piloted materials: Bishop Ireton High School, Alexandria, Virginia; Clearwater Central Catholic High School, Clearwater, Florida; Elyria Catholic High School, Elyria, Ohio; Erieview Catholic High School, Cleveland, Ohio; John F. Kennedy High School, Warren, Ohio; Notre Dame Cathedral Latin High School, Chardon, Ohio; Regina High School, South Euclid, Ohio; St. Edward High School, Cleveland, Ohio; St. Matthias High School, Huntington Park, California.

The following parishes piloted the original Abridged Lessons: Corpus Christi, Cleveland, Ohio; St. Anselm, Chesterland, Ohio; St. John Nepomucene, Cleveland, Ohio; St. Thomas More, Paducah, Kentucky.

Special appreciation and thanks to Sister M. Dolores Stanko, S.N.D., for typing the final manuscripts of the series as well as for her many helpful suggestions and her insightful editorial assistance. Deep appreciation to Mrs. Anita Johnson for research; to Sisters of Notre Dame Mary Regien Kingsbury, De Xavier Perusek, and Seton Schlather; to Robert Clair Smith for special services; and to typists Sisters Catherine Rennecker, S.N.D., Josetta Marie Livignano, S.N.D., and Ms. Charlaine Yomant.

Photo Credits

Alinari/Art Resource, N.Y., 77, 291
Arnold & Brown, 36, 41, 62, 88, 110, 120, 167, 192, 194, 224, 227, 263, 271, 273, 308, 360, 374, 376, 383, 384
Bill Aron/PhotoEdit, 65, 81
James L. Ballard, 11, 205, 222, 316
Roger B. Bean, 12, 36, 91, 208, 243, 284, 311
The Bettmann Archive, 56, 99, 105, 398, 405
Carnival Cruise Lines, 407
Catholic News Service, 68, 72, 287, 301, 304, 379, 386, 400
   J. Michael Fitzgerald, 58
   Shannon Flynn, 144
   Frank Methe, 115, 203
   Roger W. Neal, 202
   Chris Niedenthal, 298
   Gene Plaisted, 128, 136, 303
   Chris Sheridan, 216
   Ron Thomas, 66
   Paul Williams, 217
Chicago Catholic Publications, 74
Myrleen Ferguson/PhotoEdit, 43
David R. Frazier Photolibrary, Inc., 20, 104, 199
Tony Freeman/PhotoEdit, 148
Ann Garvin, 57, 232, 245, 313, 328
Gorman Typesetting, Inc., 286
Grumman Corporation, 34
Charles Hofer, 196
Impact Communications, 112
Kenji Kerins, 172, 173, 185, 213, 215, 218, 275
Erich Lessing/PhotoEdit, 30
Rick MacDonald & Co./James Carlson, 8
Stephen McBrady, 75, 83, 96, 132, 146, 154, 157, 158, 162, 250, 347
North Wind Picture Archives, 16, 18, 19, 25, 26, 27, 29, 39, 47, 48, 53, 113, 169, 235, 252, 254, 256, 302, 337, 338, 342, 343, 345, 346, 351, 352, 354, 362, 392, 395, 406
Alan Oddie/PhotoEdit, 118, 145
P&W Builders, Inc./Roger B. Bean, 318
Peoria Notre Dame High School, Peoria, IL/Arnold & Brown, 72, 125, 165, 262
Peoria Notre Dame High School, Peoria, IL/Roger B. Bean, 93, 101, 164, 174, 177, 179, 290, 296, 299
Liz Purcell, 100, 151, 255
Reuters/Bettmann Newsphotos, 229, 326, 363
Jerome Riordan, 390
Doug Schermer, 24, 40, 80, 119, 134, 135, 182, 207, 241, 261, 267, 285, 365, 366, 367, 373
St. Bernard's Church, Peoria, IL/Arnold & Brown, 147
St. Francis Woods, Peoria, IL/Roger B. Bean, 187, 297
St. Mark's Church, Peoria, IL/Arnold & Brown, 327
St. Martin de Porres, Peoria, IL/Arnold & Brown, 126, 141, 188
St. Martin de Porres, Peoria, IL/Roger B. Bean, 21, 334
St. Mary's Cathedral, Peoria, IL/Arnold & Brown, 120, 186, 280, 339, 350, 353, 356, 364
St. Thomas Church, Peoria, IL/Arnold & Brown, 84, 140, 320
UPI/Bettmann Newsphotos, 64, 324
United Nations, 6, 55
Wide World Photos, Inc., 237
Woodruff High School/Roger B. Bean, 80, 265, 319, 377
Duane R. Zehr, 90

CHAPTER 1

Seeing the Face of God

OBJECTIVES

In this Chapter you will

- Understand the meaning of mystery.

- Recognize how ancient peoples experienced the Divine Presence and see that Presence in your own life.

- Be challenged to action by the faith of the Hebrew people.

In past ages, God let the Gentiles go their way. Yet in bestowing His benefits, He has not hidden Himself completely, without a clue.
—Acts of the Apostles 14:16-17

SECTION 1
The Experience of Mystery

Sherlock Holmes, Columbo, and Hercule Poirot are popular heroes in a unique form of entertainment: the mystery. But while most people like mystery stories, many seem strangely uneasy with mystery itself.

A Sense of Mystery

On December 21, 1968, Apollo 8 blasted off from Cape Canaveral on the first journey that humans made to the moon. The crew of this mission did not attempt a moon landing. Their job was simply to circle around the moon and return the command module and its occupants safely home.

It is difficult for us to imagine how great a technological achievement this was. Back in the late 1960s, computer science wasn't as advanced as it is today. Astronauts took great risks to fly the Apollo spacecraft, and because they had to put their lives in jeopardy, everyone who took to the stars was a highly trained, scientifically minded professional.

But on the way home on Christmas Eve, the three-man crew of Apollo 8 did something that surprised everyone: they took turns reading the creation story in Chapter 1 of the Book of Genesis aloud over their radio, a broadcast directed all over the earth. They were the first people in history to see our planet from a distance, and the sight of planet earth—so fragile and yet so beautiful—moved them to experience the mysterious presence of the Creator. They realized, perhaps as never before, that their lives and all of life depended upon God's presence.

Chapter 1   Seeing the Face of God

 On the Record

Unsolved Mysteries

Most people are familiar with the four unsolved mysteries described below. Identify as many as you can by matching them with the following descriptions.

　　____ Nazca Lines
　　____ UFOs
　　____ Loch Ness Monster
　　____ Yeti

1. These are strange objects, supposedly from outer space.
2. These "abominable snowmen" are upright creatures with pointed heads and very definite humanoid features. Their twelve-to-twenty-inch-long footprints have been photographed.
3. This giant sea slug or newt was first seen in a Scottish lake by an abbot in A.D. 565. Nearly two hundred other people have since seen this creature.
4. These drawings, which are forty miles long, are in the Peruvian desert. From the air, they portray geometric figures, animals, insects, flowers and gods.

None of the science these astronauts had learned quite prepared them for this experience. They were overwhelmed at the mystery of it all, so they offered a prayer that was heard around the world.

Natural Mystery

People tend to avoid facing things that can't be explained. Mysteries—shows, movies, or books that feature unsolved cases—soon die. Whodunits must be challenging, but in the end they must also be solvable. People want answers, not further questions. They are frustrated by plots left with no resolution.

Magicians have a way of holding us spellbound. Even the simplest tricks keep us wondering how they were performed.

Worship and Sacraments: We Celebrate, We Praise

Many people insist that every mystery can eventually be fully explained. They are trained to believe that every effect has a cause. These people seem to take it for granted that someone will find the missing link, the undiscovered virus, or the unknown quantity.

To others, there is something fascinating about real mystery, even though it somehow makes them admit their limitations. Magic shows, hypnotism, demonstrations of ESP, and other evidence of the mysterious exercise a strange power over this group. Realizing that some things may be beyond them stirs these people to awe and wonder.

Recognition that some things are beyond human understanding is the beginning of the experience of what we call "the transcendent." When we speak of transcendence, we are referring to a wide range of human experiences which cannot be accounted for by simple explanations like, for example, our desire to understand the meaning of life, our capacity to love and to hope, our longing for peace and life without end, and our sense of unity with those who have lived before us. At this point, we are confronted by a great mystery—the mystery of the transcendent.

The Mystery of Life

Life itself is the greatest mystery—one that humankind has always pondered. A child begins with questions such as, "Why is grass green?" "Why does it rain?" "Where does the sun go at night?" The experiences of adolescence and adulthood prompt more challenging questions: "Why do I exist?" "Why do the innocent suffer?" "Why is there evil in the world?" "How can I be happy?" "Why must we die?" Some additional obvious problems include strife among nations, poverty, hunger, and crime.

While philosophers spend their lives trying to find answers to such questions, the rest of us are on a personal search for some framework to give meaning to the mystery of life or to reinforce our belief systems. We want to know that we have value, that our lives have purpose, and that efforts to build a better world are worthwhile. Faced with daily problems and aware that the world could be reduced to ashes in nuclear warfare, we ask, "What's it all about?"

ESP: abbreviation that means extrasensory perception.

Transcendence: the condition of being above and independent of the material universe.

The answer to the mystery of human existence has never been obvious, or there would be a worldwide consensus. As it is, there are two basic responses to our human situation, and both require faith. One response notes a lack of "observable evidence" for a divine dimension. It includes three groups: those who deny a greater-than-human hand behind the universe (**atheists**); those who decide that whether there is a Creator or not, is in all probability unknowable, so that faith doesn't make any practical difference in life (**agnostics**); and those who believe that even if there is a Creator, this maker is uninvolved in human events (**deists**). Holders of these positions constitute a relatively small minority in history.

The other response comes from the faithful: all the people who have been gifted with a more integrated view of life. In acknowledging a creative and guiding hand behind all things, these people recognize a purpose in the universe and in their own existence. In the power of knowing and being able to communicate with God to form a loving relationship, they find their lives infinitely enriched. They experience meaning in all they do, deep motivation for living in harmony with others, and the means to deal with the problems that afflict us all.

Although this is the position of the majority of people who have lived, if we opt for the existence of a caring God, we must do so by faith. Our conviction must rest on something other than merely human or "observable" evidence; it involves accepting the word of God by faith.

1. *How do you think the crew of Apollo 8 was changed by their experience of seeing earth from space?*

2. *Name some times or places when you have sensed mystery. What did this experience feel like?*

3. *Why do you think people wonder about the meaning of life instead of simply living for the moment? How, in your view, is the life of a believer different than the life of an atheist?*

Experiencing God's Presence

Almost everyone has experienced revelation in the beauties of **nature**. A Catholic and her agnostic friend were walking along the beach late one afternoon. The Catholic said that she had to go home to get ready for evening Mass. The nonbeliever, lost in wonder at a magnificent sunset, gasped, "I couldn't leave this even to pray." What he didn't realize was that, in a sense, he was being drawn to God, whose power and beauty are both revealed and hidden in the setting sun.

Others find that God is revealed through their **consciences**. Perhaps you have felt uneasy or somehow discontent when you were untruthful, dishonest, unjust, or unmerciful. This is the Holy Spirit challenging you. The world's great repentant sinners, such as Mary Magdalene and Saint Augustine, are examples of people who responded to an inner conviction to be holy like God.

A third way in which we may receive revelation occurs in our **relationships** with other people. The love others show us builds our worth and dignity, lends meaning to life, and introduces us to God's love. In the love of others, especially of those who may be unable to make little return of love, like the poor, the hungry, and the imprisoned, we also meet God in what has been called "the sacrament of the neighbor."

A fourth source of revelation is the inability of even the most ideal love to completely satisfy our **longing for happiness**. It suggests that we are made for something far beyond the best this world has to offer. Finally, the profound experiences of birth, maturation, tragedy, and death likewise show us that we are open to the transcendent. In all these ways, we recognize a divine presence in the universe by the use of our natural powers.

God's presence is often experienced through our relationships with other people.

What Is Faith?

Faith is a word that describes a complex experience. Here are a few ways in which we understand the word.

Faith is conviction. When the Wright brothers first experimented with flight, they had faith; that is, they held a conviction that if they applied certain principles or insights received as a gift from earlier scientists, they could revolutionize transportation. Religious faith can be viewed as the conviction that God's word to us in Scripture and in the ministry of Jesus is worthy of acceptance. We believe that if we apply the principles that flow from faith, life itself can be happier and more meaningful.

Faith is trust. When you fly, you put your faith in the pilot, trusting his or her integrity and ability to handle the plane. Religious faith is putting our trust in God. It is a person-to-person relationship based on trust in the power of Christ as the Son of God. But, just as it is important for a pilot to follow flight rules, it is important for us not to sit back passively and expect God to do all the work.

Parachutists put their faith into the hands of the parachute maker and the persons who packed them. This parachutist had complete trust in these people.

Faith is action. The Wrights got into their planes and flew, staking their lives on what they believed. As Christians, we stake our lives on the credibility of God's Word, Jesus. In a personal commitment to Christ, we take the initiative to feed the hungry, promote peace, and do whatever else is necessary to build God's kingdom. So, our faith must include knowledge, trust, and action. "For just as a body without a spirit is dead, so also faith without works is dead" (James 2:26).

---

4. As if you were telling a story, name the details of time, place, and circumstances of a situation in which you had to believe in someone or rely solely on someone else's word. Describe your feelings during and after the experience.

5. Describe an occasion when you experienced a need to rely on God. What inner thoughts, feelings, or memories passed through your mind?

6. Do you think that people who follow other religions have genuine faith? What reasons can you give for your answer?

Summary

- No matter how much we learn about our world, we will always sense that there is a deeper meaning or purpose to life. We call this deeper meaning the mystery of life.

- Faith is a response to the mystery of life which says that all life comes from God. God's mysterious Presence in our world invites us to understand the ultimate purpose of creation.

- Some people reject faith because they believe that some day science will be able to answer all our questions about life. This "belief" in science, however, is also an "act of faith."

SECTION 1
Checkpoint!

■ Review

1. What is meant by a "mysterious presence"?

2. How is the mystery of life different than the kind of mystery a detective tries to solve?

3. What do agnostics and deists believe? Is it the same or different?

4. In what sense is faith a gift?

5. We call the experience of God's presence "revelation." What are the four sources of revelation discussed in this section?

6. Words to Know: mysterious presence, natural mystery, the transcendent, atheists.

■ In Your World

1. Think of one or two religious people you really admire. What is it about their lives that you find attractive? Make a list of all of these qualities and compare them in class.

2. If a group of atheists or agnostics came to class one day to talk about their views of life, what three questions would you **ask** them? What three things would you **tell** them about your view?

■ Scripture Search

1. Read the two stories of Creation in Genesis. (See Genesis, chapters 1-2.) What are the mysteries explored in each one?

2. Study the story of doubting Thomas in John 20:19-29. How are we very often like Thomas? How is it possible for us to "touch" Jesus even though we don't actually see his physical body?

Worship and Sacraments: We Celebrate, We Praise

SECTION 2
The Sacred Through History

When people become aware of God's active presence in their lives, their natural response is to address God intimately and confidently. They adore and thank God and, as Christ encouraged, ask God's help for their lives. But did you ever stop to wonder how ancient people, who had never heard of the Bible, thought of God? Their encounters with God had, of necessity, to be different from those of people who have lived after Christ and who possess his revelation.

Ancient People and the Sacred

Ancient human beings were, in some ways, much like people today. They lived close to the earth and found their world charged with sacredness and mystery. They were awed by the majesty of towering mountains and the magic of moonlight on a dark lake. They feared the danger of rushing waterfalls, violent thunderstorms, fire, and wild animals. The vastness of the sky and the unending cycle of birth, growth, death, and rebirth seemed to cast a spell over them. They understood the power of sun and rain to nourish as well as destroy life. All of these experiences spoke to them of a great power or force in and beyond nature.

Worship is something basic to human nature. When ancient people encountered mystery, they associated it with the divine. They linked experience of wonder with the gods. They engaged in ceremonies and sacrifices to contact the gods, gain their favor, and ward off disaster. Their worship was not offered to the gigantic boulders, the blazing sun, or the wild animals, but to the gods beyond or within these

> **Ancient people**, or **the ancients:** here used to refer to the various tribes of people, including the descendents of Abraham (the Hebrews), who lived in the southwest section of Asia (between Egypt and Syria) about 2,000 to 1,500 years before Christ.

Chapter 1 Seeing the Face of God

things. Because these people did not separate the mystery from particular objects, they had a sun god, a water god, a moon goddess, a mountain god, an earth goddess, a harvest goddess, a monkey god, a tree god, and even deities of such human activities as childbearing and death.

Like people of today, ancient people needed to make sense of their lives. Often they found life contradictory. It seemed full of hope on such occasions as marriage, the birth of a child, or springtime and the rebirth of nature. But life also seemed threatened by despair in experiences like death, disaster, and human disharmony. To express their interpretation of the mysterious forces at work in the universe, ancient people created and handed down myths of their gods and heroes. Sometimes they spoke of their first ancestors, whose actions, struggles, sufferings, deaths, and resurrections established the basic patterns of nature.

In rhythm with the seasons, the ancients dramatized their stories of creation and eternal rebirth. They enacted rituals built around the mysterious life-giving and death-dealing qualities of water. Through the dances of their witchdoctors and the offerings of their best fruits and animals, they tried to appease the gods and win healing. They celebrated meals in which partaking of consecrated food united them with the gods or strengthened them for the return to a lost paradise. Ancient people held wedding feasts and funeral banquets to solemnize the peak moments of life and death. Although they never arrived at the knowledge of God as a person or savior, they recognized the presence of the sacred and responded to the distant call of God to union with the Creator.

7. *Does modern technology take the mystery out of life? Explain.*

8. *Several years ago, some people acquired "pet rocks." These objects held personal meaning for them. Have you ever treasured something inanimate? If so, what and why?*

Ancient peoples honored the mystery that they couldn't fully understand by worshiping gods.

Worship and Sacraments: We Celebrate, We Praise

Sacred Places

Since ancient times, people have recognized that certain places possess an unusual power to bring deep peace. The power of these places does not depend on one's mood or on personal memories, but on something more real and unchanging—a special presence of God.

You've heard of, or perhaps even experienced, what might be called a moment of truth. It happens when you encounter something or someone greater than yourself. It gathers together everything inside you and makes you feel complete. It resembles the moment of relief and joy that came to you when, after the panic of being lost, you first glimpsed your parents heading toward you.

The patriarchs of the Hebrew Scriptures (Old Testament) experienced such moments of truth when they encountered God. Just as lovers carve trees to mark the place where they enjoyed one another's company, the patriarchs placed stone markers at the sites where they had experienced God. Recognizing them as sacred places, they sometimes poured oil over the stones to consecrate them to God's worship.

Not Limited to the Israelites

Reverence for God's presence has not been limited to the Israelites. Some nomadic hunting tribes, who were recently discovered in the bush of Australia, carry around with them a long, consecrated pole hewn from a giant tree. Other people in Indonesia keep a thirty-five-foot cedar pole, more than half of which projects out of their ceremonial house.

These tribal peoples believe that their ancestors climbed these poles into the skies, the place of the gods. The poles are symbols of the ability to pierce "the heavens." The poles supposedly enabled their ancestors to share the divine power they found when they entered the "sacred space" of the upper regions. There they learned the purpose and meaning of their lives, and they were assured that the gods cared.

To these tribal peoples, the sacred pole is the pillar of the universe. It is the center or axis of their world. Without it, they cannot live. When their pole breaks or is stolen, the

---

Myths: creative stories that explain, through the actions of gods, heroes, or ancestors, what a society thinks about itself and its world.

Patriarch: a father or male leader of a tribe. Abraham, Isaac, Jacob, and Jacob's twelve sons were all patriarchs.

Nomad: someone who is homeless and who wanders from place to place.

Bush: unexplored territory.

People have built great monuments to express worship and to mark sacred places.

people are known to lose interest in everything. They refuse to eat; some simply let themselves die.

Our Own Sacred Places

Practically every day you lose things and find them. Once in a while, you even get lost yourself. Being lost is a matter of becoming separated or "unglued" from the right place—the place where you are supposed to be—the place where you feel all together. The strange thing is that places themselves have the power to make you feel found or lost.

Although some people may enjoy changing their environment frequently, there is something satisfying about being able to kick off your shoes and feel at home in a particular place. Certain places make you feel more at home because they bring back comforting memories. They are places where important events of your life happened: the place where you were born, where you spent your first day at school, your grandparents' house, the farm where you had a carefree summer, a beach where you met someone you like.

The sad fact is that you can't count on the places where you once experienced happiness to give you that feeling again. For one thing, they often change: they become shabby, are redecorated, or are even torn down. If they remain the same, you will have changed. The high swing or the corner sandbox where you spent so many happy hours

People's Response to the Sacred

Down through the ages, people have made sacred objects or images. Those listed below continue to amaze us to this day. The effort and technology that went into their construction is difficult to understand.

- *Easter Island Statues:* These two hundred long-eared sculptures can be as much as three stories tall and weigh as much as 60 tons. They were discovered in 1722, 2000 miles west of Chile.

- *Stonehenge:* Located in England, these thirty-five ton stones were transported over twenty-four miles, then precisely placed to line up with certain positions of the sun and moon to signal times of worship.

- *Pyramid of Cheops:* Built to preserve the pharoah's body during its travel to the next life, this monument required moving two-and-one-half-ton stone blocks over many miles, and then placing them precisely, without modern machines.

These statues at Ronororada, Easter Island are the only ones still erect.

of your childhood turns out, when you've grown a little, to be quite small and ordinary. The trouble with memorable places is that you can't stay in them always, and you can't carry them around with you.

9. Where do you worship God? Is this place sacred because you worship there, or do you worship there because it is sacred? Explain your answer.

10. Why do you think sacred places are important to human life?

11. Name some places that are full of memories for you. Explain why they are important in your life. If you've ever returned to that place, were you able to capture the original feelings it gave you? Why or why not?

Chapter 1 Seeing the Face of God

Touching the Sacred

Native Americans have long experienced the Presence of God whom they called the "Great Spirit." This is one of their prayers:

"O Great Spirit, whose voice I hear in the winds, and whose breath gives life to all the world, hear me! I am small and weak; I need your strength and wisdom. Let me walk in beauty, and make my eyes behold the red and purple sunset. Make my hands respect the things you have made and my ears sharp to hear your voice. Make me wise so that I may understand the things you have taught my people. Let me learn the lessons you have hidden in every leaf and rock. Make me always ready to come to you with clean hands and straight eyes, so when life fades, as the fading sunset, my spirit may come to you without shame."

Meeting God

Mountains, woods, seashores, and deserts can become sacred space. But, because of their consecration or special blessing, churches are recognized as special places for meeting the divine. A church is a house for the People of God. When you enter, the door acts as a divider. It separates you from the changing world and transports you to a place where you can more easily encounter God.

In some cultures, sacred places actually contain a second door in the form of a roof opening that symbolizes God's entrance from the world above. Smoke vents in the yurts of certain Central Asian herdsmen have this function. In other cultures, ceremonies that focus on a person's head indicate that the crown of the head is the door that leads into sacred space. This custom suggests that meeting God is more a matter of what goes on inside a person than of being in a particular place.

We do not **necessarily** encounter God in a sacred place. It is easy to become distracted and to enter a sacred

Native Americans developed special ceremonies for worship, such as this one led by Ute spiritual leader, Bear Boy.

Worship and Sacraments: We Celebrate, We Praise

Church art and architecture attempt to express people's faith in God.

place somewhat unthinkingly. For a genuine experience of meeting God, we must prepare ourselves. Only then can God be encountered.

Summary

- In their own ways, ancient peoples experienced God's Presence in the world and attempted to respond to God through rituals and prayer.

- Worship seems to be basic to human nature. For centuries, religious women and men have set aside sacred places where they believed God was present in a special way.

- Ancient sacred places were sometimes geographical locations (mountains, woods, deserts). Sacred objects included poles, altars, and special structures built by the community.

Consecrated: to be set apart for sacred purposes.

Yurts: circular, dome-shaped portable tents used by the Mongols of Siberia.

Chapter 1   Seeing the Face of God

SECTION 2
Checkpoint!

■ Review

1. What are some of the ways the ancients attempted to contact and please their gods?

2. When the patriarchs in the Hebrew Scriptures (Old Testament) poured oil over stones, what were they signifying?

3. What was the importance of the sacred poles used by some tribal people?

4. Is it necessary to have a sacred place to worship God? Why is such a place helpful?

5. Words to Know: sacred places, tribal people, sacred poles, patriarch, consecration, myth.

■ In Your World

1. Set up your own sacred place at home or in the classroom. What should be used to make it a special place to meet God?

2. Catholics usually bless themselves with holy water when entering their churches, and genuflect (or bow) before taking their seats. How do these actions suggest a separation from an ordinary place to a sacred place? What furnishings, decorations, or features of church architecture also indicate that the church is a holy place where we meet God? Walk through your parish church and make a list of all the objects there that you don't understand. Bring your list to class and compare it with those of your fellow students. If you cannot answer one another's questions, have your teacher help you find the answers.

■ Scripture Search

1. Look up the following references from the book of Genesis and find the names of the places where stones (altars) were set up to mark where God had been revealed: Genesis 12:6-8; 13:3-4; 18; 21:31-33; 26:23-26; 28:10-22; 33:18-20; 35:9-15.

2. Read the story of Elijah and the prophets of the false god, Baal (I Kings 18). Discuss how the presence of God was made known in this story and how the false prophets were exposed.

Worship and Sacraments: We Celebrate, We Praise

SECTION 3
The Hebrew People

For centuries, ancient people searched for God. But gradually the Hebrew people began to understand that God came in search of people. They began to believe that God was manifested through inspired words of prophets and through specific historical events as well as through nature.

The Chosen People

To the Hebrews, God's first direct revelation was an appearance to Abraham at the sacred tree of Moreh. Abraham heard God speak to him inwardly, calling him to move to another land. Abraham's "moment of truth" was so real to him that he risked everything to respond to God's call (see Genesis 12:6).

Abraham's experience of the divine presence was an event of saving power in his life. It set in motion a chain of events that resulted in the birth of a son, Isaac. His birth not only saved the elderly Abraham and Sarah from childlessness, which was considered a disgrace, but also insured that God's promise of descendants would be fulfilled. God's revelation also resulted in a kind of material salvation: Abraham and his clan grew prosperous.

Christians and Jews believe that in calling Abraham, God was preparing a people for salvation. To them, God's saving power has always worked through a visible human community—whether that community be the Israelites who were the descendants of Isaac or, as Christians uniquely believe, the Apostles who gathered around Jesus.

When Abraham and his descendants realized that God's plan was revealed in visible signs, they made their response of faith visible. They externalized it by building stone altars and by actually living a particular lifestyle. The Israelites believed that they were the Chosen People and that God required them to be faithful to the Covenant they had made with God. They were to perform the prescribed actions, blessings, anointings, and sacrifices as an expression of their interior faithfulness.

12. *Have you ever sensed God "speaking" in your life? If so, when? What did you hear God telling you?*

13. *How are you responding to God's call in your life? Name some ways you visibly express your faith.*

God spoke to Abraham through an angel. Abraham was kept from sacrificing Isaac by God's action.

Dealing with the Sacred

The book of Genesis, written by the descendants of Abraham, contains stories of prehistoric times dealing with creation and the entry of sin into the world. These stories describe the way ancient people interpreted God's plan for the world. Natural disasters such as famine, earthquake, and volcanic eruption were considered punishments from heaven for the growing moral corruption of the people. This corruption was seen in hatred between family members, divisions and rivalries among tribes, wars between nations, and sexual perversions.

Enoch, Noah, and Abraham represent those people who responded to God, insofar as God could then be known. The stories of the safety of Noah's Ark (Genesis 6:1-9:17) and of Abraham's escape from the destruction of Sodom and Gomorrah (Genesis 18:1-19:29) present a humanity that strayed far from God and a God who constantly brought new beginnings out of rampant evil.

Though mixed with superstitious practices, the natural inclination of these earliest peoples was to reach out toward the divine. They responded to God's dimly perceived presence with the following basic elements of worship:

- ***Intuition of a superior being.*** *Prehistoric people sensed the existence of a power greater than themselves as the source and controller of nature. It was not until God's revelation to Abraham that the power behind nature began to take on a face and become a Someone. Even in the later and more advanced civilizations of Greece and Rome, many philosophers could not reason to the fact that the "highest" god was Someone who created, cared about, and came very close to people.*

- ***Recognition of this being's transcendence.*** *Although early people associated their gods with specific things or places like rocks and mountains, they believed that the sacred presence originated outside of the natural world. In this, they had the beginnings of an insight into the true identity of God as one who is wholly other, or transcendent.*

- ***Response in hope of salvation.*** *By responding to this nameless, faceless power in rituals and sacrifices, ancient people established a saving relationship that they believed restored and increased their vitality, well-being, and favor with the divine. Through their response to the manifestation of God in nature, the ancient people were able to find salvation. In these people, God was already preparing the soil of humanity to receive the seed of the Divine Word.*

The story of Noah and the flood in Genesis 6–9 is a story of salvation.

Chapter 1   Seeing the Face of God

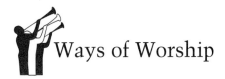

Ways of Worship

The experience of the ancient people shows that all humanity has received the call to God's communion. Those who never receive this revelation in Christ are able to find wisdom when they respond to the divine presence in creation or natural revelation. Nature, then, is sacramental in the broad sense because, through it, God extends a call of salvation to which people are capable of responding.

14. *Why do you think that modern people still engage in superstitious practices? Give some examples.*

15. *What response would you make to someone who said that religion is nothing more than superstition?*

16. *Do you think that people of other religions experience the presence of the one, true God in their lives?*

The Golden Calf

Even after being allowed to experience God's mysterious presence, some of the Israelites wanted to worship a god of their own making. When Moses delayed coming down from the mountain where God was giving him the Ten Commandments, the people grew anxious and impatient. They said to Aaron, their leader in Moses' absence, "Come, make a god who will be our leader" (Exodus 32:1). The people began melting down their jewelry and they made a golden calf. They wanted to be like other tribes they had met that worshiped gods they could see and touch. This desire to create our own gods is called **idolatry**. When Moses returned and saw the people dancing around their golden calf, he threw the tablets of God's law on the ground and broke them (Exodus 32:19).

God eventually forgave the people for their idolatry and Moses for his anger.

Even as God spoke to Moses the Hebrew people worshiped the Golden Calf.

Worship and Sacraments: We Celebrate, We Praise

God spoke to Moses through the Burning Bush (Exodus 3:14).

Moses and Sacred Places

When God spoke to Moses in the burning bush (about 1200 B.C.), God was revealed by name. From that moment, God was known as a definite person, "Yahweh," which means, "I am" (Exodus 3:14). But Moses had only heard a voice. In the strange bush that burned and was not destroyed, he could not see God as you see others. Later, in the desert, God's presence was both revealed and hidden in the pillar of fire and the luminous cloud (Exodus 40:38).

Throughout the Hebrew Scriptures, the privileged encounters with God are described as occurring on mountains because the early peoples associated the mystery of divinity with the vast heights of the sky. "Come, let us climb the Lord's mountain, to the house of the God of Jacob," writes Isaiah (Isaiah 2:3). The mountain encounter with God was an experience of deep happiness. Moses' meeting with God on Mount Sinai was far superior to what the ancients had experienced in nature. This encounter on Sinai resulted in a spelled-out, mutual contract in which God and the Hebrew People agreed, through the mediation of Moses, to be faithful to each other. The Book of Exodus says that the face of Moses was so radiant when he descended Sinai that he had to veil it (Exodus 34:33).

Sacramental: having the power to mediate God's grace or help.

Chapter 1 Seeing the Face of God

The one difference between the self-communication of God to the Chosen People and the communication through creation to people of other cultures is that God now took the initiative and started the action. Moses was not looking for God in the burning bush; God attracted Moses' attention in order to speak to him. The Chosen People didn't reach God by their own efforts of mediation or penance. God reached into their everyday lives, just as was done for Abraham. It is true that they needed faith to recognize God's intervention, but God acted in ways they could see and feel, through physically destructive plagues, blood on doorposts, a safe passage through the sea, and the conquest of their enemies.

Most astonishing of all, God communicated with Moses, revealing the divine identity and divine plans. God's revelation was concrete and specific, and based in history. It was always expressed in terms that people could grasp easily.

All God's saving interventions were for one purpose: to build a people through whom God's plan could be safely carried out and eventually transmitted to all other nations.

The Ark of the Covenant

As a visible sign of a special presence among the Chosen People, God instructed them to build a sacred place—the ark of the covenant—which was to be placed in the tent of meeting. God determined everything about the ark: its measurements, its construction, its adornments (Exodus 25:21-22). It was to be a portable chest of acacia wood overlaid with gold inside and out, about three feet nine inches by two feet three inches. A gold plate, called the "mercy seat," rested on the top of the ark. Two cherubim faced each other on either side so that their wings overshadowed the seat.

The Israelites often recalled God's wondrous deeds to them in songs and ceremonies celebrated around the ark. Whenever a decision was needed as they moved through the desert, the Israelites prayed to Yahweh at the ark. It was the ark that was placed in the forefront of the whole column of people during their many years in the desert. It was the ark, too, that was carried first across the Jordan when the Chosen People entered the Promised Land.

The Ark of the Covenant was a symbol to the Hebrew people that God was always with them.

The two stone tablets of the commandments, a vessel of manna, and the rod of Aaron were kept inside the ark. They symbolized the concern God had shown in the past. The ark was a reminder of the deepest purpose of Israel's existence—that God cared in a special way. By means of this sacred place, the Israelites addressed God whenever they wanted. This portable symbol reminded them of God's nearness.

Continuing Expressions

Jesus, a faithful Jew, visibly expressed his faith in God's call. He asked to be baptized, he preached God's kingdom, and he showed his love by dying on the cross. The early Christians showed their faith by requesting baptism and the sacrament of the Spirit and by participating in the Eucharist. Today, Christians still express their faith by associating themselves with the visible Church community and by actively celebrating the sacraments.

17. Where are some of the places you meet God?
18. Name some times when you felt God taking the initiative in your life.
19. Do you think that people are closer to God now in modern times or further away? What reasons can you give for your opinion?

Chapter 1   Seeing the Face of God

The Monarchy and the Sacred Places

When the Israelites formed themselves into a kingdom, King David saw the ark as the symbol needed to unify the northern and southern tribes. He had the ark brought to Jerusalem (about 1000 B.C.), which was to serve as the capitol and sacred center of the nation. David had hoped to build a fitting temple there to house this ark, but through the prophet Nathan he was told that, though the time was near for building such a sacred place, he would not be the one to do it.

David's son, Solomon, fulfilled his father's dream by building the magnificent Temple of Jerusalem (about 950 B.C.). The ark was placed in the Holy of Holies inside the Temple. There, in the one Temple of Israel, the Israelites worshipped Yahweh. It was every Israelite's goal to visit this most holy place at least once in the course of his or her lifetime. The psalmist composed special songs for the pilgrimage to Jerusalem, the Holy City (see Psalms 24 and 84).

The Temple was the place of worship for the Hebrews.

Summary

- Both Jews and Christians remember Abraham as the first person to receive the revelation of God that eventually led to the formation of the Jewish people.

- God gave the tablets of the law (the Ten Commandments) to Moses, which was a sign of God's covenant or special relationship with the Hebrew people.

- All ancient peoples, including the Jews, experienced the mystery of God's transcendence, but it was through the history of the Hebrew people (the Jews) that God's revelation was made known most clearly.

Worship and Sacraments: We Celebrate, We Praise

SECTION 3
Checkpoint!

■ Review

1. What do we mean when we refer to the Jews as "the chosen people"?
2. What role did Abraham and Moses have in helping their people recognize the presence of God in their lives?
3. What was the "Ark of the Covenant"?
4. Why was the Temple such an important place for the Jews?
5. Words to Know: the Chosen People, Ark of the Covenant, Hebrew Scriptures, Mount Sinai, Promised Land, manna, idolatry, sacramental.

■ In Your World

1. How can an awareness of God's presence help you establish goals in your life? How would an awareness of God affect the ways you attempt to achieve your goals?
2. Ancient people celebrated in order to honor the gods and to ask for help in the successful capture of food. After the capture, the people thanked the gods for the food, clothing, and tools provided from the animal. On what occasions do you pray in order to "psych yourself up" for the accomplishment of some goal? Which of these goals, if any, are religious in nature?
3. Make a list of all the reasons why someone would worship God. Compare your list with others in the class, and then try to rank these reasons in order of importance.

■ Scripture Search

1. Read the account of Abraham's call from God to go to a new land (Genesis 12). Discuss how Abraham's positive response took deep faith.
2. The story of God giving Moses the Ten Commandments on Mount Sinai helps us to understand how much God desires to be present to us. Read Exodus 19 and 20. Discuss the difference between this meeting of God and Moses and the revelation Moses received earlier in Exodus 3:1-4:17.
3. In Exodus 40:34-38, we see visible signs of God's presence among the Hebrew people. What were those signs? Discuss their meaning.

Chapter 1   Seeing the Face of God

CHAPTER 1 Review

■ Study

1. What is the difference between a novel called a "mystery" and the **mystery** of God's presence?

2. In what sense is life itself a mystery?

3. Name some specific things about human life that you find mysterious. How does your faith in God help you to deal with these mysteries?

4. What are some of the ways God's Presence is revealed to us?

5. What are sacred places and how did these places help the ancients experience their gods and their sense of transcendence?

6. What are some "sacred places" for Americans and how do these places help us to express our patriotism and "fidelity" to the United States?

7. What were some visible signs given to the Israelites as proof of God's continuing presence?

8. In what important way did God's revelation to Moses differ from that offered to peoples of other cultures?

9. What idol did the people make for themselves when Moses was on Mount Sinai? Why did they make this idol?

10. What is the special importance of the Ark of the Covenant for the Jewish people? Describe how the ark was constructed.

11. Why do societies and individuals lose hope without some kind of relationship with the divine?

12. Briefly outline the gradual revelation of God through the history of the Chosen People.

13. How can modern people meet God today?

■ Action

1. Robert Frost, in his poem "Stopping by Woods on a Snowy Evening," tells about a man driving along the edge of a woods on a cold, snowy night. Becoming absorbed in the sheer beauty and quiet of the snow, he experienced a strong desire to stop and watch the woods fill up with snow. The poem concludes with these lines: "The woods are lovely, dark and deep,/ But I have promises to keep, and miles to go before I sleep." Write a letter to the late Mr. Frost explaining what benefit might have come to the man in the poem by lingering a while in that sacred place.

2. Using slides from your school library or from your own collection, put together a visual presentation of scenes that might stimulate meditation on the presence of God. You might try to choose scenes that are not from nature—for instance, children playing around a water hydrant in an inner-city environment. Show your presentation to your class.

3. Bring to class a recording that helps you feel the presence of God. Before playing it for the class, present a prayer or other explanation that points to the inspirational elements it contains.

■ Prayer

This simple prayer will help you to recognize God's presence all around you. Recall that Jesus used to take time for prayer like this. After a busy day, he would invite the disciples, "Come away by yourselves to a deserted place and rest a while" (Mark 6:30).

Find a quiet place, preferably outside. If you live near water, sit by the shore. Perhaps you can offer your prayer at dawn or dusk. The purpose of this prayer is to place yourself in surroundings that suggest the beauty and wonder of creation. A garden, a park, a balcony, or a rooftop of a tall building are also good settings for this quiet time with God. Take your Bible with you.

Make yourself comfortable and, for a few minutes, simply observe your surroundings. Thank God for each beautiful thing that you see. Open your Bible to Psalm 148. Pray each verse of the psalm slowly, stopping from time to time to allow God to speak to you through the images used by the psalmist. After finishing your psalm prayer, ask God in your own words to help you be more attentive to the divine presence in your life and more grateful for the gift of creation.

CHAPTER 2

Emmanuel— God with Us in Jesus

OBJECTIVES

In this Chapter you will

- Understand that life is a journey that can lead you to union with God when you are responsive to the "signposts" of God's presence among us.

- Come to know Jesus as the way and the truth of life.

- Experience Jesus' call to seek God's Kingdom of justice, and see how living God's kingdom is the meaning and purpose of human life.

He said to them, "But who do you say that I am?" Simon Peter said in reply, "You are the Messiah, the Son of the Living God."
—Matthew 16:15-16

Worship and Sacraments: We Celebrate, We Praise

SECTION 1
Our Journey with Christ

Have you ever taken a long journey, say to a far away state or a distant country? What with the packing and preparation—maps, passports, language guides—the build up for the trip is great excitement.

Humankind has always been captivated by the journeys of daring people who venture forth on uncharted courses. Many of these journeys are recorded in the annals of history. Among the more spectacular of these voyages are the following:

- *Christopher Columbus sails across the Atlantic Ocean and "discovers" America.*
- *Ferdinand Magellan's ship completes the first circumnavigation of the world.*
- *Charles Lindbergh flies solo from New York to Paris.*
- *Neil Armstrong becomes the first human to set foot on the moon.*
- *Freed black South African nationalist, Nelson Mandela, journeys to North America to explore new ways to abolish apartheid (government supported racial segregation).*

A Pilgrim People

There is no need to envy these daring pioneers because you, as a person and as a Catholic, are engaged in a journey that is just as thrilling as those listed above. Your unique journey is called life. For many people, life is just an accident or a chance combination of the right elements at the right time. It is a meaningless sequence of joys and sorrows, successes and failures, loves and hates.

Chapter 2 Emmanuel—God with Us in Jesus

For believing Catholics, however, life is purposeful. This sense of purpose begins with the moment of conception and ends with death. For believing Catholics, every person is created by Divine Love, guided by Divine Providence, and directed by Divine Wisdom to the final goal of eternal life. Each person's life is seen as a meaningful journey, or pilgrimage.

Finding Your Way

As a Catholic, you belong to a group of people who are on the same journey together. That is why the Second Vatican Council (1962-1965) referred to the People of God on earth as "the Pilgrim Church." Because of a shared faith in Jesus, Catholic life is a pilgrimage toward eternal life in God. This pilgrimage was made possible through the life, death, and resurrection of Jesus. Just as Jesus came from God and returned to God, you were created by God and you are on a journey through life back to God.

Catholics find meaning in life because they believe life's ultimate destination is union with God. The only real failure in life is not to reach this destination. The goal of life is not "eat, drink, and be merry"; rather, it is to live in such a way so that eternal happiness is ensured.

We take many journeys in our lives, including the final one at death. The ultimate end of our journeys is union with God.

Worship and Sacraments: We Celebrate, We Praise

The older you get, the more you will realize how short life is and how important each day can be on your journey toward God. The human life span is a mere seventy or eighty years. As the psalmist writes, "We are like a breath; our days, like a passing shadow" (Psalm 144:4). Every day takes you a step closer to God or a step farther away. Unfortunately, some people go out of this world without ever learning why they came into it. Some know why they are here, but they become absorbed in distractions along the way and quit making progress, and some people are so busy pursuing popularity, money, pleasure, or position that they forget where they are going. Unless they somehow come to their senses, they may lose their way altogether.

Your Personal Journey

Your journey is similar to that of Abraham and Sarah in the Hebrew Scriptures (see Genesis 12–13). God asked Abraham and Sarah to journey to a strange land. It was no easy matter in those days to transport a family and all their belongings to another land. Besides, Abraham and Sarah had only God's word that the land existed and that it was available to them. To venture forth into the unknown was a definite risk. But because they dared to believe God and to take that risk, Abraham and Sarah received the land. Eventually all the nations of the world were blessed through them.

Acting on faith, Abraham and Sarah made a successful journey. In just the same way, God calls you to believe there is a promised land awaiting you. Like Abraham and Sarah, you must have faith to undertake the journey toward that land. Like the journey to Canaan, the journey to heaven is not an easy one. "How narrow the gate and constricted the road that leads to life. And those who find it are few" (Matthew 7:14).

As people of faith, we are pilgrims on earth. "For here we have no lasting city, but we seek the one that is to come" (Hebrews 13:14). As Catholic believers, we search for "a better homeland, a heavenly one" (Hebrews 11:16), a city that God has prepared. It is this promised kingdom of God that keeps life from being absurd. For those who believe, life's mystery is clothed with meaning.

Pilgrimage: a journey to a distant place for a devotional purpose.

Resurrection: returning to life after death. Applied to Jesus of Nazareth who was crucified as a rebel by the Romans about A.D. 30.

Seven: in number symbolism represents perfection or infinity.

Kingdom of God: refers to the new life Jesus came to offer us—a new age when sin is overcome. Justice and peace are two signs of God's kingdom.

1. *Which of the great voyages listed at the beginning of this chapter would you rank as the greatest? Why? How is the journey of Mr. Mandela different than all the other voyages on the list?*

2. *What are some of the questions that you think Abraham asked himself when God told him, "Go forth from the land of your kinsfolk and from your parents' house to a land that I will show you." (Genesis 12:1)?*

Touching the Sacred

Saint Patrick's Breastplate can be a help to us as we attempt to walk with Christ on our journey through life:

"I arise today through God's strength to pilot me; God's might to uphold me; God's wisdom to guide me; God's ear to hear me; God's words to speak for me; God's hand to guard me; God's way to lie before me; God's shield to protect me; God's host to secure me; Christ with me, Christ before me, Christ behind me; Christ in me, Christ beneath me, Christ above me; Christ on my right, Christ on my left; Christ in breadth, Christ in length, Christ in height; Christ in the heart of every person who thinks of me; Christ in the mouth of every person who speaks to me; Christ in every eye that sees me, Christ in every ear that hears me."

Guides and Provisions

It would not be fair if God asked you to make a journey and then failed to provide you with maps and provisions. As a member of the Catholic Church, you are supplied with what you need to guide and strengthen you every day of your life.

The best guide for Catholic living is the life and teachings of Jesus Christ. In Jesus' words and example you have God's road map for the traveling pilgrim. "I am the way," Jesus said (John 14:6). Through the Incarnation, God dramatically broke into history, joining the divine and the human so uniquely in Jesus that he could say, "Whoever has seen me has seen the father" (John 14:9). The key to the way God would live as a human being is summarized in one word—love. Jesus said, "As the Father loves me, so I also love you. Remain in my love. If you keep my commandments, you will remain in my love" (John 15:9-10). To come safely and surely to the end of the journey, we need only to keep our eyes fixed on Jesus.

God sent Jesus as our guide to life. Since his resurrection, the sacraments are given to us to help us live out this journey. As we look at the gifts Jesus left us, we can better understand how the sacraments support us even now.

By giving us the Bible and the Church, God is helping us follow Christ even today, centuries after his earthly life ended. These two invaluable gifts are not just two lifeless guides. They are God's providential ways of remaining with us, the pilgrim disciples.

Worship and Sacraments: We Celebrate, We Praise

Because the Scriptures were written by people who were inspired by God, they are God's living word. God speaks through them. The psalmist declares, "O Lord, a lamp to my feet is your word, a light to my path" (Psalm 119:105). The Ten Commandments of the Hebrew Scriptures and the Beatitudes of the New Testament (Matthew 5:1-12) are like road signs along the way. When we do not follow these signs, we run into detours and dead ends. Heeding them ensures a safe journey and a happy homecoming.

Through the bishops, the successors of the Apostles, together with the pope, Christ's representative on earth, Jesus continues to teach, to lead, and to sanctify his people. In fact, in his Holy Spirit, working in and through **all** the members of the Church, God guarantees that the pilgrim people are heading in the right direction.

---

3. *If you were going to drive across the United States during your summer vacation, what preparations would you make for the trip?*

Jesus left us food for the Journey in the Eucharist. The feeding of the multitudes in Matthew 15:32-39 reminds us of the Eucharistic meal.

Incarnation: to become flesh; refers to God becoming human in Jesus.

Chapter 2 Emmanuel—God with Us in Jesus

Walking with Christ

As we travel, the best companion we can have is Jesus. The Gospel story of the two disciples on the way to Emmaus is a good model for anyone who wants to walk with Jesus (Luke 24:13-35). One of the disciples is named Cleopas; the other's name is unknown. The two travelers are going to Emmaus, a town seven miles from Jerusalem. This particular Easter journey can easily be symbolic of the journey each Christian is making toward eternal life with Jesus.

As the two disciples walk along, they are engrossed in their discussion. The events of the past few days have them baffled. The man they had hoped was the Messiah had been killed. Gone were their visions of a glorious leader, a new kingdom, and an age of freedom. The cross and the tomb, it seemed, had dashed their hopes, despite the incredible stories of some women who told them Jesus was alive.

Catholics today are in a position similar to that of Cleopas and his companion. What Jesus spoke about and promised appeals to us. We hope that what he said is true, especially his assurance of everlasting life. Like the disciples, we have heard others witness to his resurrection, but perhaps we do not fully understand what resurrection means.

In the course of their conversation, the disciples are joined by a third traveler. It is Jesus who walks with them, but they do not recognize him.

Like Cleopas and his companion, we often fail to realize that God is with us. The psalmist, however, understood God's constant presence:

"Where can I go from your spirit?
 from your presence where can I flee?
If I go up to the heavens, you are there;
 if I sink to the nether world,
 you are present there.
If I take the wings of the dawn,
 if I settle at the farthest limits
 of the sea,
Even there your hand shall guide me,
 and your right hand hold me fast."
(Psalm 139:7-10)

On the road to Emmaus (Luke 24:13-35) the disciples finally recognized the resurrected Jesus in the breaking of the bread.

Checking Your Road Map

When you are making a long journey, it is wise to stop once in a while to check the road map. The same holds true for the journey of life. Much time and energy can be lost if you do not ever assess exactly where you are and the direction in which you are traveling. The following list contains practical suggestions to help you check your journey's road map.

1. For a week, keep track of how you use your time each day. Make a list of things that you would like to make top priorities in your life or that you consider important for you to spend time on. Compare the list with your record of how you spent the week. Did you make space in your life for what was really important to you?

2. Draw up a practical weekly schedule for yourself that coincides better with your priorities. Allot more time for essentials; cut time for nonessentials.

3. Try to live according to your new schedule. If you don't succeed, either adjust the schedule to make it more realistic or try harder to be more disciplined.

The Bible can serve as our road map on our journeys of faith.

No matter where you are or what you are doing, Jesus is there with you. This is what Jesus meant when he said, "I am with you always, until the end of the age" (Matthew 28:20). Even though you walk through fog or darkness, the light of Jesus' presence can comfort and encourage you. In sorrow and in joy, the risen Jesus is an abiding presence.

Chapter 2   Emmanuel—God with Us in Jesus

4. *What are some of the benefits of having a companion on a journey?*

5. *When, on your journey, did Jesus walk with you but you did not recognize him?*

Making Progress

You are a pilgrim. To progress on your journey with Jesus toward the kingdom of God that he came to announce, you must possess specific qualities and develop basic skills. Among the qualities you will need to successfully complete your pilgrimage are prayerfulness, self-control, courage, enthusiasm, confidence, and perseverance. All of these will emerge from the most essential characteristic you will need: faith—"we walk by faith, not by sight" (2 Corinthians 5:7). A strong, living faith will enable you to journey onward in wisdom, hope, and love.

There are three basic skills you will need on your pilgrimage. The first one is to **know the Catholic Faith.** A good way to learn more about this Faith is to read and to reflect on the Scriptures. The second skill is to **live the Catholic Faith.** Even a Scripture scholar with a Ph.D. in theology can lose his or her faith if it is never practiced. The way to live your faith is to pray, be conscious of God's presence, be open to God's working in your life, worship God at the Eucharistic table, and act with mercy and love towards others. The third skill is to **share the Catholic Faith.** Your faith in God can inspire others to believe also. And, as you encourage others in the Faith, your own faith is renewed.

To all appearances, the journey to Emmaus was in vain. The two disciples ended up exactly where they had started, in Jerusalem. But the stranger they met along the way had made the journey a success. This stranger explained the Scriptures to them concerning himself, and their eyes were opened. Because they realized that they were walking with Jesus, these disciples had made real progress. With him, they had walked the immeasurable miles between despair and hope.

Worship and Sacraments: We Celebrate, We Praise

Sharing the faith is a skill every Catholic needs to develop.

6. Why are the qualities of wisdom, hope, and love necessary? What other qualities would you add to the list?

7. What can you do to spread the gift of your faith to others?

Summary

- Life is a journey, and like all journeys, it involves both adventures and risks.

- The adventure in the Christian journey is the exciting new world that we can help God create. We call this brand new kind of life the kingdom of God.

- The risk we take when we journey with Christ is like the risk Abraham took when he heard God's word to him. We have to trust that God will be faithful to his promises.

SECTION 1
Checkpoint!

■ Review

1. How is a pilgrim different from a tourist or a hobo?
2. Why is the title "the Pilgrim Church" appropriate for the People of God?
3. How is your task in life similar to Abraham's?
4. What are some qualities you need to have in order to be a successful pilgrim?
5. Words to Know: pilgrim people, Pilgrimage, resurrection, Second Vatican Council (Vatican II), the Pilgrim Church, Incarnation, kingdom of God.

■ In Your World

1. What types of pilgrimages do teenagers make? Discuss one of these pilgrimages.
2. Find out all you can about the annual pilgrim of Muslims to the city of Mecca. Write a brief report on this topic.
3. In the context of the Catholic pilgrimage, explain the often-quoted ending of Robert Frost's poem, "The Road Not Taken": "Two roads diverged in a wood, and I - / I took the one less traveled by, / And that has made all the difference."

■ Scripture Search

1. Read Genesis, chapters 12 and 13. Map out the journey of Abraham and Sarah. How many different ways did God show Abraham divine protection and guidance?
2. Read Psalm 119. Draw pictures telling the story.
3. Read Luke 24:13-35. What guides did the disciples have on their journey?

SECTION 2
Jesus, An Experience of God's Presence

Who is this Jesus? How do we recognize in him an experience of God's real presence among us? These are questions with which Jesus himself confronted the disciples.

Christians know Jesus as our guide and our companion on the journey of life. His proclamation of God's kingdom gives us hope because this disclosure (revelation) of God's plan for humankind gives new meaning to the purpose of human existence. We no longer have to be afraid that sin will conquer the world. God is with us as Emmanuel in the person of his Son, Jesus Christ.

Who Do You Say That I Am?

If you've ever secretly worried about what other people think of you, you can relate to Jesus when he asked his disciples, "But who do you say that I am?" (Mark 8:29). Jesus was asking them to identify what they saw in him. When Peter answered, "You are the Messiah," it was clear that the Apostles saw more in Jesus than was visible to many others.

Many who were in contact with Jesus saw only a Jewish male in his thirties. He dressed like everyone else. He spoke Aramaic with a Galilean accent. He was a preacher.

But those close to Jesus, like Peter and the disciples, saw something different. In Jesus' words they recognized God's word. In his healing they sensed the power of God. They glimpsed the holiness of God in Jesus.

> **Messiah:** "anointed one."

> **Aramaic:** a Semitic language spoken by Jews at the time of Jesus.

Chapter 2   Emmanuel—God with Us in Jesus

Simple Human Goodness

The apostles sensed God's presence in the everyday things Jesus did and said. In the simple human deeds that Jesus did, the apostles saw complete sincerity, and practical love for those who were hurting. Jesus left people with a sense of wonder, and they wanted to be with Jesus. They wanted to hear more about what he called the **good news** of God's kingdom.

- "The people were astonished" (Mark 1:22).
- "When it was evening, after sunset, they brought to him all who were ill" (Mark 1:32).
- "Everyone is looking for you" (Mark 1:37).
- "He remained outside in deserted places, and people kept coming to him from everywhere" (Mark 1:45).

Meeting God in Jesus

Jesus himself is the place where we meet God. His words and actions all show us God in human form. Jesus is the most complete **sacred** sign or **sacrament** the world has ever known. In Jesus, all is brought to salvation, all is brought to fulfillment. When he appeared in Palestine he could rightly proclaim, "This is the time of fulfillment" (Mark 1:15).

All four Gospels and the letters of Paul were written to reflect the faith of the Apostles that Jesus did, in fact, bring us to the life of God. They record how Jesus, his personality bursting with love and kindness, changed lives through touch, word, and action.

Jesus remained faithful to his message of a trustworthy Father even until his death on the cross. As he died, Jesus spoke his conviction of God's goodness. His death shows us that when we are in touch with God, we are empowered to do things far beyond the normal capacity of human nature. In the resurrection, Jesus' trust in God was justified beyond our understanding. God raised him up to a brand new kind of life, free from death and suffering.

The emphasis here is on Jesus' fidelity even to the point of death. With every free decision he made, Jesus expressed that he was born of God as well as being the son of Mary. In this moment of total surrender, Jesus was glorified.

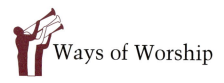

Ways of Worship

Scripture records many ways in which Jesus prayed. He celebrated the ritual feasts of the Jewish people: Feast of Tabernacles (John 7:1-13), the Passover feast (Luke 22:7-13), and the Sabbath day (Luke 4:16-22), for example.

Besides these prescribed times, Jesus is also recorded as praying on his own at important times of his life. After his baptism (Luke 4:1-12) and before his death (Matthew 26:36-46) are examples. The ways Jesus prayed, plus his very actions, have shaped the way we worship today.

With Jesus, humanity comes to share in the qualities of the divine. We call this sharing in the divine qualities the life of grace.

---

8. *Have you ever had the experience that "there's more than meets the eye" when you met someone? Describe this experience.*

9. *What special qualities would you expect to see in Jesus if he were alive today?*

10. *Describe a time when the kindness or wisdom of another person helped you to feel as if God were helping you.*

11. *Jesus showed "practical love" toward those he met. What are some examples of this kind of love?*

12. *Jesus said that we are now living in a time of fulfillment. What do people lack today and how can Christians help people experience "fulfillment" in their lives?*

"Our Savior" from a painting by Hughes Merle
The Apostles recognized in Jesus the power of God.

Something New: "Come and See"

With Jesus' Incarnation, that is, his birth as a person of flesh and blood, something new entered human history. Following his death, the resurrection also added something new. The Incarnation shows that God and man became one. If it's possible for Jesus, then it's possible for all humanity to at least share in the divine. It is mind-boggling to consider this distinctive element of Christianity. Through Jesus' resurrection, the goal of human life has changed. It is now possible to consider a shared life with God.

Jesus' death and resurrection brought us back to God. We say that Jesus saved us from sin. Following his resurrection, Jesus sent the Holy Spirit to be our guide and companion for all of history. The Spirit is God's self-giving gift to all of us. The Spirit calls us to live out the resurrection in our life, to live true to ourselves and to God. If we are true to ourselves, with the help of the Holy Spirit, then we will be true to God's will for us.

When the Apostles first showed interest in Jesus' teaching, his response was "Come after me" (Mark 1:17) or

Good News: The literal meaning of the word "Gospel."

Sacrament: one traditional definition is "a visible sign of inward grace (God's favor) that accomplishes what it signifies." A more modern definition is "a symbol of Christ's saving action reenacted by the Church."

Grace: our sharing in God's gift of divine life.

Chapter 2 Emmanuel—God with Us in Jesus

The Blessed Trinity: One, Holy God

"Ehod!" **One**! In the "Shema," the Jews have repeated their faith through the centuries: "God is one, there is no other." We believe this because God has been revealed through saving deeds and the words of the prophets. We experience God as transcendent, and yet close to us. We know God's mercy and justice.

In Christ, we learn further that the one, holy God is triune. Christ, the eternal, holy Son of God, left the inner circle of God's life to enter the circle of our world to allow us immediate access to God. Through Jesus, the Holy Spirit was given to us to continue God's divine work on earth.

Through these gestures of self-giving, the totally unified, divine inner life that would otherwise remain unknown to us has been revealed. God gives of self in the total self-expression, which is the Word (Jesus), and in the climate of eternal and personal love, which is the Spirit. So God is revealed as both Giver and Gift, and as such, serves as the image of all that we should be. By this revelation, we know that when we give of ourselves completely, we enter into the life of infinite love and become more totally who we should be.

Traditionally, God the Father is known as Creator; Jesus the Son is known as Redeemer; and the Spirit is known as Reconciler. We recognize these three distinct relationships within God, but we never claim that there are three gods! God is one. God is **both** with us **and** beyond all understanding. This is the mystery of the divine revealed to us in Jesus.

Although God is one, Catholics believe that God is experienced in the persons of Father, Son and Spirit.

"Come, and you will see" (John 1:39). If we want to follow Jesus as well, we have to do the same. Although it's not possible for us to return to Galilee in A.D. 30, we can say "yes" to Jesus as Lord. We do this through living in his

Worship and Sacraments: We Celebrate, We Praise

footsteps, following his example, and celebrating with him through the Church.

When we say "yes" to Jesus, we say "yes" to his strong faith in God. In so doing, we become one with his life-giving death and resurrection. Our union with Jesus plunges us into the actions which redeemed the world. For us, this saying "yes" is supported and celebrated by the Church, through its strong teachings on peace and social justice and through the worship of the believing community in the sacraments.

13. *Jesus may be described as a person who took commitments seriously. He was faithful to God, his Father, and he was faithful to his disciples. What are some indications that we need to take our commitments more seriously in today's world?*

14. *By his death, Jesus showed us the way to new life. Describe an experience when you let go of an attitude, understanding, or approach to life (a "death") that brought you greater joy, wisdom, or understanding ("new life").*

15. *Jesus frequently called the Father "Abba," which literally means "papa" or "daddy." What does this reveal about God's relationship to us?*

16. *The Holy Spirit was symbolized as a strong wind and as tongues of fire when the Spirit descended upon the Apostles at Pentecost (Acts 2:1-4). God, of course, is neither wind nor fire, but what do these images suggest to us about the Holy Spirit?*

Summary

- Jesus is the Son of God, the Messiah sent by God to save us from our sin and inaugurate the kingdom of God.

- Jesus accomplished his divine mission by making gestures of love which helped people to experience God's presence and action in their lives.

- By giving freely of himself, even to the point of death, Jesus showed us the power of God to bring forth new life from death and defeat.

Shema: the ancient Jewish confession of faith, taken from the Pentateuch.

SECTION 2
Checkpoint!

■ Review

1. What led the followers of Jesus to sense God's presence in him?
2. What did Jesus mean when he said, "This is the time of fulfillment" (Mark 1:15)?
3. What does "Incarnation" mean and what does the Incarnation reveal about Jesus' true identity?
4. What does the teaching of the Blessed Trinity tell us about God?
5. Words to Know: Aramaic, Messiah, Good News, sacrament, grace, Blessed Trinity, shema.

■ In Your World

1. Write an essay in which you talk about who Jesus is for you. Who do you say that he is?
2. We know that the kingdom of God includes living with God forever. But we also know that Jesus invites us to help one another make signs of the kingdom right now. How can we go about doing that? Make some specific suggestions.

■ Scripture Search

1. Read and study Peter's progression of faith in the Gospels in this order: Mark 8:27-30; Luke 9:18-22; Matthew 16:13-20. What differences do you see between the earliest Gospel profession (Mark) and the last of the three Gospels quoted above (Matthew)? Why do you think that Jesus says not to tell anyone that he is the Messiah?
2. Study and discuss John 1:1-17. What specific things does John tell us about the Incarnation?

Worship and Sacraments: We Celebrate, We Praise

SECTION 3
Building God's Kingdom with Jesus

Jesus told the Apostle Philip, "Whoever has seen me has seen the Father" (John 14:9). Therefore, everything Jesus did is worthy of our serious attention. One of the revolutionary doctrines of Jesus was his great emphasis on the dignity of every person, no matter how disadvantaged. We come to our full knowledge of the sacraments by knowing and following Jesus' actions. The more we know of how he lived, the more we will be prepared to live his life today through the sacraments.

Jesus, Our Way

Although Jesus numbered among his followers people who were wealthy and learned, he seemed to prefer the outcasts of society, especially the poor, the diseased, the sinners who were hungry for God. He excluded no one from his concern. Instead of amassing wealth and possessions, he lived simply and expected his followers to live as he did: trusting God.

Jesus' all-consuming concern was for the coming of God's kingdom; that is, the total orientation of all things according to God's plan. He prayed for the kingdom to come but also preached his unique message until he was too tired to move (see John 4:6). He cured all who came to him, ridding them of whatever burdens held them back from a life of service to God and others, whether it was a physical handicap, disease, or demons. Jesus' passion for justice and authentic love of God, as opposed to a meaningless fulfillment of laws, angered some of the religious authorities whose own political positions were threatened by his growing popularity with the masses. The confrontation was so serious that Jesus, whose whole life was a service of love and peace, was put to death in a Roman execution—on a cross (crucifixion)—a most violent official punishment.

But why was Jesus, who had acted with such power and charity, so cruelly defeated? The Apostles who had placed their hope in him had difficulty understanding this. With Jesus' resurrection and subsequent appearances, and also the outpouring of the Holy Spirit, their confidence was completely restored. They saw the meaning of his death, and they were inspired to proclaim and follow his teachings. Now we are called to bring the presence of Christ to the world in visible ways. Believing in God's universal love, Christians share their gifts until the world is totally reconciled in Christ at the end of time. He will come again, then, to hand the kingdom over to his Father (see 1 Corinthians 15:24).

17. *Why do you think Jesus spent so much time paying attention to disadvantaged people?*

The Moral Teaching of Jesus

As a good Jew, Jesus grew up with the Ten Commandments, which had shaped the wandering tribes into God's People. The main focus of this Covenant Code was on any external deeds that might injure the harmony of the Israelite community. It barely touched on personal moral obligations. In the episode of the rich man, Jesus seems to regard the Mosaic law as a taken-for-granted obligation (Luke 18:20). He mentions only a few of the commandments, and nowhere in the Gospels does he quote the code in its entirety. The Ten Commandments were not prominent in Jesus' teaching.

Jesus' moral teaching reaches beyond concern for social harmony within the small nation. The precepts of the "New

Jesus gave us the "New Law" in the Beatitudes.

Law" were to embrace the whole world. His emphasis as the founder of the New Law was on one's deepest values, attitudes, and motives. It made very high personal demands, exacting transformation from within.

Jesus Calls Us to "Metanoia"

Metanoia is the key to Jesus' moral teaching. Jesus demands a fundamental reorientation of one's whole life to faith in the Gospel of forgiveness. He condemns only the self-righteous who deny their need of redemption and he offers salvation to sinners who repent. Jesus cures and he forgives.

When Jesus called his disciples, he gave them the authority to go out and do what he had been doing (see Matthew 10:1). To be Christ-like is not just obeying laws; it is imitating Jesus. This imitation consists of putting on Jesus' mind. In the Sermon on the Mount (Matthew 5-7), Jesus revealed what the mind of a follower of his should be. He proposed a program of perfection, reaching to deep-seated attitudes (Matthew 5:48). He did not dismiss the Old Law, but advanced it to its utmost dimension. Merely avoiding murder and adultery and false witness cannot suffice for Christians whose morality extends as far as not calling someone a fool or harboring evil thoughts or confirming spoken words by oath. The healing of sin begins at its root, in the heart.

Covenant Code: refers to the Ten Commandments, a special relationship (covenant) with God.

Metanoia: (see Mark 1:15), a Greek word. It suggests a radical change in the way we think about the meaning of life; often translated as "conversion."

Chapter 2   Emmanuel—God with Us in Jesus

 On the Record

Old Testament Roots of Our Moral Code

Although people have been given an ability to recognize good and evil (through God's gift to us that we call our consciences), Scripture more clearly reveals both our purpose in life and how we are to achieve it. As Catholics, our most ancient moral roots reach back to Israel. God gave the Chosen People the Ten Commandments, which are regarded as the revealed will of God. The listing of these commandments has taken several forms, but the following is a traditional Catholic listing:

Prohibition of false or foreign gods and images;
Prohibition of the vain use of God's name;
Keeping holy the Sabbath;
Honoring one's father and mother;
Prohibition of murder;
Prohibition of adultery;
Prohibition of theft;
Prohibition of false witness against one's neighbor;
Prohibition against coveting a neighbor's wife;
Prohibition against coveting a neighbor's goods.

Rejecting God

The heart is the place where God's kingdom comes into being. It is within our power to love God because we were given the freedom of choice. But freedom also grants us the option of rejecting God. However, not all rejection cuts us off from God. Less inclusive rejection, called **venial sin,** weakens our ability to accept God's love. Serious sins threaten our relationship with God. **Mortal** or **deadly sin** is a total, conscious, and deliberate turning from God to a state of being fully alienated. Born in a state we call **original sin,** we are inclined to prefer independence to the freedom of God's love. But Christ's redemption makes it possible for all repented sin to be forgiven. Jesus calls and empowers us to practice his Law of Love. Wholehearted dedication to God and to neighbor is the summary and high point of his moral teaching (see Mark 12:28-34; Matthew 22:34-40).

Everything depends on the orientation of our heart (Luke 10:25-28). Even the most evil deeds, when repented of, can lead to love, while the most religious or heroic actions performed without love are useless (see Matthew 5:23-24; 1 Corinthians 13). At life's end, we will be judged on our practical service to others, done out of love for God. The parable of the Sheep and the Goats illustrates this, as does Jesus' own sacrificial act of redemptive love (Matthew 25:31-40).

The clearest example of Christian morality is when we forgive our enemies, do good for those who hate us, and pray for those who persecute us (Luke 6:27-28). This morality makes demands beyond mere human power. It calls us to love others as Jesus loves us. We are stengthened to live out the challenges of Christian morality everytime we receive the sacraments, especially the Eucharist. That is the ultimate sign of Jesus' love for us.

---

18. *What kind of changes do you think that Jesus is inviting you to consider in your life? In your society?*

19. *What do you think is meant by the statement, "the heart is the place where God's kingdom comes into being"?*

Worship and Sacraments: We Celebrate, We Praise

20. *Jesus asked us to forgive our enemies. If everyone accepted this challenge, think of one or two world problems that would be solved. Why do you think that people resist making this sign of God's kingdom?*

The challenge of living in the world is more difficult for some than for others. This person has overcome a physical disability to ply a trade. Sin is a similar disability in everyone's life.

Jesus, Women, and Family Life

Jesus did not enter directly into politics, yet he set revolutionary principles for the healing of society. He warned his disciples never to place anything above justice and service in their efforts to build the kingdom.

In a culture and era that placed women at the bottom of the social ladder, Jesus must have shocked everyone with his concern for the dignity of women. He traveled with women in his group and accepted their support. Women figure largely in his cures, and he violated laws concerning uncleanliness and the Sabbath in order to serve women.

Peace and Justice: Signs of the Kingdom

Service of the poor, the disabled, and all who suffer deprivation or oppression has been characteristic of Catholicism throughout the ages, even in those eras when many Church leaders succumbed to the temptation of luxury and power. Today, the forms of Christian service are undergoing change.

In response to the industrial revolution, the Church's social teaching focused on labor relations and just wages. The increasingly international nature of the human community, brought about through advanced methods of communication and transportation, triggered greater Catholic emphasis on peace and social justice. The technological revolution has focused attention on new social questions posed by a high-tech society: the development and liberation of the Third World, environmental planning, and control of the arms race. Catholic missionaries are dying while laboring in developing nations. Individually and as a conference, bishops are speaking out against social injustice, and the Holy Father himself has taken a strong position against nuclear escalation, making himself a world ambassador of peace and human rights.

Yet, Jesus did not go to the extreme of attacking the notion of private property, nor did he reject the wealthy. He was to be the Savior of all. Christians, therefore, should respect the right of private ownership, but also work for the equitable distribution of goods.

Missionaries often give their lives to bring Jesus to people around the world.

As a family you can witness to Jesus as the Risen Lord.

But Jesus' greatest contribution to the cause of women's liberation was his insistence on the permanence of marriage: wives were not to be discarded at whim, as was the custom, nor were adultery and divorce to be tolerated. Jesus based his teaching on the equality of the sexes (see Mark 10:2-12; Matthew 19:3-9).

Jesus encouraged family life by emphasizing the fourth commandment and through his warm acceptance of children, even holding them up as examples for kingdom seekers (Mark 7:10, 13-16). Even though Jesus made comments about his mother and family ties, in actuality his words only emphasized that faithfulness to the eschatological family (of the kingdom) must come before all other considerations, even ties of blood (see Matthew 12:46-50; Mark 3:31-35; Luke 8:19-21).

But the most outstanding trademark of Jesus' social ministry was respect for each individual's worth. As we have seen, Jesus made each person the focus of his concern. He identified with the poor and the worker. In a society where doing the socially acceptable thing was the highest value, and illness and poverty were taken as signs of God's disfavor, Jesus actually preferred the poor, the sinners, and the outcast whose hearts were right with God. His concern was for the whole person: physical, emotional, mental, and spiritual. He did not favor economic or spiritual poverty for them, but stated that happiness comes to those who learn by hard circumstances to give God full control of the secrets of their hearts.

Eschatological: refers to the "end time," when God's kingdom is completed.

Chapter 2   Emmanuel—God with Us in Jesus

21. *How do the Beatitudes (Matthew 5:1-12) summarize life in God's kingdom?*

22. *What does Jesus' treatment of women reveal to us about how God regards women in the divine plan?*

23. *Jesus touched and healed those who were physically, emotionally, and spiritually ill. What professions might Christians consider if they want to make their lives visible witnesses of God's kingdom?*

Knowing what Jesus taught is not enough. You have to put that knowledge to work serving others.

Summary

- In his preaching of the kingdom of God, Jesus showed a preference for the disadvantaged and the poor.

- In calling us to *metanoia,* Jesus was telling us that living in God's kingdom requires more than just keeping laws. We must also imitate Christ and his gift of self.

- People who help to promote justice and peace are living witnesses of God's kingdom.

SECTION 3
Checkpoint!

■ Review

1. How did the people of Jesus' time view sickness and poverty? Did Jesus accept this view? Why or why not?

2. Why weren't the Ten Commandments prominent in Jesus' teaching? Was he suggesting that we disobey them? Why or why not?

3. What does *metanoia* mean and what part does it play in Jesus' proclamation of God's kingdom?

4. Was Jesus against private property? Explain the balance between "having" and "sharing" for those who follow Jesus.

5. Words to Know: crucifixion, Covenant Code, *metanoia*, venial and mortal sins, eschatological.

■ In Your World

1. Each year there are thousands of suicides in the United States. What are some possible reasons why people decide to cut short their lives? What might convince someone that the journey is truly worthwhile?

2. Learn what you can about the group called "Alcoholics Anonymous." How does this group help people who have a drinking problem experience "conversion" to a new way of life?

3. Do you think that Christians are working hard enough to maintain the dignity of women as Jesus did? How would you rate our efforts to improve the status of the disadvantaged? Discuss your opinions.

■ Scripture Search

1. Read the Letter to the Colossians, chapters 1-3. How does Paul d the consequences of accepting Christ into our lives?

2. When some people see the homeless begging f they just walk by. Read the story of the G Does this story suggest that we ha do you think that Jesus' words homeless situation?

Chapter 2 Emmanuel—God wi

CHAPTER 2 Review

■ Study

1. How does Christian faith help us to see a deeper meaning to life than non-believers see?

2. Life may be described as a journey. What are some of the important guides that God has given us to show us our way?

3. In what sense is the journey of life both exciting and risky?

4. What is the kingdom of God and how can we help achieve it?

5. What do Christians mean when they say that Jesus is the place where we meet God?

6. What is the role of the Holy Spirit in our journey of life?

7. What is the Incarnation?

8. Jesus calls us to *metanoia*. Explain what this means.

9. In what sense does Jesus liberate us or set us free?

10. What is the lesson in the parable (story) of the Good Samaritan? What are some ways we can put this lesson into practice?

11. What are the two unmistakable signs of the kingdom of God? How can Christians make these signs?

12. How does Jesus' treatment of women and his concern for family life help us to understand more fully the kingdom of God that he came to announce?

13. What do you think that Saint Patrick meant when he prayed that he could see Christ "in every eye that sees me" and "in every ear that hears me"? How can we "hear" and "see" Christ in others?

■ Action

1. Collect songs and poems with a journey theme. In a sentence or two, summarize the insights each song or poem gives you about your journey.

2. Make a poster or collage that depicts two situations side by side. On the one side, show the effects of greed, selfishness, and lack of love in our world. On the other, illustrate the "metanoia effect" which occurs when people cooperate with God in building the kingdom.

3. Prepare a short dramatic presentation based upon Luke 24:13-35 (Journey to Emmaus). Adapt your presentation so that the story takes place at the end of the 20th century.

4. Find a place or two in your city that are "signposts of the kingdom" (an orphanage, a soup kitchen, Catholic charities, a homeless shelter). In class, talk about how these places can help us walk with Christ on our journey toward the kingdom. Discuss how you can find deeper meaning in your life by volunteering your services there.

■ Prayer

This prayer should be celebrated with other people, either in class or at home with your family. A Bible opened to Matthew 5:1-12, and your textbook are needed.

All who are joining in the prayer should sit or stand in a circle. Place a candle on a table in the center of the circle. Chose a prayer leader who begins the prayer.

Leader: "Let us put ourselves in the presence of God as we thank God for the gift of Jesus Christ."

All: "Praise to you, Lord Jesus Christ. You are the light of the world."

Leader: (Read slowly each verse of the Beatitudes—Matthew 5:1-12—stopping after each verse.)

After each verse, **all** respond: "Lord, lead us to your kingdom."

Leader (invites volunteers to offer their own prayers saying): "Let us ask God to hear our prayers and petitions. Please feel free to voice your prayers."

After everyone has had an opportunity to offer a personal prayer:

Leader: "Let us remember that Christ is the center of our lives as we pray the prayer of Saint Patrick on page 38 in our texts."

CHAPTER 3

Jesus Lives On in the Church

OBJECTIVES

In this Chapter you will

- Learn how the Church preserves, interprets, and teaches the divine revelation of the mystery of Jesus.

- Recognize the Church as the people of God who proclaim God's revelation in Jesus Christ and who celebrate God's love in worship.

- Recall the Church's invitation to praise God and celebrate the presence of Christ in your world.

Christ is the light of humanity, and it is. . .the heart-felt desire of this sacred Council that . . . it may bring to all people that light of Christ which shines out visibly from the Church.
—Vatican II, Opening words of the "*Dogmatic Constitution on the Church*"

Worship and Sacraments: We Celebrate, We Praise

SECTION 1
Recognizing God's Revelation in the Church

Almost everyone has experienced revelation in the beauties of nature: a beautiful sunset over the ocean, the fall foliage in Vermont, peach blossoms in Georgia. Others find God's revelation in their consciences. Perhaps you have felt uneasy or somehow discontent when you were untruthful, dishonest, unjust, or unmerciful. It is also possible to find God's presence in our relationships with others—the poor, the hungry, and the imprisoned especially. Finally, we recognize God in our inability to be completely satisfied, our unfulfilled longing for happiness.

As we have seen, God has always offered the gift of divine life to humanity through natural means, but human blindness and evil often reject this gift. Therefore, to make revelation more explicit, God broke into history, giving the prophets messages that inspired a whole community of people to put this knowledge into special religious language. It is through this revelation that we come to know Jesus "more clearly, love him more dearly, follow him more nearly" in the Church, with the sacraments.

Revelation Through God's Word

The descendents of Abraham were the first to receive the gift of this more direct revelation, which was first transmitted in oral tradition and later recorded in Scripture. The foundation event that shaped this Chosen People's subsequent perception of God was the Exodus and God's gift of

These fragments of the Dead Sea Scrolls are the oldest manuscripts we have of the Bible.

the Covenant Code, an event in which God was clearly revealed to them as a savior and liberator. Other actions of God are conveyed to us by the stories and prophecies of Israel.

Because God exercised still greater initiative, it is now possible to plumb the depths of the mysteries of human existence and even of God. In Jesus Christ, God actually walked among his people as a human being. God's very name sums up the great teaching of Israel that Yahweh is not unknowable or detached, but caring and saving. The life and death of Jesus carry that teaching to unexpected lengths. The foundational event of our Christian faith, therefore, is the life, death, and resurrection of Jesus, which revealed him as God's own Son and the very Word of God.

Those who receive the gift of faith in Jesus freely accept him as the ultimate authority and truth (Matthew 28:18). The teaching and promises of Jesus reassure us of our unique significance. What Jesus has revealed provides a worldview that glues together the pieces of life, shapes values, and directs judgments and decisions. Divine Revelation, then, transforms our awareness, our understanding, and our ability to perceive and interpret what is real. Through his Spirit-filled Church, Christ continues today to invite men and women who yearn for truth and life to come to him, the Way.

The fact that, without accepting faith in Christ, the Jewish people continued to find truth and liberation in their revelation was part of the problem that the Apostles and early Christians were forced to work out. Could there be two Gods and a double revelation? Guided by an outpouring of the Holy Spirit, the Church boldly professed faith in the one and only God who was revealed in various ways through the prophets, but who now, in the final age, was revealed more intimately in the Son and in the sending of the Holy Spirit (Hebrews 1:2).

The stories of Jesus in the early Church were, at first, delivered orally. As the Apostles died, the stories, as well as some of the Church's reflections on what Jesus had meant, were recorded in the New Testament (Christian Scriptures) that is accepted by Jesus' followers today. But the life of the early Church, its prayers and practices, its hymns and sermons also carried the Good News. Christians recognize God's revelation in the whole experience of the Church—its total tradition—the most sacred of which is Scripture.

The Jewish people continue to seek God's revelation in Scripture.

1. *The Church is sometimes referred to as "Holy Mother." What do you think that this image attempts to convey?*

2. *Describe an experience you have had of reading a poem or a story in English class and finding that you required some help in interpreting its meaning. How does this experience demonstrate some of the difficulties we face when interpreting revelation?*

Understanding God's Revelation

If God has been revealed to all people and now dwells in every Christian spirit, doesn't everyone have a right to interpret revelation? The problem of who has the right to decide what constitutes God's authentic revelation arose in the early Church when the Christian **Gnostics** claimed

Jesus: means "God saves."

Gnostics: A group in the early Church who believed a special knowledge was required for salvation.

Chapter 3 Jesus Lives On in the Church

privileged knowledge of a hidden meaning in the Gospels. They said that all matter is evil. The answer given by the Church to this claim is that true revelation, the true message of Jesus Christ, has been handed down through the generations in what the whole Church believes and teaches (the *magisterium*), not in what individuals or groups hold.

That Christ's commission was made to his Apostles, the guardians of revelation, is already indicated in the earliest years of the Church. Paul traveled from Antioch to consult with Peter, the Apostles, and the presbyters in Jerusalem to settle a controversial issue. Their decisions were always made with heavy dependence on the Holy Spirit (John 14:16-17, 26; 16:13-14). Jesus promised that the Spirit would bring to our minds all that he taught.

Although the words in which that revelation is expressed will never exhaust God's self-revelation, there will be no new revelation. The formulations of faith—the creeds that now constitute Tradition, and especially the Scriptures—are reliable interpretations. Still, under the guidance of the Holy Spirit, the teaching Church (whether the pope speaking in his office as head of the Church, or the councils—the bishops speaking officially in union with the pope) will continue to probe the mysteries contained in the deposit of faith. Thus the Church will never stagnate, but instead will continue to deepen its understanding of the unchanging realities behind the words that have been handed down from the Apostles. Our response to the gift of Divine Revelation is the leap of faith prompted by the Holy Spirit.

The bishop is the primary teacher of the faith in a diocese.

3. *Among the stories of Israel is the one about the covenant God made with Noah—a non-Israelite. What meaning do you see in this inclusion of a foreigner in the Hebrew Scripture?*

4. *In the story of the Burning Bush (Exodus 3:1-17), Moses was called by name and told to remove his sandals before approaching the presence of God. What does it tell you about God's revelation and how it should be approached?*

5. *What problems would arise if all Christians believed that they could interpret God's revelation on their own?*

The Apostles' Creed

This important statement of faith contains twelve statements of belief which coincide with the number of Apostles. It also contains the core of our faith which comes to us from the original group of Jesus' disciples. This creed (or act of faith) is shorter than the one we pray at Mass (the Nicene Creed), but it still contains the fundamental teachings of the Church.

"I believe in God, the Father Almighty, Creator of heaven and earth; and in Jesus Christ, His only Son, Our Lord; who was conceived by the Holy Spirit, born of the Virgin Mary, suffered under Pontius Pilate, was crucified, died, and was buried. He descended into hell; the third day He arose from the dead; He ascended into heaven, and sits at the right hand of God, the Father Almighty; from thence He shall come to judge the living and the dead. I believe in the Holy Spirit, the Holy Catholic Church, the communion of saints, the forgiveness of sins, the resurrection of the body, and life everlasting. Amen."

Keeping the Faith

Two distinctions here will forestall certain difficulties in regard to faith later. One is that, besides a central core of beliefs that has remained constant since the early Church, there are outer layers of beliefs that are relative to history and culture. For instance, the existence of God, the Incarnation, the Redemption, and the Spirit's work of sanctification are central dogmas of faith and part of **public revelation**, which closed with the writing of the New Testament. Public revelation contains, at least in seed, all that we need to know for our salvation. The creeds are our guide to these truths. Some teachings, like those on indulgences, are the proposals of theologians and are not essential to salvation.

Magisterium: from the Latin word for "office of a master"; the official teaching office of the Church.

Dogma: a doctrine (official teaching) that is proclaimed with the highest authority and solemnity.

On the Record

Councils of the Church are sometimes called "ecumenical" councils from the Greek *oikos* meaning "house." At the important meetings of the world's bishops, leaders of the Catholic **household** or community gather to discuss matters that affect the faith and worship of all Catholics. For this reason, bishops at a council are called "fathers." There have only been 21 ecumenical councils of the Church. The first was held in the city of Nicaea (a town in modern-day Turkey) in 325 A.D. The most recent council met in Rome, Italy, at the Vatican. It was called Vatican II and lasted three years (1962-1965). Vatican I was held in Rome in the 19th century (1869-1870). At Vatican II, 2,600 Fathers took part in the discussions and published 16 documents, including *"The Constitution on the Sacred Liturgy"* which influences the way we celebrate Mass today.

Apparitions of Christ and Mary to certain saints are matters of **private revelation**, although they may serve to popularize certain basic dogmas. Lourdes, for example, made the dogma of the Immaculate Conception widely known; however, faith in the Lourdes' apparition itself is not strictly required of Catholics.

A second distinction rests on the fact that the mysteries of faith are too large to be neatly defined, categorized, and put into mental boxes. Theology does its best to express the inexpressible, but doctrinal formulations are always less than the reality they describe. Although the truths of faith never change, new formulations may be required to meet the needs of changing times. The Holy Spirit constantly grants new insights into the mysteries, and expresses them in ways compatible with different centuries and cultures. Although there is growth in doctrinal pronouncement, no human formula can entirely capture the meaning of realities such as love, death, evil, and God.

Bishops from every part of the world participated in Vatican Council II from 1962-1965.

Scripture is the unrivaled source of our faith but, from time to time, the core faith of the Church is set into formulas like the Apostles' Creed and the Nicene Creed, which is said at Mass. Liturgy, customs, and conciliar texts also contain the teachings of the Catholic Church.

Another important way in which the Church keeps the faith alive for every generation is through councils or meetings of all the bishops in the world. At these meetings, the bishops, in union with the Pope, discuss new and better ways to proclaim divine revelation. The Second Vatican Council (Vatican II), which was held in Rome (1962-1965), gave us a fresh approach to understanding the Church, the sacraments, and the relationship of Catholicism to the world.

6. What mysteries of faith does the Apostles' Creed include?

7. Since faith is a relationship, sometimes it is strong, but sometimes it falters. When is it strengthened? When is it threatened?

Summary

- Jesus entrusted divine revelation to the Church which remembers Christ and teaches us about God and the kingdom as Jesus Christ did.

- The Holy Spirit guides the Church so that we can be confident that God's Word to us will never be lost or confused.

- In every generation, the Church attempts to proclaim God's revelation in Scripture and in Jesus in ways that can be clearly understood.

Theology: the study of revelation which attempts to help us understand our faith better.

Doctrinal formulation: a definite form of words used to express the creeds and statements of the councils.

Chapter 3   Jesus Lives On in the Church

SECTION 1
Checkpoint!

■ Review

1. How were the teachings and stories of Jesus passed down through the early Church?

2. Who were the Gnostics and what claim did they make about the meaning of the Gospels?

3. What is the difference between private and public revelation?

4. What is an ecumenical council and how do the councils help us to follow Jesus more faithfully?

5. Name a teaching that is a proposal of theologians and is not essential for salvation. Discuss the meaning of this teaching.

6. Words to Know: revelation, public revelation, private revelation, Gnostics, theologians, magisterium, dogma, creeds, ecumenical councils, Vatican II.

■ In Your World

1. Think about some gifts you have been given by the Holy Spirit. Don't be modest! What are some of the ways you can begin to use your gifts now to help proclaim that Jesus Christ gives true meaning to life?

2. Look up the purpose of the Supreme Court in the United States. Describe the High Court's function and discuss how this court operates somewhat like the magisterium; that is, as an "interpreter."

■ Scripture Search

1. For some famous faith stories, see Luke 1:34-38; 7:44-50; Matthew 9:9,18-26;14:28-32; John 6:40; 2 Corinthians 11:23-33. In each case, what difference does faith make?

2. Read Hebrews 1:1-4. What does this passage tell us about revelation and about the special place of Jesus in God's plan of revelation?

SECTION 2
The Church Proclaims Christ

The Church is the community of those followers of Jesus Christ who acknowledged him as their Lord and God. Catholic Christians carry an unbroken tradition of faith, sacraments, and ministry from the Apostles. This community of Christ's disciples is a unique witness to the presence of God in the midst of the world. It is through the Church that we can come closer to union with Christ in the sacraments.

The Church, God's People

The Church is a mystery that cannot be simply defined. It must be lived. Founded by Christ through his death and resurrection, it is guided by the Holy Spirit, whom the Father sent after Christ's ascension and entrusted to human beings until the end of time. The Church's many facets are perhaps best explored through the use of Biblical images.

Scripture reveals that, as the Father chose Israel to be God's own people by making a covenant with them, so, in Christ, God established a New Covenant with a new people. The Apostle Peter tells us, "Once you were no people, but now you are God's People" (1 Peter 2:9-10). This implies a two-fold nature. On the one hand, we are people, a visible human society governed by human leaders (the pope and bishops) and marked by all the strengths and limitations which that implies. On the other hand, we are God's people, guided by the Spirit.

The mission of the Church is to bring fulfillment to the three-fold mission of Jesus. As the Body of Christ, Christians continue the work of the Apostles, who called people

As Church, we are the People of God. We experience this most fully at the Eucharistic liturgy.

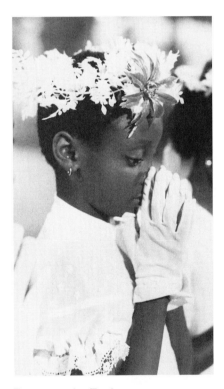

Receiving the Eucharist is an important part of what it means to be Catholic. The first reception of the Eucharist is a special celebration in all parts of the world.

to holiness by **proclaiming** the Good News, by **inviting** them to worship God in the perfect sacrifice of the Son, and by **leading** them to transform creation by the fulfillment of the kingdom, of which the Church on earth is a sign (1 Corinthians 12:29-31).

All Christians are called to share in this mission, each ministering according to the gifts bestowed by the Spirit for the good of the Church. Twenty centuries ago, Christ ordered his disciples, "Go, therefore, and make disciples of all nations" (Matthew 28:19a). Through the Church, truth and grace are communicated to all. Love for one another is the hallmark of Christ's community.

8. How does the Church proclaim the Good News and sanctify its members?

9. How does belonging to groups like the Church help to give us an identity? What groups that you belong to help you define who you are?

10. What special gifts do you have to offer the ministry of the Church?

Your Personal Call

Chances are that you are Catholic because of your family, location, and time in history. Yet, perhaps not everyone in your family, and certainly not in your neighborhood or age group, is a Catholic. By the grace of God you have been chosen for membership among Christ's disciples. Although God calls the whole Church, God personally invites you into a continually closer union with the divine self. This invitation is not a one-time call; it is repeated daily and hourly. At every stage of your life, you will be asked for a new response. This will require a constant openness and growth, ongoing prayer and study, constant self-renewal, Christian friendships, participation in the sacraments, moral decisions favoring Christ, and service to others. These are the evidence of your cooperation with God as God works in you. You are the Church, called from the foundation of the world to be God's instrument of salvation in this generation.

The "Marks" of the Church

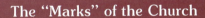

Today many people, especially teens and young adults, are searching for a way in which they can express their faith which is their own, not their parents. Often times in their search, these people run into sects or cults which proceed to lure them away from their faith through falsehoods and deceit. The search for a faith of one's own is a natural part of becoming a mature adult. The question for teens and young adults is: "How can I recognize the "true Church?"

The Catholic Church has noted certain **marks** for identifying this "true Church." Most obvious is the mark of **unity.** All members profess the same truths, celebrate the same sacraments, are guided by the same laws and leaders, and form a social unity recognizable by all. When you think of how difficult it is to maintain unity, even in a small family,

> **Ministry:** serving the needs of others in imitation of Christ. All baptized people are called to ministry.

Chapter 3 Jesus Lives On in the Church

Pope John Paul II meets with Cardinal Joseph Bernardin of Chicago. The cardinals carry on the apostolic mission of the Church in a special way.

it becomes obvious that God's Spirit is the principle of the Church's unity.

The second mark, **holiness**, derives from the Church's origin and mission, its power to sanctify, and its many saints. Although individual members may fall into sin, and even the Church itself may make human errors, the Church as a whole is guided and gifted by the Holy Spirit never to abandon its mission of sanctification.

Since it is God's will to save all peoples, the Church of Christ is **catholic**— meant for everyone, regardless of age, race, economic level, sex, or color. Therefore, to be a Christian has always implied being a missionary, zealously spreading the Gospel, but always respectful of the freedom and dignity of other people and their cultures (Romans 10:12). Universality also implies that the Church has existed in every generation since Christ, has taught all the truths revealed by God for our salvation, and can absorb goodness and beauty wherever it may be found to restore them to Christ.

Finally, Christ's Church is **apostolic**—it carries on the work of the Apostles; this includes the Twelve and others who shared their mission. The message of the Apostles has not been altered and continues to be taught by successors who form a living chain with the Apostles and faithfully interpret the Good News.

In the creed, we express our belief in the authentic Church of Christ by professing the marks that all Christian Churches have, but which are possessed in a unique way in the Catholic Church.

Because the Church is a pilgrim people not in full possession of the kingdom, we can always improve in each of the marks. As Catholics, we believe that we are especially close to Christians of other denominations who also profess belief in Christ, and we strive towards the unity for which Jesus prayed (John 17:20-23). The Church also respects the dignity and worth of non-Christians. We acknowledge a special bond with the Jewish people who were the first to receive God's Covenant. By living lives of faith, charity, and praise, the People of God are a sign to all people of the call to salvation as they work toward that day when the universe will be united in praising the Father.

A mark of the Church is being catholic, which means that the Church welcomes everyone to enter.

---

11. How can each of the Church's marks be enhanced today?

12. In what ways do you think your beliefs are different from those of your non-Catholic friends? Can you give some specific examples of these differences?

A Gifted People

In announcing salvation to the world, the Church is organized into a **hierarchy** of people. The Church is first and foremost the congregation of the laity—the People of God—whose gifts the leaders rely on heavily and call forth to serve the kingdom. Bishops, the successors to the Apostles, govern the Church and, always subject to revelation, are its final authority. They are commissioned to shepherd God's people, serving them as Christ served: teaching, leading, guiding, and sanctifying. Chief among the college of bishops is the pope, the Bishop of Rome. Just as Peter was called by Christ for a special role, his successors, the pontiffs, continue to provide leadership for the whole

Catholic: also interpreted to mean **universal.**

Hierarchy: in the Church, roles are classified from pope to laity so that all may use their particular talents, charisms, and gifts.

Pontiff: originally guardian of the state religion under Caesar, this word has been a title for the pope since the fifth century.

Chapter 3 Jesus Lives On in the Church

Church. The organization of people according to their gifts assures that people's talents will be used and that the work of the Church will go forward efficiently and effectively.

Although they have not received the full powers of priesthood possessed by the bishops, priests minister in the name of Christ by reason of the sacrament of Holy Orders. They serve the People of God in union with the bishops. Deacons, also sharing the power of the bishops, serve the Church, especially by performing charitable deeds, by preaching the Word, and by assisting in the liturgy.

One of the best gifts Christ left his Church is his Spirit who dwells in it, guiding and empowering it for God's work. To safeguard the Church's divine mission, the Holy Spirit has endowed the whole Church with many gifts. Fundamental to them all is the authority from Christ, who was given full authority by the Father. This authority should be administered in the spirit of Christ, who came to serve and not to be served.

As Church leaders, the Holy Father and the other bishops (the magisterium or teaching Church) are responsible for preserving the revelation of Christ and the Apostles. **Infallibility** is when the pope speaks **ex cathedra**, in his official capacity as supreme teacher, intending to bind all Christians in matters of faith and morals. He thus expresses the faith tradition of the whole People of God. The bishops are infallible when, together with the pope, they as a body officially pronounce on matters of faith and morals.

The entire Church was also gifted with infallibility, the special divine assistance to guarantee freedom from serious error in preserving the essential doctrines of revelation. When members of the Church teach truths held universally by the People of God, they, too, speak infallibly. Infallibility is not automatic but implies a constant listening and openness to the Spirit on the part of Church members.

By the assistance of the Holy Spirit in the characteristic known as **indefectibility**, the Church moves constantly and unfailingly toward the end of time. Jesus is not "automatically" present, but comes again and again as the Church continually reforms itself to become a purified people presentable to God.

Touching the Sacred

John 17:11-13 Prayer for the Disciples

Jesus prayed:

"Holy Father, keep them in your name that you have given me, so that they may be one, just as we are.

"When I was with them I protected them in your name that you gave me, and I guarded them, and none of them was lost except the son of destruction, in order that the scripture might be fulfilled.

"But now I am coming to you. I speak this in the world so that they may share my joy completely."

Even though the Church is a visible sign of Christ's living among us, its effectiveness is marred by the sinfulness of its members. The individuals who make up the Church are only human. This includes the pope who, like Peter, the first pontiff, makes mistakes. Infallibility, limited by the requirements described, does not extend to the pope's personal opinions or such things as his knowledge of science or other secular matters. As God worked through the Israelites and the Apostles in the past, God works today through imperfect human beings by the power of the Holy Spirit. Leaving people free to respond, God relies on them to live up to their sacred trust: to spread the divine message, to love and support one another in community, and to address the needs of all people, inviting them to worship the Father.

13. Why do you think God has chosen to work through imperfect human beings instead of the simpler method of sending a book that gives all the details humans would ever need?

"Saint Peter's Chair in Rome"
The pope speaks infallibly only when he speaks "ex cathedra," from the chair of Peter, that is as head of the Church.

Ex cathedra: literally "from the chair"; the pope speaking in his official capacity as supreme teacher.

Indefectibility: the gift of God to the Church that it (the Church) will last until the end of time, ever able to respond to the needs of people in new ways.

Summary

- The Church is a society established by God through the Son, Jesus. It is also a human society comprised of people who need guidance and direction of the Holy Spirit.
- There are four characteristics of the Church called "marks." The Church is **one**, **holy**, **catholic,** and **apostolic.**
- All members of the Church have been gifted by the Holy Spirit. Sharing these gifts is called "ministry."

Chapter 3　Jesus Lives On in the Church

SECTION 2
Checkpoint!

■ Review

1. What is the three-fold mission of the Church?

2. Explain the meaning of each of the four marks of the Church.

3. What is meant by the terms "indefectibility" and "infallibility"? What do they refer to?

4. What is meant by "the hierarchy"?

5. Do you have to belong to the hierarchy to be a "minister" in the Church? Explain.

6. Words to Know: church, hierarchy, infallibility, "catholic", ministry, marks (of the Church), ex cathedra, indefectibility.

■ In Your World

1. Discuss why you are a Catholic. Is it simply because you were born into a Catholic family? Do you feel strong enough in your faith to remain a good Catholic after high school?

2. Some religious people (like the Muslims in Iran) believe that their religious leaders should also be the country's political leaders. Do you agree or disagree with this opinion? Why?

■ Scripture Search

1. Discuss 1 Corinthians 12. What image does Paul use to describe the Church? How can this image help us to work together more effectively?

2. Read Romans 10:1-13. What attitude regarding different nations and religions is evident? Make a list of three things you would say to people who are prejudiced against other races and religions.

SECTION 3
The Church Celebrates Christ

Most people would rather hear a voice over the phone than get a letter. But more than that, most people would like to see and be with their friends. People are happier in the actual presence of friends than with any gift or message sent in their place, and yet, people don't long for mere physical nearness. You would be disappointed if your friends were asleep or consistently ignored you whenever you visted them. You want to feel their interest and affection. You value the love in their eyes and the smile on their lips. But more than anything else, you feel the need to communicate with them personally and intimately.

So it is with Jesus. Through the Church and the sacraments we can experience Christ's presence with us throughout our lives. As students, as brothers and sisters, as sons and daughters of our parents, and as people active in bringing Jesus to the world today, we need to take advantage of the Church's celebration of prayer and sacrament.

Celebration

A celebration is a time out from the daily grind, a pause for the purpose of rediscovering who you are and what you are about. For example, the routine of countless classes, pages of notes, cramming for exams, trips to your locker, dreaming out the window in spring—all end in the "time out" of graduation. This is a celebration of the fact that you did what was required to become free to read, write, and think on your own.

It is right that you celebrate this event in the company of all who made the day possible. There are special robes, long

Chapter 3 Jesus Lives On in the Church

We communicate best with friends when we see them face to face.

speeches, processions, music, and awards in a ceremony at which everyone gathers to ackowledge your good fortune. There are further parties, gift-giving, and good food at home to emphasize the significance not only of what you've become but of what your achievement promises for the future.

Graduation from high school or college is a time for great celebration.

Worship and Sacraments: We Celebrate, We Praise

It is typical to mark the important occasions of life with celebrations: birthdays, anniversaries, passing tests, winning games and awards. These occasions are milestones of growth into the person you are meant to become. It is likewise typical to celebrate what gives you your deepest identity—your relationship with God.

Since the beginning of history, people have celebrated their religious identity. To celebrate their special closeness with God, the Israelites annually held a Passover festival that extended over a full week (Exodus 12). The center of the feast was a meal of lamb and, later, unleavened bread, which brought to mind the original event of the Passover. This commemoration was more than a simple retelling of the story: it was a reenactment of the event, and the Jewish people actually felt God's saving power among them in the symbolic actions.

Every week, this feast was celebrated in miniature at the Sabbath supper. As time went on, other feasts were added to bring out different aspects of the great and complex Passover event. The Feast of Weeks, or Pentecost, commemorated the Covenant with God. During the Festival of Tents, the Israelites thanked God for feeding and caring for them in the wilderness.

14. Why do so many families gather on Thanksgiving or other holidays? Why do these reunions so often center on a meal?

15. Why do people like to talk about "the good old days" when they get together? What other achievements do people celebrate? Why do these celebrations seem to be so important for people?

For Example

The Jewish people left the door open and a seat empty at Passover to make room for the possible return of the prophet Elijah.

Passover is a time of special celebration for the Jews. Passover reminds us of the saving power of God.

Chapter 3   Jesus Lives On in the Church

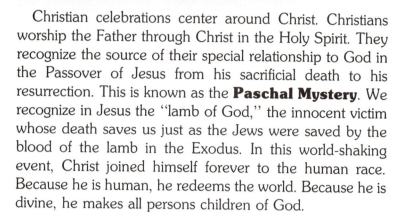

Christian Celebration

Christian celebrations center around Christ. Christians worship the Father through Christ in the Holy Spirit. They recognize the source of their special relationship to God in the Passover of Jesus from his sacrificial death to his resurrection. This is known as the **Paschal Mystery**. We recognize in Jesus the "lamb of God," the innocent victim whose death saves us just as the Jews were saved by the blood of the lamb in the Exodus. In this world-shaking event, Christ joined himself forever to the human race. Because he is human, he redeems the world. Because he is divine, he makes all persons children of God.

After Pentecost, with the help of the Holy Spirit, the early Church understood the Last Supper as a new Passover meal to commemorate Jesus' saving action on Calvary. Jesus' followers broke bread together on the first day of every week, the Lord's Day, to bring into their midst his death and resurrection. They not only recalled the Paschal Mystery, they actually made it **present**.

Foremost among the sentiments of the first Christians was thanksgiving. They were grateful for God's continued presence and saving acts, first for creation, but above all for the gifts of redemption through his Son and the Holy Spirit. To show their wholehearted participation, the assembly of the early Church would enthusiastically stamp their feet, shout glad alleluias at the conclusion of the Eucharistic Prayer, and sing out the Great Amen. Something of this spontaneous spirit can be seen today in the applause of a congregation when a new member is added to the Church by baptism, a couple is married, a minister is ordained, a bishop is consecrated, or a new Holy Father is elected.

The singing of songs and hymns played a large part in the early liturgies. When the first Christians sang Christ's own prayer, the Our Father, they stood with arms extended to praise God with their whole bodies as well as their voices. Their enthusiasm was infectious. The great happiness shown in the assemblies of these early communities attracted many new converts.

Eventually, each Sunday became a small paschal celebration. The early Christians called these celebrations

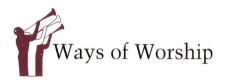

Ways of Worship

Worship in the Early Church

"They devoted themselves to the teaching of the apostles and to the communal life, to the breaking of the bread and to the prayers. Awe came upon everyone, and many wonders and signs were done through the apostles. All who believed were together and had all things in common; they would sell their property and possessions and divide them among all according to each one's need. Every day they devoted themselves to meeting together in the temple area and to breaking bread in their homes. They ate their meals with exultation and sincerity of heart, praising God and enjoying favor with all the people. And every day the Lord added to their number those who were being saved" (Acts of the Apostles 2:42-47).

Worship and Sacraments: We Celebrate, We Praise

When you celebrate the Eucharist you participate in the paschal mystery.

ministry—that is, "official service." At the season of the Passover, Christians remembered Jesus' paschal sacrifice and victory over death in a special way.

In the centuries that followed Jesus' departure from earth, the weekly and annual Easter celebrations were the only liturgies of the Christian communities. As time marched on, Christians understood more and more what Jesus had accomplished by his life and death. As their realization became clearer, the Church added daily celebrations of praise and joy that extended through the entire year.

16. What do you think attracts converts to the Faith?
17. It has been said that, for the Jews, the greatest sin was to forget all that God had done for them. That's why they gather for celebrations: to remember. How is this also true of all celebrations, especially Christian celebrations?

Paschal Mystery: the event of Jesus' death and resurrection.

The Lord's Day: the day on which Jesus rose from the dead, Sunday.

Eucharist: based on a Greek verb meaning "to give thanks."

Chapter 3 Jesus Lives On in the Church

Holy Days

In the United States, there are six special celebrations called "Holy Days." On these days, Catholics are obliged to celebrate Mass just as they are on Sundays.

January 1: The Solemnity of Mary. We begin the new year by honoring our Blessed Mother.

Ascension Thursday: The sixth Thursday after Easter, which celebrates Jesus' return to the Father. Because the date of Easter changes each year, so does the date of the Ascension.

August 15: The Assumption of Mary into heaven after her death.

November 1: All Saints' Day, the celebration of all the holy women and men who have gone before us.

December 8: The Immaculate Conception of Mary, which celebrates the fact that Mary was conceived without Original Sin.

December 25: Christmas, the birth of Jesus.

Greeters at mass welcome people into the worshiping community.

Summary

- Celebration is a normal and necessary human activity. Through celebrations, we recall the important things in our lives.

- Christian celebration focuses on God's great gift of Jesus Christ to us. It helps us to remember him and experience his presence in our world.

- From the very beginning of Christianity, followers of Christ gathered to celebrate Jesus' death and resurrection by sharing a common meal.

Worship and Sacraments: We Celebrate, We Praise

SECTION 3
Checkpoint!

■ Review

1. Why do people celebrate special events in their lives and in the history of their countries?

2. What is the Passover celebration and what event does it remember?

3. What is meant by the "Paschal Mystery"?

4. What are Holy Days and why does the Church invite us to celebrate them?

5. Words to Know: Passover, Paschal Mystery, Eucharist, Holy Days, the Lord's Day, Sabbath.

■ In Your World

1. How are **Holy** Days in the Church like civil **holi**days that we celebrate?

2. Why do you think that the Church invites us to celebrate Mass on Holy Days? What do these special celebrations help us to remember about God and Jesus?

3. Write a letter to a non-Catholic friend describing the importance of the Church and it celebrations.

■ Scripture Search

1. Read Exodus, chapter 12. What were the Jews celebrating at Passover and how does this celebration resemble a celebration of Christ in the Catholic Church?

2. Study and discuss 1 Corinthians 11:17-34. What problems was Paul trying to correct at the Sunday celebrations in Corinth? What advice did he give?

CHAPTER 3 Review

■ Study

1. What is the Apostles' Creed and why is this prayer an important statement of faith?

2. After Jesus left the earth, how did God and his Son provide a guide for Christians? What event recalls God's sending us this helper?

3. What are Church councils and how do they help us interpret God's revelation?

4. Who founded the Church? Why was it founded?

5. How would you define the Church?

6. We say that the Church is holy (second mark), but we also say that it is a pilgrim people (not in full possession of the kingdom). Are these two beliefs contradictory? How would you reconcile them?

7. Who are "the hierarchy" and "the people of God"? What is their relationship in performing the works of ministry?

8. What is the purpose of Christian celebration?

9. How did the early Church celebrate God's revelation in Jesus Christ?

10. In what ways do you think God is calling you to be a disciple of Christ?

11. What are some of the difficulties young people face as they try to be good Catholics today?

12. What advice would you give to someone who is having questions about their faith or the Catholic Church?

■ Action

1. Find out from one of the priests in your parish how the parish's ministry is organized. Make a chart that shows all of the ministries and what service each one provides.

2. Talk to your parents about the importance of religion in their lives. Ask them if there have been any changes in the way they view religion now compared to how they viewed it as a teenager. If you feel comfortable doing so, share with them some of your questions about your faith. Believe it or not, they may be able to offer you some pretty good advice!

3. Consider having a guest speaker come to class—someone who can speak about the Church and its history. Prepare questions in advance and use the time to gain a better understanding of how Jesus lives on in the Church.

■ Prayer

An old Christian hymn begins with the words, "The Church's one foundation is Jesus Christ, the Lord." We remember Christ, our foundation, not only by how we live but also by how we pray. Notice how many prayers of the Church end with the words "**through** Jesus Christ, our Lord."

This prayer activity will help you focus on Jesus, the foundation of our lives and of the Christian community. It's a good prayer to say before going to bed or in the morning before beginning the activities of your day. It is simple enough to memorize.

> Creator of the day and night,
> You give us love and hope and life,
> Through Jesus Christ, our Lord.
> Be my guide, my strength, my light,
> Help me to know the wrong from right,
> Through Jesus Christ, our Lord.
> And when my days on earth are done,
> May I then live with Mary's Son,
> Through Jesus Christ, our Lord.
> All glory, praise and honor be
> To you, great God, both One and Three
> Through Jesus Christ, our Lord. Amen.

CHAPTER 4

Signs and Symbols: Language of the Heart

OBJECTIVES

In this Chapter you will

- Explore the meaning of symbols in your life.

- Examine sacramental symbols and experience their real and true presence.

- Understand how symbols are encountered everyday, and the important role they play in human living.

The thing which becomes a symbol retains its original form and its original content. It does not become, so to speak, an empty shell into which another content is poured; in itself, through its own existence, it makes another reality transparent which cannot appear in any other form.
—G. Scholem, *Major Trends in Jewish Mysticism*

Worship and Sacraments: We Celebrate, We Praise

SECTION 1
The Language of Signs and Symbols

Have you ever spoken with someone, and knew what they were going to say before they said it? Or have you had a feeling that something was going to happen, and then it did? Although some people may communicate by ESP, it certainly is not the ordinary way people get across to others what is in their minds and hearts. Communicating without the use of the senses may work for angels; for humans, however, ideas and emotions are nontransferable unless they are embodied. They must be packaged in signs that can be unwrapped by another's eyes, ears, taste, smell, or touch.

In a Dream

Juanita woke with a start. "Dave Michaels. . . Dave Michaels. . ." The name rolled around in her mind awhile before she was awake enough to remember that Dave was her new student who had been admitted to her history class the week before.

Juanita glanced at her clock. Its illuminated dial showed 2:30. Why did she have so strong a sense of Dave Michaels at 2:30 in the morning? She had hardly said a word to him since giving him his text and an outline of the course. "Maybe he's in trouble," Juanita thought. She whispered a quick prayer for him, rolled over, and fell asleep again.

The next morning there was a flurry of excitement in the teachers' lounge. Everyone was talking about how Dave Michaels had been killed in an auto crash. Juanita turned pale. "When?" she murmured, almost afraid to ask. "His car went out of control, hit a guard rail, and exploded sometime around seven last night," Jim Hoover, the geometry teacher, answered. Juanita relaxed slightly. Then Jim added, "He died at 2:30 this morning."

1. Do you think Juanita was actually being told of Dave Michael's accident in her dream? Why or why not? How would you have felt if you were Juanita? Explain.

Sign Language

A sign is something that suggests the existence of something else that cannot be known exactly. For example, if you want to let others know you're tired, you have to make sounds and signs such as saying, "I'm tired," yawning, slouching, or sleeping.

Human beings are expert sign-makers. Daily they make hundreds of body-signs and action-signs: they wave, drum their fingers, salute, and eat. They make many sound-signs: they speak, whistle, or give a cheer. They make written signs: they record messages on paper, wood, glass, plastic, and metal. They also use images as signs: they relay messages by depicting fire, a skull and crossbones, or people.

Humans communicate through many ways. These students are speaking in American Sign Language.

My Beloved Philomena

Not many people answer to the name Philomena these days, though it's actually a very beautiful Greek name. At any rate, a teacher who was trying to help his students understand the meaning of symbols started his class one day with the words, "My beloved Philomena is a red, red rose." His astonished students tried to be polite, but before long they started to laugh uncontrollably.

"We didn't even know you had a girlfriend," one student said. More laughter. "It sounds pretty silly," the teacher answered. "Not the part about my having a girlfriend, but the fact that I called her 'a red, red rose.' " The laughter began to taper off as the teacher continued.

"If someone asked you to describe a person you loved and cared about, and you talked about all the standard information relating to her or him that goes on job applications or on student records, you'd know that you have failed to communicate the power and the beauty of your relationship. All that data is correct, but none of it tells the whole truth about the person." The class fell silent.

"Before long you would be groping for words—symbols—describing the indescribable. Of course, Philomena is no rose. She's the person I hope to marry. But then, again, she is a rose. A red, red rose." And at that point, everyone in the class knew exactly what their teacher was saying. They couldn't wait to meet the rose with the name, Philomena.

Roses are often given as gifts to show affection.

Simple Signs

All signs point to something beyond themselves. A **simple sign** conveys a single idea to the mind in a one-to-one relationship. Once the sign gets its message across, its work is finished. It says what it means and it means what it says. End of discussion! A traffic light, a barber pole, and a "wet paint" sign are some examples of

For Example

The "wet paint" sign is not wet, and the sign itself may remain posted long after the paint has dried.

Chapter 4   Signs and Symbols: Language of the Heart

simple signs. Remember that even simple signs point to something beyond themselves.

Complex Signs

The second kind of sign, a **symbol**, is richer and more complex in both its meaning and what it can do. It represents something else by association or resemblance. Like a simple sign, a symbol is a form of communication that points to something outside itself. But unlike a sign, a symbol also contains within itself something of the meaning it conveys. A symbol somehow brings about what it represents. Your body, for example, is a symbol of your invisible spirit. It outwardly shows interior poise or nervousness, love or hate.

A sign appeals to the mind. A symbol stimulates the imagination by carrying with it a whole background of feelings, memories, and sense experiences. A sign conveys an idea; a symbol conveys an experience.

The Meaning Behind Symbols

Your school jacket is an example of a sign and a symbol. To people who are not well acquainted with your school, your jacket is, first of all, a sign. It identifies the name of the school you attend. But if your school has just won the state championship in football, that jacket becomes the symbol of everything your school stands for: discipline, achievement, courage, excellence, school spirit, self-control, responsibility, initiative, and leadership. Its colors will remind you of your school years for the rest of your life. Because many people in the school wear a school jacket, you feel a oneness with them.

If you paid for the jacket yourself, wearing it gives you a sense of independence. In some ways, the jacket is part of your own identity, and its symbolism has the power to stir up all sorts of feelings and memories. If the losing team were to drag it through the mud or set it on fire, you would feel it very personally.

Symbols can grow in meaning. For example, your school jacket may mean more to you as a senior than it did when you were a sophomore. Long after graduation, seeing a picture of yourself wearing the school jacket may bring back the joys, excitement, and fun of high school. If, for some

 On the Record

Meet Karl Rahner

Karl Rahner, a twentieth-century Catholic theologian from Germany, used the language of symbol to talk about the sacraments. Like all Catholic theologians, he believed that God's grace was really present and available to us in the sacraments. Rahner described the sacraments as symbolic actions of Christ and the Church in which we go beyond ourselves through the power of the Holy Spirit to grow in love and grace. Jesus, Rahner said, is the fullness of grace, and the Church is where we meet him in his life of self-giving, demonstrated most dramatically in the Paschal Mystery. To celebrate the sacraments, therefore, is to meet Jesus Christ and to be touched by Christ's offer of new life.

Besides your school jacket, what other examples of signs can you name which identify your school as a special place?

reason, during your high school years you got into trouble with the administration or were expelled from your school, the sight of your jacket might arouse bitterness, rebellion, or shame.

2. What are some examples of simple signs that people use to communicate? Choose any five signs and tell what they suggest.

3. What are the signs of a cold? Fear? Rain? Sorrow? Spring? Joy?

Summary

- Signs simply point out something. Their meaning is clear, and once they are understood, there is no need for further discussion about what they intend to communicate.

- Symbols are also signs—complex signs—but they not only point out something, they also contain within themselves the reality of what they symbolize. They make what they symbolize real and present.

- Symbols grow in meaning. Unlike simple signs, the meaning of symbols is never fully grasped. There is something truly mysterious about them.

SECTION 1
Checkpoint!

■ Review

1. Why must human beings communicate using signs and symbols?

2. Your body is a symbol of your invisible spirit. In what sense is this true?

3. Explain this statement: "All symbols are signs, but not all signs are symbols."

4. In math, the word "symbol" is often used for certain quantities or relations. When your math teacher uses the expression "mathematical symbol," she or he is really talking about what we call a (simple) sign in religion. Why?

5. Words to Know: simple signs, complex signs, symbols.

■ In Your World

1. At John F. Kennedy's grave, his widow lit an "eternal flame." What did she mean the flame to symbolize? Why is a flame a good symbol for the risen Christ? Think of some ways that flames are used in church.

2. On a piece of paper, write the word "flame." Think about any ideas it generates. Next, place a lit candle in a darkened room. Experience it. What difference did you notice between this experience of a flame and the first experience on a piece of paper? Which was more alive for you? Which of the following do you think a burning flame symbolizes? Why?
   Zeal, creation, love, knowledge, hate, peace, punishment, friendship, an old person, the Spirit, wisdom, patience, self-giving, goodness, courage, jealousy, fear, faith, youth, prayer.

■ Scripture Search

1. Read Genesis 1:1-8. Describe some of the symbolic images used by the author of the text to describe God's creative act.

2. Read Psalm 148:1-10. Psalms are really hymns that were sung with musical accompaniment. They are, therefore, a kind of poetry, and they use language figuratively. What do you think the "poet" of Psalm 148 was expressing? In what sense is the language of the psalm "symbolic"?

SECTION 2
Sacramental Symbols

You have seen that human beings have always used symbols to express their faith. After some time it became clear that nature was not to be worshipped because God has an existence separate from creation. God became so distinct in this identity that, through God's inspiration, the Chosen People constructed symbols, like the ark and the brazen serpent, in order to experience God's specialized presence. Natural and man-made symbols continue to speak today of God's presence, goodness, beauty, and creativity.

The Meaning of Sacramental Symbols

Sacraments are rich symbolic actions that make use of words, symbols, and simple signs. For instance, the sanctuary light reminds us of God's presence. The paschal candle recalls the Paschal Mystery. The celebration of the Eucharist, with all its gestures, is the richest symbolic action human beings can ever experience. Yet, you may be confused by the fact that sacraments are sometimes called signs even though they are not simple idea-bearers, such as a green light. When applied to a sacrament, the word "sign" is used in a broader sense to mean its total action—words, gestures, prayers, and symbols.

If you have seen *Fiddler on the Roof,* you may have been struck by the intimate friendship the Jewish people have with God. They bring God into every cranny of their lives, whether in the joy of a wedding, the anguish of exile, or the routine of their daily work. The many ceremonies and blessings of the Jews are symbolic. Jesus brought the Jewish symbols and rituals to an even fuller development by his gift of the sacraments, especially the Eucharist.

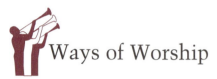

Ways of Worship

Praying Twice!

You may have heard the expression, "Whoever sings, prays twice." That's because music itself is a symbolic language that can place us more fully in God's presence. This is what the Church says about music in our worship:

"Liturgical worship is given more noble form when it is celebrated in song, with the ministers . . . fulfilling their ministry and the people participating in it.

Indeed, through this form, prayer is expressed in a more attractive way" —*Instructions on Music in the Liturgy*, Paragraph 5, 1967.

The priest at the Eucharist lifts the consecrated bread and wine in a symbolic gesture. What does this gesture say to you?

Sacramental symbols can have layer upon layer of meaning. Bread, for instance, has a symbolic tradition reaching back to the beginning of recorded time. Bread has nourished billions of people since creation. For Christians, the Eucharistic bread symbolically reflects the traditions of Israel going back to Melchizedeck's blessings of Abram, the unleavened bread eaten in haste by the Hebrews on the night of Passover, and God's great gift of manna that saved the Israelites in the desert (see Genesis 14:18; Exodus 12:37-39, 16:1-8). Eucharistic bread also reminds Christians of the times Jesus fed the thousands with a few loaves, and of Jesus' last meal, when he consecrated the bread as his own body.

Then, too, the Christian community has a two-thousand-year tradition of sacred bread. Countless Eucharistic meals have been celebrated from the time of the Apostles—in the private homes of the early Christians, in the catacombs, in the great medieval cathedrals, in small country churches, in large parishes, at formal high Masses, in secret hiding places, in the glorious setting of the Vatican, and in the foxholes of war.

Besides all these associations, each Christian has his or her own personal memories of Eucharistic bread. There are memories of special occasions such as First Communion, Confirmation, Matrimony, Religious Profession or Ordination. There are also memories of intimate, peaceful communions of ordinary days, and the soul-shaking liturgies of the high feast days.

The concrete symbols used in the sacraments—water, bread, wine, and oil—are laden with meaning and associations. But the entire action of each sacrament, from beginning to end, is a sign with rich symbolic overtones as well.

---

4. *Take a few moments to think about each of the following symbols. What do they reveal to you about God? A) a sunrise; B) the moon; C) a mountain; D) water.*

5. *Which Eucharistic celebrations are most vivid in your life? Recall your own associations with and memories of each of these symbols: water, wine, bread, oil.*

6. *What actions of Jesus symbolize God's love? What actions of the liturgy celebrate these events?*

Symbolic Actions

When revealed to the Chosen People, the prophets described God through symbols. As one prophet wrote, "For who can see him and describe him? Or who can praise him as he is?" (Sirach 43:33). God came to the Hebrews **through** visible actions that actually saved them from

Catacombs: large underground cemeteries in Rome that extended for great distances. During times of persecution, Christians used to celebrate Mass there, especially at the graves of women and men who died for their faith.

Liturgy: a public act of worship, from the Greek "the people's work."

Chapter 4 Signs and Symbols: Language of the Heart

different kinds of evil: slavery in Egypt, starvation in the desert, defeat by enemies, and idolatry. All of these actions symbolized a God who was gracious to the Chosen People without any merit on their part.

Above all, the Hebrew people kept sacred the memory of the Covenant that God had made with them. Through rituals—the symbolic actions of what God had done for them—the Israelites reminded themselves again and again of God's faithful love. In this way, they recalled the past. Over the centuries, their liturgies continually renewed the memory of God's saving acts. These actions helped them to receive God's deliverance in their present lives. They also provided a way for the Israelites to look ahead with the expectation that God would send a Savior to end their hardships forever.

---

7. A man who had been married to the same woman for 40 years said, "A kiss on the way out of the door does not in itself make a marriage work. But forget the kiss for a long enough time, and you're in trouble!" What do you think he meant?

Symbolic Words

Words are symbols. Because they are personal and direct, they are clearer than objects and events. They make the meaning of symbols specific. Many people don't like to be asked to explain their meaning when they speak because they expect words to be plain. But they don't mind being asked what symbols mean because symbols can be ambiguous.

An angry wife might interpret the box of candy sent by an estranged husband on their anniversary as a bitter mockery of the candy he brought her on their first date. By his addition of the four small but powerful words "I still love you," the intended meaning of the candy cannot be mistaken.

Symbolic Postures

Words and objects can be symbols. So also can gestures that we make with our bodies, as we can easily see in symbolic postures used by Muslims when they pray.

Each Muslim believer sits and kneels on a small, beautifully-designed rug during the five required daily prayer rituals. Each prayer ritual, called a **rakah**, consists of seven body positions and six prayers.

Position	*Prayer*
The worshiper stands facing Mecca with hands raised along the side of the face. The fingers point upward.	Allahu Akbar—God is most great!
Hands are placed on stomach, right on top of left.	Praise be to Allah, Lord of the Worlds, the Beneficent, the Merciful.
Hands are placed on knees, while the worshiper bows.	Glory be to my Lord, the Great!
The worshiper stands, letting arms dangle at his or her sides.	Glory be to my Lord, the Great!
Worshiper kneels, touching rug with forehead, nose, palms of hands, knees and toes.	Glory be to my Lord, the Most High!
With hands on top of knees, the worshiper, still kneeling, sits upright on heels.	Allahu Akbar—God is most great!
Repetition of positions five and six, with face turned to the right.	Peace be with you.

The next time a Protestant friend asks you why Catholics stand and sit and kneel and go through all those complicated body postures at Mass, you can tell them about the Muslims! You might also suggest that he or she pay attention to the bodily postures, expressions, and gestures that fans demonstrate at a football game, or even at his or her own church. This is the language of symbols and everybody speaks it! It's only human.

Muslims at prayer assume many different body postures.

Ambiguous: not clear.

Estranged: separated or become like strangers.

Chapter 4   Signs and Symbols: Language of the Heart

The inspired words of the prophets in the Hebrew Scriptures clarified the meaning of God's symbolic actions in Israel. Over and over, the prophets repeated how God had chosen and saved the Hebrews and how, even in calamities like the destruction of their Temple, God was blessing them.

Because the Hebrews considered God as one, they could not separate the communications of God from the person of God. God was the Word. Therefore, when God spoke, God was present to the People in the Word.

The word of the sacraments is God's Word, even though it is spoken by the human voice. It makes the symbols and symbolic actions of the sacraments definite and clear. What is more, God comes through this Word. But the word of the sacraments is more than God's presence. When God speaks, the Word always makes things happen. The Word of God is the vehicle and cause of God's power. The prophet Isaiah explains it this way:

"For just as from the heavens the rain and snow come down And do not return there till they have watered the earth, making it fertile and fruitful, Giving seed to those who sow and bread to those who eat, So shall my Word be that goes forth from my mouth; It shall not return to me void, but shall do my will, achieving the end for which I sent it" (Isaiah 55:10-11).

Word and act are one in God. As the Book of Sirach states, "At God's Word were his works brought into being; they do his will as he has ordained for them" (Sirach 42:15). God both speaks and acts through the word of the sacraments, and he both speaks and acts through the actions of the rite. God's Word is expressed in the human word and in the human action.

The prophet Isaiah compared God's Word to life-giving water.

8. *Describe the action and the meaning Jesus gives to it by his words in these passages: Luke 18:15-17, 19:1-10, 22:17-20; John 13:1-17.*

9. *How is God shown to have created the world in the first chapter of Genesis?*

Prayer in front of the Tabernacle is a special way of recognizing the presence of God in the Eucharist.

Summary

- Sacraments may be described in the language of symbol, but this in no way suggests that sacraments are not a real meeting with Christ. If an action is symbolic, that which it symbolizes is really present.

- The ancient Israelites celebrated God's presence through many symbolic actions and when they did so, they believed that God was living and acting among them.

- All words are symbolic. The Word of God is even more so. When we celebrate God's Word, we allow God to change our lives and overcome our human sinfulness.

Rite: the set of words and actions that make up a sacrament or other religious ceremony.

Chapter 4 Signs and Symbols: Language of the Heart

SECTION 2
Checkpoint!

■ Review

1. What do we mean when we say that sacramental symbols can have layer upon layer of meaning?

2. What are some of the important symbolic actions celebrated by the Jewish people?

3. In what sense is God's Word a powerful symbol for people of faith? How can hearing and living God's Word affect us?

4. How can bodily postures be symbolic gestures?

5. Words to Know: ritual, liturgy, rite, catacombs.

■ In Your World

1. Explain this statement: "There are two ways of spreading the light—to be a candle or the mirror that reflects it."

2. Explain this passage (John 1:1-3): "In the beginning was the Word, and the Word was with God, and the Word was God. He was in the beginning with God. All things came to be through him, and without him nothing came to be."

3. What is the Word of God? What is the relationship between God's Word and action?

4. How can the birth of Jesus be symbolized as light coming into darkness? Why can it be said that the darkness did not overcome the light?

■ Scripture Search

1. Find the words of God which Saint Paul speaks of in the following texts: 1 Corinthians 1:18; Acts of the Apostles 13:26; 2 Corinthians 5:18. In each case, what synonym do you find for "word"?

2. Read Sirach 42:15-25. How does Sirach relate the Word of God to God's works in creation?

SECTION 3
Encountering Symbols

Symbols are not magic. What is experienced as a powerful symbol by one person may appear to be a simple sign to someone else. If, for example, a Buddhist came to Mass with you and saw you genuflect before the Blessed Sacrament, she or he would say, "Oh yes, Catholics believe that the tabernacle of their churches contain holy bread." For the Buddhist, the Blessed Sacrament is a sign. It is simply a reminder of what Catholics believe. For Catholics, however, the Blessed Sacrament is the real presence of Christ. The difference between the Buddhist and the Catholic in this example is the faith of the Catholic. Because of faith, the bread in the tabernacle is far more than bread. It is the Body of Christ.

The Case of Mr. Spock

If you've ever seen an episode of "Star Trek" or one of the movies about the Enterprise going boldly "where no one has gone before," you are familiar with Mr. Spock. Spock seems to be a nice enough person. He never lies. He's brilliant. He shows uncommon bravery. Spock is also the definition of logic. Everything he does has to be completely logical. When another member of the crew cracks a joke, he looks puzzled, raises an eyebrow and remarks, "I fail to see the logic of that statement."

Because he is a good Vulcan, Mr. Spock thinks his way through life. He almost never smiles and he would sooner die than cry. He is perplexed when people thank him for doing what he believes is only his job. Even when Spock plays his Vulcan stringed instrument, something is missing. He gets all the notes right, but there's no light in his eyes. He creates sound, but he does not make music.

Buddhist monks dress in distinctive looking clothing and assume definitive prayer positions for worship.

Buddhist Symbolism in Worship

Buddhists center their religious practices around the life and teaching of their founder, Siddhartha Gautama, a rich prince who renounced his kingdom to search for truth. In festivals, parades, and dances, they honor the Buddha—the Enlightened One—who, while meditating under the Bodhi tree, discovered, and then spent his life teaching, the meaning of life.

In a community ceremony, young boys are dressed in princely clothes such as those worn by Siddhartha before his conversion, only to strip them off as a sign of rejection of the world. In imitation of the original Buddha, the boys put on the tea-colored robes of the strict monks with whom they live and through whom they hope to learn the truth and the path of the Buddha. On the days of the Buddha's birth and death, April 8 and February 15, his followers make offerings at his altars in their homes and temples. The daily reading of the *sutras*, the Buddhist scriptures, and the saying of grace before and after meals, are other practices that keep devout Buddhists mindful of the Buddha and his teachings.

Some Japanese sects hold thanksgiving worship in the *hondo* (temples) every Sunday morning. When they enter, they make a *gasho* (bow), offer incense, and take their places at the sound of a gong. The priest reads scripture and gives a sermon. They wrap *ouizu* (prayer beads) around their folded hands, especially during *gasho*. By their worship and by living in accord with the way of the Buddha, believers hope to reach *nirvana*, the place of perfect peace.

♦

If you have followed "Star Trek" on film, television, or in novels, you know why Spock is as he is. He's half human. His mother is from Earth and his father came from the planet Vulcan. Through Vulcan training, Spock learned to overcome the human trait of "understanding with his heart." For him, all truth and reality must be the result of pure intellectual inquiry. In a way, he gathers information and comes to conclusions more like a computer than like a human.

This fictional character is not entirely unreal. Some people try to go through life as if they were all head and no heart. When this happens to people, they find it very difficult to encounter symbols, for the language of the symbol is, in a sense, the language of the heart. Yes, God gave us our intellects and we must use them. But God also created us with an ability to "see into" the meaning of things—to understand truth and reality without sometimes being able to account for this understanding in coldly logical terms—like when we fall in love, appreciate a work of art, or say, "I believe in God."

It's only when head and heart work together that we are fully human. And it's only when we are fully human that our faith allows us to speak and interpret the language of symbols.

The character of Mr. Spock in "Star Trek" emphasizes logic over emotion.

10. What do you think allows a "simple sign" to become a powerful symbol of God's presence in our lives?

11. If you are familiar with Mr. Spock's character, give some other examples of his Vulcan logic. What problems might a Spock-like person run into with love, marriage and belief in God?

12. How do you think Spock would react to Jesus if the Enterprise went back in time and landed in Palestine when Jesus was alive?

Openness and Imagination

The Statue of Liberty, which raises its lamp of freedom and justice over the New York harbor, has stirred hopes and dreams in the hearts of thousands of immigrants. Most Americans who witnessed the telecast of the planting of the Stars and Stripes on the moon were moved with emotions of patriotism. Symbols greatly enrich life, but they speak only to those who listen.

Touching the Sacred

In prayer, we let the Sacred touch us. Our hearts are moved and our hope is renewed. In this prayer from the Book of Psalms, let the "images" that are used speak to your imagination. Try to hear God's Word—not just the words of the Psalm.

"The Lord is my shepherd; I shall not want. In verdant pastures he gives me repose; Beside restful waters he leads me; he refreshes my soul. He guides me in right paths for his name's sake.
Even though I walk in the dark valley I fear no evil; for you are at my side
With your rod and your staff that give me courage.
You spread the table before me in the sight of my foes
You anoint my head with oil; my cup overflows.
Only goodness and kindness follow me all the days of my life;
And I shall dwell in the house of the Lord for years to come" (Psalm 23).

Because they are capable of many possible interpretations, symbols ask us to use our imagination. They require faith in their power to call forth our deepest human emotions. A gift of flowers or a single dew-trimmed blade of grass has no symbolic meaning at all unless we actively exercise our belief in the reality of the love that someone (or Someone) means to express by it.

To experience symbols fully, we need to cultivate openness and imagination. Being too scientific or too logical can make us miss their many dimensions. Instead of thinking too precisely about symbols, analyzing and dissecting them like frogs in a biology lab, we need to cultivate a sense of wonder and alertness to the possibilities of things. We need a readiness to let their meaning penetrate our hearts. Sometimes we may completely overlook a breathtaking sunset or the magic of a starlit sky simply because we're too busy to give it our attention.

In other words, symbols are empty and lifeless when we are unwilling to take the risk of faith, when we are closed or negative to their many possibilities, or when we refuse to let them into our hearts. If we approach symbols with the simplicity of children and allow ourselves to respond to them freely, they can become bridges between each of us, and between us and the Spirit at work in the world.

13. *Do you think Americans are good at responding to symbols? How do they show their response to symbols publicly?*

Summary

- The language of symbol is language that speaks to our imaginations, not just to our intellects.

- We encounter symbols every day. They can communicate to us a whole world of meaning that we would miss if we could not understand them.

- In order to grasp the meaning of symbols and experience reality through them, we must be open to their unique form of communication.

SECTION 3
Checkpoint!

■ Review

1. Why can we say that people who rely only on their intellects are not open to hearing God's Word in its fulness?

2. Explain this statement: "Some day, we may be able to build a computer that knows everything and can actually think, but it will never be able to understand the meaning of what it 'knows.'"

3. What is the role of our God-given imaginations in our journey of faith?

4. Do you agree with those who claim that the product of our imaginations is always fantasy and, therefore, should be regarded with suspicion by mature adults? Give reasons for your opinion.

5. Words to Know: imagination, *sutras*, *nirvana*.

■ In Your World

1. Rate your own involvement in Sunday worship on a scale of one to ten, ten being the greatest degree of involvement and one being no involvement. Explain why your rating is what it is.

2. Some thinkers have said that the emphasis in the past century on scientific fact, industrialization, and computerization, together with a lack of interest in history, make the modern generation unsuited for symbolic communication. Others claim that because of these impersonalizing trends there is a renewal of involvement with symbolism, shown in an upswing of interest in new religions, the occult, dream interpretation, prayer, and Pentecostalism. Which position would you agree with? Why?

■ Scripture Search

1. Study Revelation 1:9-20. Describe some of the images John used there to tell us about his vision.

2. Find a Bible that has extensive notes interpreting the texts or use a Bible Commentary like the *Jerome Biblical Commentary*. Write a brief report on Revelation 1:9-20 in which you give an interpretation of the symbols used in this passage.

CHAPTER 4 Review

■ Study

1. Why do human beings need to communicate by signs?
2. What is the difference between a simple sign and a symbol?
3. Why are symbols known as "experience-bearers"?
4. How can symbols grow and change? What "layers" do the Christian sacraments have?
5. What are symbolic actions? What was the purpose of ritual in Israel?
6. What does the spoken word add to everyday actions?
7. In what way is God's Word different from ordinary words?
8. How can you learn to experience symbols better?
9. What is the difference between a simple sign and a sacramental sign?
10. Describe the character of Mr. Spock in "Star Trek." Why might he find much of this chapter difficult to understand?
11. What are some of the symbols used in Buddhist worship? What do they mean?
12. Who was Karl Rahner and how did he describe sacraments?
13. How do Muslims use symbolic postures in their prayer?

■ Action

1. Ask a Jewish friend or rabbi to explain the symbols of Hanukkah (Feast of Lights).

2. Make a list of signs that appear around your school. Then make a list of symbols. Compare these with the lists of others in the class.

3. Write a poem or short essay, using a symbol to explain your present experience of God.

4. View one of the old "Star Trek" television programs or one of the movies. Discuss the character of Mr. Spock, especially when (on those rare occasions) he responds to his "human side."

5. Read the following passages from the Old Testament that speak of the worship of the Chosen People, and then match the type of worship with the correct Scripture readings. Genesis 1:1-2, 4a; Leviticus 23:33-44; Exodus 23:16, 34:22; 1 Kings 8:31-40.

■ Prayer

Plan a prayer service with your class in which you use images, symbols, and music to help create a climate of prayer. The preparation for your service can be made by a number of groups. As many people as possible should participate in leading the parts of your prayer, since it is a prayer of your "classroom community."

Practically any format can be used for your prayer. Here is only one suggestion:

- Song or music with presentation of special symbols
- Opening prayer
- Scripture reading(s)
- Shared psalm response
- Petitions and/or music
- Silent reflection and/or recitation of the Lord's Prayer
- Closing Prayer
- Song or music

CHAPTER 5

Sacraments and Christian Worship

OBJECTIVES

In this Chapter you will

- Understand the nature of sacramental presence and the importance of sacraments in Catholicism.

- Recognize Jesus as the primary sacrament revealing to you God's desire to heal you and welcome you into the kingdom.

- Experience the Church as a sacrament which proclaims and manifests Christ in the world.

Sacraments are actions of Christ. They are actions of the Church, actions of those who celebrate them. Jesus makes sacraments happen, and the celebrating community makes sacraments happen—at one and the same time. The sacraments are a joint enterprise of Jesus and his people.
—Fr. Eugene Walsh, *Ministry of the Celebrating Community*, Pastoral Arts Associates, page 12

Worship and Sacraments: We Celebrate, We Praise

SECTION 1
Sacramental Presence

A soldier in Saudi Arabia wired flowers back home. Wouldn't it have been better if she could have gone home herself?

God uses more than symbols to show people the way to peace and meaning in their lives. God also gave the Son. In Christ, God's plan was no longer secret, but fully revealed. By Christ's death and resurrection, the human race is now liberated. Sin is overcome and people are free to become their true selves in Christ.

More than Symbols

Christ is our companion on life's journey. As we will see in this chapter, he is the sacrament of God's real presence among us and he calls us, in turn, to be sacraments for others. But in order to understand Christ in this way, it would first be helpful to learn more about what might be called the "sacramental mentality" of Catholicism.

The Sacramental Mentality

Probably the most outstanding characteristic of Catholicism is its sacramental mentality. For Catholics, the world is permeated with the presence of God. Every star, leaf, and flower bears the divine signature. History and events speak to us of a mysterious dimension in the universe.

This privileged perception of the world is the result of a three-thousand-year heritage experienced first by Israel and communicated to us through the Hebrew Scriptures. In the Judeo-Christian tradition, the entire universe is sacramental because everything in it is capable of bringing us into contact with God. In its widest sense, a **sacrament** is God's love reaching out to us in signs and waiting for our free response.

Chapter 5   Sacraments and Christian Worship

All of creation announces the wonder of God's love.

The uniquely "Catholic thing," if we can call it that, is the belief that the Creator has chosen to be present to us in and through creation. When we were discussing Revelation in Chapter 1, we saw that nature itself can be a place to meet God and begin to understand the divine love for us.

The things of the earth and the people who use these gifts of God to nourish and promote life are like windows through which we can see the face of God. As the Fathers of Vatican II taught in *"The Constitution on the Sacred Liturgy,"* "There is scarcely any proper use of material things which cannot . . . be directed toward the sanctification of people and the praise of God" (Paragraph 61).

This means that using things properly makes us holy and, at the same time, gives God praise. Unlike some religions which believe that matter, people, and creation are distractions for those who hope to share in God's holiness, Catholicism holds that the material world can draw us closer to God.

But we must use the things of this world, which God has created and given to us, **properly.** There's the catch. We are not a sacramental people when we hoard the things of the earth at the expense of others who are in need or in poverty. We cannot see God's face in creation if we abuse the planet by poisoning its air and polluting its oceans. This improper use of things insults God and makes us anything but holy.

God's Challenge to Us

It's almost as if God is offering us an opportunity and a challenge. We have the opportunity to praise God and grow in holiness by sharing the fruits of the earth with all people, just as God has shared them with us. If we take this opportunity, we will know that the bread we have is not just for keeping ourselves. It is also for breaking and giving away. We will look for new and better ways to serve people by making more "proper" uses of material resources. And, as we have seen, when we do these things in faith, we become holier in God's sight.

But this is also a challenge. Like Adam and Eve, we often prefer to be masters ("gods") of creation, rather than sons and daughters of God. We want to enjoy the benefits of

Institution and Number of Sacraments

Did Jesus institute seven sacraments? Yes. By the mystery of his death and resurrection, Christ made us sharers in divine life. In this he is the author and source of the sacraments. But the word **sacrament** does not appear in Scripture. There was no such thing as a sacrament before the time of Christ, and although Jesus performed many saving actions, he did not prescribe the formulas and gestures used in the sacraments today. The infant Church was quick to recognize that certain of Jesus' actions were more purposeful than others. Some of these were his baptism by John, his miracle at the wedding feast at Cana, and his blessing of bread and wine. The young community carried out the commission of Jesus to continue his mission by beginning at once to perform these "signs," or symbolic actions, in memory of him. They did this to bring his saving presence into their midst.

If you consider every personal encounter with the risen Lord as a sacrament, there are more than seven sacraments. But the Church has come to identify seven vital saving actions in its worship as especially powerful bearers of divine life. Of these, Baptism and Eucharist are the most important, although the others cannot be dismissed. The form of the sacraments may have changed somewhat through the centuries, but their power has not.

With his baptism in the Jordan River, Jesus set an example which all Christians now follow.

creation or make ourselves rich from the land rather than taking the time to preserve life and make it multiply for others in imitation of God. If this is our attitude, we will never be able to experience God's presence in the created world. Instead of worshiping God by using creation, we will find ourselves worshiping creation. This false worship is called **idolatry.**

 On the Record

Describing Sacraments

Throughout the centuries, Catholic thinkers and leaders have made their contributions to understanding the sacraments. Here are a few of their ideas.

Saint Augustine (354-430): Sacraments are visible signs of invisible grace.

Saint Thomas Aquinas (1225-1274): A sacrament is a sign which causes the grace it signifies; expresses our participation in Christ's worship of the Father; reveals the unity of the Church through the common faith it shares.

The Council of Trent (1545-1563): Lack of holiness of the minister does not hinder the effects of the sacrament. Personal merit in the recipient does not cause grace, but lack of the proper disposition can hinder the grace of the sacrament.

Vatican II (1962-1965): Sacraments are signs which instruct us; they presuppose faith, but they also express and strengthen faith; through the sacraments we receive the share in God's life called grace.

---

1. *Where do you experience God most personally and intimately?*
2. *Why do you think that some people believe the material world distracts us from "Godly concerns"?*
3. *Think of some examples of how people today seem to worship creation and not the creator.*
4. *In what sense is sharing the things of the earth an act that praises God?*

Sacraments: People and Things

Sacraments can be described in many different and enlightening ways, but no matter how they are defined or explained, one fact remains: there can be no celebration of the sacraments unless people of faith use material things.

Taking our cue from Jesus and the Father, we use water to celebrate new life in Baptism. We use bread and wine to help us experience Christ's real presence in the Eucharist. Oil is a sacramental sign in Baptism, Confirmation, Holy Orders, and the Anointing of the Sick. Each sacrament also includes the use of ordinary speech which becomes extraordinary when our voices proclaim the Word of God in the Scriptures that are read during all sacramental celebrations.

As we continue our study of the sacraments, you will notice this respect for and use of material things. You will also notice that the sacraments are not simply these **things.** They are rituals or celebrations that involve an **activity** of Christ and the Church, and, in the course of this activity, simple, ordinary things like bread and wine, water, and oil are used.

For this reason, it is more proper to speak of sacraments as actions or gestures that use the things of the earth than it is to focus exclusively on the sacramental signs which are necessary for sacraments. We believe that the actions or gestures, such as welcoming a child into the Christian community or breaking and sharing the Bread of Life at Mass are the actions of Christ himself. We continue to

Worship and Sacraments: We Celebrate, We Praise

celebrate God's presence among us in these ways for one simple reason: Jesus instructed us to do so.

After giving us his Body at the Last Supper (which was also the first Eucharist), Jesus told us, "Do this in memory of me" (Luke 22:19). After rising from the dead, he instructed us to "make disciples of all the nations, baptizing them in the name of the Father, and of the Son, and of the Holy Spirit" (Matthew 28:19).

In a sense, Jesus is the first sacrament of the Church. Though he was the Son of God, he was also a human being whose humanity, his flesh and blood, manifested God's presence among us. Jesus is God's gift of grace to us in human form. Jesus also taught us how to use the things of the earth properly and to make of them gifts that we share with others. Everything we know and say about the Church's sacraments depends upon our knowledge and proclamation of Christ. He is the key to understanding the sacraments and the grace we receive through them.

---

5. *If you have witnessed the celebration of Baptism, describe some of the gestures (actions) and symbols that you saw. Discuss their meaning.*

6. *An old Catholic catechism book of religious instruction describes sacraments as "outward signs, instituted by Christ, to give grace." How would you explain this description to someone who is not a Catholic?*

Summary

- Catholicism is distinguished by its belief in sacraments. Sacraments manifest God's love for us and they invite us to make a response.

- Sacraments use created things to help us experience the presence and action of God in our lives through Jesus Christ.

- Sacraments are also actions—actions of Christ and of the Church. When we participate in these activities, we grow closer to Christ and to one another.

The making of bread is an ordinary, everyday task throughout the world. In the sacrament of Eucharist this ordinary bread becomes the Body of Christ.

Sacrament: an encounter between a person and the risen Christ through the symbolic actions of the Church.

Chapter 5   Sacraments and Christian Worship

SECTION 1
Checkpoint!

■ Review

1. What do we mean when we speak of the Catholic "sacramental mentality"?
2. Explain what the Fathers of Vatican II meant when they said that "there is scarcely any proper use of material things which cannot . . . be directed to the praise of God . . . "
3. Why should we be careful not to confine our discussion of the sacraments to the things that we use to celebrate them? What else should we also emphasize?
4. Did Jesus institute the sacraments? Explain your answer.
5. Words to Know: "proper" use of things, idolatry, sacrament, sacramental signs.

■ In Your World

1. How can the contemporary interest in caring for the environment help us to gain a deeper appreciation of our Catholic faith?
2. How can our ordinary, everyday actions help people to experience the love that Christ shared with us? Give some specific examples.

■ Scripture Search

1. Study Luke 22:14-20. What is it that Jesus is commanding us "to do" (22:19)? Compare this passage with 1 Corinthians 11:23-29. How are the two sets of passages similar? How are they different?
2. In what ways does Jesus show us that he is the first sacrament of the Church in these Scripture verses: Matthew 15:32-39; Mark 7:31-37; Luke 8:22-25; John 9:1-41?

SECTION 2
Jesus as Sacrament

Because Jesus is God in our very midst, he is the greatest sacrament. With one glance, he could call people away from their means of livelihood (Matthew 4:18-20) or melt their hearts with repentance (Luke 15:1-10). The mobs jostled one another to experience his healing touch, and the Apostles would gladly have brushed aside others, including children, to have him to themselves. Everyone wanted to be drawn into Jesus' mysterious sphere of influence.

God's Grace in Jesus

Encounters with Jesus of Nazareth were encounters with God. When Jesus cured people, the love of God was visible in his human actions. When Jesus was friendly with Mary and Martha (Luke 10:38-41) and when he patiently taught Nicodemus in the middle of the night (John 3), God's personal love for human beings was no longer hidden as in a sunset or pillar of fire. Yet none of these actions so clearly revealed the incredibly selfless and other-centered love of the Father as did the Paschal Mystery—Jesus' death on the cross and his resurrection. In loving the human race to his death, Jesus expressed God's infinite yearning to share his life and love. His resurrection was the greatest sign of God's intention and power to give eternal life.

Jesus' risen and glorified presence among his Apostles ended with his return to the Father. Yet he did not come to serve as the sacrament of God only to those few who had the privilege of living with him. Before Jesus' resurrection, he, like you, could be personally present in the fullest sense only to the people he met and to whom he talked. When he left the earth to take his rightful place at the Father's side, his risen humanity became present in the Holy Spirit. From the moment of his glorification, Jesus' range of contact became

> **Glorified presence:** the way Christ was present to the disciples after his resurrection. He was no longer bound by the limitations of time and place.

unlimited. He received the power to be personally present in the Spirit to everyone who believes in him to the end of time.

---

7. Name some people who tried to get physically close to Jesus. Why did they? Who tried to understand his thinking?

8. Before his ascension, Jesus said, "I will be with you always to the end of the ages." How can someone "go away" and yet remain?

9. How can Christ be the sacrament of God to those who live after his return to the Father?

10. How many ways can you name in which Christ is present to you today?

Jesus, A Sacrament of Healing

To call Jesus a sacrament is to say that people experienced God's grace and presence in all the things that Jesus said and, perhaps more importantly, in all the things that he did.

But what did Jesus do during the short time he was with us? We know that he proclaimed what he called a piece of "good news." He told us to take a fresh look at what life was all about, to "repent," because God's kingdom was close at hand (Mark 1:15).

There's more to the sacramental story of Jesus, however. He not only **told** us that God's kingdom was about to begin, he also **showed** us through tangible, visible signs (**sacramental** signs) what God's kingdom was like. These signs demonstrated the effect of the kingdom on our lives. They showed us how different we and our world could be if we followed Jesus. In this, he helped people experience God's grace and presence.

What kinds of signs did Jesus make? Practically all of them can be described as signs of healing. That's why it is proper to speak of Jesus as God's sacrament of healing among us.

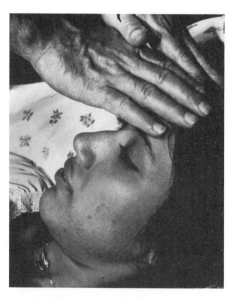

Jesus healed through the power of touch. How can you be a healer today?

Worship and Sacraments: We Celebrate, We Praise

Jesus, Sacrament of God's Kingdom

Jesus was the sacrament of God's kingdom. This means that he was also the sacrament of our salvation because the kingdom of God frees us from our sins. By accepting the offer of God through the Son to live a life of peace and justice, we allow God to reconcile all things to himself (2 Corinthians 5:19). Jesus is the beginning of this new life for us.

The Gospels give us many specific examples of how Jesus was the sacramental presence of God's kingdom among us. Review the examples below and ask yourself the question: "How can I imitate Jesus, the sacrament of the Father, so that I too can be a living sacrament of God's kingdom?"

- *Jesus fed the hungry (Matthew 14:13-21).*
- *Jesus continued with his mission even when his relatives tried to dissuade him (Mark 3:31-35).*
- *Jesus was compassionate and forgiving (Luke 6:27-38).*
- *Jesus showed hospitality (John 2:1-12).*
- *Jesus paid attention to people that even the disciples were not interested in helping (Matthew 19:13-15).*
- *Jesus knew the Scriptures, and because he did, he knew that the greatest Commandment is love (Mark 12:28-34).*
- *Jesus raises us up to new life (John 11:1-27).*

Practically every page of the Gospels proclaim Jesus as the sacrament of God's kingdom. Do you have any favorite passages that proclaim this "good news"?

Sometimes everyone experiences being separated from a friend or loved one. Through the sacrament of Penance, this separation can be healed.

Touching the Sacred

Sacramentals are not sacraments, but, like the sacraments, they involve the use of things and actions to praise God. The Stations of the Cross is a sacramental. It is used to remember Jesus' suffering, death, and resurrection.

I—Jesus is condemned
II—Jesus takes the cross
III—Jesus falls the first time
IV—Jesus meets Mary
V—Simon of Cyrene helps Jesus
VI—Veronica wipes Jesus' face
VII—Jesus falls a second time
VIII—Jesus meets the weeping women
IX—Jesus falls the third time
X—Jesus is stripped
XI—Jesus is nailed to the cross
XII—Jesus dies
XIII—Jesus is taken off the cross
XIV—Jesus is buried
XV—The Resurrection

When people were sick in mind and body, he made them whole. When their lives were off-course, Jesus showed them the way back to the Father. When he met the hungry, he fed them. When he saw that people were mourning, he comforted them. These signs of God's loving compassion are all signs of healing.

It's as if Jesus were trying to show us by his actions that the kingdom of God was far more than just a pious wish for the future. It was real and present. All that was necessary was for people to accept Jesus and his gift; those who did were healed.

11. *What are some signs showing that our contemporary world has experienced healing in recent years? Do you think that the liberation of Eastern Europe from Communism is one of these signs? Why?*

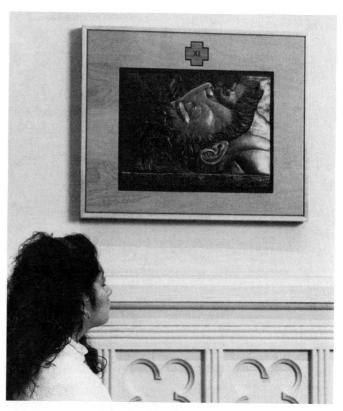

Praying the Stations of the Cross can be a time of quiet, meditative prayer for you.

Worship and Sacraments: We Celebrate, We Praise

12. *What response would you make to those who say that the world will never experience the two most important signs of God's kingdom—peace and justice?*

The Function of the Sacraments

Meeting Christ in the sacraments, therefore, affects our lives profoundly, not only weakening the grip of evil over us, but gradually transforming us into instruments of peace and reconciliation. This happens because, through the sacraments, we are connected with the key action of Jesus' life, his ministry of healing. Participation with Christ in this action draws us closer to him and makes us holy. We make this contact through Christ's community and in the sacramental signs that bring about **inwardly** what they **externally** signify. For instance, in Baptism, the water poured on a person's head and the baptismal words signify the divine life that floods our being. We are given new life, and in this sense, we are healed and reconciled to God.

Each sacrament meets a specific need and confers a particular form of divine help known as **sacramental grace.** The sacraments of Baptism, Eucharist, and Confirmation launch people into the mystery and life of Christ. The sacraments of Penance (Reconciliation) and Anointing of the Sick also heal us. Matrimony and Holy Orders assist in life vocations. At every turn in life, Christ is with us, offering us the opportunity to participate more fully in the life of God's kingdom.

Summary

- Jesus revealed the compassionate love of the Father by his preaching and by the way he dealt with others.

- Because Jesus made signs of God's care for us, we call him the sacrament of God's kingdom.

- All the sacramental signs that Jesus made may be understood as signs of healing. He made it abundantly clear to us that God was acting through him to reconcile (to heal) the world.

Sacramental grace: the gift of God received through the sacraments.

SECTION 2
Checkpoint!

■ Review

1. Why can we say that encounters with Jesus are encounters with God?

2. Now that Jesus is risen and glorified, he is no longer bound by time and place. What does this mean? What are the consequences of this for us?

3. What kinds of signs did Jesus make? Why do we call these "signs of God's kingdom"?

4. What is the function of sacraments in our lives?

5. Words to Know: glorified presence (of Christ), sacramental grace, sacramentals, Stations of the Cross, sacrament of the kingdom (Jesus).

■ In Your World

1. The miracles were special healing signs that Jesus made. How can we perform healing "miracles," even though we cannot physically cure people as Jesus did? Give some specific examples.

2. If you marry and become a parent, what kinds of things would you do for your children to help them become aware of Christ's healing presence in their lives?

■ Scripture Search

1. What sacramental signs does Jesus make in John 2:1-12, and how do these signs help us to see that we are called to be signs of hospitality?

2. Study these passages (John 20:19-23; John 21:1-19; Acts 1:1-11) which describe the glorified presence of Jesus. What do they tell you about the new life Jesus enjoyed after the resurrection?

SECTION 3
The Church as Sacrament

Jesus promised to remain with us until the end of time (Matthew 28:20). Although it is true that God is present in nature and events, the Church is the sacrament of Christ's saving action in the world. It is in the sacraments, where he acts in and through his people, that Christ most clearly continues to manifest God's saving love. As he did in his Palestinian ministry, in the sacraments Christ makes simple gestures and ordinary objects the vehicles of his powerful presence and healing love. In virtue of the Holy Spirit, the sacraments are truly Jesus living and acting among us.

Christ, Joined with Us in the Church

But because Christ is joined with his Church, the sacraments are at the same time signs of **our** loving response to God. United with Jesus, we joyfully remember what he did for **us,** we celebrate the faithful goodness of our Father, and we look forward in hope to being united with God forever.

The sacraments are more than gestures of God's love to us and of our return of love. They are joyful acts of worship. Just as people celebrate birthdays, anniversaries, and graduations to remind themselves of their daily blessings while strengthening bonds of love and marking their personal growth, Catholics set aside key moments of their lives to gratefully remember and celebrate the continual flow of God's blessings and to grow in faith and love.

13. *What are the key moments of every human life? What sacraments celebrate each of them?*

14. *Why do people bother to celebrate at all? Isn't it enough to simply say what we believe is important in life and dispense with all the rituals we use in Church and in society?*

Ways of Worship

Liturgical Celebrations

Originally, **liturgy** meant any work undertaken for the welfare of the whole people—a public work. As Christianity flourished, liturgy came to mean the public worship the People of God offered in union with Christ. The Eucharistic celebration was the main liturgical action, but the Jewish converts added the morning and evening psalms and other prayers of Judaism to their official liturgy.

Because he is God, Jesus' sacrifice on the cross is the eternal divine worship. By sharing in Jesus' risen life, Christians become his very body, continuing through time his mission of perfect and unceasing praise. Although the language and prayers of worship may change from time to time, Christian worship does not change, for "Jesus Christ is the same, yesterday, today, and forever" (Hebrews 13:8).

Members of Christ's Body

Christ's presence in the world today is a living presence based on a unity of hearts—a unity of love and life in the Holy Trinity. Christ lives in the world today through the Church.

At Pentecost, when Christ poured out the Holy Spirit on those gathered in the upper room, he made them a mysterious embodiment of his risen life through time. Just as Christ is the sacrament of God (God made visible in Christ), the Church is the sacrament of Christ (Christ made visible in his Church).

Christians—members of Christ's body—together with the risen Christ are the **sign** of God's plan. Their faith is the route by which God comes to the world, as well as the way by which humanity can respond to God. At the same time, the Church has the power to bring about the close union of which it is the sign. Christians are invited by their baptism and confirmation to do what the risen Lord does. They praise God for the divine goodness through the perfect worship of the Eucharist. They also continue God's work of spreading the kingdom by building up the community of life and love, by deepening their own holiness which is union with God, and by going out into the world to spread the Gospel.

God wants everyone to enjoy the gift of eternal life. The Church's work is to continue to build God's kingdom until one day all nations join the Body of Christ. The life of the Holy Trinity, a relationship of eternal love, will then permeate all things. Saint Paul puts it this way:

"He is before all things, and in him all things hold together.

The Body of Christ is made up of believers of every race and nation of the world. Men and women, young and old, lay or ordained, all are equal members of Christ's Body.

He is the head of the body, the Church. He is the beginning, the firstborn from the dead, that in all things he himself might be preeminent. For in him all the fullness was pleased to dwell, and through him to reconcile all things for him, making peace by the blood of his cross [through him], whether those on earth or those in heaven" (Colossians 1:17-20).

Followers of Jesus are not simply signs of Jesus, nor do they suggest or recall his presence. They **are** Jesus to the world, by both their presence and the power of their example to lead others to God. The Church can be defined as a visible union of those who publicly say to the world, "We are Christ for you today." Every individual Christian, too, is a visible manifestation of Christ. You might even define a Christian as "a sacrament of Christ in the world." This means that when you serve your neighbors, you are Christ serving people today. And whatever you do to others, as Jesus said, you do to him (Matthew 25:40).

15. Based on the above usage of "Church," to whom or to what is being referred?

16. If Christ were with us today working through the Church, where would you expect to find him and how do you think he would spend most of his time?

17. In what ways can you be Christ to others at home? At school? At work? At play?

18. If God wants us all to enjoy the gift of eternal life, do you think that God loves those who do not accept Jesus any less than Christians? Can the unbaptized demonstrate signs of God's kingdom too? If so, how?

Eternal Life Through the Sacraments

The Church continues Christ's risen life through all its various actions. Among the most important of these actions are the sacraments. A sacrament is an encounter between a person and the risen Christ brought about by Christ through the symbolic action of the Church. In these encounters, Christ acting in his Church saves us by bestowing eternal life. But since life has many needs, each sacrament

We encounter the risen Lord each time we celebrate the Eucharist.

Restoring Christian Unity

The Second Vatican Council made some astounding statements about how the Church can become a more visible sacrament of Jesus Christ. In the document called the "*Decree on Ecumenism*," for example, the Fathers of the Council addressed the question of Christian unity and they talked about ways for the Catholic community to heal the divisions that still exist between themselves and other religions. The statement below helps us understand that reconciliation often requires a "continual reformation" of God's pilgrim people.

"The concern for restoring unity involves the whole Church, faithful and clergy alike. It extends to everyone, according to the talent of each, whether it be exercised in daily Christian living or in theological and historical studies. This concern itself already reveals to some extent the bond of brotherhood existing among all Christians, and it leads toward full and perfect unity, in accordance with what God in his kindness wills.

"Every renewal of the Church essentially consists in an increase of fidelity to her own calling. Undoubtedly, this explains the dynamism of the movement toward unity.

Christ summons the Church, as she goes her pilgrim way, to that continual reformation of which she always has need, insofar as she is an institution of [people] here on earth. Consequently, if, in various times and circumstances, there have been deficiencies in moral conduct or in Church discipline, or even in the way that Church teaching has been formulated—to be carefully distinguished from the deposit of faith itself—these should be set right at the opportune moment and in the proper way" (*"Decree on Ecumenism,"* Paragraphs 5 and 6).

produces the particular effects that it symbolizes. The seven sacraments serve the main life processes of the Church: bringing forth new members, offering means of nourishment and growth, building up the community of faith, and blessing her members in death.

Sacraments make God's life available to us, but they also require the cooperation of those who participate in them. Christ may come to someone who receives communion at Mass, but if the person inwardly rejects Christ, the effect of the sacrament will not take place. Sacraments also express the faith of the community. If there is only one person present to celebrate a sacrament (such as a priest offering Mass alone), the communal aspect of the celebration is lost. At least one other person should be present.

Because the sacraments are personal actions of Christ who lives in eternity, as well as of the Church which lives in time, they have elements of time and of eternity. Each sacrament contains three time elements:

1. It calls into the present the **past** offering that Christ once made in the one Paschal Mystery.
2. It is an encounter with the risen Christ in the **present** to bring his saving action to the participant.
3. It is a pledge and an actual bringing about of **future** glory and eternal salvation.

Summary

- The Church is the sacrament of God's saving activity in the world. It is a sign of healing and reconciliation.

- All baptized Catholics, as members of the Body of Christ, must participate in the work of bringing Christ to the world. When we do this, we become living witnesses to God's plan for humanity.

- The seven sacraments of the Church are acts of public worship which celebrate Jesus' mission and the mission he gave us. When we worship God this way, we profess and strengthen our faith and we receive God's grace.

The anointing during the sacrament of Confirmation marks you as a person who has committed his or her life to God.

Worship and Sacraments: We Celebrate, We Praise

SECTION 3
Checkpoint!

■ Review

1. After studying this section carefully, write a definition of the Church in your own words.

2. Why is it necessary for us to celebrate what we believe in how we live our lives and worship God?

3. What does it mean to "be Christ" for the world today?

4. What three time elements do the sacraments contain? Explain each one.

5. Words to Know: sacrament of Christ, liturgy, *"Decree on Ecumenism."*

■ In Your World

1. Write an essay in which you attempt to explain the meaning of sacraments to non-Catholics.

2. Discuss in class how Christians can be better sacramental signs of God's kingdom. What issues regarding peace and justice should be the special concern of the Church?

■ Scripture Search

1. At the Last Supper, Jesus asked the Father for unity between himself and his followers. Saint John stresses this unity at the beginning and end of his Gospel. Tell the point John makes in each of these passages: John 1:12, 14, 16; 14:23; 15:4, 7; 17:21, 23.

2. Study the "Great Commandment" in Matthew 22:34-40. What does this commandment tell us about the life of the Christian? How can celebrating the sacraments help us to live this life more fully?

CHAPTER 5 Review

■ Study

1. Describe what is meant by the Catholic "sacramental mentality"?

2. What does an appreciation of sacraments have to do with learning how to use created things properly?

3. In what sense are sacraments activities?

4. Why do we call Jesus a sacrament?

5. What specific healing activities do we associate with the ministry of Jesus? How do these activities put us in touch with the kingdom he preached?

6. How does meeting Christ in the sacraments affect our lives?

7. What is the role of the Church in spreading the good news of God's kingdom?

8. Explain what we mean when we say that sacraments both express our faith and make our faith stronger.

9. To what does the term "liturgy" refer?

10. In what sense is reconciliation with God or our neighbor a kind of healing? Have you recently experienced reconciliation in your life? How did this experience help to heal you?

11. What are sacramentals? Explain the sacramental called "The Stations of the Cross."

12. We are all called to carry on Christ's work of making sacramental signs of God's kingdom. Give some examples of how an individual can do this.

13. What is meant by the statement "The Church is the sacrament of Christ"?

■ Action

1. Prepare a prayer service around the theme, "Unity in Christ." Choose Scriptures, write petitions, select songs and compose prayers which focus on this theme. Perhaps you can celebrate your service in church or at school with other classes.

2. Give a report to the class on a person that you think is a living sacrament of Christ. Show how his or her life helps people experience God's kingdom.

3. Have a session of your class's own "Vatican Council." Discuss the topic "Making Christ Live in Our World," and prepare a class "document" on this issue.

4. See if a local pastor is available to visit your class. Ask him to discuss some of the changes he has seen in the Church during his life. Use this occasion to gain a deeper appreciation of how the Church continues to grow and develop under the guidance of the Holy Spirit.

■ Prayer

Besides offering God praise and worship through the seven official sacraments of the Church, Catholics can also praise God through the objects or activities called "sacramentals." One of the most beautiful of the sacramentals is the rosary.

Take some time for this simple prayer. If you are not familiar with it, you will find this outline helpful.

With your fingers on the crucifix of the rosary, say the Apostles' Creed. Then move your fingers to the next rosary bead and pray the Our Father. On each of the next three beads, you say a Hail Mary and conclude your beginning prayers with: "Glory be to the Father, and to the Son, and to the Holy Spirit. As it was in the beginning, is now, and ever shall be, world without end. Amen" (The *Doxology*). Then begin the five "decades" (series of ten Hail Marys) of the rosary. Each decade begins with an Our Father, followed by the ten Hail Marys, and ends with the "Glory Be." Use the beads to keep track of how many Hail Marys you have said. As you pray each decade, think about one of the five mysteries of Christ's life, using your choice of the Joyful, Sorrowful, or Glorious mysteries.

CHAPTER 6

Sacraments of Initiation

OBJECTIVES

In this Chapter you will

- Become familiar with the Rite of Christian Initiation of Adults.

- Learn more about the sacraments of Baptism and Confirmation.

- Understand the Eucharist as a sacrament of initiation.

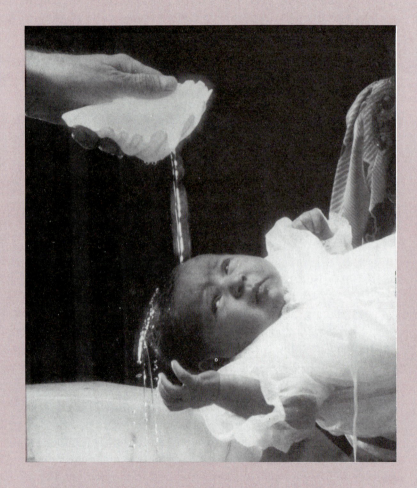

Let us profess the truth in love and grow to full maturity. You must put on that new person created in God's image.
—From Ephesians 4:15, 24

Worship and Sacraments: We Celebrate, We Praise

SECTION 1
Christian Initiation

Andrew had been baptized as an infant, shortly after he was born. Now that he is in high school, Andrew is angry with his parents for having him baptized. He says that because of his parents' action, he has missed out on the experience of making an adult commitment for himself.

Andrew's concern is not new. Many people for centuries have raised this same question. Is Infant Baptism necessary? Should baptism be delayed until at least the teen years so that a person can choose to receive the sacrament for himself or herself? Is the commitment of Baptism so serious that it should be delayed until later in adulthood? What do these questions have to do with being initiated into the Church?

We begin our discussion of the seven sacraments of the Church with a few reflections on the process of initiation into the Catholic community of faith. Though Catholics who were baptized as infants already enjoy full membership in the Church, learning more about the process of initiation will deepen their appreciation of the Church. As we look at how men and women are initiated into the Church today, we will learn about Jesus, the Gospel, and Catholicism in more detail. Christian initiation doesn't just welcome new members into the Body of Christ. It also is an opportunity for "cradle Catholics" to renew their commitment to Christ.

Initiation

At your high school there are probably many different types of clubs and organizations. Some of these groups may be open to all—if you want to join, all you have to do is come to a meeting. Other groups, especially sports teams, make you prove your worth before you are allowed to join. A teen who wants to join the Latin Club, for example, might

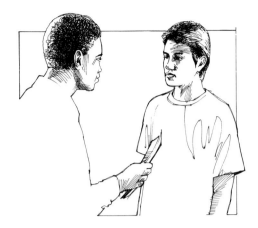

Have you ever experienced an initiation ceremony into a group or a club? Some initiation rituals are quite demanding.

be required to memorize a page of Latin verse before he or she can gain admittance. On a team, the student has to prove that he or she can shoot a basket, kick a ball, balance on the beam, or use a hockey stick.

Why are initiation periods necessary? Sometimes, initiations are used to keep undesirable people out. This can be discriminatory because of race, sex, or religion, which a Catholic would find unacceptable. If a particular skill or talent is needed to fully participate in or benefit from the group, such initiation practices make sense. In other cases, initiations are held to help the initiate come to appreciate the rules and regulations of the group in order that the initiate knows what is expected of members. If done honestly, this is a crucial step for an individual's decision whether to join a particular group or not. Finally, membership in a group often includes responsibilities and rewards. The group may limit its membership to those people who are willing to freely accept the consequences of their decisions. Initiations are important to the life of any group.

All organizations which have rules and regulations also have initiations. Sometimes the initiation ceremony is secret and complex—like for a college sorority or fraternity—and sometimes the initiation is simple—show up at the meeting, give your name, address, and phone number, volunteer to help, and you're in. It often seems that the more secretive, difficult, and complex an organization's initiation process is, the more people want to go through it to become a member.

A person can believe in Jesus without belonging to a church and without going through an initiation process. However, it is not possible to belong to a church—with all of the benefits a church community has to offer—without some initiation process. Every church has one, and, just like private groups or organizations, some initiations are complex while others are simple.

The Catholic Church uses an initiation program to assist members to enter the Church Community. This initiation process is known as the RCIA.

1. *Name some groups that you are aware of which practice initiations. Discuss how the initiations are handled, and what the groups hope to accomplish through their initiations.*

2. *Have you ever been initiated into a club or group? Discuss what happened (if you can) with the class. Describe why you went through this process.*

The RCIA

The Rite of Christian Initiation of Adults—often referred to as "the catechumenate" or RCIA—is a period of inquiry and study about the Catholic Faith. It takes place in several stages, each celebrated and sanctified by its own rite. This step-by-step approach to initiation is based on the fact that conversion is a gradual process and a lifelong journey.

In the past, the initiation of adults into the Catholic Church was a simple matter, done without much celebra-

The Catechumenate is a time of preparation prior to receiving the sacraments. As a period of initiation, it helps a person become familiar with the Church.

Chapter 6 Sacraments of Initiation

tion. A person interested in becoming a Catholic would be instructed for anywhere from several weeks to two years by a parish priest. The candidate and the priest would meet in private or in "inquiry" classes with other people preparing for Baptism. The text used during this study would be a catechism containing the doctrines of the Faith. Then, in a private ceremony, with only a few people present the candidates would receive the sacraments of Baptism, Eucharist, and Confirmation. Sometimes these adults were confirmed at the same time as the school-aged children. There were no stages of initiation.

The Second Vatican Council called for a renewal in the way adults become Catholics. The Council recognized initiation as a process—a process requiring time and involving the entire Catholic community. Thus the bishops of Vatican II called for a revision of the rite of Baptism for adults and for the restoration of the catechumenate.

In response, the Sacred Congregation for the Sacraments and Divine Worship promulgated, in 1972, a revised rite entitled "The Rite of Christian Initiation of Adults" or RCIA.

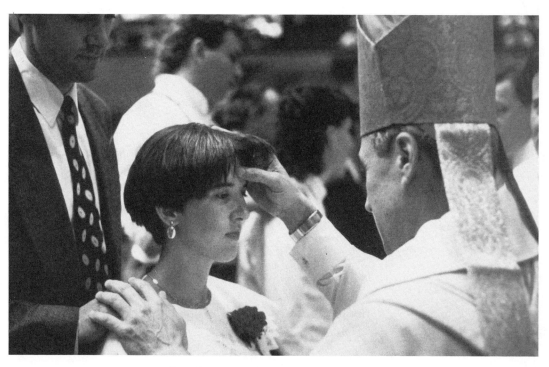

People who are baptized after childhood (including teens and adults) are confirmed during the same ceremony.

The RCIA Process

The Rite of Christian Initiation of Adults takes place step by step in the midst of the Catholic community. The process itself has four periods.

The first period, the **precatechumenate,** is a time of inquiry on the part of the candidate and on the part of the Church. In this period, candidates have the Gospel preached to them so they can learn more about Jesus. It is a time of loose association with the Church when the candidates have no rights, privileges, or duties. Once they make their decision to follow Jesus as members of the Catholic community and then go through the Rite of Catechumens, they become catechumens.

The second period, the **catechumenate,** admits the person into the Church, which can last for several years. This period includes catechesis, or learning about the Catholic faith, and discovering what life as a Catholic is all about. It is completed on the Day of Election when the third period begins.

The third period—shorter in length and called **enlightenment** or **purification**—is a time of more profound spiritual preparation—purification and enlightenment or "illumination." It usually coincides with the Lenten season. After the Rite of Election, presided over by the bishop, the former catechumens are known as the elect. Together with the Catholic community, the elect decide whether or not they are ready for baptism. If the preparation seems adequate, the elect receive Baptism, Confirmation, and Eucharist, the sacraments of full initiation.

The final period, known as **mystagogia** or **postbaptismal catechesis,** is a time of deepening the Catholic experience. The new members continue to receive the sacraments and begin to participate fully in the life of the community.

Chapter 6 Sacraments of Initiation

 On the Record

Obligations of Catholics

Whenever we become part of a group or organization, we accept the responsibility of abiding by its standards. While becoming a Catholic means far more than following a set of "rules and regulations," those who are or who wish to become Catholic should be aware of what are sometimes called "the six commandments of the Church." These obligations were published for Catholics in the United States by the Third Plenary Council of Baltimore in 1884 (not an Ecumenical Council).

1. To celebrate the Eucharist on Sundays and Holy Days.
2. To observe the laws of fasting and abstaining from meat on certain days.
3. To receive the Sacrament of Penance at least once a year.
4. To receive Communion during the season of Easter.
5. To support the parish.
6. To keep the Church's marriage laws.

A person becoming a Catholic through the RCIA comes away with an understanding of Christianity as a way of life and as a commitment to the person of Jesus. The RCIA encourages a change of heart and a transformation of the human spirit. Like the formation given to candidates entering religious communities, the new process of initiation stresses the formation of the entire person until he or she is able to become one with the community of Christ, sharing its life, worship, faith, and mission.

To begin the Catholic journey and to persevere in it often is difficult in today's society. With the restored catechumenate, used in the early Church when people also faced hostility against the Catholic Faith, the Church has provided people seeking baptism a revitalized method of preparation and a system to turn to in support when they have questions or doubts. Through the catechumenate, converts and those desiring one of the sacraments of initiation are prepared and motivated to continue their journey of faith.

An important dimension of the RCIA is that it reveals Christ's Church as a loving community of believers. The candidates are inspired and encouraged throughout their period of initiation by people who are eager to share the Catholic faith with them. As the candidates progress through the different stages of initiation, they in turn remind the parishioners of the meaning of Christianity. The new faith of the candidates often strengthens the faith of parishioners and reawakens in them renewed dedication to the Gospel. Because the RCIA provides a process whereby candidates and parishioners support one another, it is a powerful agent in transforming the local Church into a vibrant faith community of caring people.

Another feature of the RCIA is that it focuses the Church's attention on the importance of the Easter mystery. Lent, the time of immediate preparation for the catechumens, becomes a period of dying to one's old self and becoming a new person in God. The Easter Vigil, the time when Catholics celebrate Christ's rising to new life, becomes a celebration of full membership in the Church as the catechumens receive the sacraments of initiation.

Every member of the parish is involved in some way with the preparation of Catechumens, especially through prayer and example.

6. *If you were a godparent, how could you be of help to a candidate before Baptism? After Baptism?*

7. *If you were in charge of a meeting to introduce catechumens to the life and work of your parish, what could you tell them about your parish?*

Summary

- The Church welcomes new adult members through a process called the Rite of Christian Initiation of Adults (RCIA).

- The RCIA involves the cooperation of many different parish members and leaders who share their own talents and experiences of faith with those who have expressed an interest in becoming Catholic.

- The RCIA process helps life-long Catholics appreciate their faith better and grow closer to God and Jesus.

SECTION 1
Checkpoint!

■ Review

1. What is the difference between the RCIA and the way adult converts used to become Catholics? What are the advantages of this new approach?

2. Name the seven "traveling companions" for those who are on their journey to full membership in the Body of Christ through the RCIA.

3. Who are "catechists" and what is their task in the RCIA?

4. What four periods does the RCIA involve and what happens in each one?

5. What are the six commandments of the Church?

6. Words to Know: RCIA, sacraments of initiation, catechumen, catechist, conversion, pre-catechumenate, mystagogia.

■ In Your World

1. Write an outline of the important things about being a Catholic that you would share with someone who was involved in the RCIA process.

2. How can the RCIA be an opportunity for the members of **your** parish to continue growing in an understanding of Christ and the Church?

■ Scripture Search

1. Read the story of the Call of Levi (Luke 5:27-32). How does this story help us to see that Jesus calls all kinds of people to be his disciples?

2. What is the role or mission of those who accept Jesus' call to follow him? (Matthew 9:35-38 and 10:1-42).

Worship and Sacraments: We Celebrate, We Praise

SECTION 2
Baptism and Confirmation

The three sacraments of initiation are Baptism, Confirmation, and Eucharist. For adults who join the Church through the RCIA process, the order in which the initiation sacraments are celebrated at the Easter Vigil is Baptism, if the catechumen has not already been baptized; Confirmation; and Eucharist, when the new members receive their first communion.

For Catholics who were baptized as infants, the order of receiving the other two sacraments of initiation is reversed. First Communion is usually received when a child is 7 or 8 years old, and Confirmation is celebrated some time later.

In this section, the RCIA order is followed, and the sacrament of Baptism is discussed with the sacrament of Confirmation. This approach will show the important relationship between these "first" two sacraments of initiation.

New Life Through Baptism

In many times and cultures, the rite of baptism has been a sign of commitment to a new way of life. The baptism of John the Baptist had a similar meaning. It signified repentance and a willingness to change. It was not until Christ began his ministry, however, that baptism became a powerful action that actually brought about forgiveness. Jesus' baptism by John marked him as the Messiah and signaled the beginning of his Messianic mission (Mark 16:15-16 and Matthew 28:19-20).

Christian baptism gives the baptized a new life, identity, and mission. Baptism marks a conversion to Christ in a

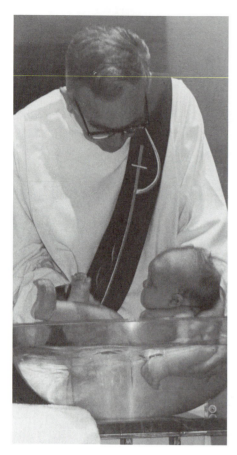

In the sacrament of Baptism we die to sin as we pass through the waters to new life with Christ.

For Example

At the very beginning of time, God moved over the formless **waters** and brought forth all living creatures (Genesis 1:2, 24-27). When the People of God were slaves in Egypt, God led them to freedom and new life through the **waters** of the Red Sea (Exodus 14).

covenant of friendship. Conversion, a turning or *metanoia*, reflects the change in a person's life. The person turns completely away from his or her past and turns completely towards Jesus. This event is sometimes called "christening" because the baptized person becomes united to Christ and, by a commitment to him and his teachings, shares in the risen life of Christ—the new life of the Spirit. The Christian thereby becomes a member of God's priestly people, empowered to worship the Father through participation in Christ's Paschal Mystery. In this, Baptism is a sacrament of welcome into the Christian community as well as a sacrament of commitment.

Baptism imparts a **character** that seals a person forever as belonging to God. **Character** is a word taken from antiquity where it referred to the seal by which a soldier or slave might be identified as belonging to the service of the emperor or the owner. In Christian usage, it describes the permanent effect of the sacrament—membership in the Church and responsibility for its mission. The sacrament marks a person as belonging to God, opening the door to holiness, and sets a person on a lifelong journey of growth in God's presence. Even the decision to marry, to remain single, to join religious life, or to be ordained for priesthood is a living out of the graces of Baptism.

During a baptism celebration, all Catholics present renew their own faith in God. They are reminded of the constant need for conversion in remaining faithful to Christ. Parents renew their own faith as well as learn their responsibilities in rearing their children as Catholics.

The Sign of Water

Water is one of God's greatest natural gifts. It is the original material from which all life has emerged. Without it, plant, animal, and human life would disappear. Water, in the form of oceans, rivers, and lakes, covers seventy percent of the earth's surface. It also makes up fifty-seven percent of the human body.

From the beginning of time, people have recognized water as the source of life. Without water, they would die. Thus people have organized their lives and have built their dwellings around permanent water sources. In addition to

Worship and Sacraments: We Celebrate, We Praise

using water for drinking and for cultivating crops, people use water for washing off dirt. Water is not only the source of life, but the restorer of life as well. As a natural purifier, water is a symbol of cleansing.

Water as a powerful energy source can be a positive symbol. But it can also be a negative symbol. If you have ever come close to drowning, been stranded in a car during a flash flood, or been caught in a storm in a small craft, you understand how destructive water can be. In a few hours, water can sweep away whole cities and can destroy the achievements of centuries.

Celebrating Baptism

While the Church gladly welcomes adults to profess their faith and to join the community through the Rite of Christian Initiation of Adults (RCIA), most Catholics were baptized as infants. Our description of the celebration of this sacrament, therefore, assumes the baptism of a child, though the adult baptism follows a similar format.

- *The celebration of the sacrament begins with a blessing of the baptismal water. This blessing reminds the assembly of God's use of **water** in the great events recorded in sacred history.*

- *As the rite of Baptism continues, the celebrant asks the child's parents and godparents to reject sin and to profess their faith in Jesus.*

- *The actual baptism may take place by pouring water on the head of the child or by immersion (putting the child into the baptismal font of water). If the baptism is by immersion, the child's clothes are removed. This stripping symbolizes the "putting off of the old person." Immersion symbolizes the dying to one's former self. In baptism, the child is plunged into the death of Jesus on the cross. Rising from water is a symbol of rebirth in the resurrection of Christ. In the rite of the sacrament, the celebrant immerses the child or pours water over the infant's head three times, saying, "I baptize you in the name of the Father . . . and of the Son . . . and of the Holy Spirit."*

- *After the baptism, the child is anointed with **chrism.** This oil prepares the child for Confirmation. Chrism, once used to anoint kings and priests, indicates that*

After being baptized, the person is anointed with chrism—blessed oil.

Anointing: a sign of setting something aside for sacred purposes.

Chapter 6 Sacraments of Initiation

every Christian shares in the priesthood of Christ and is responsible for bringing others to new life in Christ.

■ Next, the child is clothed in a white garment, which suggests the transformation that has occurred by "putting on the new person in Christ."

■ The priest or deacon then lights a baptismal candle from the Easter candle. He hands the baptismal candle to the child's parents or godparents, saying, "Receive the light of Christ." This light recalls Jesus' words, "I am the light of the world" (John 8:12). Through Baptism, every Christian shares the light of Christ's life and truth.

The newly baptized person is given a lit candle to symbolize that she has received the Light of Christ.

8. How do the waters of Baptism bring forth life, and how do they purify (cleanse)?

9. What are examples of water as a destructive natural element? Does water symbolize destruction in Baptism? Explain.

10. In the above discussion on the celebration of Baptism, it was assumed that the person being baptized was an infant. What adaptations do you think are made when an adult is being baptized?

Some Questions and Answers about Baptism

You may still have some questions about the sacrament of Baptism. Here are some of the questions most frequently asked:

- **Who can be a godparent?** According to canon law, there may be one or two godparents (one of each sex). Godparents must be at least fourteen years of age, and preferably already confirmed in the Catholic Faith. These people should be baptized Catholics in good standing in the Church. Non-Catholics can serve as Christian witnesses, although sponsors are always Catholic.

- **Why are infants baptized?** Although infants cannot understand what the Faith means, they can begin to receive God's graces through the sacrament. Infant Baptism can also be an occasion for a renewal of faith by parents, godparents, and the local community.

- **Can only a deacon, priest, or bishop baptize?** No. In case of necessity or emergency, anyone can celebrate the sacrament—even someone who is not a Christian. Ordinarily, however, an ordained minister of the Church baptizes.

- **Is it true that Baptism is supposed to remove Original Sin and, for adults, all sins that the person previously committed?** Baptism does indeed remove sin because, like all the sacraments, Baptism celebrates the healing and reconciliation with God that Jesus promised. It gives us the new life of grace. This may be easier to understand in the case of the forgiveness for their sins that adults receive than in the case of the infant whose Original Sin is "removed" by the sacrament. The sinful condition which all humans inherit is removed by Baptism so that the grace of God may no longer be impeded. He or she, therefore, receives God's grace and is reconciled to God through the gift that Jesus made to the Father.

Although a priest or deacon usually celebrates the sacrament of Baptism, in time of need, anyone may baptize.

Chapter 6 Sacraments of Initiation

Confirming Our Commitment to Christ

At the Last Supper, Jesus made a promise to his disciples: "And I will ask the Father, and he will give you another Advocate to be with you always . . . it remains with you, and will be in you" (John 14:16-17).

This Spirit would help the disciples be Christ's witnesses to the world. Before his ascension into heaven, Jesus commissioned his Apostles with these words: "Go, therefore, and make disciples of all nations, baptizing them in the name of the Father, and of the Son, and of the Holy Spirit" (Matthew 28:19).

From that time onward, the Apostles fulfilled Christ's wish. They baptized people and imparted the gift of the Holy Spirit by the laying on of hands. By the third century, the laying on of hands was regarded as the second sign of Catholic initiation—after Baptism with water and before participation in the Eucharist.

The Holy Spirit continues to play an important role in the life of the Church today. The Spirit gives us the insight and ability to believe in Christ, in his Church, in the Scriptures, and in the sacraments. The Spirit is first given in Baptism; we receive the **power** of the Holy Spirit, which strengthens us to continue Christ's mission and to build God's Kingdom. Then through the sacrament of Confirmation, the Spirit

Through the sacrament of Confirmation the Holy Spirit sustains you for your journey through life.

Worship and Sacraments: We Celebrate, We Praise

further **sustains** us on the journey toward God as full members of the Church who actively assume our Christian responsibilities of proclamation, witness, and transformation of the world through service.

In the sacrament of Confirmation, the Spirit recreates us in Christ's image. "Do you not know," Saint Paul writes to the Corinthians, "that you are the temple of God, and that the Spirit of God dwells in you?" (1 Corinthians 3:16). This Spirit can make us more truly ourselves, the person we are meant to be. The actions of the Holy Spirit are not limited to the rite of Confirmation. The Spirit continues to function when we read Scripture, celebrate the sacraments, pray, and go about our daily activities. In every event of our lives and in every person we meet, the Spirit works to make Christ's message clearer to us.

11. *When and where were you confirmed? What did this sacrament mean to you then? What does it mean to you now?*

Gifts of the Spirit

The Holy Spirit is exciting, creative, loving, enthusiastic, exuberant—every quality that describes life at its best. The Spirit, given to us in Baptism and increased in Confirmation, becomes the motivation for our attitudes and actions. Just as a person with a stingy spirit acts out of stinginess, so confirmed Catholics with a loving spirit act out of God's Spirit. Their actions are performed with the kind of ease that comes to athletes with strong and supple limbs or to people of great talent. We say they are "gifted." A gift of the Spirit is a **charism,** a spiritual quality given by God to serve and build the body of Christ.

In Confirmation, the Spirit provides us with gifts that help us to live more Christ-like lives. These gifts are based on a passage from the prophet Isaiah: "A shoot shall sprout from the stump of Jesse, and from his roots a bud shall blossom. The spirit of the Lord shall rest upon him; a spirit of wisdom and of understanding, a spirit of counsel and of strength"

Advocate: an intercessor.

Chapter 6 Sacraments of Initiation

Touching the Sacred

Gifts of the Holy Spirit

The Church speaks of seven gifts of the Holy Spirit which God offers us as we grow in commitment to Christ through Confirmation.

Wisdom: The ability to see life through the eyes of faith.

Understanding: Taking the facts we have learned and applying their meaning to living life with deep faith.

Counsel: The capacity to see the difference between right and wrong; good judgment in moral decision making.

Fortitude: Courage; the strength to overcome obstacles that stand in the way of right action.

Knowledge: The gift to study and learn the message of Jesus.

Piety: Reverence toward God and toward others whose lives are a gift of God.

Fear of the Lord: Wonder or awe at the marvelous love that God shows us.

(Isaiah 11:1-3a). The person is confirmed for a special purpose: to go forth and proclaim the Gospel by living a life of service. Confirmation prepares you to use the gifts of the Holy Spirit for the benefit of the world. They strengthen you for the journey of life, and support the good that you already do.

Throughout the Hebrew Scriptures, the spirit was seen as the impersonal power of God. The spirit creates, removes obstacles, guides the People of God, brings about salvation, and reveals God's activity in creation, in the historical events of the Chosen People, and in the lives of particular personalities.

Although the spirit in the New Testament still refers to God's power and activity, this Spirit has become personal—a Person. It is no longer just any spirit, but God's Spirit, the Holy Spirit. Through the sacrament of Confirmation, we invite this Person to become a greater part of our lives.

The concrete signs of the sacrament of Confirmation are the bishop laying hands upon the person, and annointing him or her with the oil of Chrism. As in baptism, the person being confirmed has a sponsor from the community, often the person's baptismal godparent(s).

There is an ongoing debate in the United States concerning the age when the sacrament of Confirmation should be celebrated. Should it occur at the time of Baptism, or should it happen at puberty, or should it take place towards the end of high school or even later? The following arguments are offered for each position in this ongoing debate.

- ■ *At Baptism*—This is when Confirmation was celebrated during the first five centuries, and when it is celebrated in many Spanish speaking countries around the world. This would bring the practice in line with the other sacraments of initiation.

- ■ *At puberty*—This argument is for celebrating Confirmation at the age of ten or twelve, as a Catholic rite of passage. This is the time when many American dioceses now celebrate the sacrament. The idea behind this argument is that it confers the sacrament in the seventh or eighth grade, thus insuring that the child will receive it before leaving school or religious instruction. This also celebrates the youth's transition from childhood into young adulthood, a major step toward maturity.

Worship and Sacraments: We Celebrate, We Praise

- ***Early Adulthood***—*Several dioceses have begun to celebrate the sacrament of Confirmation toward the end of high school, or even later. The argument here is that Confirmation is a time to make an adult commitment to the faith, accepting for one's self what was accepted for him or her at Infant Baptism.*

There are no quick and easy solutions to this discussion. Does it really matter when Confirmation is received? It certainly does to scholars, catechists, and bishops. As far as the sacrament itself is concerned, each of the positions has equal merit. The important thing is that the sacrament be received and lived.

12. Look up the word "enthusiasm" in the dictionary. What does it mean to be "enthusiastic" about something?
13. If Confirmation helps us to become more **enthusiastic** about our faith, what does it mean to say that you are "enthusiastic about your mission in life"?
14. When is the most appropriate time to receive the sacrament of Confirmation? Debate this issue in class.

In the forest, dead and rotting trees provide a rich environment for new growth. Our new life in Christ springs forth from our death to sin.

Summary

- The three sacraments of initiation are Baptism, Confirmation, and Eucharist.

- Through Baptism, we are welcomed into the Christian community and become a member of the Body of Christ. Baptism marks the beginning of our journey with Christ as we die to our old selves (sin) and rise with him in glory (grace).

- Confirmation is the celebration of God's Holy Spirit in our lives. The Spirit enables us to follow Christ more faithfully and offers us gifts that strengthen us in our journey to God's kingdom as we live a life of service in the Christian community.

SECTION 2
Checkpoint!

■ Review

1. What are the sacraments of initiation?

2. What do the two sacraments discussed in this section celebrate?

3. What does water symbolize in the sacrament of Baptism?

4. Confirmation is celebrated by the "laying on of hands." What does this ancient gesture of blessing signify, and how is it related to the role of the Holy Spirit in Confirmation?

5. Name the gifts of the Holy Spirit, and discuss how each gift helps us grow more deeply in our commitment to Christ.

6. What are the concrete signs of the sacrament of Confirmation?

7. What are the three arguments for the appropriate time to receive the sacrament of Confirmation?

8. Words to Know: character, chrism, immersion, anointing, advocate, gifts of the Holy Spirit, Original Sin, charism.

■ In Your World

1. When were you baptized? Do you know who baptized you or who your godparents were? Find out as much as you can about your Baptism by asking your parents or godparents. (Maybe ask them why they wanted you baptized, who was present, what their thoughts and feelings were when you were being baptized.) Write a prayer which expresses your gratitude to God for your gift of faith.

2. How do you think that God's Spirit works through the Church today? Be specific.

3. How has confirmation empowered you for mission? Talk to friends who have been confirmed and find out how they are presently active proclaiming the Gospel.

■ Scripture Search

1. What does the story of Noah (Genesis 7, 8, 9:11-17) suggest to us about the meaning of Baptism?

2. How is the celebration of Baptism similar to the Passover event described in Exodus 14?

SECTION 3
The Holy Eucharist

The Eucharist, which is also a sacrament of initiation, is the heart of the Christian community because it gives us entry into the Paschal Mystery—the redeeming act of Christ that restored our friendship with God. "For as often as you eat this bread and drink the cup, you proclaim the death of the Lord until he comes!" (1 Corinthians 11:26). Although God blesses us with divine friendship throughout our life journey in all the sacraments, in this sacrament God gives us "direct passage" to our destination (God) and brings our destination to us even as we travel.

As the ritual which celebrates Christ's death and resurrection, the Eucharist is central to Christian life. It sums up perfectly what all the other sacraments do in part. Like Baptism, the Eucharist builds the Body of Christ, uniting the members to one another. The words of consecration, "This is my body, this is my blood," are as much a prayer to transform the community into the Body of Christ as to change the bread and wine. In the Eucharist, as in Confirmation, the Holy Spirit's presence is deepened in us. The Eucharist is the chief sacrament of reconciliation, uniting us with God and with one another.

Signs of God's Concern for Us

The Eucharist is the most obvious sign of God's concern for and acceptance of us. While it seals our acts of dedication and thanksgiving, it is the stimulus for our outreach to the world in the same spirit of concern that we have experienced in Jesus.

The celebration of the Eucharist also expresses and fosters love among the family members of Christ's community. "Because the loaf of bread is one, we, though many,

The celebration of the Eucharist begins with a Rite of Gathering.

are one body, for we all partake of the one loaf" (1 Corinthians 10:17). Just as God sustained the Chosen People in the desert with bread from heaven, we are fed on the way today, being bound together by God's love. Sharing one vision of life and a common heritage, the Church journeys toward the kingdom of God of which the Eucharist is but an anticipation. A sign of freedom and hope, the Eucharist motivates Christians to conquer evil by working to unite the entire world into God's family. The ultimate purpose of the Eucharist is to hasten the day when God will be the homeland of all peoples (1 Corinthians 15:28). This fills our lives with a satisfying significance that is not often realized by unbelievers.

---

15. *How do the meals that we share with others help us to draw closer to one another?*

Entering God's Presence as Friend

In the Hebrew Scriptures, relationships were sharply defined and tasks unevenly distributed. The priest was the only one authorized to offer sacrifice to God. Only those appointed by God could speak on behalf of the people. The High Priest alone could enter the Holy of Holies once a year. Today, in the age of the Church, that is not the case. All Christians can worship God. Jesus has demonstrated God's respect for each individual. Because Jesus Christ is our High Priest, whose perfect sacrifice was found pleasing to the Father, we can enter God's presence with confidence, intimately talk to him, listen to him, and share his very existence.

Knowing that, despite personal shortcomings, you are redeemed and acceptable to God does not guarantee a problem-free life, but it gives your life a sure direction: it places you in a relationship with God. People are made for relationships because it is only through friendships with mutual give and take that we grow. The relationship that is most essential to our growth is friendship with our God. With God's unfailing support, we can find on our journey the strength we need to triumph over our own tendencies to detour; we can avoid the roadblocks placed by the world; and we can guide others along with us as we make our way to the Father.

◆

16. Can you recall a particularly memorable celebration of the Eucharist? What made that particular Eucharist so special?

17. Why is it appropriate to celebrate important family events like wedding anniversaries with the Eucharist?

18. What are some symbols related to the Eucharist? Explain their meaning.

Ways of Worship

There are several introductory prayers (called Prefaces) that the priest can use to begin the Eucharistic Prayer. In the Preface below, notice how this simple prayer helps us to understand the sacrifice of Christ that we are invited to participate in at Mass.

"Father, all-powerful and ever-living God, we do well always and everywhere to give you thanks through Jesus Christ our Lord.

By his birth we are reborn. In his suffering we are freed from sin. By his rising from the dead we rise to everlasting life. In his return to you in glory we enter into your heavenly Kingdom.

And so, we join the angels and the saints as they sing their unending hymn of praise" (Preface for Ordinary Time IV).

Joining Our Lives with the Church

In the simple forms of bread and wine, which become for us the Body and Blood of Christ, Jesus reveals the love of God. In the Eucharist, the sacrifice of Calvary is made present again in a special way. Jesus' one sacrifice saved the world. Sacramentally, in the Eucharist, we share in that saving action. There we experience God's power and love in our lives.

At each Eucharistic celebration, we join our sacrifices with the offering of our risen Lord. In the Mass we look back to Calvary as we journey with Christ to our reunion with God at the end of time. Although we meet God in faith, it is by God's own power and initiative, working through the ordained minister who leads us in worship, that God is made present among us. And that presence transforms us, readying us to share our gifts more freely with others, to live our lives in the spirit of the Paschal Mystery, and to participate in the life of God's kingdom proclaimed by Jesus.

---

19. *Distinguish between Memorial Day, when we remember the deeds of those who gave their lives for our freedom, and the memorial of the Eucharist.*

20. *How does the Eucharist "initiate" us into the dying and rising of Christ?*

Eucharistic Prayer II

The priest uses more than one prayer to express our gratitude to God for the gift of Jesus, but the one called "Eucharistic Prayer II" is probably used most frequently. Read this prayer carefully and notice how it expresses many of the ideas discussed in this section of the chapter.

Presider: "The Lord be with you."

Congregation: "And also with you."

Presider: "Lift up your hearts."

Congregation: "We lift them up to the Lord."

Presider: "Let us give thanks to the Lord our God."

Congregation: "It is right to give him thanks and praise."

Presider: "Father, it is our duty and our salvation, always and everywhere, to give you thanks through your beloved Son, Jesus Christ. He is the Word through whom you made the universe, the Savior you sent to redeem us. By the power of the Holy Spirit he took flesh and was born of the Virgin Mary. For our sake he opened his arms on the cross; he put an end to death and revealed the Resurrection. In this he fulfilled your will and won for you a holy people. And so we join the angels and the saints as we say:"

All: "Holy, holy, holy Lord, God of power and might, heaven and earth are full of your glory. Hosanna in the highest. Blessed is he who comes in the name of the Lord. Hosanna in the highest."

Presider: "Lord, you are holy indeed, the fountain of all holiness. Let your Spirit come upon these gifts to make them holy, so that they may become for us the body and blood of our Lord, Jesus Christ.

"Before he was given up to death, a death he freely accepted, he took bread and gave you thanks. He broke the bread, gave it to his disciples, and said: 'Take this, all of you, and eat: this is my body which will be given up for you.'

"When supper was ended, he took the cup. Again he gave you thanks and praise, gave the cup to his disciples, and said: 'Take this, all of you, and drink from it: this is the cup of my blood, the blood of the new and everlasting covenant. It will be shed for you and for all so that sins may be forgiven. Do this in memory of me.'

"Let us proclaim the mystery of faith."

All: "(A) Christ has died, Christ is risen, Christ will come again."

"(B) Dying you destroyed our death, rising you restored our life. Lord Jesus, come in glory."

"(C) When we eat this bread and drink this cup, we proclaim your death, Lord Jesus, until you come in glory."

"(D) Lord, by your cross and resurrection you have set us free. You are the Savior of the world."

The priest lifts the sacred bread for all to see after the words of institution: "This is my body which will be given up for you."

Presider: "In memory of his death and resurrection, we offer you, Father, this life-giving bread, this saving cup. We thank you for counting us worthy to stand in your presence and serve you.

"May all of us who share in the body and blood of Christ be brought together in unity by the Holy Spirit.

"Lord, remember your Church throughout the world; make us grow in love, together with N. our pope, N. our bishop, and all the clergy. Remember our brothers and sisters who have gone to their rest in the hope of rising again; bring them and all the departed into the light of your presence.

"Have mercy on us all; make us worthy to share eternal life with Mary, the virgin Mother of God, with the Apostles, and with all the saints who have done your will throughout the ages. May we praise you in union with them, and give you glory through your Son, Jesus Christ.

"Through him, with him, in him, in the unity of the Holy Spirit, all glory and honor is yours, almighty Father, forever and ever."

All: "Amen."

---

21. Break Eucharistic Prayer II down by paragraphs and discuss the key idea stated in each.

These familiar objects are used to celebrate the Eucharist. Why are special books, cups, and platters used during the Eucharist?

Summary

- The Eucharist is the sacrament of initiation that sums up what all the other sacraments do. It joins us to Christ and his saving activity.

- In the Eucharist, God expresses divine love and concern for us and invites us to show these same expressions of self-giving toward others.

- When we celebrate the Eucharist, we join our sacrifices with those that Jesus offered the Father on our behalf.

SECTION 3
Checkpoint!

■ Review

1. In what sense is the Eucharist our "direct passage" to our final destination as Christians?
2. How does the Eucharist unite us more closely to God and to one another?
3. What effect should the Eucharist have on our lives?
4. How does the Preface of the Eucharistic Prayer that you read help to express the meaning of Eucharist?
5. Words to Know: Eucharist, Eucharistic Prayer, blessing, preface.

■ In Your World

1. Discuss why the Eucharist is so essential to Catholic life.
2. Help prepare yourself to celebrate the Eucharist this weekend by finding out what the three Scripture readings are and discussing them at home or in class. This is an excellent practice to keep up with every week.

■ Scripture Search

1. Read John 6:47-56. What startling things does it say? What consoling things does it say?
2. Study 1 Corinthians 10:17, 11:26, and 15:28. What do these passages tell us about the meaning of the Holy Eucharist?

Chapter 6   Sacraments of Initiation

CHAPTER 6 Review

■ Study

1. What is the RCIA and why is it called a "process"?

2. Why are so many different people involved in the RCIA?

3. Describe the RCIA "periods" and explain how they mark the progress of a person who is seeking full membership in the Church.

4. What relationship does Baptism have to the death and resurrection of Jesus?

5. What does water signify in Baptism? The white garment? The candle?

6. Baptism removes Original Sin. Explain.

7. What does Confirmation celebrate and why is it closely linked to the action of the Holy Spirit?

8. What are the signs of Confirmation?

9. How does Confirmation prepare you for mission?

10. What three ages are proposed as most appropriate for Confirmation? What arguments are used to support each age?

11. Why can we call the Eucharist the "table of fellowship"?

12. We call the Eucharist a sacrifice. Whose sacrifice? Why do we speak of the Eucharist this way?

13. How does the Eucharist help to build the Body of Christ?

14. How does the Eucharist give our lives a significance they might not otherwise have?

15. What are the six obligations of Catholics, sometimes called "the commandments of the Church"?

16. What are the Eucharistic Prayers?

■ Action

1. Ask your teacher to help you find the name of someone who is involved in the RCIA process. Write him or her a letter of support and welcome into the Catholic community.

2. Invite to class a catechist who works with a Confirmation program in a local parish. Ask her or him to discuss with you the importance of this sacrament.

3. Prepare a class Eucharist. Choose readings, songs, and special prayers that focus on our commitment to Christ.

4. Pay special attention to what's going on around you at Mass next weekend. Write your reflections on this Eucharist and bring them to class for discussion.

■ Prayer

This prayer can be said either privately or in common with your family or class. Use it often to thank God for your own gift of faith and for those who will soon join you at the table of the Eucharist.

Opening Prayer: The Apostles' Creed (or an informal prayer expressing your faith)

Celebration of God's Word: Matthew 28:16-20

Litany for the Catechumens: (A litany is a prayer of praise and petition which uses one or more responses that are repeated throughout.)

    The **response** for the litany is: "You save us, Christ Jesus."
    By the gift of our life . . . (Repeat the response for each prayer)
    By your dying and rising . . .
    By your sending the Spirit . . .
    By your Church here on earth . . .
    By your sacraments of love . . .
    By the example of Christians . . .
    By our hope for eternal life . . .

The Prayer of Jesus: "Our Father . . ."

Closing Prayer: Loving Father, we thank you for the gift of faith. We pray for our sisters and brothers who are joining us in the Body of Christ. Help us to support and encourage them as you support us, through Christ, our Lord. Amen.

Chapter 6   Sacraments of Initiation

CHAPTER

7

The Table of Unity

OBJECTIVES

In this Chapter you will

- Recognize the Eucharist as a communal meal, the Lord's Supper which nourishes the community of faith.

- Explore the order of the Mass and become better acquainted with each part of the "Eucharistic Meal."

- Experience the Liturgy of the Eucharist as a prayer of thanks, a sharing of food, and a sacrifice to God offered by Christ and his people.

The celebration of the Eucharist nourishes the faithful with Christ, the Bread of Life, in order that, filled with the love of God and neighbor, they may become more and more a people acceptable to God and build up the Christian community with the works of charity, service, missionary activity, and witness.
—"National Catechetical Directory," #121

SECTION 1
Table Fellowship and the Eucharist

"Sarah has soccer practice until 6:15, while Peter has it until 6:30 tonight, dear," Mrs. Mulhall said. "If you'll pick Peter up on the way home from work, I'll get Sarah. That way, you can get to Mass for the Feast of All Saints. I guess you will have to eat after Mass. I'll eat with the kids before practice."

People today don't often have the opportunity to sit down together and share a meal. Social, recreational, and church activities use up much of the family's time together. The pressures of work make this problem even more challenging. Yet, humans have always had the need to share meals together. For Christians this shared meal is the Eucharist.

As the only sacrament of initiation which is repeated, the Eucharist holds a central place in the life of the Church. This suggests two things. First, the fact that we celebrate the Eucharist daily in our churches indicates its importance in Catholic life. A church without the Eucharist is not the Catholic Church!

Second, by having a repeatable initiation sacrament, the Church is telling us that initiation into the Body of Christ is not a once and for all activity. We must begin to celebrate and foster our faith over and over again. There's no end to beginning and renewing our relationship with God. If we fail in our commitment, the Lord is always prepared to welcome us back. If our faith begins to grow weak, Jesus offers himself to us as our nourishment and strength.

The Lord has set a table for us, the table of the Eucharist. Every time we accept his invitation to come to the table, we

Chapter 7   The Table of Unity

celebrate our invitation into his way of life and we praise the Father, who calls us all to live in the kingdom.

The Power of Table Fellowship

One of the most natural moments of the day to feel unity with others is during mealtime at the dinner table. People seem instinctively to sense the close association of food with friendship. Wherever two or three friends are gathered, food almost always seems to make a miraculous appearance. But because of the rush of modern life, few people now know the satisfaction that leisurely eating can provide. A four-hour multicourse dinner in a European restaurant or a traditional tea ceremony in Japan would demonstrate the love and worship that a meal can provide.

Jesus could have chosen to deliver his message of love by gathering people around him as a teacher gathering students in a class or as a corporation holding its committee or sales meetings. But he was working toward something more than mere instruction. In carrying out his mission, Jesus often ate with others because eating together creates a feeling of unity. It has greater possibility for the experience of love than does a class or a meeting.

The Eucharist is the most powerful means of unifying individuals, both within themselves and with one another, because it brings Christ's actual presence to their relationships. The warm fellowship of the Last Supper was a culmination of Christ's entire mission. He brought a great heart to that momentous meal with his closest friends because he had made a practice of loving and serving others all his life. He had always been able to think of the needs of others before his own. That night was no different. Despite his own heaviness of heart, Jesus put his Apostles first. He showed them the depths of his great desire to be one with them and with all humanity.

The Passover Meal

Every November, the United States observes the national holiday of Thanksgiving, which celebrates the blessings of freedom and plenty that came together in a festive meal. While remembering the past, Thanksgiving Day also cele-

Gathering together to share a meal is one of the simple pleasures of life.

The Christian Community gathers to share in the Eucharistic meal to express its thanks for God's gifts.

brates God's continued gifts to the country as symbolized by the abundant food on the table.

Similar to Thanksgiving, the Passover was the most sacred annual festival for the Jews in Jesus' time. The high point of the feast was a family meal commemorating the great historic events of the past. The family recognized God's continued blessings in the food they enjoyed together, and their meal symbolically expressed their reliance on God's faithfulness and their hope of receiving even greater blessings in the peace of the Messianic Age to come.

The Jewish Seder celebration, as the Passover Meal is sometimes called, focused on the theme of liberation. Early in the meal, the youngest member of the family asked, "What is so special about this night?" The leader or head of the family then joyfully proclaimed God's mighty deeds in the history of their ancestors and their deliverance from bitter Egyptian enslavement.

Passover and Salvation

"Passover" is a complex word that has many associations. Basically, it refers to the liberation or salvation the Israelites won from their oppressors when God's vengeance slayed the eldest born of the Egyptians while passing over

Names for the Lord's Supper

At the beginning of the Church, the Mass was known as the "Lord's Day," the "Lord's Supper," or the "breaking of the bread." This was because it continued what Jesus did with bread and wine at the Last Supper. At first an entire meal was celebrated, with the bread and cup introducing and closing the celebration, but soon the essential actions connected with special blessings were separated from the eating of the main dish.

Before long, the word frequently used for the Mass was *eucharistia,* a Greek word meaning "thanksgiving," which referred to the Jewish *berakah.* The early Christians followed the Jewish custom that Jesus had used at the Last Supper of pronouncing the *berakah* over the bread and wine, which represented all things in creation. The first prayers over the gifts in the Liturgy of the Eucharist today closely imitate this *berakah.*

Some names for the Eucharist—stressing that the Mass is a celebration of the entire Christian community—are *collecta* (a gathering together) and *processio* (a marching forward together). As a sign of being pilgrims, the people formed a procession to enter the Church. *Liturgia* (work or service performed with or for the people) was the word the Greeks settled on for the Mass. This was because the people shared Christ's priesthood in offering Christ's sacrifice and because it was offered for all the people. Occasionally, early terms like the Lord's celebration, the table of the Lord, divine service, the holy sacrifice of the Mass, and the sacrificial banquet were used.

The word **Mass** itself became popular around the fifth century. Since then, it was practically the only term used for the Lord's Supper until this century, when the reform of Vatican II reintroduced **Eucharist** or Eucharistic Liturgy.

and sparing their own firstborn sons (1230 B.C.). It also recalls the Israelites' safe passage through the Sea of Reeds when the Egyptians, pursuing them in royal chariots, were drowned. It includes the Covenant on Sinai that God made with his People through Moses, as well as the religious ceremony of the sealing of the Covenant in blood. The Passover was a remembrance of God's guidance through the barren desert to the Promised Land (1200 B.C.). Finally, in the years preceding the coming of Christ, the Passover commemorated the Israelites' release from exile after the Babylonian Captivity (587 B.C.).

The memory of these unexpected liberations called forth in the Jewish people a feeling of exaltation at God's power to bring their impossible dreams to realization by the Word. They became convinced that they were special, a chosen race, loved above even the greatest nations. They were filled with awe and gratitude that, although high above them in holiness, their God had entered their lives to make them more livable and more human.

In blessing God for past favors, the Jewish people felt God's saving power in their midst again, strengthening them in their present trials. At the same time, the Passover meal expressed their eager hope and longing for the final coming of God's kingdom, the time of peace foretold by the prophets. When they blessed and drank the customary cups of wine, they launched a week-long celebration of joy and thanksgiving.

1. If you have experienced any kind of elaborate meal, tell the class about it. What ceremonies accompanied the meal? What did they mean?

2. How important is the common meal to your family? What happens to the relationships in the family when eating together is pushed aside by other activities?

3. In what ways was the Passover meal a celebration of unity?

4. Sometimes, Catholics celebrate the Seder meal on Holy Thursday besides celebrating Mass that day. Have you ever attended a Seder? Can you recall any parts of the ceremony?

Family celebrations are often connected to a shared meal. How does your family celebrate with a meal?

Chapter 7   The Table of Unity

 On the Record

The Passover Meal
The Jewish Passover meal consists of three parts:
Blessing and Remembering. The meal always begins with the *berakah* (or Blessing Prayer) over the cup of wine. A dish of bitter herbs is then served, but not eaten. There follows a washing of hands and the breaking of bread, after which an explanation of the reason for the feast is given by the head of the family. A second cup of blessed wine is shared.
A Sharing in the Sacrifice of Praise. The main dish is the Passover lamb, which has been sacrificed. It commemorates the lamb whose blood, sprinkled on the doorposts of the Israelites at the time of the Exodus, saved them from the destroying angel. It also recalls Moses' sealing of the Covenant by sprinkling the blood of the sacrificed animal.
A Closing Blessing. The meal closes with a blessing said over a third cup of wine and the singing of hymns.

The Most Momentous Meal

It was in the consciousness of this heritage that Jesus and the Twelve sat down to table that night before his death. According to the Gospel of Saint Luke, Jesus sent Peter and John ahead to make the customary preparations for the feast. The Apostles certainly expected to follow the form of the meal they were familiar with since childhood.

The meal indeed opened in the ordinary way, but Jesus introduced something new. The Gospel accounts say that while giving thanks, he took the unleavened "bread of affliction," broke it, and said, "This is my body that is for you. Do this in remembrance of me" (1 Corinthians 11:24).

Jesus did the same with the cup of wine. After the supper, using the "blood of the grape," which, according to Jewish ritual, was always red, he said, "This cup is the new covenant in my blood. Do this often as you drink it, in remembrance of me" (1 Corinthians 11:25).

The intention is clear. The Hebrews had always offered real lambs and bulls, not mere signs of them. This bread and wine was not to be a sign only, but the true body and blood of Jesus, who would soon be sacrificed on the cross. Bread, either in itself or as a symbol, could hardly have been "given for you," nor could regular wine be "shed" for the forgiveness of sin. Only by becoming Jesus could this bread and wine have been connected with the events of Calvary. Only the real, personal presence of Christ, the lamb of sacrifice, could make this meal a way of uniting worshipers with their God.

Jesus' gift to the Apostles and to all his followers was not something he had made or bought. It was himself, his body and blood, his very life. As Jesus himself explained, "There is no greater love than this: to lay down one's life for one's friend" (John 15:13). This meal was to be the way Jesus' closest friends would celebrate for all ages to come his greatest act of love: his passion, death, and resurrection.

At that Passover meal with his disciples, Jesus devised a way for his followers to remember how he had given himself. In the Eucharist, they were to commemorate not only his death but also what his death won: God's acceptance as shown in the resurrection, ascension, and sending of the Holy Spirit. Jesus commanded that his followers together celebrate his self-gift "in memory" of him to the end of time.

The Church has taken Jesus' words very seriously. It is obvious from the entire setting of the Mass (the bread and wine, the plate and cups, the table with its covering, the priest as host, the congregation as invited guests, the great Eucharistic prayer of thanks, and the reception of the food) that the Eucharist is basically a meal commemorating the Last Supper. It contains the main rituals of the Passover meal: a retelling of God's saving deeds in the Scripture readings, a solemn prayer of thanksgiving in the Eucharistic Prayer, and the sharing of food.

5. *The Last Supper that Jesus ate with his disciples suggests a new sacrifice that Jesus was about to offer God on our behalf. What was this sacrifice and how did it liberate us?*

6. *Why do you think that Jesus used wine at the Last Supper? What was he telling us?*

Christians believe that Jesus gave us the Eucharist at the Last Supper.

Summary

- The Eucharist is the one repeatable initiation sacrament. This suggests our need for constant nourishment on our journey towards God's kingdom.

- Our celebration of the Eucharist is a fellowship meal, much like the Jewish Passover which Jesus celebrated with his disciples on the night before he died.

- We also call the Eucharist a sacrificial meal because when we celebrate it, we participate in the supreme sacrifice Jesus made to God on our behalf. We also offer God our own gifts of bread, wine, and our lives.

Chapter 7   The Table of Unity

SECTION 1
Checkpoint!

■ Review

1. Why is it important to have a sacrament of initiation that we repeat over and over again?

2. What do the Jewish people celebrate at their Passover meal?

3. Why do we call the Eucharist a fellowship meal? A sacrifice?

4. What are some of the other names used for the Mass over the years?

5. Words to Know: fellowship meal, Passover, Seder, the Exodus, *Eucharistia, berakah*.

■ In Your World

1. Some people believe that Latin preserved a sense of mystery and reverence in the Mass. Others say that English makes the Mass more meaningful. Organize a debate over the pros and cons of celebrating the Mass in a universal language such as Latin as opposed to a vernacular language such as English.

2. Plan a special meal with your family. Do whatever you can to help. Spend some time during the meal recalling special memories that your family shares. Make it a kind of mini-Thanksgiving with a special blessing over the food before the meal and a prayer of thanksgiving after it.

■ Scripture Search

1. Skim the texts given below to find instances when Jesus, while eating or drinking with others, listened to their complaints, shared his thoughts, and was aware of the thoughts and feelings of those present: Matthew 9:9-13, 16:5-12, 26:6-13; Mark 2:13-17, 8:14-21, 14:3-9; Luke 5:27-32, 7:36-50, 19:1-9; John 12:1-8, 2:1-12, 4:1-26.

2. In Luke 11:29-32, the Jews ask Jesus for a sign. What sign does he say will be given them? Do they accept it? What is the connection between that sign and the Eucharist?

3. Read John 13. Discuss the significance of the Washing of the Feet being used instead of the Last Supper story of the other Gospels.

The Gathering Rite

In some parishes, provisions are made for the people to gather before the service to greet one another. Before Mass begins, it is the function of "hospitality ministers" to help everyone find a place in the Church and to feel at home in this place of worship.

The entrance song is a call to worship and a means of focusing the congregation's attention on the celebration at hand. A joyous song may be sung as the priest and ministers process to the sanctuary. If no song is sung, a leader may lead the congregation in reciting a short verse or psalm that has the same function as a song.

It is the celebrant's right and duty to greet the People of God as they come together with him to worship. One official greeting is "The Lord be with you," to which the people respond "And also with you." This greeting acknowledges the presence of the congregation and reminds everyone that the Mass is not simply the actions of the priest himself. Christ is present where his People pray.

A joyous song is sung by the choir and congregation to begin the Eucharistic gathering.

Chapter 7   The Table of Unity

People often fail in their attempts to be loving. The penitential rite is a time in the Mass for reconciliation with others and with God. There are different options for this rite.

Prepared now for worship, the congregation joins in praying or singing the Glory to God, a hymn of praise for God's goodness. Except on the Sundays in Advent and Lent, the Gloria is always prayed.

The opening prayer of the priest focuses our attention on the reason we have gathered together. The prayer also helps us in preparing to open ourselves to listen to God's Word.

About the Liturgy of the Word

The main part of the Liturgy of the Word is composed of readings from Scripture and chants between the readings. The homily, profession of faith, and general intercessions (prayers of the faithful) complete the Liturgy of the Word. In the readings, God speaks to the community about the mystery of salvation. The priest's homily then explains what these readings mean. Through the chants (responsorial psalm and Gospel acclamation) and the profession of faith, the People of God formally accept God's Word. Having reflected on this Word, they then pray for the needs of the Church and of the world.

On Sundays and feastdays, there are three readings: the first from the Hebrew Scriptures (Old Testament), the second from the writings of the Apostles, and the third from the Gospels. There is an order of ascending importance in these readings. Like a family record, the first reading reaches far back into the history of Israel to show how, for centuries, God prepared for the coming of Jesus. The New Testament reading is usually a comment on the meaning of what God did for humanity in Christ. The Gospel proclaims the good news of Jesus himself.

After the second reading, a Gospel acclamation prepares the people to hear the Gospel. This acclamation is also called an "alleluia," which comes from the Hebrew words *hillel* (praise) and *Yah* (Yahweh, or God). If there is only one reading before the Gospel, as is normally the case on weekdays, the congregation can respond with both a responsorial psalm and an alleluia, either the responsorial

The role of the Lector is to make God's Word come alive for all those present at Liturgy.

Liturgical Roots

More and more people today are interested in tracing their roots. In the Church, too, there has been a trend toward studying the first days of its existence. The basic shape of today's Mass seems to have been set before the end of the first century. One of the earliest known written records of liturgical custom comes from Saint Justin Martyr (100-165 A.D.) who summarized a second-century Sunday liturgy in his First Apology.

"On the day named after the sun, all who live in city or countryside assemble, and the memoirs of the Apostles or the writings of the prophets are read for as long as time allows. When the lector has finished, the president (priest celebrant) addresses us, admonishing us and exhorting us to imitate the splendid things we have heard. Then we all stand and pray, and, when we have finished praying, bread, wine, and water are brought up. The president offers prayers of thanksgiving, according to his ability, and the people give their assent with an "Amen!" Next, the gifts over which the thanksgiving has been spoken are distributed, and each one shares in them, while they are also sent via the deacons to the absent brethren.

"The wealthy who are willing make contributions, each as he pleases, and the collection is deposited with the president, who aids orphans and widows, those who are in want because of sickness or other cause, those in prison, and visiting strangers; in short, he takes care of all in need."

psalm or the alleluia, or just the responsorial psalm. The alleluia should be sung. If not, it should be omitted. In Lent, the alleluia verse is replaced with a more subdued response.

In the prayers of the faithful, the people exercise their priestly powers by praying for all humanity. In general, the

Ways of Worship

Liturgical Dress

Until the fourth century of Christianity, the dress worn by the clergy for liturgical functions was the same as the ordinary clothes worn by the people. The regular dress of the Greco-Roman civilization at that time consisted of an undergarment fastened at the neck, a tunic (a loose-fitting garment with or without sleeves and extending to the knees), and the mantle (an ample outer garment wrapped around the body). When fashions changed during the barbarian invasions, the clergy kept the old styles. These styles became symbolic, much as the uniforms of airline attendants, nurses, and the military are today.

In the Middle Ages, vestments became so ornate and heavy that their size had to be reduced. Although there has been a reduction in the number of vestments to be worn since the 1950s, there has also been a return to the free-flowing, ample styles of earlier times. Contemporary vestments like the chasuble—the outer vestment—are made of light materials.

types of intentions that should be included are the needs of the Church and of civil authorities; the salvation of the whole world, including the oppressed and those in any kind of need; and the needs of the local community. The priest usually introduces and concludes the petitions. The community responds vocally or silently after each petition.

---

7. *Some churches are being built with large lobbies in which parishioners can socialize before services. Why do you think this is the trend?*

8. *What part does the entrance song play in setting the mood of the Mass?*

9. *What symbolism do you see in the entrance procession?*

10. *Suggest some constructive ways to improve the way the Word of God is proclaimed so that people can hear it better and act on it more easily.*

Liturgy of the Eucharist

In the Liturgy of the Eucharist, Christians give thanks for both God's Word and action. The Liturgy of the Eucharist has three main parts: the Preparation of the Gifts, the Eucharistic Prayer, and the Communion Rite. During the Liturgy of the Eucharist, the sacrificial and meal aspects of the Mass become apparent.

Preparation of the Gifts

Earlier in Church history, great emphasis was placed on the bread and wine as sacrifices Christians offered to God. Today, the bread and wine are seen as God's gifts to the People, for which they give thanks. These gifts also symbolize the total dedication of the worshipers to Christ. During this part of the Mass, the gifts are placed on the altar. They should not already be on the altar, but at some other place. The gifts may be brought to the altar by an acolyte or may be presented by members of the congregation in a procession.

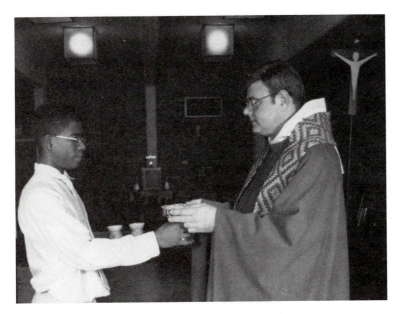

The gifts of the community are gathered and celebrated at every Eucharist.

In times past, the offertory procession was a high point of the liturgy. People brought chickens, lambs, bread, eggs, and other items to be left at the altar. Today, a monetary offering symbolizes our self-gift and our willingness to support the work of the Church. This procession has reduced importance today, and the emphasis is once again where it belongs: on the Eucharistic Prayer.

In the last part of the preparation of the gifts, the priest prays over the bread and wine. He asks the people to join him in praying that these gifts—this Eucharistic sacrifice—may be acceptable and pleasing to God.

The Eucharistic Prayer

The Eucharistic Prayer begins with a prayer known as the Preface. The Preface is a prayer of glory. Full of thanks and praise, it sets the tone for the most solemn part of the Mass when Christ, in his sacrifice, becomes personally present in the midst of his People. The Holy, Holy, Holy imitates the spirit of the crowd who welcomed Jesus in his triumphant entry into Jerusalem. At the same time, it recalls the vision Isaiah had of the holiness of God that filled the whole Temple.

Acolyte: a minister of table service, sometimes called an altar server.

The Eucharistic Prayers used at Mass are based on the ancient Jewish *berakah* prayers of praise and blessing. They consist of eight parts: Thanksgiving (the Preface); the people's Acclamation of Praise (Holy, Holy, Holy); the *Epiclesis* (the invocation of the Holy Spirit to bless the gifts and the members of the Church); the Narrative of the Last Supper, instituting the Eucharist (consecration); *Anamnesis*, the memorial prayer expressing faith in Christ's Real Presence; an Offering of the Sacrifice to God; Intercessions for the whole Church; and a Doxology of praise.

At the end of the Eucharistic Prayer, the people respond with a heartfelt "Amen!" This amen is called the Great Amen because it affirms everything that has taken place throughout the Eucharistic Prayer. For the Jews and early Christians, a prayer was not complete or "validated" unless it ended with an "amen." This is another reason why the Great Amen is considered so important and should have a place of prominence in today's liturgies.

The Communion Rite

The Communion Rite begins with the Our Father. Even in Communion services outside of Mass, the Our Father is included as a preparation for reception of the Eucharist.

The Sign of Peace occurs after the Our Father, but may occur at anytime throughout the Mass preceding the reception of Communion. This gesture of reconciliation is based on Jesus' instruction to his followers, "Therefore, if you bring your gift to the altar, and there recall that your brother has anything against you, leave your gift there at the altar, go first and be reconciled with your brother, and then come and offer your gift" (Matthew 5:23-24).

Just before Communion, the priest breaks the bread and drops a small part into the chalice. This action is known as the fraction rite. At this time, the priest may also break up the bread into smaller pieces for Communion. The priest reminds the people that Jesus is the Lamb of God who takes away the sins of the world. The faithful then approach the altar to receive Communion, the body and blood of Christ.

Offering the sign of peace to someone with whom you are angry can begin the process of reconciliation.

11. *Have you been at Masses where other symbolic gifts were presented? Describe the meaning of the practice.*

12. *Why is it important for us to participate in the prayers of the Mass set aside for the people? What does an active participation symbolize?*

13. *Why is the Our Father a good preparation for Communion?*

Summary

- The Eucharist should be considered a single action of the worshiping community. Though it has many different parts, each part celebrates the Church's praise and worship of God as a single prayer of thanksgiving.

- The Liturgy of the Word proclaims God's mighty deeds and confronts us with the challenge to live up to our obligations as Christians.

- In the Liturgy of the Eucharist, we share the bread and wine that Jesus gave us as his own life and as the gift of himself to the Father.

Doxology: a short hymn of praise to God.

Chapter 7 The Table of Unity

SECTION 2
Checkpoint!

■ Review

1. What does the Gathering Rite suggest about the importance of our sisters and brothers in the celebration of the Eucharist?

2. How does the Sign of Peace emphasize the relationship we have to those who worship with us?

3. Why is the Liturgy of the Word an integral and necessary part of the Mass?

4. The Eucharistic Prayer is a *berakah* prayer. Explain.

5. Catholics are encouraged to receive communion as frequently as they can. Why? Why do you think that some people stay away from Communion?

6. Words to Know: Liturgy of the Word, Liturgy of the Eucharist, Gathering Rite, Alleluia, *Epiclesis*, *Anamnesis*, Doxology, Great Amen, acolyte, chasuble.

■ In Your World

1. What are some positive ways you could work to make the Liturgy of the Word in your parish more meaningful?

2. Jesus did not wear vestments at the Last Supper, and during the first four centuries of the Church priests did not wear vestments. List the advantages and disadvantages of wearing or not wearing vestments.

■ Scripture Search

1. In every Eucharistic acclamation, you affirm your faith in Christ's Second Coming. Several of Jesus' parables use the figure of a banquet to show what the joy of his kingdom will be like in the life beyond death. Read the following parables: Matthew 22:2-14; Luke 14:7-11, 12-14, 15-24, 16:19-31. From these parables, what "hints for happiness" does Christ give about the kingdom-banquet you experience in the Eucharist? Compose a "Dear Abby" letter asking for advice about happiness. Submit it to someone else in the class who volunteers to answer your letter on the basis of the "hints for happiness" suggested in the parables above.

2. Read Exodus 12:1-28. Why is the Passover such a special celebration for the Jewish people? Why is it a celebration of liberation and of sacrifice?

SECTION 3
Jesus' Gift of Himself in the Eucharist

The Eucharist is more than just a meal; it is **the** great sacrament of reconciliation. It is Christ's sacrifice. Some Christians believe that it was simply Jesus' death on the cross that saved the world and brought about union with God. They wrongly hold that Jesus died because his Father, angered by the rebellion of the human race, demanded the death of Jesus in order to make up for sin. Jesus' teachings say something different. He says time and again that his Father is a loving God, and such a Father would never destroy his Son.

Loving Obedience

Jesus' loving obedience to God brought about forgiveness of sin and humanity's reconciliation with God. The role of Savior that Jesus accepted from the Father did eventually lead to his death. It was not just this death, however, that "made up" for sin. Rather, reconciliation was won by the attitudes and dispositions Jesus had throughout his life and he embraced even in death.

Jesus' total cooperation with his Father's plan sprang from a deep inner attitude of absolute trust in God's goodness. Jesus' mind, heart, and instinct told him that God would never use almighty power to inflict evil on God's creatures. He lived in the confidence that God, as a divine Father, could and would bring good from every event. Jesus' response was profound thanksgiving and love, even in the unjust suffering he endured.

Chapter 7 The Table of Unity

Touching the Sacred

Prepositions in our Prayers

Hardly anyone pays much attention to grammar these days, but sometimes it can make a great difference.

At Mass, the prepositions used are important. In many prayers of the Eucharistic celebration, the prepositions follow this order: from, through, in, to. **From** God the Father, **through** Christ, **in** the Holy Spirit, back **to** the Father.

This order may not seem important, but it expresses God's entire plan for the world. Every good thing comes from the pure goodness of the Father, through Jesus the great mediator. Without Jesus, no one can receive anything from the Father or even approach God. The Holy Spirit, sent by Christ and the Father, is present personally with gifts. It is in the Spirit that we are united with Christ. Our response to the Father works in reverse order: it is by the presence of the Spirit within that we return back to the Father, through Christ.

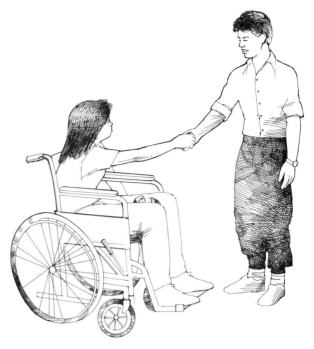

The Eucharist is the great sacrament of reconciliation.

Jesus' inner disposition was revealed in the words he pronounced at the Last Supper over the bread "given for you" (Luke 22:19) and over the wine "shed on behalf of many for the forgiveness of sins" (Matthew 26:28). In these two simple phrases, Jesus showed that he was fully aware of what was ahead, and that he deliberately and consciously offered his life for the world's salvation. He, the divine victim, was also to be the priest, the human offerer of the sacrifice. His altar was to be the cross.

Jesus prayed to his Father at the Last Supper, "And I consecrate myself for them" (John 17:19). The Last Supper and Calvary were two moments of the same act of perfect love.

14. *What things are teenagers tempted to rebel against? Which of these "rebellions" are sinful?*

15. *Submission is not always virtuous. Was Christ always "passive"? Was he a "rebel" in any way?*

Christ's Sacrifice Made Present

Instead of offering an animal victim as Moses had done, Jesus set apart bread and wine as the signs of the gift of himself. But in naming them his body and blood, he did not create a merely psychological, spiritual, or symbolic memorial. By his divine word, through the power of the Holy Spirit, Jesus' presence took over the bread and wine completely. He changed their meaning so radically that they were no longer what they had been. They became, instead, truly his body and blood, signs of his actual presence.

Through the Eucharist, Jesus' sacrificial act becomes present, too. Christ comes to his People not merely in memory, but truly in his risen, bodily state. The Eucharist is the death, resurrection, ascension, and pentecost of Christ brought to believers under sacramental form.

To grasp somewhat how Christ is present, Christians must realize that, although God is present everywhere, the risen Christ is, by his nature, only in heaven. But his risen life permits him to be present wherever he wills to be, in the way he wills. But his presence in the Eucharist is not a physical confinement of his earthly body to the area of the bread and wine. When you receive the consecrated bread or drink the consecrated wine, you receive the risen Christ really and truly present in the bread and wine, whole and entire, body and blood, soul and divinity, as he is in heaven. This is called being "sacramentally present."

The Real Presence

In the Eucharist, the Christ who offered himself on the cross is the same Christ who now, through the ministry of the priest, offers himself on the altar. Under the Eucharistic species (the exterior signs of bread and wine), he comes in the way that is most satisfying—as a human person. He is present in a unique way—whole and entire, God and man. This presence is also called **Real Presence**, not because the other ways of being present are not real, but because this way of being present surpasses all the others. It is the personal presence of Christ's glorified body. He makes himself truly present in a sacramental way in the Eucharist through the instrumentality of his Church.

When Jesus comes to us in Communion, he knows and loves each of us personally. As the food of divine life, he deepens his eternal life in us, transforming the human things we do into the true worship of God in the Spirit. Our words and actions become his proclamation of the Good News. Our service of others is both his service to them and our service to him, for "Whatever you did for one of these least brothers of mine, you did for me" (Matthew 25:40). Through the Eucharist, the world is daily recharged with the current of Christ's love until the final day when God's love will be the light and warmth of both heaven and earth.

The Mystery of Christ's Presence

How the change in the bread and wine by the words of consecration takes place is a mystery. No explanation can clarify it completely, but, from the beginning of the Church, theologians have labored to find words that attempt to explain what Jesus did that night of the Last Supper.

While bread is a basic, ordinary food, it contains many meanings. It is the symbol of all God's gifts of creation and also all "the work of human hands." The crushing of the many grains to make flour is an image of human interdependence.

Jesus did not merely strengthen these meanings. He gave the bread an entirely new meaning. Jesus broke the bread to share it, to show that all present were one in spirit: Jesus with his disciples and they with one another. He changed the bread completely from a gift—a thing given—to the very giver himself. Although the appearances of the bread remain in the Eucharist, the reality of bread is changed into the personal, actual, and real presence of Christ himself.

To describe this change of bread into the body of Christ, official Church teachings use the technical word **transubstantiation.** It means the change of the substance of bread into the body of Christ. The bread and wine are not annihilated or wiped out of existence. Instead, they are transformed. All their physiochemical properties—color, taste, bulk, minerals, carbohydrates—remain. It is faith alone that tells us that what we eat and drink is the risen Lord Jesus.

Catholics believe that the bread and wine of the Eucharist become the body and blood of Christ.

Because of developments in physics and philosophy in the last two hundred years, the word **substance** has undergone a shift in meaning. As a result, Catholic theologians of this century have been prompt to search for more suitable words to reinterpret the doctrine of the Real Presence.

Thus far, however, no word is so helpful as transubstantiation, first used by the Council of Trent in the sixteenth century, to describe the "how" of the Eucharist. Although the term is not in the Bible and was never used before A.D. 1150, it has served for centuries to express what happens at the words of consecration. As Christians, we have the obligation to be careful of the words we use to express this mystery. The great truth that we must always remember is that in giving the Eucharist, Christ gave not merely a proof or symbol of his love, but his very self to be the sacramental food.

16. *Jesus set apart bread as a sign of his gift of self to God and to us. Why is bread a particularly good sign of what Jesus means for us?*

17. *Besides his sacramental presence in the consecrated bread, how else is Christ present to us at Mass?*

> **Substance:** a word that, in philosophy, always meant the total reality or essence of a thing. Today it can mean the physical material of which a thing is made, or it can mean whatever is of importance, as in "you grasped the substance of the message, but not the fine points."

Chapter 7 The Table of Unity

Simplicity in Church Furnishings

The reform of Vatican II has suggested that the altar should be the most noble, the most beautifully designed, and the most well-constructed table the community can provide. It symbolizes the Lord, so it should not be used as a resting place for papers, notes, cruets, or even candles or flowers. Because it is the focus of attention during the Eucharistic Prayer, it should be covered with a handsome altar cloth and hold nothing but the chalice, the book, and the bread and wine. Ideally, the altar should be large enough for only one celebrant.

Perhaps the best word to describe the present thinking in liturgical furnishings is simplicity. The celebrant's chair should have a place of convenience in the sanctuary, and the placement of pews (or chairs) should foster a spirit of community. Each person in the congregation should have a clear view of all the movements of the celebration, as well as of other members of the community.

The ambo, or lectern, is the stand from which the readers proclaim God's Word. It should be dignified in design and, like the altar, constructed of fine materials. This stand should be used only for reading the Word of God and preaching. Another lectern may be used by song leaders or for making announcements.

Fine furniture, of course, does not guarantee fine celebrations of the Eucharist. But the way we furnish our churches can help to enhance our liturgies and highlight the signs we use to celebrate Christ's presence among us.

◆

The ambo, the stand from which the Gospel is read, should be dignified in design and constructed of fine materials.

Worship and Sacraments: We Celebrate, We Praise

Source of Healing and Life

All during his life, Jesus healed people by his presence. Now his sacramental presence brings healing to the people of every generation by making his supreme act of healing—the sacrifice on the cross—sacramentally present on the altars of the world. These symbolic actions do not repeat Jesus' total self-offering on Calvary; they continue it. Because of Christ's personal presence under the appearance of bread and wine, he—through the priest together with the people—offers himself anew to the Father as he did on Calvary and as he does eternally.

Although Jesus actively surrendered to death, all the emphasis in his sacrifice was on life. In submitting to death, Jesus actually chose resurrection. Jesus accepted death as the means to the greatly amplified life of union with God. It is for the sake of this life of love, this new union of humanity with God, that the Eucharist exists at all.

By bringing the Eucharist to those confined to the home, the Church proclaims Jesus as healer.

Jesus' sacrifice is an accomplished historical fact that can never be repeated. He will never die again. In the repeated consecration of the bread and wine, Jesus does not relive or repeat his passion. Rather, he continually offers himself to the Father. Because of his divinity, Jesus' inner decision of obedience is a glorious, eternal act.

While Christ, the eternal high priest, has been victorious over evil once and for all, each Eucharist gives us a share in his offering. Every Mass is the bringing before God of Jesus' saving actions and a bringing to us of that one past action.

18. Why is it impossible for someone who truly understands the Eucharist not to become involved with the needs of others?

19. The Eucharist is a sacrament of reconciliation. What kinds of reconciliation does it accomplish?

20. The Eucharist is sometimes called a "sacrifice of praise." How does our celebration of the Eucharist praise God?

What are some of the ways people show reverence while receiving the Eucharist?

Summary

- In the Eucharist, Christ's sacrifice on the cross is made present to us as a divine gesture of healing and reconciliation.

- We speak of God's presence at Mass as the real presence. He is with us in his Risen Body under the forms of bread and wine.

- After the priest prays the words of consecration, Catholics believe that the bread and wine become the Body and Blood of Christ. This change is called **transubstantiation.**

SECTION 3
Checkpoint!

■ Review

1. How does Jesus' gift of himself reconcile us to God?

2. What is meant by Christ's sacramental presence at Mass and how is this an experience of his real presence?

3. What does "transubstantiation" refer to?

4. Why is it necessary to pay attention to the furnishings used in our churches for the Eucharistic celebration?

5. Words to Know: Real Presence, sacramental presence, substance, transubstantiation.

■ In Your World

1. What groups of people in your parish do you think are most lonely? What can you do to restore their sense of community?

2. Some people criticize the recent Catholic emphasis on the Liturgy of the Word, saying that it is "too Protestant." What role does the Liturgy of the Word play in the Eucharistic celebration? How does it relate to what Jesus did at the Last Supper?

■ Scripture Search

1. Explain the Catholic belief in the real presence of Jesus in the Eucharist using John 6:44-59 and Luke 22:14-20.

2. Read Exodus 16:4-15 and discuss how this Scripture text prepares us to accept Jesus' great gift of the Eucharist.

CHAPTER 7 Review

■ Study

1. What are the three parts of the Jewish Passover meal and how do they express the meaning of the celebration?

2. Why were the changes that Jesus made in the Passover meal he shared with the disciples the night before he died important?

3. What is the *berakah* prayer and how is this prayer incorporated into the Eucharist?

4. After the Gathering Rite, there are two major parts of the Eucharist. What are they, and what does each celebrate?

5. What is the "Great Amen," and what does it signify?

6. According to Saint Justin Martyr, what were the important parts of the Eucharist as celebrated in the second century?

7. What did Jesus' obedience to his Father's will consist of? Why was he obedient?

8. In what ways is Christ present at the celebration of every Eucharist?

9. How does the Church's teaching about transubstantiation help us to appreciate Christ's sacramental presence?

10. Why is it incorrect to say that the Mass **repeats** the death of Christ on Calvary? What is a more accurate way of stating the relationship of the Eucharist to the sacrifice of Christ?

■ Action

1. Organize a discussion on the topic: "Sacrifice is necessary for true love."

2. Write a prayer service which thanks Jesus for his willingness to sacrifice for you.

3. Find a reference to the Holy Spirit in one of the Eucharistic Prayers. Describe the meaning of the reference.

4. Look up the etymology of the word "*epiclesis.*" Discuss your findings with the class.

■ Prayer

This *Agape* Service is not a Mass. It is a celebration of our **love** (the meaning of the Greek word *agape*) for God and for one another. As you celebrate this *agape*, recall the "table of unity that Jesus sets for us in the Eucharist.

Gathering Open with a song or recorded music, welcome, and statement of the event we celebrate.

Reading 1 Corinthians 11:17-29 ("abuse" of *agape*/mockery of the gift).

Prayer (Leader) Let us pray. Father, we thank you and praise you for the gift of love you freely share with us in creation and especially in Jesus, your Word. We remember that Jesus told us not to make our gift of thanks and praise to you without first being reconciled to our brothers and sisters.

Sign of Peace (Leader) May the peace and *agape* of the Lord be with you always. Let us now share a sign of the Lord's own love with one another.

Reading Mark 6:30-44 (After the reading, everyone can share reflections about the meaning of this story.)

Berekah Prayer (Prayer of blessing over the bread and over the people who share it—prayer to be offered by the Leader).

Blessed are you, Lord God of all creation! Through your goodness we have this bread and wine, and the bread of our lives, to offer you as we share with one another what you have freely given to us. You have even more richly blessed us with the gift of Jesus, your living and true presence in our lives and in the world.

Blessed are you, Lord our God, for raising Jesus up on the third day. Blessed are you for working the same miracle in us. Blessed are you for your Word Jesus, who now invites us with his word spoken at the Last Supper: "Do this in memory of me."

Blessed are you, Lord God of all creation! Amen.

Sharing of Bread (Leader instructs people to break the loaves and give bread to **someone else** in silence: no one should keep the piece of bread she or he breaks off. This is an "untidy" arrangement, but that's the way it often is with *agape*. No one eats yet. When all have bread, the Leader speaks.)

We are the Body of Christ when we break and share the bread of our lives in memory of him. (All eat.)

Song or recorded music (All join hands as the Leader ends the service by inviting everyone to join hands and say the Lord's Prayer.)

CHAPTER

8

Sacraments of Vocation

OBJECTIVES

In this Chapter you will

- See that every person has a vocation or calling from God to live the life of grace.

- Recognize marriage and family life as a vocation and a sacrament.

- Understand more about the vocation of those who serve Christ and the community through the sacrament of Holy Orders, and consider your own vocation.

Father, you are holy indeed, and all creation rightly gives you praise. All life, all holiness comes from you through your Son, Jesus Christ, our Lord, by the working of the Holy Spirit. From age to age you gather a people to yourself, so that from east to west a perfect offering may be made to the glory of your name.
—From Eucharistic Prayer III

Worship and Sacraments: We Celebrate, We Praise

SECTION 1
Our Vocation, The Life of Grace

Coletta jumped in the back of the truck with the others in her club. They were going to pick berries on a nearby farm. Suddenly the farmer motioned through the back window of the cab. She wanted Coletta to sit up front with her. Puzzled, Coletta dismounted and climbed into the cab section with the farmer. Mrs. Hernandez told Coletta that she reminded her of a daughter who had gone off to college. Mrs. Hernandez wanted the pleasure of speaking with Coletta. Although she missed the fun of riding in the back with the others, Coletta felt special for being singled out. It was a privilege to ride with the owner of the farm.

Having a vocation is like that. God singles us out of millions of others to be born, filled with love, and able to share the divine life offered to us through Christ. Each person has a special vocation, and every person shares a common vocation. The word "vocation" means "calling." When we speak of our vocation as Christians, we are referring to the invitation that God offers to all baptized people to be disciples of Jesus. The sacraments of initiation celebrate our acceptance of this invitation through the life of grace.

In Baptism and Confirmation, we begin living out our Christian vocation. We accept Christ's way of life as our own. The Eucharist further strengthens us in our efforts to be more Christ-like as the on-going sacrament of our initiation into the company of Jesus' disciples.

Exercising Our Christian Vocation

Just as we have been given sacraments which celebrate the beginning of a life that demonstrates a willingness to hear God's call and respond in faith, so too has the Lord given us sacraments that celebrate specific ways of exercising our Christian vocation. These two sacraments, Matrimony and Holy Orders, may be called the sacraments of Christian vocation.

Regardless of whether we are chosen to marry, to remain single, to live a vowed or consecrated life, or to seek Holy Orders, our **Christian** vocation remains the same. That vocation or calling from God is to live the life of grace as fully as possible.

There are no first-class or second-class citizens in the kingdom of God. There is no **one** way of being faithful to our Christian vocation that is intrinsically better than any other. Any way we choose to lead our lives can lead us to God, and we go "first class" as long as the life choices we make help us to be the image of God that we were created to be (Genesis 1:26).

This is what we mean when we say that our vocation is always to live the life of grace. Whether we sell cars or run corporations, whether we get married or not, whether we join a religious order or become an astronaut or a teacher, we all have the same vocation. God calls each one of us to be witnesses and ambassadors of the divine life we share through Jesus, the Son of God.

God's Spirit living in us makes this possible. Permitting the Holy Spirit to guide us allows us to be women and men who are full of grace, holy people in God's sight.

When you show concern for the earth and its resources, you are practicing the Christian vocation.

---

1. *What problems do you think people face these days as they attempt to be faithful to Christ in their chosen careers?*

2. *Can you think of a person that you particularly admire? What is it about his or her life that demonstrates the power of God's grace?*

Worship and Sacraments: We Celebrate, We Praise

3. Why do you think that fewer people are choosing to live out their Christian vocations as sisters, brothers, and priests today?

_____

Grace

God calls each and every person to live out his or her life as completely as possible. While you won't always succeed in everything you try, you are called to make the attempt as fully as your gifts allow. Because nothing is impossible with God, with God's help you can succeed at practically anything you attempt. God's help comes to us through Grace. Grace is the free gift of God's self-communication to us. The Holy Spirit invites us to share in God's divine life. If we believe, we become transformed into people cleansed of sin and responsive to God's action in our lives.

In Baptism and Confirmation, the Spirit offers us strength beyond ordinary human attainment. This strength is called "the virtues," which may be described as "spiritual habits." Virtues make us people of character, able to recognize and avoid evil. Not content merely to obey laws, we make the right decisions out of personal conviction. It is character that gives direction and shape to our lives.

At no time can we sit back and say that our character formation is ever finished. Since it is closely linked with personality, and since personality is unique, each person must develop in his or her own way. Character unfolds by the exercise of **virtue:** power rooted in grace to carry out morally good actions with a certain ease and perseverance, even in the face of obstacles and at the cost of sacrifice. The opposite of virtue is **vice,** a habit of bad action. Virtue leads to wisdom, vice to destruction.

Christian Virtue

Some areas of psychology refer to virtue as ego-strengths or positive forces originating in the unconscious. These keep the **id** (the irrational and destructive forces of the self) from leading us away from becoming our true selves. In Christian thinking, the movement toward true fulfillment is the same as salvation or union with God.

For Example

Marc practices the virtue of patience. He refuses to get upset when things don't happen as he plans. When he studies the wrong chapter for the test, he doesn't panic. He patiently works through what he remembers, answers the questions that he can, then explains to the teacher he studied the wrong chapter.

Martha practices the vice of haste. She is always rushing through things haphazardly. When she studies incorrectly for the test, she panics. She rushes to answer the questions, sees none that make immediate sense, and turns in her paper. She screams at the teacher for making her fail. Which person accomplishes more in the long run?

Religious order: a group of women and men who remain unmarried and promise (vow) to live, in community, lives of poverty, chastity, and obedience in the service of Christ and the Church.

Character: the self, regarded in its ethical or moral dimension.

Personality: the dynamic self or psyche that makes a person a unique individual.

How are the students in this photo practicing the virtues of prudence and justice?

In Christian living, these forces include the **theological virtues** of faith, hope, and love, which give us the ability to relate to God in a person-to-person encounter (1 Corinthians 13). **Moral virtues** give us the power to relate to others in a Christ-like way, with the key (or cardinal) virtues being prudence, justice, fortitude, and temperance.

Faith grants us the ability to accept the worldview revealed by God's word: to trust God and to act out of our convictions. Through **hope,** we expect from God forgiveness, divine help, and eternal life, and thus we are enabled continually to reorient ourselves and our relationship to the world in the light of the coming kingdom (Romans 15:13). **Charity** (love) is our personal participation in the divine life. It moves us to total dedication to God and to the welfare of others for God's love. As the animating force of all other Christian virtues, love is willing to suffer, if necessary, to build the kingdom.

All the moral virtues hinge on the four **cardinal virtues** by which God guides and assists us in facing life's hardships. **Prudence** is the cardinal virtue that enables us to choose what is best in specific situations. Right judgments result in the blessings of charity, joy, and peace.

The Life of Grace

Stuart has the gift of song. Everyone tells him so. When people are sad, he sings just the right song to cheer them up. People like to be around Stuart because he shares his gift with them freely. When asked where he learned to sing so well, Stuart answers, "It's God's special gift to me. I thank God for this grace."

Because grace refers to the mysterious action of God in our lives, it is not easily defined. The word comes from a Latin noun, *gratia*, which means something that is **freely given.** Grace, therefore, is a **gift** which allows us to enjoy and participate in God's own life.

We **experience** God's grace (we never **earn** it) when we turn to God in prayer, when we imitate the activities of Jesus, and especially when we celebrate the sacraments. This gift of God changes us for the better and challenges us to live even more faithfully.

We experience **sanctifying grace** when we receive the sacraments. We call this moment of grace "sanctifying" because it leads to holiness, which is a quality of God (see Isaiah 6:3). Each time you celebrate the sacrament of Eucharist you are filled with this grace. This grace helps you to grow more deeply in love with God, and is further strengthened by prayer and imitating the works of Christ. So sanctifying grace helps you live a more Christian life, and living this life strengthens the grace within you. While it is possible for us through sin to turn our backs on God and live apart from divine grace, God will **never** abandon us. In fact, when we sin, God offers us the grace of forgiveness even before we seek reconciliation (Luke 15:11-32).

Actual grace is God's way of being present to us at all times, not just when we celebrate the sacraments. As Jesus told us, "know that I am with you always until the end of the world" (Matthew 28:20). Actual grace is the fulfillment of that promise.

Justice empowers us to do our duty and to accord others what is their rightful due. Social relationships demand commutative justice (individual to individual), distributive justice (government to individual), legal justice (individual to government), and social justice (individual to society at large).

Fortitude provides courage to overcome obstacles to salvation, especially fear and rashness. It is exercised either actively, by taking energetic action on behalf of the kingdom, or passively, by enduring hardship, suffering, and even death for its sake.

Temperance regulates the bodily drives by facilitating the self-denial and renunciation required to bring our disordered tendencies into balance.

The Christian virtues are ours to live through the sacrament of Baptism. Through the other sacraments we receive the ongoing grace to live these virtues, and so shape out life as true followers of Christ. Practicing the virtues without the sacraments is difficult. Receiving the sacraments without living the Christian virtues would be an empty gesture. It is through living out the Christian virtues that we bring God's grace to the world; that we bring the sacraments alive to others.

Growth Through Transformation

Grace is not forced upon us; it is God's love alive and active within us. Grace causes a transformation within us that helps us truly recognize that we are forgiven, and loved as fully as God can love. We do not earn grace. It is given to us because of Christ's redeeming sacrifice and it helps us in whatever we do, but especially when we celebrate the sacraments and perform other religious actions. We cannot even live without it.

Grace is like sunlight that we do not directly perceive, yet through which we see things clearly. If we are open to God's presence in all things, we experience God. We are not forced to respond to the divine invitation to love. God's love is not imposed upon us; instead we are drawn to God. We come to Baptism through grace, and through Baptism, we accept the responsibility of Christian love. Our relationship with God depends on how faithful we are to the law of love

Touching the Sacred

A Woman Full of Grace

Besides Jesus, Mary is the only human being to have lived the life of grace completely. We believe that she was without sin, and because of this, Mary is the model of Christian vocation.

We call Mary our Blessed Mother, Mother of God, and Mother of the Church. Her example helps us to conform our lives to that of her son, Jesus Christ.

We honor Mary with a special prayer that is based upon the angel's visit to her before Jesus was born (Luke 1:26-38).

Hail Mary, full of grace. The Lord is with you. Blessed are you among women, and blessed is the fruit of your womb, Jesus. Holy Mary, Mother of God, pray for us sinners, now and at the hour of our death. Amen.

through the Eucharist, the sacraments, prayer, and good works. But this life of grace is threatened by our tendency to oppose God or to be independent of God. Actions, omissions, and attitudes that are inconsistent with our role as God's People and that weaken our bonds with God tend to diminish our ability to be faithful to our Christian vocation.

No one is ever fully faithful to Christ. No one ever lives a completely virtuous life. Over and over we need conversion of heart; we seek forgiveness, are reconciled, and make atonement. Even when we have sinned, grace is available to us, and as the conversion of the thief on the cross demonstrates, it is never too late to say yes to God and begin to live a grace-filled life.

---

4. *Find a news story about a criminal that reveals the trail to violence or tragedy.*

5. *Which of the three theological virtues do you think is most needed today?*

6. *In your attempt to fulfill your Christian vocation and live the life of grace, which of the four cardinal (moral) virtues have you found most helpful?*

7. *If it is our Christian vocation to live a grace-filled life, do you think that God never forces grace upon us?*

The Christian virtues require us to act for others.

Summary

- No matter what profession or way of life they choose, all Christians have the same vocation or calling from God, which is to live the life of grace as perfectly as possible.

- Grace is God's free gift of divine life. The Holy Spirit helps us to accept this gift and strengthens our life of grace.

- God never forces grace on us. Like every gift, it must be accepted freely and with gratitude.

SECTION 1
Checkpoint!

■ Review

1. What is meant by the statement: "There are no first-class or second-class citizens in the kingdom of God"?

2. What are virtues? What are the theological virtues? The moral (cardinal) virtues?

3. What is the difference between sanctifying grace and actual grace?

4. Why do we say that Mary was "full of grace"? What are some special names or titles that we give Mary?

5. Words to Know: vocation, Religious order, grace (sanctifying and actual), character, virtue, personality, theological virtue, moral (cardinal) virtue, commutative justice, distributive justice, legal justice, social justice.

■ In Your World

1. Think about some ways that you would be happy living out your Christian vocation. Set some goals for your life as you think about a possible profession and whether you plan to get married or not. Write these goals down and show how you plan to accomplish them as an adult disciple of Christ.

2. Write an essay on the four cardinal virtues and show how living these virtues can help people be better witnesses of God's kingdom. Discuss your essay in class.

■ Scripture Search

1. The vocation of teenagers is usually related to their family life and responsibilities to their parents. Study Sirach 3:1-16. In what ways is this advice helpful even today? Is any of it "outdated"? Also consider and discuss Sirach 1:1-29. Which pieces of advice found in this passage are you attracted to?

2. Read Luke 23:39-43. How is this a story about the power of God's grace to transform us?

SECTION 2
The Vocation of Marriage and Family Life

William and Delbert were seminary classmates. Shortly before ordination, Delbert decided to leave the seminary in order to seek his true vocation. He loved what he was doing at the seminary, but recognized that he did not have the vocation to be a priest. A few years later Delbert married. His good friend William, now a priest, witnessed Delbert's marriage. It was a joyous day for both friends.

Vocation and Sacrament

For Catholics, marriage is both a vocation and a sacrament. It's a vocation because not everyone is "called" by God to live the life of grace as a husband or wife and as a parent. While it is true that most people feel drawn to married life, Catholics recognize that accepting the conjugal obligation of being faithful to one spouse for life is a special gift. So is the capacity to be a good parent. Although the Church does not celebrate a specific sacrament for men and women who never marry, it does recognize this life style as a vocation as well.

Marriage is also a sacrament in the Catholic Church. It is a promise that two people make to each other and, according to Catholic teaching, it is a bond of love that reflects God's own love for creation. This means that when two people get married, their union is more than a contract "signed" by the partners. It is also a **sacramental sign** of

> **Conjugal:** refers to the intimate physical, spiritual, and emotional union of husband and wife.

Prior to marriage, couples are now required to meet several times with the priest to discuss the meaning of sacramental marriage.

the covenant God made with us through Jesus Christ. Like the covenants found throughout Scripture, the marriage covenant binds two people together through life in a mutual partnership: for better or worse. As a covenant it is not dependent on the partner. Each spouse commits himself or herself fully to the relationship, come what may.

To live married love, therefore, is to experience God's mysterious presence through every gesture of self-giving that a husband and wife offer to each other. When they face hardships in their marriage or when they have to make sacrifices for one another or their family, God is with them offering divine strength as sacramental grace.

Developments in the Church's Teaching on Marriage

Jesus did not create the institution of marriage. Marriage is of divine origin, practiced long before Jesus lived, since the creation of the human race, in fact.

But from the way Saint Paul speaks of Christian marriage, we know that Jesus' teaching in regard to marriage represented a radical departure both from Israel's long

The Marriage Covenant

Covenant is not an everyday word in our times. But people acquainted with it through the story of God's dealing with us find it just about the best word for describing the marriage pact or pledge between Christians. Marriage vows are not only like the Hebrew Scripture Covenant, they are a living symbol of God's pact to love the Chosen People "for better or for worse." In fact, Christian marriage is a sign of Jesus' New Covenant made in the total gift of his life. Like him, spouses pledge their unconditional love.

Because we participate in God's spiritual nature, the intimate physical union of human intercourse demands complete psychological and spiritual union. Our songs and poetry sing of the need and desire we have for this complete communion. Marital union based on anything less results in the disintegration and loss of human dignity. It is because God has made us so that the parties cannot dissolve a marriage covenant.

In today's world of broken promises and longer life, it is a relief to realize that a covenant is held together not only by the mutual commitment of the parties, but by the strength of God who witnesses to and participates in the unique relationship by his continued presence. For Christian marriage has God as author, witness, and guarantor. As a sacrament of graced covenant, it is a living sign of Christ's love. The couple receives the same faithful love that binds Jesus to his body, the Church. From his redeeming power, they are empowered to live as equals in unity, fidelity, and permanence. It is not a civil law or social custom or mutual consent that creates the unbreakable bond, but rather the involvement of God in the marriage union.

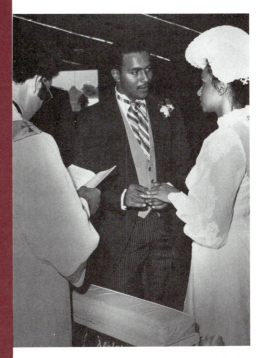

Rings are exchanged as part of the wedding ceremony as signs of commitment to the marriage covenant.

 On the Record

Jesus Teaches the Sanctity of Marriage

At the time of Jesus there were two schools of thought among the rabbis on justifying divorce. Rabbi Shammai allowed divorce strictly because of adultery. Rabbi Hillel allowed a **man** to divorce his wife for anything that might cause him displeasure.

The stand Jesus took was so revolutionary that the disciples were surprised and had difficulty accepting it (Matthew 19:10). Jesus opposed both schools and reverted to God's original command as given in Genesis:

"Have you not read that at the beginning the Creator made them male and female and declared, 'For this reason a man shall leave his father and mother and cling to his wife, and the two shall become as one'? Thus they are no longer two but one flesh. Therefore, let no man separate what God has joined" (Matthew 19:4-7; Genesis 2:23-24).

By preaching the sanctity of all marriage, Jesus not only declared the equality of men and women, he also proclaimed their dignity.

tradition and from the contemporary Roman understanding of marriage.

Paul asked the Christians in Ephesus to "defer to one another out of reverence for Christ" (Ephesians 5:21). He reminded them that once baptized, their relationship to one another in marriage takes on a new dimension. They are Christ to one another. "Husbands should love their wives as they love their own bodies...nourish and take care (of her) as Christ cares for the church, for we are members of his body" (Ephesians 5:28, 30).

Paul's careful responses to questions about marriage addressed to him by the new converts in the city of Corinth (1 Corinthians 7:1-16) show that from the beginning, the Church was concerned that Christians make their married lives worthy of their intimate association with Christ.

Gradually the Church began to express its concern in a more formal way. As early as 110 A.D., a letter written by Ignatius of Antioch speaks of some couples getting the bishop's consent for their unions, and by 210, Tertullian refers to a special blessing ceremony imparted at a Eucharist held to celebrate a couple's marriage performed earlier by mutual consent within the family.

The discussion of marriage continued for several centuries in the Church. New customs and laws, introduced by the Germanic tribes that conquered the Roman Empire in the middle of the fifth century, led to heated debates over precisely what constituted a valid or legitimate marriage. Was it the consent of the couple (Roman custom) or their sexual intimacy, called "consummation" (Germanic custom)?

By the twelfth century, however, the Church declared that matrimony was a sacrament, a permanent sign of God's faithful love, and the necessary elements for Christian marriage were defined once and for all.

The Church taught that the couple administered the sacrament to each other through their promises of love. Although the promises were to be "sanctified" by the Nuptial (wedding) Blessing and the Eucharist, the blessings and Mass were not essential to the validity of the marriage.

Marriage was defined as a **contract** in which the couple pledged to each other exclusive and perpetual marital rights and openness to children. This is what made the union a sacramental marriage. Three "goods of marriage" were identified: (1) the procreation and education of children, (2) the fidelity of the partners, and (3) the indissolubility of the bond, meaning that the marriage could not be dissolved or broken up. The notion of marriage as a covenant was not emphasized, though it is the proper way of speaking about the marriage bond today.

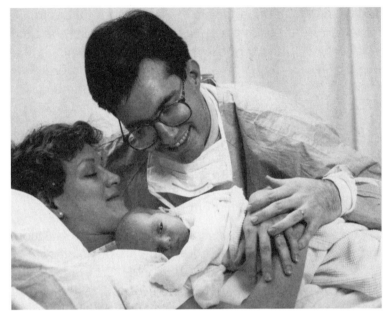

The birth of a child is a joyous occasion for married couples. Having children is a sign of their love and fidelity.

8. What reasons can you give for taking your time with a decision to marry?

9. The intimacy of a healthy sexual relationship is an important and necessary part of marriage, but why is it correct to say that marriage is far more than just "making love"?

10. Why does the Church teach that the bond of marriage is indissoluble?

11. What is the difference between the ideas of "marriage as a contract," and "marriage as a covenant relationship"? Discuss your answer in class.

Vatican II: Marriage Today

Under the leadership of Pope John XXIII, the Fathers of Vatican II updated the Church's teaching on marriage. They adopted a more personalistic approach. No longer was marriage treated simply as a matter of rights and duties. Instead, the Council spoke of it as a covenant of personal consent.

This view represents a radical renewal which is consistent with the Council's focus on the call of the laity to holiness. Marriage today is clearly an agreement between two people to live in intimate partnership. To emphasize that marriage consists essentially in the consent of two people, the ritual allows the couple to choose their songs, to shape their own ceremonies, and even to formulate their vows according to their unique relationship. Their covenant has three essentials: it must be **permanent, exclusive,** and **open** to children.

Marriage is for life. In an age when people are living a lot longer, lifelong fidelity in marriage requires daily effort and prayer. Older couples, surrounded by generations of children, testify to the wisdom of this arrangement.

Many people today look at the growing world population, the poverty of so many, and the threats of pollution and armed conflict with a sense of despair. "Why add to the confusion by adding people?" they ask. It takes faith to reach beyond these objections to find the wisdom of God's plan in requiring that married couples be open to children. As Catholic Christians, we are called to preserve our tradition which leads to life. We can never be on the side of death. The social sciences point out that maturity consists in the creative sharing of life. It is healthy, normal, and holy to love life so much that we want to pass it on. The world's problems need to be solved in other ways than by curtailing the conception of human beings. Abortion, casual sex, avoiding the sacrifices involved in having children: all these things frustrate God's desire to bring forth life through us. They cannot do our world any good either.

While Vatican II and the Revised Rite of Marriage affirm the indissolubility of marriage as never before, the personal approach also lets us recognize instances when what appears to be a marriage isn't a marriage at all. A person

How many children do you hope to have? Who will pay the bills? Where will you celebrate holidays: her parents or his? These are just some of the questions couples consider in marriage preparation.

may be physically mature and all decked out in a tuxedo or wedding dress and yet be an infant psychologically, emotionally, or in the ability to assume adult responsibility. Marriage is only for adults. The immature cannot enter into it.

Preparing for Marriage

For these reasons, along with the revision of the rite, the Church is calling for better preparation for marriage. High schools and colleges offer courses in marriage, and Pre-Cana classes are obligatory for couples planning marriages. The Christian Family Movement, Marriage Encounter, Natural Family Planning, Renew, and other groups support Christian marriage.

Today, with so many challenges facing couples, the Church continues to encourage its married people who are the backbone of the Christian community. All of us long for

Pre-Cana classes: a program designed to help engaged couples understand the obligation of Christian marriage. Jesus performed his first miracle, according to John, at a wedding feast in the city of Cana (John 2:1-12).

Chapter 8 Sacraments of Vocation

marriages that radiate the love of God, for, in the long run, it is only in seeing examples of good family life that good family life is learned.

We also need to support those who suffer one of the greatest tragedies of our time: divorce. We have to show understanding and compassion toward both the adults and the children who are victims of broken marriages. It has often been said that a divorce is like a death for those who endure it. There is often no explanation for it, just mourning and profound respect for the suffering of those involved.

Marriage: A Ministry of Hope

The hope and happiness that fill the dreams of marrying couples are often shadowed by fear of the difficulty of long-term fidelity and unselfish, dedicated love. Yet through the graces of this sacrament, Christ assists married couples to love each other as he loves us. By dying daily to the selfishness and weakness that plague us all, couples rise in the power of Christ to faithful love in his Spirit as they assist each other and their children to grow in faith and love of God. These daily death and resurrection experiences create a bond between husband and wife that imitates the union

Sacramental marriages are a bond between husband and wife that imitates the union between Christ and the Church.

between Christ and his Church and the covenant of love between God and God's people.

The ministry of married couples consists of fostering mutual love and personal holiness as a means of building God's kingdom. Christian families give hope to society by the witness of faithful love, Christian values, and intimate union with Christ.

12. Find the Vatican II document, "The Pastoral Constitution on the Church in the Modern World." Study Chapter 1, especially section 48. How does this document describe marriage? Can you find the language of "covenant"?

13. Someone once said that "tradition isn't wearing your grandfather's hat. It's having children." What do you think this means?

14. We probably all know someone whose parents are divorced, perhaps even our own parents. What are some of the problems the children face, and how can the Christian community be more supportive?

Summary

- Christian marriage is a vocation and a sacrament. When we answer God's call to live married life faithfully, the covenant we make with our spouse is a witness of the covenant God made with the Chosen People through Christ.

- The Church's understanding of marriage developed through the centuries, but from the beginning our attitude toward marriage has been grounded in Christ's call for a lifelong union.

- Because of the many challenges facing married couples today, marriage should not be taken lightly.

SECTION 2
Checkpoint!

■ Review

1. How did Jesus change the understanding of marriage that was popular in his day?

2. In what sense is marriage a covenant?

3. Who "administers" the sacrament of Matrimony and what does this suggest about the Catholic understanding of this institution?

4. What are the three "goods of marriage" identified by the Church?

5. Why shouldn't we say that any **one** good is "better" than another? Explain your answer.

6. Words to Know: conjugal love, marriage consent, marriage consummation, goods of marriage, marriage covenant, indissolubility of marriage, pre-Cana classes.

■ In Your World

1. What are some of the important ingredients of a good Christian marriage? Discuss whether there's such a thing as an "ideal couple."

2. Give reasons why you think that the way sexuality is often portrayed in the movies and on television is not consistent with the Church's understanding of married love. What are some examples of this different approach to sexuality in the media?

■ Scripture Search

1. Read 1 Corinthians 7:1-16. How does Paul's advice to married people offer some important guidelines for us today? Does Paul's advice raise any questions in your mind?

2. What reasons does Jesus give for not getting divorced in Matthew 19:3-12? Discuss the issues Jesus raises for us today in this passage.

SECTION 3
Serving Others as Ordained Ministers

"Why are you a priest, Uncle Bob? Are you married to Jesus?" The questions tumbled out as four-year-old Theresa crawled up on her uncle's lap. Father Bob whistled softly through his teeth at the challenge his little niece presented. After a bit he said, "No, I'm not married to Jesus, but I guess you could say my main job is getting people together with God."

Father Bob not only brought his job description down to the child's level, but he also summed up the mission of the Church and the job description of Jesus himself.

Just as the vocation of married people is to help each other to experience God's love and to strengthen the Body of Christ by the witness of their marriage and by the education of their children, so too does God call ordained ministers to build up the Body of Christ and to help people find the love of God in their lives and in the Church.

The Development of Ordained Ministry

About twenty years after Jesus' ascension, Saint Paul wrote this practical and yet profound description of those who provided leadership and service in the first years of Christianity.

"And he gave some as apostles, others as prophets, others as evangelists, others as pastors and teachers to equip the holy ones for the work of ministry, for building up the body of Christ" (Ephesians 4:11-12).

Chapter 8   Sacraments of Vocation

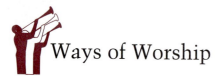

Ways of Worship

The Ordination of a Priest

The sacrament of Holy Orders is celebrated at Mass by a bishop. Only a bishop can ordain a priest. The Church teaches that when an ordination takes place, the authority given by Christ through the Apostles to celebrate the Eucharist and to preach the Gospel is handed on to the new priest in an unbroken succession of ordination that goes back to Christ himself.

The sign that this authority is being given by God is the gesture of the bishop's imposing hands on the head of the man being ordained. Through the imposition of hands, the Holy Spirit gives the priest the sacramental grace necessary for the exercise of his ministry. No words are recited when hands are imposed. No prayer is said at that moment. It is the simple act of imposing hands that signifies the ordination.

From the beginning, Church ministry was exactly as Paul describes it: service to the members of the Church. What service? Paul focuses on three things that Church ministers are called to promote: unity among Christ's followers, knowledge of Jesus as God's revealer and savior, and actions that continue Christ's presence in the world. We are to promote these "till we become one in faith and in the knowledge of God's Son, and form that perfect person who is Christ come to full stature" (Ephesians 4:13).

You may be surprised to learn that, even though the Apostles and leaders of the early Church were very conscious of their mission to minister in Christ's name and to lead the new Christian communities, they never thought of themselves as priests. The reason for this is simple. At least until the destruction of the Temple in 70 A.D., the first Christians were Jews who had accepted Jesus as the Messiah, and Judaism already had a well-developed priesthood.

Saint Luke tells us that many priests were among the early believers in Jesus, but they did not offer sacrifice for the Christians as far as we know (Acts 6:7). Another factor that discouraged using the title "priest" for Christian ministers was the fact that the Greek-speaking converts to Christianity tended to consider the priests of their former religions as imposters, that is, people who pretended to possess special knowledge and powers. Of course, no one in the Christian community wanted ministers of the Church to be confused with those kinds of priests!

Overseers, Elders, Deacons

Although Jesus had commissioned the Apostles to carry on his ministry, he did not leave them a detailed description of how to organize the ministry after his death. Under the guidance of the Holy Spirit, the Apostles had to work out these details as various needs arose. When a Christian community formed and had gained a certain stability, the Apostles appointed leaders or overseers *(episkopoi)* and elders *(presbyteroi)* to initiate new members, preside at the Eucharist, preach, and guarantee that the teaching and moral conduct of the community remained true to what had been delivered to them by the Apostles.

Worship and Sacraments: We Celebrate, We Praise

One of the first new offices that developed after Jesus' death was that of deacon, from the Greek work *diakonia,* meaning service. The Apostles felt that serving the needs of everyone in the community was so important that when they recognized a problem in the distribution of food among the Greek-speaking converts, they delegated the leaders of these people to see that no one was overlooked. To commission them officially and to call down on them the power of the Holy Spirit, the Apostles laid hands on these deacons (Acts 6:5-6). Their job description was not confined to table ministry. Both Stephen and Philip engaged in preaching and evangelizing (Acts 6:8-9 and 8:4-5). Like the Apostles, they were called to further the mission of Jesus in special service to the Church.

The Language of Priesthood

By the end of the first century more and more of the ministries originally performed by Church members were turned over to the bishop. The role of the elders all but disappeared until finally, by the third century, the bishop was the sole leader of the Eucharistic community. As Church membership continued to increase and the Eucharist came to be thought of as a sacrifice instead of a communal meal, the bishops used deacons as their personal representatives to perform the ministries they could not do. The bishop's role was associated more and more with offering the sacrifice as the priests of the Hebrew Scriptures had done.

Priests are often turned to in time of need. These men are often prepared to be good listeners.

In the early Church, the Apostles and other leaders were almost completely taken up with evangelizing and serving the needs of their people. Now the clergy understood their roles in terms of the Hebrew Scripture priesthood. The bishops were set apart from the laity. As preparation for the Eucharist, they were to abstain from sexual intercourse as the priests of the Old Covenant had done to observe ritual purity. Soon there was a rule that they could marry only once. By the year 1139, it became universal Roman Church law that no ordained person could be married.

As Christianity moved outward from the large cities to the rural areas, deacons were ordained to the priesthood and were delegated to perform some of the rituals outside the

Episkopoi: the Greek word that eventually became "bishop."

Presbyteroi: the Greek word for "elders," which we now use to refer to presbyters or priests.

cities. Now that Christians had become disassociated from Judaism, Christians felt free to use Israel's language of priesthood. The three orders of the Jewish priesthood (high priest, priest, levite) were paralleled in Christianity by bishop, priest, and deacon.

15. Think of a priest you admire. What is it about his life that you respect most?

16. In what ways was the life of Christ an example of service to the needs of the people?

17. How do priests help us to reach "the extent of the full stature of Christ" that Saint Paul spoke of in Ephesians 4:13?

18. Why do you think that bishops began to speak of the celebration of the Eucharist as the "offering of the Sacrifice"? In answering this question, recall what you learned about the Eucharist in Chapter 7.

The Priesthood Today

Even though the word "priest" was not used for Christian ministers in the letters of Paul or in the Gospels, the Church teaches that Jesus gave us the sacrament of Holy Orders at the Last Supper. By commanding the Apostles to remember him by celebrating the Eucharistic meal, the Church understands that Jesus wanted the Apostles to select certain men to serve as leaders of worship and as preachers.

Today we call this selection of leaders "ordination." Those who are ordained to administer the sacraments and to preach the Gospel celebrate their vocation by receiving the sacrament of Holy Orders.

Deacons, priests, and bishops receive this sacrament, and the difference among the three groups of ordained ministers is the role each has in providing leadership in the Church. Deacons serve the community by assisting the bishop. Sometimes called "permanent deacons" to distinguish them from the "transitional" status of deacons who are

Priests today have demanding jobs. They must administer the physical aspects of parish life as well as care for the spiritual needs of parishioners.

studying for the priesthood, these ministers can preach at Mass, witness weddings, lead funeral services, and baptize. Deacons are also involved in many acts of Christian service, and they are the only ordained ministers who are normally allowed to be married while serving as a deacon (as long as they were married before they were ordained).

Priests normally exercise their leadership role in parishes as pastors and sacramental ministers, though many priests work as teachers or chaplains. When a priest exercises his ministry in a geographic area which we call a "diocese," he is known as a diocesan priest (sometimes referred to as a "secular priest"). These priests are responsible to the bishop of the diocese. Some priests are members of a religious community or "order" such as the Franciscans, Dominicans, or the Jesuits. "Order priests" are responsible to the leadership and the mission of their community, and they engage in a variety of ministerial roles.

Bishops are leaders of dioceses. Their chief role is that of teacher. Together with all the bishops of the world in union with the Bishop of Rome, the Holy Father, they are the official teachers of faith and morals in the Church. That's why a bishop is sometimes called the "shepherd" of his diocese.

Pastor: in Latin, "shepherd." Jesus called himself the good "pastor" (John 10:11).

Chapter 8 Sacraments of Vocation

While unusual, former Anglican priests who have become Catholics may be ordained even though they are married.

Married Priests?

Many dioceses in the United States now have married priests. "What? I thought priests were not allowed to marry," you say. Normally, you might be correct, but not always. Since 1980 men who have been ordained to the priesthood by the Anglican Church may, after they have become Catholic, ask the bishop of their diocese for permission to be ordained in the Catholic Church. After special seminary preparation, they may then be ordained Catholic priests. If they have been married while they were Anglican priests, they are allowed to be married and priests in the Catholic Church at the same time.

How is this possible? First, celibacy is a charism, a gift from God. For nearly a thousand years, it has been a requirement for men in the Roman Catholic Church that they must remain celibate if they wish to be priests. Remember, however, that many of the Apostles were married, as were many priests during the first centuries of the Church. This same rule of celibacy is not required in the Anglican Church, or even in Orthodox Churches which remain in full communion with Rome. Most Anglican priests are married.

The Roman Catholic Church has decided to allow an exception to the rule of celibacy for men who had been Anglican priests. It is considered unfair to deprive these men of their priesthood. Thus married Catholic priests have become a reality.

This same dispensation is not possible for men who are Catholic who wish to be married and priests at the same time. These men must recognize the vocation that God has given them and choose between priesthood or marriage. If they wish to be married and a priest, they must wait until their marriages end when their wives die. This happens occasionally. One family in Los Angeles has both the father and two sons as ordained priests.

Worship and Sacraments: We Celebrate, We Praise

Unlike deacons, neither priests nor bishops are allowed to be married. This practice of remaining single is known as the "law of celibacy." Its purpose is to allow priests and bishops the opportunity to witness the kingdom of God more fully and more freely by giving their undivided attention to the ministry.

Becoming a Priest

A man is eligible for ordination when he receives a **call** from a bishop. This official **selection** is actually the end of a long process that begins when a man is accepted for training at a seminary (a school for future priests).

Though there are still a few high school seminaries and several college seminaries left in the United States, the preparation for priesthood begins for most men after they have graduated from college and enter a four- or five-year post-graduate program called a "theologate." During these years, a man studies the Church's reflection on the meaning of faith (theology). He also studies Scripture, morality, history, sacraments, and a wide variety of topics that relate to his future work as a pastor and a teacher. During his years in the seminary, a student has ample time for prayer and reflection, and for "hands-on" experience working in a variety of ministries. In some seminaries, students take an entire year away from their books to work in local parishes. During the summers, all seminarians are encouraged to do some kind of work related to the ministry.

Men who wish to become priests study for eight years beyond high school before they are ordained.

An Insight from Vatican II

Vatican II taught that priests are chosen from the People of God to serve the community, but that their ordination does not separate them from the community or make them any "better" than the people they serve. As the Fathers of the Council put it, priests could not serve the people "if they remained aloof from their lives and circumstances" ("*The Ministry and Life of Priests,*" # 3).

In the same document quoted above, the Council outlined the relationship of priests to the rest of the community.

"Priests are to be sincere in their appreciation and promotion of lay person's dignity and of the special role the laity have to play in the Church's mission. They should also

> **Lay people:** the laity; members of the Body of Christ who are not ordained. The term "laity" comes from the Greek word for "people," *laos*.

Chapter 8   Sacraments of Vocation

have an unfailing respect for the just liberty which belongs to everybody in civil society (Paragraph 9).

In recent years, fewer and fewer men have decided to enter the seminary. As a result, the number of ordained priests has dwindled. In 1990, for example, there was one priest for every 2,000 Catholics in the United States. It is predicted that by the year 2005, there will be only one priest for every 3,100 Catholics. Yet, as the Council's teaching on ordained ministry indicates, the priesthood can be a challenging and rewarding life for those who feel called by God to accept it.

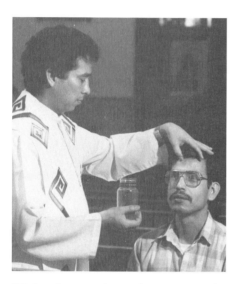

While the number of priests in the United States is declining, the number of Catholics is increasing. How will this change the role of priests?

19. Why do you think that we call priests "father"? Does this title help you to understand the role of the priest?

20. Some people today believe that priests should be allowed to get married. What do you think? Would your parish welcome a married priest?

21. Do you know any seminarians? If so, explain the kinds of things seminarians do in your parish.

22. Why do you think that fewer men are entering the seminary these days in the United States while vocations to the priesthood are growing in Eastern Europe and Asia? Explain your answer.

Summary

- In the beginning of the Christian tradition, the word "priest" was not used for those who provided leadership in the Church's ministry according to their gifts.

- The Apostles appointed "overseers, elders, and servants" who later were called "bishops, priests, and deacons." At first, only the bishops led the community in its celebration of the Eucharist. Later, priests were also ordained for this ministry.

- Men who wish to become priests today prepare for their ordination by training at a seminary where they study theology and learn the skills they will need for their work.

SECTION 3
Checkpoint!

■ Review

1. What three things did Paul say that ministers were called to promote?

2. What do these terms refer to: *Episkopoi, Presbyteroi, Diakonia?*

3. What is the role of bishops, priests, and deacons today?

4. How is it possible for a man to be a Roman Catholic married priest?

5. Words to Know: ministry, *episkopoi, presbyteroi, diakonia*, celibacy, ordination, imposition of hands, diocesan and order priests, *pastor* (Latin word), the "call" to priesthood, seminary, lay people or laity.

■ In Your World

1. Discuss in class what it would be like to have a married priest in your parish. What are the positive and negative aspects of married priests?

2. Write a short paper about why men decide to become priests and why many more do not. Discuss it in class.

■ Scripture Search

1. Read and study the "Good Shepherd passage in John 10:1-21. Use this text to make a list of the qualities a good pastor should have. (Recall that the word "pastor" is the Latin word for "shepherd.")

2. Read and study the following Scripture texts: Acts 6:1-7; 1 Corinthians 12:27-31; 1 Timothy 3:1-13; Titus 1:5-16. Make a chart that outlines the ministries described in these texts and indicate how these ministries are exercised in the Church today.

Chapter 8   Sacraments of Vocation

CHAPTER 8 Review

■ Study

1. What is meant by the statement: "The vocation of all Christians is to live the life of grace"?

2. What is "grace"?

3. How do the virtues demonstrate strength of Christian character?

4. Why is Mary called a "model of Christian vocation"?

5. Why does the Catholic Church consider marriage a sacrament?

6. What are the obligations of those who choose to marry and how are these obligations related to the "three goods of marriage"?

7. Why can we call marriage a "ministry of hope"?

8. Describe the meaning of the marriage covenant and its obligations.

9. What two reasons can be given for the Church's decision not to use the word "priest" for its ministers in the early years of Christianity?

10. What three groups of leaders did the Apostles appoint and what ordained ministries have these groups developed into today?

11. What is the law of celibacy and how does it relate to the role of ordained ministers (especially priests and bishops) in the Church?

12. Some married men have recently been ordained as Roman Catholic priests. Explain how this is possible.

13. What sacramental sign is used in the ordination of a priest and what does it signify?

■ Action

1. Videotape parts of two TV programs: one which portrays Christian love in a positive manner and one which fosters other views of love and sexuality. Show these tapes in class and discuss their messages.

2. Invite a priest to your class. Ask him to talk about his ministry. Share some of your questions about the priesthood with him.

3. Talk to a priest about the Church's prohibition against divorce. Also ask him what an "annulment" is and how it is possible for divorced Catholics to receive an annulment and be married in the Church. Report to the class what you have discovered. This activity can be shared by several students who could make this report as a panel.

4. If a camcorder is available to you, videotape "person in the street" interviews of your fellow students at school. Prepare some questions about Christian vocation that interest you. After you have completed your taping, prepare a summary of your interviews and present your video and summary to the class.

■ Prayer

Plan to have a Day of Recollection which focuses on the theme *Accepting My Vocation*. A "Day of Recollection" is kind of a mini-retreat that lasts only one day or even a short period of the day. Normally, these days are made with a group of people under the leadership of a teacher, chaplain, or spiritual director. The day includes time for common prayer, group discussions, talks by the leader, quiet reflection or reading, and Mass. This makes an excellent class activity.

Prepare for your "day" in advance. Choose some audiotapes that help you reflect on life choices. Find a book in the library that discusses married life, priesthood, or religious life. Bring your Bible and a notebook for writing your reflections. Make sure that the place you will use is quiet so you don't get distracted.

CHAPTER 9

Our Need for Healing

OBJECTIVES

In this Chapter you will

- Explore the bright and dark sides of life in an effort to face your imperfections and gain the courage to deal with them.

- Understand the nature of sin and see how it affects our world.

- Gain a deeper appreciation of personal sin and its devastating results in our lives.

To err is human. To forgive, divine.
—Alexander Pope

While he was still a long way off, his father caught sight of him and was deeply moved. He ran out to meet him, threw his arms around his neck, and kissed him.
—Luke 15:20

SECTION 1
Facing Our Imperfections

Anyone who has tried to lose weight knows how challenging the simple resolution to eat less can be. Even with strong motivation, such as pressure from the wrestling coach or the desire to fit into a smaller size, people still find themselves weakening now and then, and defeating their own purposes.

This same weakness is found in every human being. For some it is a temptation to eat, for others it is a temptation to drink, and for still others it is a temptation to steal or fight. What causes these problems in human nature, and how can we learn to confront them as Christians?

Our Bright Side

Like most people, you have ideals for your life. You may not frame them into resolutions, but underlying your actions are strong desires. You need to be a self-directed individual, trusted and trustworthy. You want to make your own decisions and not be merely someone else's tool or puppet. Above all, you do not want to just follow the crowd.

You also have an intense need for relationships. In our high-tech society, where it is so easy to become a number instead of a name, you experience the urge to share your deepest self with someone and to give your life to something profound and meaningful. You want your life to have a purpose. You want to feel that you are part of a caring community, valued for yourself as well as for your positive contribution to the community.

You like to think of yourself as basically a good person. You may not always jump for joy when people let you know you can improve, but in the long run you will be grateful. Even though at the moment you may not always show it,

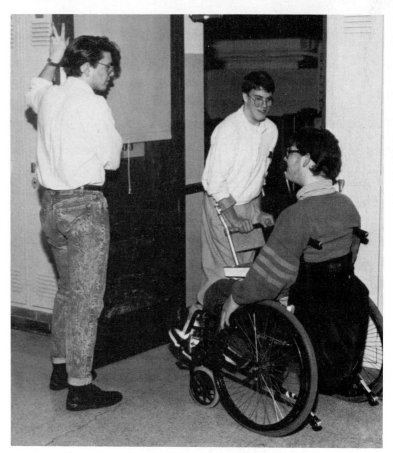

Helping others is a simple way of living the Gospel message.

you do listen to sound advice. There are times, such as New Year's and Lent, when you make resolutions to do better.

Maybe because television and other modern means of communication have brought people everywhere closer together, you somehow feel a part of, and responsible for, the world family. You pray for a better society in which everyone can enjoy a life worthy of human beings. You are encouraged when you hear of people who return lost wallets with the money left in them. You admire people who generously donate their services to the poor and people who risk their lives for others. You are strongly on the side of truth, justice, and peace.

In your more reflective moments, you probably are grateful to God for calling you into existence. You can believe that you have a unique purpose that no one else on earth can fulfill. You love Christ and honor him as your God and Savior, and you try to worship regularly and keep the laws of God and the Church.

1. *Share with someone your success—or lack of it—in carrying out some resolution.*

2. *What are some examples of the "bright side" of human nature? Recall an experience you have had when someone did something that restored your confidence in the human race.*

3. *On the whole, do you think that films and television today portray our bright side? If you think they do, give examples. If you think they don't, why do you suppose they choose not to?*

Our Dark Side

And yet, your life journey isn't always smooth and easy. Even with a solid belief in Catholic teachings, you feel pulled in another direction. Modern psychologists speak of it as the attraction of the dark side of personality.

When you face yourself squarely, you know that you aren't always one hundred percent trustworthy. There are times when you haven't finished a job and when you have done things you wouldn't have done if someone had been watching. You don't want to follow the crowd, and yet peer pressure has led you to actions you otherwise would never have chosen. Looking back, how many of your New Year's or Lenten resolutions have you actually kept?

You desperately need friends, and yet selfishness or laziness often stands in the way of your entering into really rewarding relationships. Sometimes it's just too much trouble to use your gifts for others. In class discussions, you passionately are in favor of the rights of the oppressed and the disabled. But how often have you visited someone in a convalescent home or actually given up something you value for the benefit of the poor? When is the last time you carried the books of an injured classmate or someone else who couldn't manage alone? Are you enough in favor of the rights of the oppressed, disabled, and unborn to do something about it?

As you hear and read about the skirmishes and wars that are constantly erupting, as you witness the racial and class

 On the Record

Anxiety and Hope

The modern philosopher Martin Heidegger, who died in 1976, came to the conclusion that life is experienced as a series of **polarities.** By polarities, he meant two seemingly opposite experiences. The one polarity illustrates our "bright" side, the other, our "dark" side.

One of these polarities is anxiety and hope. We have a sense of anxiety, we feel threatened and overwhelmed by forces in and around us that cannot be controlled. When we experience hope, we have the opposite feeling. We believe that nothing can stand in our way. For us, the sky's the limit!

Heidegger's point is that both polarities are "real," and that if we wish to be happy, we must learn to accept and integrate both. Denying anxiety (or our "dark" side) can be just as destructive as denying hope (or our "bright" side).

Everything is simply **not** beautiful all the time. Nor is everything rotten all the time!

hatred that may be practiced even in your school, and as you review the fate of millions of babies who have been aborted, and of other millions who have perished in massacres such as the holocaust, or the killing fields in Cambodia, you may suddenly experience a mysterious sense of evil or free-floating guilt. You hurt because you can't stop thinking about the situations for which you feel guilty, and yet you don't do anything to correct them. Furthermore, you know that, although you are keenly aware of your own right and need for freedom, you have at times stepped casually on the rights of others when it was to your advantage; you realize that you sometimes contribute to the injustice in the world.

You have probably observed relatives and friends who for years have religiously gone to Church, but have continued to argue, hold long grudges over petty things, and have been unfaithful to their commitments to married fidelity or to religious vows. Fearing the same fate, you might face a painful crisis in your own faith. You might even be tempted to imagine that if you belonged to another "persuasion," you'd be free of the guilt of sin that Catholics seem to suffer. You see other young people apparently happy and totally dedicated to the new cults. Eastern religions seem to cut through the modern confusion to a transcendent peace. You might be tempted to take a temporary vacation from the Church or from God.

Looking honestly at yourself and the world, you may find that the "heaven-bound" journey we are all supposedly engaged in sometimes grinds to a halt. You ask yourself: Why is it all so complex and difficult? Why aren't things working out according to my resolutions and dreams? Is the journey to God really possible in the real world? And if it is, is it worth the trouble?

4. *How can we become discouraged when we see the dark side of our friends or family? How have you coped with this feeling?*

Facing Imperfection

Thousands of years ago, people had the same questions as you do about the meaning of life. Aware of the roadblocks and detours in the human journey, certain theologians of Israel courageously set out to describe the route as it really was. They recorded knowledge of their observations in the first chapters of Genesis in stories as important for today's pilgrims as maps are to sailors, or blueprints are to builders. Although written long ago, these pages are so profound and timeless in their insight that only God could have been their source. No other religion has come anywhere near them in revealing the deepest truth about the universal human condition. We will be taking a closer look at Genesis later in this chapter.

It is human to err—to sin. Every generation has to grapple with the problem of sin in the light of its own times (1 Corinthians 10:12-13). The temptations of your day differ from those your parents faced. However, the solution to the problem remains the same.

The images used in the New Testament of passage from death to life, from darkness to light, and of change of heart, all tell us of our fundamental need to be healed of sin and to grow. Spiritual maturity is not a station we arrive at to rest forever in peace. The passage from death to life is the

The temptation to use drugs can be very powerful. Learning how to overcome temptations is part of becoming morally mature.

Persuasion: as used here, belonging to another tradition or faith; believing differently than another.

Chapter 9 Our Need for Healing

Our Twofold Reality

Although not a Christian, Carl Jung (1875-1961), the Swiss psychologist, concluded, after working with thousands of cases of disturbed people, that every person experiences deep within the unconscious of the psyche (soul), a double invasion from the numinous (spiritual) world. One is disintegrating. It originates from an outside evil force. The other, *Das Selbst*—German for "The Self"—is an outside good force, which is the Deepest Self working to integrate and heal the person in an orbit of love and transformation.

- *Archetypes are symbols for universal realities. For instance, in a dream, a car might symbolize your ego. Archetypes have dark and light sides. Thus, domination can be protective like a good father, or destructive like a dictator.*

- *For other ways of depicting the perilousness of the Inward Journey, read* Pilgrim's Progress *by John Bunyan.*

pilgrimage. It is a state of striving—a pilgrim state—a continuing journey upward and onward. To develop our potential then, we must look more closely at the **way** we are to travel.

You hear people casually say, "Face reality!" But it isn't the easiest thing to do. One of the touchstones of emerging maturity is a growing ability to cope with the imperfections we find in ourselves and others. As children, we believe the world is perfect. Our parents can do no wrong, our teachers know everything, and priests are always holy. Our first encounter with imperfection is a rude awakening. We go through stages. First, there is denial. Many a nose has been bloodied in defense of a loved one whose faults have been exposed. Then, fear and anger may arise as our worst suspicions are confirmed. Rebellion is characteristic of a beginning acceptance of the negative side because it represents resistance to a recognized reality. During adolescence, we vacillate between extreme idealism—expecting perfection of ourselves and those we care about—and bitterness or wholesale condemnation of the least flaw.

The eminent psychologist Jean Piaget defines a mature person as one who can differentiate interior experiences in a practical manner. Differentiating implies recognizing and accepting the fact that nothing is pure black or white. There are thousands of shades in between.

Just as it takes a deliberate intelligence to distinguish the many tones of gray in the clouds, so it takes mental, emotional, and moral discipline to live with ambiguity in ourselves, in other people, and in our institutions. To face ourselves as we are takes courage. Without this courage, we might end up resorting to drugs, alcohol, over-working, or even suicide to block out our consciences.

5. *Do you think people have lost a sense of sin? Give some reasons for your answer.*

6. *When someone says, "Face **reality**!", which of our two "sides" is apparently "reality" for him or her? What would lead people to draw this conclusion?*

Because we live in a world affected by sin, we are often called to make moral decisions. Even though war is horrible, Catholic Tradition recognizes that fighting is sometimes necessary.

Summary

- We sometimes experience life as a series of endless possibilities and we are impressed by the good we see around us.

- We also know that our world is far from perfect. At times we can be overwhelmed by the evil that exists in society.

- Learning to face imperfection involves a process of maturing. Mature people don't **condone** evil. They make efforts to **confront** it with a hope which comes from their faith in God.

Ambiguity: being open to a variety of interpretations.

Chapter 9 Our Need for Healing

SECTION 1
Checkpoint!

■ Review

1. What is the "bright" side and the "dark" side of the human experience?
2. In what sense is it human to err?
3. How does the psychologist Jean Piaget define the mature person?
4. According to Martin Heidegger, what are the polarities of life and how does the anxiety-hope polarity illustrate his philosophy?
5. Words to Know: polarity of human existence, "bright" and "dark" side of personality, ambiguity, anxiety, archetype.

■ In Your World

1. Review the steps in maturing listed below. Imagine that a prominent citizen in the community is a child abuser. Give concrete examples of how people would react to the news, based on the steps below.

   Steps in Maturing
   1. Child: perfect world
   2. Denial of evil
   3. Fear and anger
   4. Rebellion
   5. Vacillation between idealism and condemnation
   6. Acceptance of ambiguity

2. Sometimes people give up on religion because they get to a point where they simply do not believe that religious faith changes anything in the world. What would you say to a person who has left the Church for this reason? Write a letter to a friend who is in this situation.

■ Scripture Search

1. Study John's Gospel, 12:44-50. How does Jesus use the images of light and darkness in this text to talk about living the light of faith? How do Jesus' words apply to us today? Write a one-page report on your study.

2. Read the story of the Prodigal Son (Luke 15:11-32). Look up the meaning of "prodigal" in the dictionary. Then rewrite this story about our bright and dark sides using modern characters and contemporary situations. Read your story to the class or act it out.

SECTION 2
Sin in the World

In one of Shakespeare's greatest plays, the Danish prince Hamlet, suspecting that his father had been killed by his present stepfather, says, "Something is rotten in the state of Denmark." Over the centuries, social commentators and philosophers have come to interpret "the state of Denmark" to mean "the world." Thus, Hamlet's deduction, when applied to present-day happenings, means that the world is basically rotten or crooked, that things just aren't right with individuals or society.

Society of Negative Values

Sadly, there is more than a germ of truth to Hamlet's perspective. Many children come into families that lack harmony: tensions between parents reach a baby before birth; rivalries between brothers and sisters scar the young in their earliest formation; physical abuse turns a home into a prison of fear; hostile divorces or family ruptures can sow the seeds of lifelong emotional problems. About us, we see a society charged with negative values: infants are aborted, abandoned on random doorsteps, or dumped in garbage cans; most cities cannot pass through a night without a robbery or murder; fraud and deceit stain our highest circles of government; and, while adults may walk with confidence on the moon, too often their children cannot walk alone safely to the corner store.

People who experience the "rotten" side of human nature are understandably appalled and often turned off by the world around them. They shake their heads and mutter that there must be something better (after all, there is a loving God!) than what they have encountered thus far.

Just as this house has fallen apart through lack of care and abuse, so too can sin wreck people's lives.

The world's web of disorder is the result of what is called "sin." Hebrew Scripture writers defined sin as *hatta:* "missing the mark" or "being deceived by the evil one or by oneself." This understanding of sin still holds true in describing the disharmony we experience when we yearn to do what our best selves tell us to avoid.

Christians attribute the world's disharmony to original sin. Such sin is called "original" not so much because it was the first sin, but because it describes the original or root condition that separates people from God. Original Sin is a complex term. It can mean the basic rebellion against authority and human unwillingness to accept God's commands. Original Sin can refer to the web of sin active in society, the disruption of nature that seems to act against good, and the personal lack of integrity that results from the failure to live up to one's best impulses.

7. *From your experience, reading, or study, would you say that people are generally good, generous, and concerned with others? Or are they more inclined to be cruel, greedy, and selfish? Give reasons for your stand.*

8. *What things and characters in fairy tales symbolize the evil in the world? What part of the stories represent your longing for something better?*

9. List the tendencies that draw you away from following the promptings of your conscience. (For instance, greed may lead you to avoid paying taxes or to ignore the needs of a neighbor.)

10. How does the material universe seem infected by the corruption of human sin?

Scripture Tells the Story

The Biblical stories of the Fall and the spread of sin are parables of the conditions we find ourselves in today. From the different accounts of these events (Genesis 1-11), we know that the authors weren't interested in recorded history but in wisdom, which is God's revelation of what life is all about. Under the guidance of the Holy Spirit, the authors describe and interpret what we now call the **state of Original Sin**. The state of Original Sin is our human condition of alienation from God, our lack of integrity, and our tendency toward evil and disharmony with other people. From his experience of imperfection, Cardinal Newman concluded that the doctrine of Original Sin was almost as certain as the existence of the world and the existence of God! But it is in Genesis that its nature is spelled out.

The theology of Genesis can be summed up in four words: **creation, election, fall,** and **reconciliation.** When we are conceived, God **creates** us, personally calling us into existence. "God created man [and woman] in the image of God...male and female God created them" (Genesis 1:27). With great love, God gifts us with God-like powers that make it possible for us to commune with God: knowledge and free will, as well as a body through which revelation is made known. Having the destiny of living with God is known as **election**—God's choice of an individual for a particular work, or for salvation and eternal life. It is something like a man or woman choosing a marriage partner. We are created for the purpose of sharing God's life here and hereafter.

One of the deepest mysteries is that instead of responding to God with faithfulness and love, we tend to desire

The Traditional Meaning of Sin

To the Jews, sin was defined as "missing the mark." The "mark" was happiness, and happiness rested in a friendship or covenant with God. Thus, sin was a violation of the covenant.

In German, the word **sin** is *Sunde*. It indicates that sin **sunders** or **tears** us apart: from God, within ourselves, and from right relations with others and creation. The invitation to repentance is not so much a call to **do** as a call to **be** someone untorn—whole, healed, and active in loving relationships with others.

But the clearest understanding of sin comes from Saint Paul in the letter he wrote to the Romans. The Greek word he used for sin was *hamartia*, which means pretty much what the Jews understood sin to be—"off the mark." What is interesting about Paul's discussion of sin in Romans is that in this letter, he seemed to be using *hamartia* (sin) to refer to what we call Original Sin. This suggests that after the Fall, all human beings are born "off course" and we need the guidance, direction, and assistance of God's Son to get back on our proper course—toward God.

This is how Saint Paul spoke of sin and our salvation through Christ:

"Just as through one person sin entered the world, and through sin, death,...death reigned from Adam to Moses, even over those who did not sin after the pattern of the trespass of Adam, who is the type of the one who was to come.

For if, by that one person's transgression many died, how much more did the grace of God and the gracious gift of the one person Jesus Christ overflow for the many (Romans 5:12, 14-15).

The story of Adam and Eve in Genesis is an attempt to explain, through the use of story, how sin entered the world.

independence—to determine our lives apart from our Creator's plan. Our pride allows us to think we know what is best. This constitutes the root of our **fallen** condition. The tendency to rebel against the laws which God ordained for our good leads to all our problems, and it results in alienation in our relations with one another and with creation. These evils are not only manifest in each **individual** life, but also in **families,** as illustrated in the Cain and Abel story; in **neighbors,** as seen in the increasing vengeance of Lamech; and in the whole structure of **society,** as shown in the story of Babel (Genesis 4:24 and 11:1-9).

Thus Original Sin is the deep state of alienation from God in which we all come into existence and which is reinforced by the sin of others, including our family, friends, neighbors, and society. As human beings, then, when we enter the world, we are confronted with the tendency to sin within ourselves, and we find ourselves out of harmony with the world, other people, ourselves, and God. Additionally, the evil actions of others and the unjust structures of society exert a strong influence on our lives.

But all is not "doom and despair." Genesis promises **reconciliation.** God does not condemn Adam and Eve to death, but promises them a savior. Cain is not killed, but is given a "mark" to protect him from all who would kill

Chapter 9 Our Need for Healing

him. In fact, Catholics read the Scriptures as the salvation history of how God brought reconciliation into the world in many ways, finally through Jesus.

 **Touching the Sacred**

11. *In Genesis 3:7-24, what actions indicate the punishment of sin? What actions show God's kindness and mercy? What is the relation between the serpent (an outside evil force) and God's mercy?*

The Prayer of Saint Francis

This prayer is usually considered a prayer for peace, but it also demonstrates the attitude of those who want to cooperate with God in defeating the power of evil. It is certainly a prayer worth learning.

Make me, O Lord, an instrument of your peace.
Where there is hatred, let me sow love;
Where there is injury, pardon;
Where there is doubt, faith;
Where there is despair, hope;
Where there is darkness, light;
Where there is sadness, joy.

O Divine Master, grant that I may not so much seek to be consoled as to console; to be understood as to understand; to be loved as to love;

For it is in giving that we receive; it is in pardoning that we are pardoned, and it is in dying that we are born to eternal life. Amen.

Becoming Sensitive to Sin

Television and radio news programs and daily newspapers seem to overflow with depressing news. But this does not necessarily prove that the world is more bad than good. It only shows that bad news gets more attention. If we open our eyes, we can point to dozens of fine people we know and hundreds of kind acts being performed all the time—in families, schools, hospitals, businesses, and other institutions. If we can scan our acquaintances, we will definitely find people who are loving and good.

It takes sensitivity to see the good that is in the world, in others, and in ourselves. Likewise, it takes great sensitivity to recognize evil. Some people don't see anything wrong with abortion or other actions against life. Even highly-developed peoples like the Greeks and the Romans accepted infanticide (the killing of unwanted infants), suicide, slavery, and illicit sensuality. Not that long ago, slavery was still a part of life in the United States. During World War II, a supposedly Christian nation supervised the extermination of millions of Jews and other races in concentration camps.

Sensitivity to sin comes to the Christian through the vision of faith. Unless we have "eyes to see," as Jesus said, we will be blind to the sense of sin and its terrible power to destroy individuals as well as our society. People with a sense of sin are sensitive to the often invisible—but very real—destructiveness of anything that is contrary to God's design for the human race.

Besides recognizing the existence of Original Sin, persons of faith go further and take the giant step of admitting that they themselves are sinners. This disposition, which runs contrary to human pride, is a gift of the Spirit. It is in facing this truth that people find God, who is truth, and open themselves to receive divine pardon and reconciliation.

This tremendous breakthrough doesn't happen just because people say, "Lord, have mercy on us" or make an act of contrition. As Jesus said, "Not everyone who says to me 'Lord, Lord,' will enter the kingdom of heaven" (Matthew 7:21). People must have a sincere inner conviction that things aren't completely right. They must know that they are torn and wounded and at cross purposes with themselves and their universe. And they must realize that they can't reach wholeness by themselves. They need God's help. They need a Savior.

12. *Some people believe that our misuse of the earth's resources through pollution of the environment is an example of insensitivity to sin. Do you agree? What other ways are we insensitive to sin in the modern world?*

13. *In what sense is the "sin of humanity"* **more** *than the personal sinful deeds that people do? Can you think of some common attitudes of people that demonstrate the tug of Original Sin without actually being a sin? (Example: "It's not my turn to take out the garbage. Let someone else do it.")*

This machine was designed to help people easily commit suicide. Such inventions seem to make people less sensitive to evil.

Summary

- We call the human condition of "missing the mark," or being caught up in the web of evil, "Original Sin."

- Scripture links Original Sin to the fall of Adam and Eve from God's grace. Because we share in humanity, we share this original "flaw" of our Biblical first parents.

- Gaining a sensitivity to our human sinfulness is the first step in overcoming the effects of Original Sin in our lives. Through our life in the Church and our celebration of the sacraments, we increase this sensitivity.

Chapter 9   Our Need for Healing

SECTION 2
Checkpoint!

■ Review

1. How does Hamlet's statement, "Something is rotten in the state of Denmark," describe the condition of Original Sin?

2. In what ways does Original Sin promote disharmony in the world?

3. Describe how the effects of sin are talked about in Genesis.

4. What do we mean when we say that we need to develop a sensitivity to sin?

5. Words to Know: Original Sin, the Fall, *hatta, hamartia.*

■ In Your World

1. Spend part of an evening watching television. Write down the names of two or three programs that you watch and the basic plot of the shows. Then write a brief paper in which you discuss the attitude toward life that was evident in the programs. Was the "bright" side of life portrayed? The "dark" side? Both sides? Compare notes with your classmates.

2. Make a list of ways to increase your sensitivity to sin. They don't all have to be "religious." For example, recycling paper can help sensitize you to the sin of waste. Some religious activities, however, should be included.

■ Scripture Search

1. Read Genesis 3:7-24. What things symbolize the following human conditions: alienation from God, a sense of guilt and lack of self-worth, disturbance in relations with others, isolation from nature, frustration in masculine and feminine (societal) roles?

2. Study Genesis 4:24 and 11:1-9. What do these passages tell us about the power of sin to affect the structure of society?

SECTION 3
Our Personal Participation in Sin

Hugh McEvoy, age sixteen, a wild wit and school clown, died in the intensive care unit of Manhattan's Saint Luke's Hospital. A respirator had kept him alive since the previous Sunday night, when a thirteen-year-old gunman had put a bullet in his head.

Six hours after watching his son die, Leo McEvoy faced the press. He knew that neither the thirteen-year-old gunman nor his sixteen-year-old accomplice had shown any remorse at having fired a pistol into his son's temple as he was walking and laughing with a friend. Yet the victim's father, a state parole officer, said, "Toward the two boys charged with the crime, I have no hatred. They should be given an opportunity to rehabilitate themselves...I hope they can fulfill their lives. My son's attitude today would be one of forgiveness."

Mr. McEvoy's soft-spoken words seemed to touch the city's conscience. More than a thousand New Yorkers wrote consoling letters. The mayor and the governor attended the funeral. Cardinal Cooke, who had blessed the dying boy, later wrote his parents: "You have given New York a powerful witness on the meaning of forgiveness and compassion." A noted Scripture scholar said, "I have learned more about Christianity from you in the past few days than from all my reading."

Sin and Its Results

All people are expected to promote the general good of society, but the actions and attitudes of Christians carry an even greater responsibility. As members of the Body of Christ, they are to be signs to each other and to the world of God's special love. As "other Christs," their mission is to join together as God's people and to hasten the fulfillment of the deepest purpose of all creation—the worship of God and the building of his kingdom "on earth as it is in heaven."

But sin places an obstacle to this mission of the Church in the world; it promotes the power of darkness rather than of light. It tears apart, breaks down, and disunifies instead of reconciling all things in love as God wills.

Every act of evil, whether public or private, leaves its effect on the individual and society. Mortal sin or "sin unto death" destroys all relationships by seriously eroding the love and unity that God gives. If one were to die in such a state, he or she could be eternally alienated from God. Saint Teresa of Avila once said that hell is the inability to love yourself, others, and God. Traditionally, we call this the "eternal punishment of sin."

This effect is easy to see in the case of such criminal acts as murder, rape, and theft. However, it is not so clear how a person's secret suicide wish, inner jealousy, or anger harms others. Even when "interior sin" never comes to light, it changes the quality of the sinner's life. Essentially a break with God, this kind of sin makes us less able to relate to others, to work within God's plan, or to cope with success or failure. Our personal defectiveness is carried into social life, affecting everything it touches.

Personal Sin

Personal sin cannot be the effect of immaturity, weakness, ignorance, or discord. Age, as well as mental and emotional stability, must be taken into consideration.

If, for instance, as a child, you confused fantasy with reality and told others about an imaginary friend who followed you, that was not a sin; your imagination was developing. Or, if out of a great desire to love everyone, you announced to all your little friends that you were having a party when your mother knew nothing about it, that wasn't a sin. If someone suffers severe mental problems and tries to kill a national leader, that isn't a sin.

People who are trapped in a cycle of evil by sin are afraid to face the light of truth.

Breaking Our Relationship with God

Sin is not simply breaking a law. It's also the breaking of a relationship. Sin is a deliberate turning away from God's friendship, a conscious rejection of his love—an offense against God and other people. This implies two things: (1) to sin, you have to be capable of a full human/divine relationship—old enough, mature enough, emotionally stable, and mentally sound; (2) there is a domino effect from sin because all creation is related. The Danish religious philosopher, Soren Kierkegaard, said that self-actualization is being that self which one truly is—a child of God.

Chapter 9 Our Need for Healing

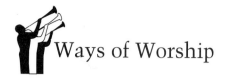

Ways of Worship

The Penitential Rite

Every time we celebrate the Eucharist, we have an opportunity to call to mind our sinfulness.

This part of the Mass is called the Penitential Rite. There are three forms of the rite that can be used, but the one that appears below is particularly beautiful.

Priest: My brothers and sisters, to prepare ourselves to celebrate the sacred mysteries, let us call to mind our sins. (Time for silent reflection.)

Priest: You were sent to heal the contrite: Lord, have mercy.

People: Lord, have mercy.

Priest: You came to call sinners: Christ, have mercy.

People: Christ, have mercy.

Priest: You plead for us at the right hand of the Father: Lord, have mercy.

People: Lord have mercy.

Priest: May almighty God have mercy on us, forgive us our sins, and bring us to everlasting life.

People: Amen.

Severing or weakening our relationship with God or others or creation disturbs all our other relationships. If it damages our best self and blocks self-actualization, it introduces disharmony between us and our neighbor and even puts us at odds with creation. If we do violence to creation, we do ourselves and others damage, which affects our relationship with God.

Although Original Sin orients us toward evil, we have the freedom to choose good. But, from the widespread existence of corruption, it is clear that we can't make the right choice alone. It takes God's initiative and our cooperation.

---

14. *What things do you think helped the elder McEvoy to forgive such a cruel hurt as his son's murder in New York City? If you were Mr. McEvoy, how would you respond in this situation?*

15. *Someone has defined forgiveness as showing mercy even when the injury has been deliberate and there is no excuse for it. Do you agree or disagree with this definition? Explain what you think forgiveness is.*

16. *How does one family member's thinking of jealous or gloomy thoughts affect the other members, the plans and dreams of the group, and the things the family can do?*

17. *Why can't a small child commit sin? What tendencies toward evil can you recognize even in a small child? What tendencies toward good?*

Conditions for Sin

If you are not free to act, if someone forces you to pull a trigger, or if, through no fault of yours, something wrong happens, you are not held responsible for your actions. Neither are you guilty if you do something that you didn't intend to do. For instance, no one would blame you if, in pushing someone to protect him or her from a falling object, you caused that person to fall and break an arm. These three things, then, are necessary for human actions to be virtuous as well as sinful: freedom, knowledge, and willingness.

For a sin to be serious, it must involve a complete rejection of a moral law. Our actions must show a serious neglect of the honor due to God, grave irresponsibility in family obligations or in the respect due to our own life or toward the life or property of others, or deliberate deceit on a grand scale. When we deliberately and knowingly choose to take or omit a course of action that wholly divorces us

Outside help, like this couple is receiving in marriage counseling, is often needed to overcome the power of sin.

Chapter 9   Our Need for Healing

from God, others, or the Christian community, we sin mortally. The sin is in our intention. Even if we never get to carry out a scandal we deliberately planned, our decision to do so mars our character and harms our relationship with others and with God.

Mortal and Venial Sin

The gravity of sin is understood by dividing sins into two major categories. **Mortal sin** is a complete break with God and the Church. It is a personal, definite decision to do or not to do something that one knows for sure is a serious betrayal of loyalty to Christ. Every other sin is called a **venial sin**, which can also be quite serious, though it does not completely destroy our relationship with God.

These categories might be compared to degrees of fracture in a marriage relationship. After a difficult day with the children, a wife might slam a milk carton on the table in annoyance at her husband. That might be called a venial offense, one that is easily forgivable. It in no way seriously threatens the marriage.

If there is a bitter exchange of name-calling and physical assault during an argument, that would be much more serious. Yet even that situation could conceivably be patched up and excused. However, in cases of long separation or divorce, the basic marriage relationship is ended completely.

That is an analogy of how mortal sin breaks one's friendship with God. It is the whole self turned away from God in a rejection of the divine gift of love.

God's Love Never Fails

The more integrated we are as persons, the more we relate everything we do to our deepest core. That's why sometimes the saints considered their small faults to be serious failings. That is also why some criminals can experience no guilt for serious sin.

But no matter how grievous the sin, God's love never fails. Because of this, our very sins can be a way to increase our love. Jesus taught this lesson while having dinner with

Modern Insights into Sin

Psychologist Erich Fromm says that we feel lonely and isolated because we are separated from nature and others. To be human means to be aware of self—to be in and part of nature and yet to be able to transcend it. The ongoing task of maturity is to continually overcome our sense of separation. Fromm suggests that there are two ways to do this. The first—unacceptable but frequently followed—is by **regressing** into nature, that is, symbolically never severing our umbilical cord to become human and independent. We do this by submerging ourselves in a group so that we lose our individuality in the security of the crowd. In this way we don't ever have to make deliberate decisions.

The other way to overcome our sense of separateness is by **individuation**. In this process, from childhood we learn about the outside world and sharpen our distinction from it as we distinguish ourselves from one another, and yet grow so strong physically, mentally, and emotionally that we can reach out in deliberate decisions of love to embrace others. Jesus' teaching on love suggested that we be one with God and others and yet, God considers every individual to be sacred.

Sin is the root of all our other separations. It spells disintegration and frustration. It threatens our relationships with others. It builds up an evergrowing contradiction in one's innermost being.

There is no sin that does not affect our whole being. Through sin, we become the embodiment of selfishness and close-mindedness. This disintegration doesn't happen all at once; it is gradual. It is not repetition of sin, but lack of repentance that erodes our moral freedom and the effectiveness of conscience.

Reaching out in love to another person or thing is known as individuation.

a Pharisee named Simon, who had criticized Jesus for allowing a sinful woman to wash his feet (Luke 7:41-47). From this story, we learn several startling facts:

- *The kind of sin we commit is not really the crucial issue.*
- *No one can make up for even one sin. God's forgiveness is a pure gift.*
- *Acceptance of God's forgiveness frees us to be truly kind, loving, and sensitive people.*
- *As human beings, we tend to express inner attitudes, like sorrow, outwardly.*
- *Those who can open only a small part of their sinfulness to God's mercy will be only partially freed to be better people.*

18. One of the cruelest of human actions is the rejection of a gift. Describe a time when a gift you or someone else gave was rejected. Since, strictly speaking, God cannot be hurt by sin, why is rejecting God's love such an evil?

Summary

- Our personal participation in sin affects not only ourselves but the people around us. In this, sin not only damages our relationship with God, but also with our sisters and brothers.

- In order to be guilty of sin, three conditions must be present: freedom to sin, knowledge that a particular action is sinful, and a desire to commit the sin.

- Not all sins are equally serious, though we should never feel comfortable with sin—even if the sin we commit is a venial sin.

SECTION 3
Checkpoint!

■ Review

1. What is mortal sin and how does it differ from venial sin?

2. What three conditions must be met before we are guilty of commiting a sin? Give an example of how this principle applies in the case of a four-year-old who kicks her sister. How about the case of a starving man who steals a loaf of bread?

3. What do we mean when we say that sin is more than breaking a law? How else can sin be described?

4. What insights into sin can be gained from contemporary psychology?

5. Words to Know: personal sin (mortal and venial sin), conditions for sin, the Penitential Rite, individuation.

■ In Your World

1. Write an essay with the title: "Some of the Greatest Sins in Our World." Use newspapers and magazines to provide examples of the sins you identify.

2. If you know someone who "reformed" or converted from a life of sin, tell how he or she now reveals a deeper devotion to Christ. Is this person happier than before?

■ Scripture Search

1. Read about Abel and his brother Cain in Genesis 4:1-16. How do these two Biblical characters portray the tendencies toward good and evil in us all?

2. Discuss Paul's understanding of sin in Romans 6. What does he mean when he says: "the wages of sin is death" in verse 23?

CHAPTER 9 Review

■ Study

1. What is it about human nature that prompts us to speak of our "bright" and "dark" sides? Are we really split into two separate kinds of people? Explain.

2. Give an example from recent events in the world that illustrates the dark side of humanity.

3. How might Martin Heidegger's discussion of the polarities of human existence help us to deal with the "dark" side of our lives?

4. Define "ambiguity" and describe how coping with ambiguity takes courage.

5. What is Original Sin?

6. What image do the Biblical words *hatta* (Hebrew) and *hamartia* (Greek) suggest about the nature of sin?

7. Why is it important for us to develop a "sense of sin"? How can this sensitivity affect the way we live?

8. How would you differentiate personal sin from Original Sin?

9. Are there different grades of seriousness in sinful acts or are they all equally serious? Explain.

10. What is the German word for sin? What does this word indicate?

11. Can we be guilty of sin if we do not intend to commit an offense? What reasons can you give for your answer?

12. When does sin hurt? What does sin have to do with damaging relationships?

13. Now that you have completed this chapter, write and discuss **your** definition of sin.

■ Action

1. Write a Penitential Rite that expresses sorrow for sin and asks for God's forgiveness. You can model your rite after the one in this chapter or you can create a new format for this prayer.

2. Prepare a prayer service that focuses on helping us become more sensitive to sin in our lives and in the world. Use the service for a class prayer.

3. Make a poster using words and pictures that illustrate the "bright" and "dark" sides of human existence.

4. Discuss the Prayer of Saint Francis in class. See if you can come up with some suggestions about how we can sow love where there is hatred, pardon where there is injury, and so on.

■ Prayer

This private, informal prayer activity is an examination of conscience. According to Catholic tradition, there are four steps that we take to form our consciences well. We can also use these steps to help us evaluate our spiritual health, much like physicians examine patients before determining their physical condition.

The four steps that we will use are
1. Reflection on the Word of God;
2. Careful consideration of the teachings of the Church;
3. Taking advice from recognized experts in spirituality, morality, or theology; and
4. Prayer.

Find some time when you can be alone, undisturbed. Bring your Bible and this book.

Begin your examination of conscience by reading these Scripture passages: Genesis 3 and Luke 7:41-47. Ask God to help you become more sensitive to your sins and to the loving mercy of Jesus.

Ask yourself if you have been faithful to the teachings of the Church. Have you kept the Ten Commandments? Are you trying to learn more about your Catholic tradition? Do you help to work for justice and peace in your world? Is there any major sin in your life that you should overcome now? How can you do better? In your own words, ask God to help you be an instrument of peace and reconciliation.

CHAPTER 10

Sacraments of Healing

OBJECTIVES

In this Chapter you will

- Explore God's offer of forgiveness and call to conversion in the Scriptures.

- Gain a deeper understanding of the sacrament of Penance (Reconciliation).

- Recognize the sacrament of the Anointing of the Sick as a celebration of healing and reconciliation.

My heart is overwhelmed, my pity is stirred. I will not give vent to my blazing anger, I will not destroy Ephraim again; For I am God and not man, the Holy One among you; I will not let the flames consume you.
—Hosea 11:8b-9.

SECTION 1
A Forgiving God

There is an old saying, possibly from the days of conflict between settlers and Native Americans, that concerns itself with forgiving and forgetting. This saying is "burying the hatchet." Unfortunately, some people who "bury the hatchet," never forget where they bury it. They never really forgive because they are never able to forget. Sometimes, because people find it hard to forgive, they often picture God as having the same difficulty in burying injury. The problem is that human beings, who have never seen God, can only think of God as someone like themselves.

But there is someone who has actually seen God and who knows what God is really like. Jesus said, "No one knows the Father but the Son, and anyone to whom the Son wishes to reveal him" (Matthew 11:27). Jesus reveals the Father in human language because he is God become human. What Jesus touches with his human hands, God touches. What Jesus cures, God cures. What Jesus speaks is the very Word of God.

Forgiveness and Healing in Scripture

A careful reading of Genesis reveals that even though sin clearly has a strong attraction to us and we are trapped in weakness and limitations, God does not abandon us. Saint Paul says, "Despite the increase of sin, grace has far surpassed it" (Romans 5:20). God triumphs over evil. There are four indications of redemption in the first eleven chapters of Genesis and many others throughout the Bible that explain our human condition. Already in the Garden, before the expulsion of Adam and Eve, God made a veiled promise of redemption to Eve—the prediction of the woman whose child would crush the serpent (Genesis

3:15). Then, as a sign of mercy, God tenderly made leather garments to clothe Adam and Eve in their bodily embarrassment (Genesis 3:21).

Although Cain killed Abel, God showed forgiveness by marking Cain so that he would not be killed for his deed (Genesis 4:15). When the whole earth became corrupt, God again came to the rescue by saving Noah (Genesis 7:1, 23). In Noah and his wife, God began a new creation. When humanity again turned from God, the story focuses on Abraham, whose family was spared in the destruction of Sodom and Gomorrah. From Abraham's descendants would come the more immediate revelation of salvation. The climax of salvation occured in Christ, the Savior of the world. Throughout the Bible, God is presented as constantly recreating a humanity who had turned aside from his true purpose. Thus, we come into the world confronted by sin but also surrounded by redemption.

The message of the Bible from the beginning is that we are not alone. We don't have to pull ourselves up by our own bootstraps. There is Someone who loves us in spite of our sin. God's love is encompassing enough to absorb the evil of sin, to triumph over it, and to forgive us. Without forcing us, God draws us back.

The story of Cain and Abel shows God as one who forgives. Cain is marked so that he, in turn, will not be murdered.

Jesus' Teachings on God's Forgiveness

Jesus taught God's love for the sinner by his actions. Every cure was a sign of the inner healing God wills for us. Leprosy and possession by the devil were the very figures of sin. To the paralytic, Jesus said directly, "Give up your sins so that something worse may not overtake you" (John 5:1-15). The man's newfound physical freedom symbolized the spiritual freedom that God's power releases in remitting sin. Mary Magdalene was prompted to greater love because of her sins; the Samaritan woman who had five husbands became a fervent disciple because of the great relief she experienced in the acceptance and compassion of Jesus.

Even the chosen Apostles experienced the control of evil: Peter denied Jesus; some of the disciples deserted Jesus in his crucial hour; and Thomas lost faith. Only the one who could not repent was swallowed up in evil's power; the rest experienced the fact that the power of evil is not absolute. In their encounter with the risen Jesus, they were freed from slavery and sin. Jesus' crucifixion teaches us that God is willing to release us from the chains of sin and destruction (see John 20:22-23). The gift of the Spirit on Easter night indicated the forgiveness of sin.

Jesus the Healer

Before his birth, Jesus' name and mission were given by the angel. He was to be the "Savior," the one who would "save his people from their sins" (Matthew 1:21). John the Baptizer pointed him out as the "Lamb of God" who would "take away the sin of the world" (John 1:29). Jesus' ministry of healing was directed against the ancient Jewish symbols of sin: sickness, leprosy, and possession by the devil. Repeatedly, Jesus claimed the power to forgive sin, sought the company of sinners, and acted out God's loving attitude of gentleness, compassion, and understanding toward wrongdoers.

The heart of Jesus' message about his Father is contained in one word: forgiveness. From the first pages to the last, the Gospels proclaim God's desire to forgive sin. The parables of the Lost Sheep, the Lost Coin, and the Prodigal Son (or Merciful Father) show God's concern for and loving

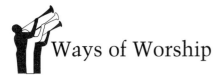

Ways of Worship

Lifelong Conversion

We praise God by accepting the call of Jesus to conversion. Here are some actions that express a spirit of repentance and demonstrate to God our desire to worship only God.

Faithfulness to duties: Accepting obligations is the surest way of doing God's will and avoiding temptation.

Works of charity: Love of neighbor is a sign of our love for God. To love others is to imitate God and to offer praise.

Forgiving others: In forgiving others, we allow God to forgive us. Recall the Lord's Prayer.

Prayer: Prayer flows from our desire for friendship with God. We express our desire for conversion through private prayer and the Liturgy, the public prayer of the Church.

Accepting suffering: Suffering in itself is not good, but the way we deal with suffering can help us all to mature.

Fast and abstinence: These disciplines are meant to sharpen our sensitivity to God and to make us more focused on the holy.

Jesus was recognized for his ability to heal. People went to great lengths to have Jesus simply touch their sick relatives or friends.

welcome of the sinner (Luke 15). Jesus' farewell gift of the Eucharist is his blood shed "for the forgiveness of sins" (see Matthew 26:28). Even on the cross, he forgave both those who executed him and the repentant thief who died with him.

---

1. What power does the serpent have in Genesis 3:15? What do you think is being promised?

2. What does God's willingness to give humanity a second chance (and a third, fourth, or fifth) reveal about God's nature?

3. In defiance of religious custom, Jesus constantly spent time with sinners like Mary Magdalene and the Samaritan Woman. Why do you think that Jesus risked his reputation (and his life!) by associating with people like that? What should our attitude toward sinners be?

4. Recall a time when you were worried about something you did. What effect did you experience when you learned that you had been forgiven?

Conversion

When Jesus appeared on the banks of the Jordan, he asked only one thing as the proper response to God's merciful love. That one thing was **conversion**. Jesus did not expect the Jews to change their religion. He expected something else.

Jesus summed up this expectation in two words: "Follow me." In this, he asked only for faith and for a complete dedication to himself. Unlike the religious leaders of the day, Jesus did not lay down a lot of small, isolated rules. He knew that once a person's heart was given to someone, everything else would follow. This is because a person operates as a unity. Everything we do and say reveals who and what we are. If we are dedicated to Christ, our actions will follow our heart. We cannot **follow** and **not follow** at the same time.

Just as an engaged person no longer feels interested in other possible mates, so the person converted to Christ experiences a certain settling and feelings of wholeness and healing. A conversion is a special moment, an awareness of a new direction in life. It may come as the result of some crisis, tension, failure, or problem.

Those who cannot pinpoint a definite turning point but who know that their lives are Christ-centered may find, upon close examination, that their conversion came about in small, almost invisible, stages. Perhaps their conversion began with an enlightening word, or perhaps a picture, prayer, program, or book opened the personal realness of Christ's love to them. Even those who have dramatic conversions can usually look back and recognize events that led to their peak moment of total acceptance.

The most mysterious thing about conversion is that, even though one definitely chooses Christ, the choice is more a form of "letting go" or surrender. It is an act of love expressed in trust and openness, allowing Christ to work actively in our lives, rather than a "doing" of something specific.

Conversion, like human love, is God's love taking hold of us at so deep a level that we can't fully contain it at any given moment. A lifetime is not long enough to express it

What would it mean for you to change your life for God?

Chapter 10   Sacraments of Healing

David and Bathsheba

One of the stories in the Hebrew Scriptures that best reveals God's position in regard to sin is that of David and Bathsheba. David had been chosen and anointed and graced by superior gifts of leadership. God had helped him in battle to turn aside his foes. To his house was promised an everlasting dynasty. All that David did seemed touched by God. Then, at the height of his career, although he had many wives, David desired Bathsheba, the wife of one of his soldiers, whom he proceeded to consign to the front lines to be killed (2 Samuel 12:7–20). When corrected by God through Nathan his prophet, David repented and God forgave. God let David live but allowed him to be punished for what he had done.

The consequences of his sin affected not only David but his family, his kingdom, and his people. The child born of David and Bathsheba's love died. His own son Absalom rose against him in rebellion and then was murdered. The bloodshed that marked the monarchy for generations afterward so weakened the throne that eventually the nation of Israel split apart. First Israel and then Judah were captured by enemies. God loved and restored David but God did not love David's sin. God allowed the consequences of sin to take their natural course. God repeatedly restored the Chosen People. Many other stories show the rhythm of Israel's sin, punishment, repentance, and forgiveness. God does not change.

King David experienced great remorse when he became aware of his sin.

adequately. Nor can we know with certainty how complete our response is to God. The actions we perform are only signs pointing to the reality of our personal relationship with Christ. They are like the top of an iceberg that does not always reveal its true dimensions hidden underwater. However, if our actions are predominantly hateful, bitter, or self-centered, they reveal that our relationship with divine love is faulty. If tendencies of concern for others, joy, peace, and other good things come from within, we know that God's love is alive in us.

5. *Conversion is sometimes described as a "change of heart." What do you think that this description intends to suggest?*

6. *Other than through the Scriptures, in what specific ways does God call us to conversion?*

Summary

- Throughout the centuries, God has demonstrated a willingness to give creatures a fresh start—to allow them an opportunity to seek reconciliation with God and with one another.

- Jesus is God's Word of forgiveness spoken to us in the healing works of his Son. Even when he was on the cross, Jesus forgave the repentant thief.

- Our willingness to let God offer us a fresh start and forgive our sins is called conversion. Conversion involves a change that we are willing to make—a change in attitude and behavior.

SECTION 1
Checkpoint!

■ Review

1. Give some examples of God's forgiveness in the Hebrew Scriptures. How do the examples indicate that God is all-loving?

2. The story of David and Bathsheba is a story of divine forgiveness. It's also a story about the ugly consequences of sin. God surely forgives us, but we are always still responsible for the consequences of our sins. Explain.

3. Why didn't Jesus lay down a lot of small, isolated rules? Was he saying that we could do whatever we want and still be his disciples?

4. Why can we say that conversion involves "letting go"?

5. Words to Know: faithfulness, charity, conversion, "Follow Me," forgiveness.

■ In Your World

1. Jesus taught us to be compassionate and forgiving, yet, in our society, we punish criminals. We even execute some of them. This leads to some disagreements among Christians. Should we parole dangerous criminals? Is capital punishment acceptable? Should teenage offenders be tried as adults? Discuss these issues in the context of what you have studied in this chapter.

2. Discuss how conversion involves a kind of "death" to our old selves (our old attitudes, habits, way of life). In what ways does this help us understand why people often resist the call to conversion as, for example, in the case of the alcoholic or drug addict? How can we help people like this "let go" and experience healing?

■ Scripture Search

1. Read the following passages: Matthew 9:9-13; Luke 7:36-50, 19:1-10; John 8:1-11. Which of these Gospel incidents of Jesus' dealing with "public sinners" appeals most to you? Why?

2. Read the story of David and Bathsheba (2 Samuel 11) and its consequences (2 Samuel 12:1-20). Discuss how this story illustrates the consequences of sin even though David was forgiven.

SECTION 2
The Sacrament of Penance

"God's gift and his call are irrevocable," said Saint Paul (Romans 11:29). What God did in Jesus on the cross, he does in Jesus today through the Church. Although Baptism restores us to friendship with God, the effects of Original and personal sin remain. We still make errors of judgment as Adam and David did. We still experience a lack of self-worth and confusion in our emotions. We still feel the pull toward evil. Children die and crime goes on as it did in David's house, but every Eucharist is a reminder that all creation is reconciled with the Father in Jesus' sacrifice. We also have the special sacrament of Penance. Designed to forgive sins committed after baptism, this sacrament is a visible sign that God continually forgives us.

The Church and Forgiveness

The sacrament of Penance also heals some of the alienating effects of sin. When we restore our relationship with God, other things fall into place, beginning with the hardest restoration of all, the reintegration or conversion of our fractured selves *(metanoia)*. Psychologists affirm that much emotional disturbance and psychological unrest come from repression of guilt. Ironically, it is by admitting our guilt that we become free because it is the truth that frees us.

God does not force us to avoid evil. We are still free to sin. As long as we are drawing breath, we won't be free of temptation and, perhaps, even of sin. But God's love is constant. Whenever we stray, God is there waiting for us in the sacrament of Penance, which alerts us to the sin in and around us, sharpens our perception, and makes us more sensitive to the least wind which might take us off course.

On the Record

History of Penance

Early Years: Christians were simply encouraged to remain faithful to their baptismal promises.

2nd-6th Centuries: Canonical penance for adultery, murder, and abandoning Christ. A seven-year period of public penance before absolution—only once in a lifetime!

6th-9th Centuries: Practice of seeking private spiritual help from monks or spiritual directors developed.

9th Century: Private confession called Penance. Confessors consulted "penitential books" that listed the proper "penalty" for each sin.

16th Century: Penance was declared a sacrament of the Church (Council of Trent, 1545-1563). Annual confession was made compulsory.

20th Century: Vatican II emphasized the reconciliatory aspect of the sacrament rather than juridical (judgment-centered) aspect. Communal celebrations of reconciliation became popular.

Knowing that We Are Forgiven

One Protestant minister who grew up with Catholics said he always envied the certainty Catholics have in knowing they are forgiven in the sacrament. We usually think of forgiveness as something that is God's job, not ours. And it **is** God who forgives. However, the problem is within ourselves; we can't always believe that we are forgiven.

The rewards of the public act of repentance are tangible: through the words and absolution of the priest, we have the assurance of Christ's word that we are truly reconciled with God and with our Christian community, both of whom we have alienated by our sin. This is in addition to psychological and human support we may gain through the guidance of the confessor. But the main effect—peace—can be seen in the reaction of a certain truck driver who had his marriage validated. After confession he just simply said, "Boy, does that feel good!"

Contrition

In order to seek sacramental reconciliation, we must begin with contrition for our sins.

Contrition is, first, a recognition that we have sinned or done something that keeps us from becoming the person God intended. Contrition is not necessarily a feeling of hatred for sin; it is, rather, a cold, clear judgment that sin is evil. Second, contrition is sorrow for having allowed evil an entrance into our lives. This sorrow, however, is not bitter like remorse or despair. It believes fully in God's love and mercy. Third, contrition is an act of will, a determination to turn away from sin and to turn toward God. The sincerity of this determination is tested when we avoid those persons, places, and things that we know will lead to the same sins already confessed in confession.

Since we cannot grow in Christ's life so long as our friendship with God remains severed, each of us should try to repent—that is, to bring our mind and will around to God. Setting a time every day for personal prayer and meditation can help cultivate the habit of quickly returning to God. If we remember that God waits with open arms to receive us at every hour of the day or night, we will not waste time worrying about whether we are worthy to come

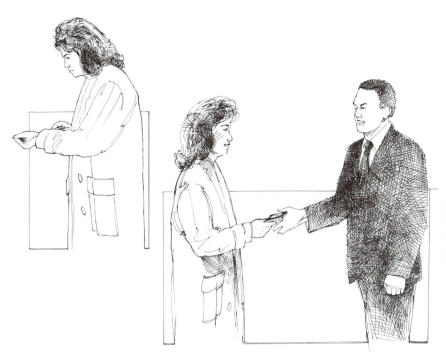

For whatever reason, some people steal by shoplifting. Contrition requires that the goods taken be returned to the rightful owner.

to God. The fact is that God doesn't take us back because we are worthy, but because we are loved.

One important fact to remember is that God is not angry or hurt when we sin. God cannot hate anyone. God cannot be hurt. God is perfectly happy and loving. What sin changes is the effect of divine love in us as we pull away or reject God.

---

7. Discuss the meaning of contrition and ways that you can show it.

Benefits of Confession

The sacrament of Penance is the Church's way for us to express contrition. It brings about a reconciliation between the penitent and God through a visible reconciliation between the penitent and the Church.

Since every sin affects both the individual and the community (others), it is not enough for the individual to

Validate: to make something legal or lawful.

Penitent: the person who is confessing his or her sins.

Chapter 10   Sacraments of Healing

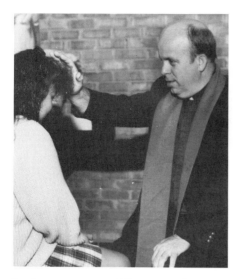

In the sacrament of Penance, the priest absolves a person of his or her sins.

ask God's pardon in personal prayer. Neither is it sufficient to ask forgiveness of the particular people our sins may have wounded or scandalized. Our reconciliation must be made in a way that the community or its official representative can see. Our encounter with the risen Christ in the sacrament of Penance satisfies all these needs.

People can experience deep comfort by the humble confession of their sins. It is psychologically helpful to talk over our intimate failures and self-doubts with someone who will not condemn us. We experience a sense of relief at sharing our burden of guilt. We receive encouragement in our efforts to overcome our selfishness and rebellion.

Confessing our sins is, above all, a religious action. It expresses our love of God, which in itself forgives sin and remits some of its bad effects. Through admitting our guilt, we can grow in self-knowledge and humility. Humility does not mean putting ourselves down. Rather, it means facing our good and bad qualities in truth. Through confession, we begin to see the patterns our bad habits take, and we can systematically work to root them out. We become better at recognizing the slightest whisperings of conscience. We pray more easily, do our work more responsibly, and see God more clearly in our daily joys and sorrows. As we grow in a sense of our own littleness before God, we worship better, love and respect others more, and so become more Christ-centered people.

Two Kinds of Confession

The sacrament of Penance can restore a serious break in our relationship with Christ. In this case, the sacrament is known as a **confession of necessity.** It is necessary because, under ordinary conditions, it is the only means for Catholics who have sinned seriously after baptism to be healed.

But penance is not only for sinners in need of "major surgery" for salvation. Christians may regularly approach this sacrament to confess their less serious sins, much as they would go to a doctor for a regular medical checkup. Such confessions are known as **confessions of devotion.**

The sacrament of Penance preserves and builds spiritual health. Frequent self-examinations can deepen our life with

God and lead to greater consciousness of our strengths and weaknesses. The graces of sorrow and repentance provide courage to cope with particular moral problems.

What to Confess

When our confession involves mortal sins that have totally severed our relationship with God and others, then the sacrament of Penance becomes a second baptism—with this exception: in baptism, there is no need to tell or make up for any sins that may have been committed before the sacrament. But, because we knowingly went back on our baptismal promises to Christ, we must now mention *every* serious sin that we can remember by its correct name, give the number of times we have committed it (as far as we know), and explain any circumstances that make it serious. If we deliberately omit some serious sin or fail to mention, for instance, that the amount of money we took was very large, we would not be reconciled with Christ and the Church because our sin has not truly been confessed.

Unless we are confessing mortal sins, it is not the exact number of sins that we should be concerned with so much as a growing and understanding of what is keeping us from

Seeking forgiveness for the times when we have hurt others is an example of things we might confess in the sacrament of Penance.

Chapter 10 Sacraments of Healing

the wholeness that will attract others to us and, through us, to Christ. Because our venial sins have probably been forgiven by our sorrow before we confess them, the sacrament does not reforgive our sins. Rather, it gives us a deeper share in the life of the Spirit, making us better worshipers and more effective laborers in God's kingdom.

Deep sorrow and charity also forgive our mortal sins, but we cannot be reconciled with the Church community unless we publicly celebrate the sacrament of Penance. This means that if we have committed mortal sin we cannot receive Communion unless we first confess our sins. The sorrow we express in confessing our sins and the making of an act of contrition, together with the celebrant's absolution, actually bring about the forgiveness of sin. We are then reconciled with God and can fully worship with the Church.

There is no strict obligation to confess sins that are doubtful. For instance, if we are not sure whether we freely consented to thoughts that gave us sexual pleasure, we don't have to mention them. However, talking the problem over with the confessor may put us at ease. He may ask us questions about our intentions when we get into situations of temptation and then assures us that we really are doing the best we can to love God. This in itself will help us in the next temptation, by relaxing us and increasing our trust in Christ, who is with us as we struggle to act according to God's will.

If we forget to tell a serious sin after reasonably careful preparation, the forgotten sin is forgiven with all the others. If, later, we remember that we forgot to confess something, we should mention it in our next confession. We should never be phony, however, by accusing ourselves of things we know we are not responsible for.

Our confession can deepen our union with God and with our sisters and brothers. The closer we draw to God, the more we will realize how great the evil of sin is and the more we will want to turn even more seriously to God for assistance.

---

8. *What would you think of someone who seriously hurt you and felt sorry in his or her heart, but never showed this sorrow or any change of attitude in word or action?*

9. *Just as it is best to have a regular doctor, it is advisable to have a regular confessor. What advantages can you see in such an arrangement?*

10. *The encounter with the confessor is truly an encounter with the living Christ. Which three qualities would you consider most Christ-like in a confessor? Why?*

11. *Sin sets up ripples of fear in society. What changes would take place in your home or school if everyone suddenly discovered that someone within the group was a thief? A liar? Determined to murder someone?*

Penance and Atonement

The prayers we are given to say in confession for the people we have harmed change us so that we may be better able to relate to those people. But the limited prayers assigned to us as "satisfaction" are only a beginning. The point of penance is to launch us in the direction of genuine love, as a fulfillment of God's plan.

It is not the number or length of penances we are given to do, but the depth of our willingness and sincerity to do them that atones or makes satisfaction for our sins. If our heart is truly converted to Jesus, we won't feel limited by the penances given us. We will work until we arrive at a true "at-one-ment" with both God and our neighbor.

The best satisfaction for sin is doing whatever is necessary to correct the harm done by the sin. If we have been selfish in the use of our stereo, then lending that same stereo or practicing some other act of unselfishness can correct the evil done.

Although we may perform the penance imposed in the sacrament anytime, we must have the **intention** of performing it at the time we confess. Without this intention, our sorrow would not be sincere. It is advisable to perform the penance as soon as possible, preferably in the church immediately after confession. Of course, some penances—

How can helping others be an appropriate penance?

Confessor: the priest who hears the confession in the sacrament of Penance.

The Rites of Reconciliation Today

Today, there are three rites of reconciliation available to Christians. An overview of these rites reveals that the emphasis has been taken off the penitent's confession of sins and is now focused on the warm, human, and divine reconciliation the sacrament brings about.

The **first Rite of Reconciliation** is for individual penitents. The person can choose to go to confession either anonymously behind a screen or face-to-face in a room designed for that purpose. The four parts of the rite are the same for all three: (1) Introductory Rite, (2) Liturgy of the Word, (3) Sacramental Celebration, and (4) Proclamation of Praise and Dismissal.

To bring out even more clearly that penance is not merely the action of one individual seeking personal forgiveness, the Church has drawn up a **second Rite of Reconciliation** that involves communal penance. This rite follows the same order as the Rite of Individual Confession, except that most of the ceremony is performed together with others. Only the actual confession and absolution of each penitent is individual.

A **third Rite of Reconciliation** involves general confession and absolution. It does not replace individual confession but may be used in cases involving danger of death or in places where confessions would be overheard. It may also be used if there are large numbers of penitents and an insufficient number of confessors or if people would otherwise be deprived of reconciliation or reception of the Eucharist for a long time. The common absolution does not relieve the penitent of the obligation to observe the precept of the Church that requires individual confession to a priest of all grave sins at least once a year.

such as the doing of good works or the saying of certain prayers daily—cannot be carried out at once. We sin if, through our own fault, we fail to do the given penance because the willingness to do penance is at the very heart of the conversion that the sacrament brings about.

---

12. *What penances do you find least meaningful? Why? Which seem most helpful?*

Experiencing the Rite of Reconciliation face to face is a very freeing experience.

Summary

- Admitting sinfulness is important for psychological health. It is also a religious act in that confession brings about a reconciliation with God and our neighbors.

- Contrition, or true sorrow for sins, is necessary for the celebration of the sacrament of Penance.

- We may confess our sins out of devotion, but we are obliged to seek reconciliation if we commit mortal sins. We express sorrow for our sins by completing the penance given to us by our confessor.

SECTION 2
Checkpoint!

■ Review

1. Why should the sacrament of Penance be viewed more as a **benefit** for us than as an **obligation** imposed upon us?

2. What is contrition and what role does it play in celebrating the sacrament of Penance?

3. Name the two kinds of confession and indicate when each is appropriate.

4. What should we confess when we celebrate the sacrament of Penance?

5. Words to Know: contrition, penitent, confessor, confession of devotion, penance, canonical penance, reconciliation.

■ In Your World

1. Write an essay on Matthew 5:39: "When someone strikes you on [your] right cheek, turn the other one to him as well." Discuss whether this is a command that Christians can always follow.

2. Discuss in class whether you think that God forgave Adolf Hitler. Give as many reasons as you can for your position.

■ Scripture Search

1. Read and study Matthew 16:13-20 and John 20:19-23. What do these passages tell us about the role of the Church in helping us experience reconciliation to God?

2. The sacrament of Penance is a sacrament of healing. In what important ways does the story in Mark 2:1-12 demonstrate this important description of sacramental reconciliation?

SECTION 3
The Sacrament of the Sick

Julie was a bright, engaging, sixteen-year-old camp counselor. She was active in all of the events at the camp, and was looking forward to her family's visit that weekend. But before her family arrived, tragedy struck. While building a campfire, Julie's clothes caught on fire and she was burned severely. The pain was so intense that Julie was afraid that she was going to die. Hope was not much better at the hospital where they gave her less than a 20% chance of living. Her parents didn't leave her bedside for a week.

Then, when all hope seemed lost, she got better. Sure she had lots of scars, but they were covered by her clothing. She missed a semester of school, but she was ready come January. On Julie's first day back, the first boy who saw her fainted. When he was revived, he said, "I thought you were dead."

Healing the Pain

Young people don't easily dwell on the thought of sickness and death because youth is a time of growth. Yet, every hospital has its children's ward, and accidents and diseases have no age restrictions.

Baptism and Confirmation are clearly sacraments of Christian vocation or calling. Matrimony and Holy Orders are sacramental invitations to a vocation within the larger Christian calling. What is not evident is that the sacrament of the Sick signals a vocation as well.

To be holy, we need to be whole, each strand of ourselves fitting in to work smoothly with the others toward our proper goal—God. The problem is that, because of

Original Sin, none of us is perfectly whole. We all stand in need of healing: physically, mentally, and spiritually. In the sick, one's need of a Savior becomes especially apparent.

The vocation of the sick is not to physical suffering itself because, however you look at it, pain is an evil to be avoided. The sick are called to the privileged vocation of healing and being healed by a close union with Jesus in his suffering and death. We gain understanding as we learn to identify with Jesus through his pain.

When we are seriously ill or in pain, our defenses are lowered, we become more vulnerable, and we reach out with a sincerity that comes only in a time of real need. God responds and we are healed. However, the healing might not always be physical. Our submission to the will of God makes us less selfish, and our illness leads to a trusting, loving acceptance that gives our lives maximum meaning.

Anointing, as the sacrament of the Sick is sometimes called, restores in us whatever is the greatest need. If God sees fit, we may get well and return to our work for the kingdom. Or, we may not recover and yet be healed of our bitterness or discouragement by the gifts of courage and insight into our role of "wounded healer" in the Church. We will receive the strength to help us face whatever happens.

Anointing, then, consecrates us for a special participation in Christ's Paschal Mystery. Our "rising above" sufferings becomes a reminder to the community of their need to "rise above" daily trials by accepting them wholeheartedly. It is a sign of the permanent deliverance from death in our resurrection. Suffering borne in Christian faith then becomes the beginning here on earth of the full coming of God's kingdom.

---

13. *Besides his death on the cross, how did Jesus endure suffering throughout his life?*

14. *If you've ever been in the hospital or confined to bed at home for a while, describe the experience. Besides your physical illness, what other kinds of "suffering" did you face (e.g., loneliness)?*

15. *Describe someone you know who, through his or her sufferings, brings joy and edification to others.*

Worship and Sacraments: We Celebrate, We Praise

As members of the Christian Community we care for those who need help in many ways.

Anointing: Christ's Continuing Action

This deeper sign of the total rescue Christ accomplishes in the community of the Church is illustrated in one of the stories he told.

While traveling, a certain man was attacked, stripped, beaten, and left for dead. Several people walked by, avoiding him. Then a compassionate man washed the victim's wounds, poured healing oil on them, and took him to a nearby inn, where he cared for him until the next day. The Good Samaritan left, but he promised the innkeeper that he would pay all the expenses incurred by the victim (Luke 10:30-35).

We might compare the bleeding man lying by the roadside to the sorry condition of humanity whose disease, pain, hunger, accidents, danger, weakness, aging, and death all image what sin does to us.

In the story, the victim is restored by the concern of someone who has just what he needs—oil and wine and

Chapter 10   Sacraments of Healing

the money to pay the innkeeper. In our lives today, that someone is Christ, who by his own suffering and death won the power to restore us to full health. The Church, like the inn, has been entrusted by him with the healing of needy travelers on the road of life.

By the oil of the anointing and the wine of love, Christ, through his members, heals the sick of each generation as a sign of the total healing work he accomplishes for all humanity.

Thus, the sacrament of the Sick is the continuation of Jesus' ministry of healing. Jesus understood the hardships of illness and death. Out of compassion for the afflicted, he reached out and tenderly touched them, imparting concern and strength through his hands. He sighed deeply over their sorrow and even cried with them.

Speaking through his actions, Jesus, the image of God, revealed that the Father is a healing God who cares for our whole person. Although people left his presence physically healed, this was not the only object of his healing. The people Jesus cured eventually died—even Lazarus. Christ healed bodily disorders to restore people to the total harmony needed to live the God-life. His cures are a sign of his power. If we follow Christ, partake of his Body, and live in him, he promises that we will experience life, not death, even if we should die. Because of Jesus' resurrection, our bodies will rise glorious and triumphant. Every anointing furthers the growth of the resurrection seed planted at our Baptism.

The Rite of Anointing

The primary signs of the sacrament of the Sick are the laying on of hands and the anointing. The priest lays his hands on the sick person. If there are several priests present, they all impose their hands as a symbol of the concern of the Church and the ministry of the Holy Spirit. The priests may take part in the introductory rite or the readings and explanations, but the celebrant offers the prayers, dips his thumb in oil, and anoints the forehead and upturned palms of the sick. In cases of necessity, only the forehead need be anointed. The number of body parts anointed may be increased if different cultures and traditions favor it.

Sacrament of Compassion

Christians show compassion to their sick because they believe in the dignity of every human being. They have the personal concern Christ has for them. Saint Matthew sums it up: "Jesus went around to all the towns and villages...curing every disease and illness" (Matthew 9:35). A few verses later, Christ is shown entrusting his ministry to the Apostles: "Then he summoned his twelve disciples and gave them authority over unclean spirits to drive them out and to cure every disease and every illness" (Matthew 10:1). Saint Mark adds, "They...anointed with oil many who were sick and cured them" (Mark 6:13).

Although it wasn't until after Pentecost that the sacrament of the Sick came into existence, its origins can be seen in this early rite practiced by the Apostles. The power that they received from Christ to assist the sick is the same power Christ entrusts to his priests today. The Epistle of Saint James says, "Is anyone among you sick? He should summon the presbyters of the church, and they should pray over him, and anoint [him] with oil in the name of the Lord, and the prayer of faith will save the sick person, and the Lord will raise him up. If he has committed any sins, he will be forgiven. Therefore, confess your sins to one another and pray for one another, that you may be healed. The fervent prayer of a righteous person is very powerful" (James 5:14-16).

In the same letter, James advises his readers to pray and sing (James 5:13). The early Church held liturgies that were vibrantly alive. What better way to help the sick than by praying and singing with them? Communal anointing services make this possible today, and many families lovingly pray and sing at the bedsides of their sick relatives.

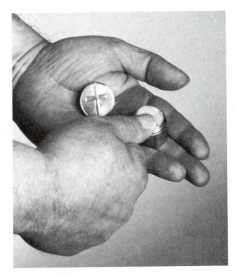

Sacred Chrism (blessed oil) is used for anointing the sick. What is the significance of blessed oil?

The prayers throughout the rite bring out the two-fold healing of the sacrament—physical and spiritual. The revised rite recommends olive oil in ordinary cases, but another plant oil is permitted if olive oil is not available. Oil blessed by the bishop at the Mass of Chrism during Holy Week is preferred, but if it is not available, the priest may bless the oil.

Change in Emphasis

Changing the name of this sacrament from **Extreme Unction** (anointing in the last moments of life) to sacrament of the Sick focuses on the original intent of healing. The sacrament is for the living rather than primarily for those who are near death. The sick are encouraged to participate in the ceremony, not only by requesting the rite or coming to the place of the celebration, but also by uniting their sufferings with the passion of Christ.

It should be noted that the sacrament of the Sick is not given for less serious illnesses like measles, or before routine surgery, although sick people may be anointed before surgery whenever a life-threatening illness (such as a serious heart condition) is the reason for the operation. Susceptible to death at any time, the elderly or those with a chronic illness may be anointed regularly. The sacrament may be repeated if the sick person recovers after the anointing or if, during the same illness, the danger becomes more threatening. Seriously ill children who are old enough to appreciate the meaning of the sacrament can also receive it.

Anointing is the sacrament expressly used for illnesses which might result in death. For this reason, soldiers, people facing execution, and those already dead may not be anointed. The sick who have lapsed into unconsciousness may be anointed if it is presumed that they would have wanted to receive the sacrament.

---

16. *Have you ever witnessed an anointing of the sick or have you celebrated the sacrament yourself? Describe your experiences.*

Touching the Sacred

The sacrament of the Sick includes a prayer of blessing for the oil that is used to anoint the patient. This simple prayer illustrates the faith which we profess in our concern for the sick:

"Let us pray.

Lord God, loving Father, you bring healing to the sick through your Son, Jesus Christ. Hear us as we pray to you in faith, and send the Holy Spirit, our Helper and Friend, upon this oil, which nature has provided to serve the needs of all. May your blessing come upon all who are anointed with this oil, that they may be freed from pain and illness and made whole again in body, mind, and soul. Father, may this oil be blessed for our use in the name of our Lord Jesus Christ who lives and reigns with you for ever and ever. Amen."

Viaticum: Sacrament of the Dying

Some people erroneously believe that in the final moments of life God or the devil will succeed in snatching the dying person away from the other. Actually, we die as we live. Death is an important time because even then we have the freedom to choose or reject God. But it is highly unlikely that a lifetime direction of our hearts will change.

As he does all during life, Christ comes to our help in our final hours through the three "last" sacraments: Penance for the forgiveness of sin, Anointing for counteracting the weaknesses that may lead a person away from Christ, and the final Eucharist. Viaticum, the name we give to the last Eucharist, is so important that it is the only one of the three "last sacraments" that is of obligation when there is opportunity.

During life, every Christian's reception of the Eucharist is an attempt to unite with the total commitment of the dying Jesus to his Father. But at no point along the way are we mature enough to attain that degree of love. Only the supreme sacrifice of death permits us to give our very life to God.

It is possible to let death triumph over us, to die because we are forced into it, as if we had no other choice. That is

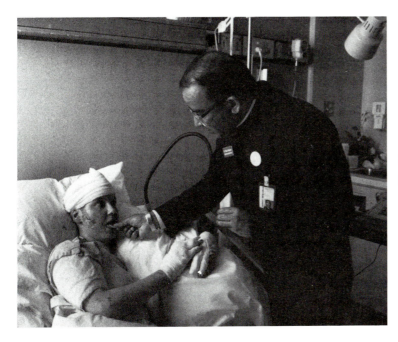

Viaticum, or last Eucharist, is given to people on the verge of death.

Chapter 10   Sacraments of Healing

the less than human way. But because we are human and therefore free, like Christ, we can accept death, own it personally, and bring our lives to complete fullness by trustful surrender to the Father.

Viaticum means provisions people take with them on their journey. Uniting our weak desire to love God with Jesus' perfect offering, we will be led by him through the door of death to our God. As we repeatedly offer ourselves to God in life in our daily morning offering, in our many other prayers, and in the sacraments, we will then give ourselves totally. We will arrive at the moment of supreme achievement: eternal life.

You might wonder how this kind of fulfillment can be ours if we should die suddenly or after a long period of unconsciousness. Jesus' warnings are full of urgency. He says over and over again that, because we don't know when death will come, it is important to reach out toward God and keep our hearts turned away from sin. We should live each day as if it were to be the last (see Romans 13:11-14 and 1 Thessalonians 5:8-10).

17. What do we mean when we say that people die as they live?

Summary

- While suffering is never welcomed, it can invite us to the Paschal Mystery of Christ. It is, therefore, proper to speak of our suffering as part of our Christian vocation.

- The sacrament of the Sick carries on Jesus' own ministry of healing. When celebrating this sacrament, Christians pray for physical healing as well as for the spiritual and moral healing that humans desire.

- The primary signs of the sacrament of the Sick are the laying on of hands (sign of concern) and anointing with oil (sign of strength).

SECTION 3
Checkpoint!

■ Review

1. What is the "vocation" of the sick and how does this vocation relate to Christ's Paschal Mystery?

2. How did Jesus minster to those who were ill in spirit and body? Give some specific examples.

3. Why was the name of the sacrament of the Sick changed? What did it used to be?

4. What is Viaticum?

5. Words to Know: anointing, Extreme Unction, Viaticum.

■ In Your World

1. What things might deprive a sick person of peace and a sense of dignity?

2. Write a letter to a hypothetical (fictional) friend who is dying. Share your faith, compassion, and concern for her or him.

■ Scripture Search

1. Jesus often showed sympathy and compassion. Note which of the following groups he healed in the texts listed below: (a) older people; (b) the young; (c) lepers; (d) bereaved families.
Luke 5:12-14; 7:11-15; 8:40-56; 9:37-43; 13:10-13; 17:11-19. John 5:1-15; 11:1-44.

2. The Apostles possessed astonishing healing powers. To what did they attribute their gift in Acts 3:11-16?

CHAPTER 10 Review

■ Study

1. Some people say that the God of the Hebrew Scriptures is a God of judgment and that the God and Father of Jesus Christ is a God of mercy and love. Why is this simply not true?

2. In what specific ways does Jesus show us forgiveness and healing?

3. What kinds of things does lack of forgiveness cause people to do?

4. What is conversion? Why is conversion a lifelong process?

5. Describe the meaning of the sacrament of Penance in your own words. In what sense can we say that Jesus gave us this sacrament himself?

6. How would you answer someone who said confession is useless because you just fall back into the same old sins anyway?

7. Why isn't it possible to be forgiven for our sins if we are not sorry for them? What is this sorrow called?

8. List six stages in the historical development of the sacrament of Penance.

9. What are the three reconciliation rites in use today?

10. What epistle (or letter) provides the Scriptural foundation for the practice of anointing the sick in the early Church? What specific actions were involved in this practice?

11. "The sacrament of the Sick is the continuation of Jesus' ministry of healing." Explain.

12. "Viaticum" means "food for the journey." What journey? Why is this food helpful?

■ Action

1. Prepare a celebration of communal reconciliation for your class using music, Scriptures, prayers, and art of your own choosing. Celebrate your prayer.

2. Talk to someone who has lost a close friend or relative and ask what role his or her faith played in this painful event.

3. Role play a "private" confession in class. Take turns being the penitent (Don't tell your real sins!) and the confessor. Discuss your experience of this exercise. Did it help you feel more comfortable with the sacrament of Penance?

4. In many parishes, Eucharistic Ministers also bring communion to the sick. Invite a person who does this to come to your class to discuss her or his experiences.

■ Prayer

Sometimes the simple prayers that we learned as children take on new and deeper meaning as we get older and learn more about our faith. The "Act of Contrition" is one of these prayers.

If you have forgotten it (and it's surprising how many Catholics have), now is a good time to make this prayer a part of your life. It can be said at night before going to bed, and it is always an appropriate form of prayer for expressing sorrow for our sins in the sacrament of Penance.

When offering this prayer, it may be helpful to divide its phrases and pause after each one to consider carefully how God is calling us to repentance.

The Act of Contrition (Sorrow for Sin)
O my God, I am heartily sorry for having offended you...And I detest all my sins because of your just punishments...But most of all, because they offend you, my God, who is all-good and deserving of all my love...I firmly resolve, with the help of your grace, to confess my sins...To do penance... And to amend my life...
Amen.

CHAPTER

11

Cycles of Time in the Worship of the Church

OBJECTIVES

In this Chapter you will

- Understand how the Church celebrates faith in Christ through the cycle of time called the liturgical year.

- Explore the meaning of the Advent/Christmas season.

- Recognize Lent, Easter, and Pentecost as the most important worship times in the Church year.

In the course of the year...she [the Church] unfolds the whole mystery of Christ from the Incarnation and Nativity to the Ascension, to Pentecost and the expectation of the blessed hope of the coming of the Lord.
—"Constitution on the Sacred Liturgy"

Worship and Sacraments: We Celebrate, We Praise

SECTION 1
The Liturgical Year

Some ancient peoples looked at the seasons as a continuing war between the gods of light and the gods of darkness. In spring, they celebrated the fullness of life and light in joyous festivals. In winter, toward the end of December, they marked the shortest day of the year and celebrated the triumph of light over darkness; from that day onward, the hours of light begin to increase.

"Year" is a term people invented to deal with the repetitious flow of the seasons. Nature divides itself naturally into four distinct "times." Spring, a time of increasing light and warmth, is known for its new life and regeneration. Summer, a time of maximum light and heat, is a time of growth and leisure. Fall, a time of decreasing days and longer nights, is a time of harvest and reaping. Winter, a time of darkness and cold, is a time of quiet and hibernation.

Sacred Time

When Christians looked at the events of Jesus' life, they saw in them similarities to the pagan feasts of seasons. They celebrated the birth of Jesus, light coming into darkness, shortly after the winter solstice, the shortest day of the year. As Saint John describes this event, "The light shines in the darkness, and the darkness has not overcome it" (John 1:5).

Likewise, when Christians looked for a time to celebrate the great feast of Easter, the resurrection and new life of Jesus, they chose springtime, the season of flourishing life. This feast is marked with the exuberance of life eternal, the resurgence of hope, and the celebration of joy. Winter is over. Jesus has triumphed forever over the powers of death.

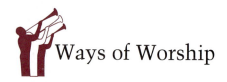

Ways of Worship

Hourly Celebration

Even the daily liturgical celebrations are not enough to express the fullness of the mystery of Jesus. The Church, in obedience to Jesus' command to pray always, established the Liturgy of the Hours (Luke 18:1). This is a collection of psalms, readings, hymns, and prayers chosen to develop the themes for the seasons and feasts of the liturgical year. It is designed to be prayed with others at various hours throughout the day in order to consecrate time and all human activity as well as to foster a sense of Christian community.

This form of prayer developed in the monasteries, and later became a required daily prayer for all clergy. More and more parishes today are prominently celebrating the Morning and Evening Prayer from the Liturgy of the Hours, especially on Sundays.

Besides being a way to offer God praise, this little-known liturgy also fosters a deeper sense of community since it is a public prayer, offered in common.

It is around these two great feasts, Easter and Christmas, that the liturgical calendar is built. Although Easter is the highest feast of the Church year, the liturgical seasons begin with the first Sunday of Advent. Advent is a four-week period of preparation for Christmas. It prepares for the celebration of Christ's first coming and also looks forward to his coming at the end of the world. Advent is followed by the Christmas season, which begins with Christmas and lasts until the Sunday after Epiphany.

The Church also spends time preparing for Easter. This time consists of forty days called Lent, reminding Christians of the forty days Jesus spent in the desert before his active ministry and of the forty years the Israelites spent wandering in the desert before entering the Promised Land (Matthew 4:1-2 and Numbers 14:33, 32:13).

The last three days of Lent, known as the Easter Triduum, are the climax of the entire liturgical year. They commemorate the passion, death, and resurrection of Christ—his great passover from death to eternal life. The fifty days between Easter Sunday and Pentecost are known as the Easter Season. They are like one long feast day, sometimes called the "Great Sunday" of the Church year.

Besides the seasons of Easter, Lent, Christmas, and Advent, there are thirty-four weeks during the year that do not stress the Paschal Mystery. Instead, they dwell on the life and teachings of Christ and celebrate the fullness of grace gained by redemption. This season is known as Ordinary Time.

Ordinary Time begins on the Monday after the Sunday following Epiphany and continues until the beginning of Lent. It resumes again on the Monday after Pentecost Sunday and ends on the Saturday before the first Sunday of Advent.

1. *What is your favorite season of the year? Why?*

2. *What has been the best year in your life? The worst year? Why?*

Reenacting the Mystery of Christ

The liturgical year, the annual cycle of seasons and feasts that reenact the mystery of Christ, is designed to: 1. instruct the faithful; 2. help them become an ever holier people; and 3. unite them in Christ, whom they encounter in the midst of their celebrations. While recalling the events of Jesus' life, these celebrations bring the effect of those events into the present. Christians actually encounter the risen Christ and are healed by his sacramental presence and action. Moreover, these celebrations look to the future, containing in themselves the promise of the eternal celebration in which all the faithful will share in the future resurrection. This threefold dimension of sacramental celebration is referred to as Christ's coming in history (time), mystery (sacrament), and majesty (at the end of the world).

From the Middle Ages to Vatican II, the Church looked at the celebrations of the liturgy as a historical representation of Christ's life and the years preceding it. The liturgical year was divided into five segments: Advent, Christmas, Lent, Easter, Ordinary Time. These five segments are seen as telling the story of Jesus in a one year cycle.

- *The four weeks of Advent represented the thousands of years before Christ, in which people looked forward to a Messiah.*
- *The time from Christmas to Pentecost (Lent and Easter) in the liturgical year represented the life of Christ from his infancy to his ascension and the sending of the Holy Spirit.*
- *The weeks after Pentecost represented the period from the birth of the Church to the second coming of Christ (Ordinary Time).*

Vatican II introduced a sacramental dimension to the liturgical year. In this sacramental interpretation, it is easier to see that the Paschal Mystery, the great event of redemption, is the center of the Church year. All the seasons and feasts unfold that mystery, keeping Christ and his life, teachings, and saving action in the midst of his people always. The *"Constitution on the Sacred Liturgy"* explains it this way: "Recalling the mysteries of the redemption, she [the Church] opens up to the faithful the riches of

Easter Triduum: (tri = three; duum = days): refers to Holy Thursday, Good Friday, and Holy Saturday which lead up to Christ's resurrection.

her Lord's powers and merits, so that these are in some way made present for all time; the faithful lay hold of them and are filled with saving grace" (#120).

Keeping the Lord's Day

Each Sunday is a mini-celebration of the Paschal Mystery. From the time of the Resurrection itself, this day has been "the Lord's Day." Because a day has been traditionally measured from sundown to sundown, many Catholics begin their celebration of the Lord's Day on Saturday evening. They gather in community, listen to God's Word, and participate in the sacrament of the Eucharist. Through extra rest and time spent eating and relaxing together, they make Sunday truly a day of rest and family togetherness.

During the first several centuries of worship, Christians celebrated the Eucharist only on Sunday. Gradually, the Church discovered that the single annual celebration of Easter was not enough to express the mystery of Jesus' life, death, and resurrection, and so added a number of feasts, extending aspects of the Paschal Mystery through the year. The Church added special days to celebrate the way certain saints lived out the Paschal Mystery. Now Fridays, especially during Lent, remind Christians of the passion and death of Jesus. Saturdays are dedicated to Mary, the Mother of God.

Somewhere in the World

Because of the eternal and unending mystery of Christ, the Church celebrates the Eucharist every day. Somewhere in the world at all times, Christ's sacrifice is being offered. Through the Eucharist, God continually lives among us, revealing and communicating the Divine Presence in Christ's one sacrifice. Although people are physically limited to the number of Masses they can attend, they can feel assured that, as members of Christ's Body, they are included in every Mass throughout the world.

For nearly two thousand years Christians have kept the Lord's Day in their homes or parishes as a mini-Paschal feast by celebrating the Christian's highest act of worship to God: the Eucharist. Today, they rejoice to hear God's Word

For Christians in the Northern Hemisphere, Easter is celebrated in the spring. When is it celebrated in the Southern Hemisphere?

Worship and Sacraments: We Celebrate, We Praise

and to have it explained to them at Mass. They enter into close union with other members of the community by praying and singing together, and they renew their deep communion with Christ.

Sunday Rest

There is a human need for regular periods of rest and recreation. If we set aside such a time, we may enjoy the fruits of a balanced life. With family life threatened today by the many things that draw people away from the home during the week, Sunday is an ideal time to enjoy good meals and recreation together or to visit relatives and friends. Engaging in parish services or neighborhood activities can strengthen the life of the larger community as well. Thus refreshed in spirit, you will be better prepared to face whatever challenges the next week may hold in store.

Sunday is a traditional time for family celebration, recreation, and prayer.

"Sun-day": suggests the powers of light and warmth.

Chapter 11   Cycles of Time in the Worship of the Church

Order of Importance in Liturgical Time

Each day of the year is ranked in order of its importance. For example, some days may have two or more coinciding feasts. Which one of these feasts or important celebrations will be celebrated is determined by certain rules regarding the liturgical year. Each feast is given one of the following ranks: Sundays, Solemnities and Feasts, Obligatory Memorials, and Optional Memorials. These ranks are given in the Sacramentary, the liturgical book for Roman Catholics containing the formulas and rites for the celebration of Mass.

Sundays are major days of the year. Each Sunday has its own readings and prayers that rotate on a three-year cycle. The liturgy of Sunday must always be celebrated, unless Sunday is also a Feast or Solemnity of the Lord. For example, the Baptism of Jesus, the Transfiguration, and Christmas would take precedence over the regular Sunday liturgy. However, the liturgies of the Sundays in Advent, Lent, and Easter take precedence over Solemnities. The liturgy of the Solemnity is then moved to the preceding Saturday.

Solemnities and feasts have their own "propers" (prayers and preface) and take precedence over weekday Masses.

Memorials are the Church's celebrations of the lives of the saints. Prayers appropriate to the saint are inserted into the regular Mass of the day. **Obligatory memorials** (important saints) must be observed unless they occur in privileged seasons, when the Mass of the day takes precedence, but the opening prayer of the memorial may be used. Privileged seasons include Advent weekdays, December 17-24, days within the Octave of Christmas, and Lenten weekdays, except Ash Wednesday and the days of Holy Week. **Optional memorials** list the saint's name in the calendar, but give no rank.

THE LITURGICAL SEASON

A — Advent
B — Christmas Season
C — Ordinary Time
D — Lent
E — Easter Season
F — Ordinary Time

This pie chart illustrates the length of the various liturgical seasons. The Church year begins with Advent (A). Ordinary Time (C and F) is the longest season.

In a growing secular world, where shops are kept open on Sunday and people are expected to work straight through the week, the day of rest runs the danger of becoming extinct. Groups of Christians who understand the purpose of Sunday are gathering in one another's houses for Scripture study, holding religion classes for the young, and joining to pray the Liturgy of the Hours together on Sundays. They recognize the symbolism of the first chapter of Genesis: that every celebration of the Lord's Day acknowledges that the purpose of all creation is sabbath—praise of the Creator.

3. *Find out which days of the week are holy days for Jews and for Muslims.*

4. *How does your family celebrate Sunday? What can you do to keep its spiritual purpose uppermost?*

5. *What are some things that keep you from observing Sunday as a day of rest? How can you overcome these obstacles?*

6. *Write down some of your feelings about the Sunday observances.*

Summary

- The annual cycle of worship and remembrance in the Church is called the Liturgical Year. Each year, five seasons are celebrated to help us recall Christ's saving activity in our lives.

- The Liturgical Year also reenacts the mystery of salvation through Jesus Christ.

- Sundays are important and special times in the liturgical cycle, for each Sunday is a mini-celebration of Jesus' dying and rising.

Sunday is a time for the community to gather for prayer.

Chapter 11   Cycles of Time in the Worship of the Church

SECTION 1
Checkpoint!

■ Review

1. What are the two great feasts (liturgical celebrations recalling events in Christ's life) that the liturgical year is built around?

2. Name the five seasons of the liturgical year. What does each celebrate?

3. Why do we call Sunday "the Lord's Day" and what do we celebrate each Sunday?

4. What is the Liturgy of the Hours?

5. Words to Know: liturgical cycle/time, liturgical seasons, Easter Triduum, Liturgy of the Hours, memorials, "propers," privileged seasons.

■ In Your World

1. Write an essay in which you explain how each liturgical season celebrates some aspect of the Paschal Mystery and how these celebrations can help us grow closer to Christ.

2. What season commemorates Christ's coming to earth to show God's will and to bring peace to all nations? The fullness of the Christian life in the Spirit? Christ's passover from death to life? The longing of all people for a Savior? One's repentance and desire to be converted to a wholehearted following of Christ?

■ Scripture Search

1. Take turns reading the verses of Ecclesiastes 3:1-15 in class. Discuss how these verses help us appreciate cycles of time in our lives.

2. What important lessons can we learn about the season of Lent from the time Jesus spent in the desert (Matthew 4:1-11)?

SECTION 2
Advent and Christmas

Celebrations such as weddings and graduations involve a considerable amount of planning and behind-the-scenes organizing. There are three stages to a celebration: the preparation, the actual celebration, and the period of grateful, quiet fulfillment following the festivities.

The liturgical year follows a similar pattern of buildup, high festivity, and fulfillment, particularly around the feasts of Christmas and Easter.

Seasons and Feasts

The Church year opens with Advent, a season of joyful preparation for the feast of the Lord's birth. In the first two weeks, the readings are directed to Christ's second coming at the end of time. The poetic and appealing passages used in the Masses of the third and fourth weeks are filled with longing for his birth. Mary's peace and interior reflection as she awaited her holy child serve as a model for all people as they await the Savior.

The Christmas season brings this period of hope to fulfillment in Christ's birth at Bethlehem. His epiphanies—the occasions when Jesus was revealed as the Messiah—are celebrated on the following two Sundays. The feast of the Epiphany celebrates the Three Kings, or Magi, who represent God's revelation of the plan of salvation in Christ to all the nations of the world. The feast of the Baptism of the Lord celebrates Christ's baptism in the Jordan when he was revealed as divine. During these three weeks of Christmas, the Church honors Mary, the virgin mother, and recognizes the Holy Family as the example of all Christian family life.

Advent: Preparing for Christmas

Most people today like to see quick action and instant results. But God, to whom a thousand years are as one day, is patient. Advent is the season when patience is needed. It is a season of waiting. God waits for our response, even as we wait for God's appearance. Mary's call at the Annunciation seems to have been a sudden revelation, yet Christ took his time: nine months to be born and thirty more years to prepare for his public life (Luke 1:26-38). He continues to wait for the response of each person.

Finding Christ During Advent

Advent is not only a time of waiting for Christ to come but also a time for finding and worshiping him. We find him not in the poor stable of Bethlehem but in our own cities. Jesus may be found everywhere: in the members of our family or neighborhood, in our brothers and sisters, and in our parents.

During Advent, Jesus is born and grows within us—in the wisdom we gain from mistakes and in our service to others. It's a time for following the "magi star": in Scripture Matthew 2:1-12, which tells us Christ will come again; in daily inspirations to do good; and in friendships that develop our best assets.

Advent Training

Most athletes go through rigorous physical training to prepare for their sports. Christians need a similar training as well. The preparation needed for the Christian life is spiritual rather than physical. Nevertheless, it is a training and it does involve discipline.

A good way to start off the Church's new year and "get into shape" for the coming of the Lord is to spend five minutes a day with him in meditation with Scripture. If your school has a chapel, this can be done before school, during the lunch hour, or right after classes. Just before going to bed is another good time for this practice.

Begin by taking a minute to quiet yourself. Close your eyes. Remember that God is present with you. Next, spend some time reading the Bible or the Scriptures for Mass the following Sunday.

Sharing prayer and Scripture study are practical ways for you to prepare for Christmas.

Getting into the Christmas Spirit

A lot of Christians are surprised when they learn that it took a while for the Church to get into the Christmas spirit! Because there is no record of when Jesus was actually born, and because the major liturgical celebration of the Church has always been Easter, early Christians, as far as we know, simply did not recall the birth of Christ with a special feast.

But in 215, Clement of Alexandria (in Egypt) suggested that a day be set aside to honor the Incarnation. He chose November 17th. In Rome, Christmas eventually became an annual religious event celebrated on January 6th, and that date was not changed until some time in the fifth century.

By the middle of the fifth century, December 25th had gained acceptance as the day to celebrate the birth of the Messiah (except in the city of Rome where December 25th was not accepted until 534).

If the actual date of Jesus' birth was unknown, why did the Church settle on December 25th? The answer seems to be that this particular date was already a "sacred time," the time of the winter solstice or beginning of winter.

For centuries, people celebrated one of the shortest, coldest days of the year by having a feast which the Romans called the *Saturnales* after the god of agriculture, **Saturn.** By worshiping Saturn during the cold season of darkness, they reasoned, he would hasten the coming of spring and see to it that the earth would warm and the crops would grow.

By selecting December 25th as the day to recall the Incarnation, Christians were proclaiming that Jesus, not Saturn, gives light to the world. It is Jesus who nourishes us and none other. With the birth of the Savior, there was no longer any need to rely upon the old Roman gods. The one true God is with us, Emmanuel.

Artists for centuries have attempted to capture the joy of Jesus' birth.

 On the Record

The Christmas Crib

Today, almost every Catholic home puts up a Christmas crib during the season of the nativity. This was not always the case. Although representations of the Christ Child and the Madonna were used in churches from the earliest centuries of Christianity, the crib scene was the inspiration of Saint Francis of Assisi.

In a famous Christmas Eve celebration in 1223, Saint Francis created a life-size representation of the nativity scene, including live animals. In a vivid and deeply moving sermon, he made the events of Christmas come alive for the villagers. Since then, cribs of every size, material, and style have been used in churches and homes.

The importance of this religious symbol lies in its power to remind people that humility and poverty need not spoil their peace.

This is an excellent way to celebrate Advent and to learn more about God's Word.

---

7. *What is it like to wait for someone if the person you're waiting for is someone you don't particularly care for and he or she is late? What is it like if you are early and the person you're waiting for is someone you like?*

8. *What qualities did Mary need to respond as she did to her call?*

9. *What other ways besides the ones mentioned in the text can be used to celebrate Advent?*

10. *Can you understand why helping the poor might be excellent "Advent training"?*

Christmas: Feast of the Incarnation

The word **Incarnation** means "to become flesh" (John 1). Jesus, who is also God, became physically human on Christmas. This fact has important implications for the way one views one's self and Christianity.

To illustrate the implications of the Incarnation, a small comparison is in order. For centuries in the liturgy, the prayer before Communion recited by the congregation read: "O Lord, I am not worthy that you should come under my roof. Speak but the word, and my soul shall be healed." Today's liturgy reads: "Lord, I am not worthy to receive you, but only say the word and I shall be healed."

The word to notice in the second version is the **I** that replaces "my soul." Jesus did not come simply to save our souls. He came to save each of us as a total person, body and soul.

Our union with Christ in Communion is bodily. Our worship at the Eucharist must likewise be whole. It is meant to involve our mind and will, body and emotions, smell, sight, taste, touch, and hearing.

Stories of Jupiter, Atlas, Hercules, Venus, Cupid, Helen of Troy, and Pandora are fictional accounts found in ancient Greek and Roman myths. They dramatize certain universal truths of life. That's where the stories of Christianity are different from other stories. When we commemorate Christmas, we remember the actual birth of a real baby, the Son of God. He was the son of a Jewish girl named Mary whose carpenter-husband was called Joseph. All three belonged to a people whose stories were not fantasies, but the real history of their human ancestors. In God's designs, these stories contain the deepest truths known to the human race: God's love, self-revelation, and the Incarnation of Jesus, God's Son.

It all began with the historical fact of Christ's birth, but the most amazing thing is that Christmas is still going on today. The Son of God takes on new flesh with every human being who accepts him. What is more, the process will never end until every last person is born. Only then will the birth of Christ be complete—when everything in heaven and on earth is brought back to the Father to praise God forever.

---

11. *Jesus came to save, not just our souls, but our **entire lives**. What elements of the liturgy appeal to each of your senses? What elements appeal to your emotions? To your mind?*

12. *How do the people express their wholehearted devotion to Christ at public ceremonies?*

13. *A lot of people go overboard with Christmas gift-giving. How might we simplify this practice and better celebrate the true meaning of the season?*

Summary

- Just as it is important to prepare for other events, Christians mark the importance of Christmas by a special season of preparation called Advent.

- Advent means waiting. During Advent we await the birth of Christ. We also continue our preparation for the fullness of Christ and God's kingdom.

- Christmas is the feast of the Incarnation, the moment in time when the Word of God became flesh and made his home among us.

SECTION 2
Checkpoint!

■ Review

1. Read the "Infancy Narratives" in Matthew and Luke (chapters 1 and 2 in each Gospel). List the details found in each story—the events as Scripture reveals them. Be sure to write the Scripture passages that apply next to each event.

2. Who was the real Father of Jesus? What event in the life of Mary recalls this fact? How does the term Incarnation relate to this event?

3. What does the word Advent mean and how can we celebrate it well?

4. During Advent we await the liturgical celebration of Jesus' birth. What else do we wait for?

5. Words to Know: Advent, the Incarnation, winter solstice, *Saturnales*.

■ In Your World

1. Advent is a time of preparation for Christmas. It's a time to "get ready for Christ." Think about some school or family event that you helped plan. Write down and discuss some of the details involved in the preparations. Why is planning and preparation so important for the success of events? Describe an experience you have had of being part of a poorly-planned event. Talk about the consequences of poor planning. Make a list of some ways you can plan to celebrate Christmas well.

2. Christmas is a time when people spend a lot of time shopping, and they often become irritable. What do you think is the best way to handle someone who cuts in front of you in line? The clerk who makes a mistake? Someone who dents your car?

■ Scripture Search

1. Read John 1 and write a paragraph that describes the meaning of the Incarnation for Christians.

2. What does the story of the magi tell us about Jesus Christ and his mission? See Matthew 2:1-12 for details. What is suggested by the fact that Jesus was literally born in a barn (Luke 2:6-7) and that his birth was first announced to poor shepherds (Luke 2:8-18)?

SECTION 3
Lent, Easter, and Pentecost

A football coach was trying to encourage his squad to work harder in the weightlifting room. Many of the future gridiron heroes could be seen pumping weights many hours after school. One young player complained to the coach. "I want to quit," he said. "It hurts too much." The coach's only response was "When it hurts, son, it does you good."

Nobody likes pain or humiliation of any kind. Yet the reply of the football coach and the marathon runner's motto, "No Pain, No Gain," are true throughout life. If you want to accomplish anything worthwhile, you must work at it. If you want to pass a test, you must study. If you want to drive a car, you must pass the test and get your license.

In Lent, Christians reflect on the tremendous courage with which Christ entered into his passion and death. It wasn't that he didn't understand or feel the pain, and he certainly didn't want suffering. He prayed so long in the garden to be relieved of it that his disciples fell asleep. His prayer was an agony in which his whole body sank to the ground, sweating blood at the thought of the torture and humiliation that lay ahead. Jesus did not appreciate pain. He was not in love with the idea of his death. But he believed in God's promise of eternal life.

Lent: A Season of Repentance

Lent is a season of self-denial and penance that culminates in the Easter joy of Jesus' resurrection and victory over death. The first Lent was only three days long, the time between Jesus' capture and death and his reappearance among his followers in a new and different life.

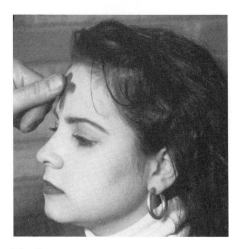

The Lenten sign of ashes reminds us of our need for conversion and forgiveness.

Today, Lent stretches over forty days, not including Sundays, which are considered separate from the forty-day period. They are called Sundays **in** Lent, not **of** Lent. Lent is not only a period of sorrow and mourning such as the Apostles experienced, but it is also a period of self-examination. It is meant to result in the conversion of our minds and hearts to Christ so that we become our true selves.

Ash Wednesday marks the beginning of Lent. The blessed ashes placed on each person's forehead are a call to "turn away from sin and be faithful to the Gospel." They remind each person of his or her humanness and eventual death. The ashes set the tone for the annual forty days of Christian renewal before Holy Week.

The Gospels of the Sundays in Lent include the accounts of Jesus' temptation in the desert, the transfiguration of Christ, and incidents in which Jesus condemned sin, cured sinners, raised the dead, and predicted his own death and resurrection.

Three Purposes of Lent

The Lenten season has three purposes: 1. to be an immediate preparation for catechumens asking to be baptized at the Easter Vigil; 2. to call sinners to return to God by means of the sacrament of Penance; and 3. to deepen the spiritual life of the devout by a renewal of their baptismal promises.

Holy Week, which brings Lent and the liturgical year to a climax, begins with the Gospel of Jesus' entry as the Messiah into Jerusalem amid waving palm branches and shouts of "Hosanna" ("save us") by the crowds. During the week, the passion account is read in its entirety on Passion Sunday and Good Friday. The week moves solemnly from a commemoration of Jesus' gift of the Eucharist on Holy Thursday to the celebration of the Lord's passion on Good Friday. Good Friday is the only day in the year when Mass is not celebrated; there is a Communion service, however.

The Positive Side

The cross, the main sign and greatest mystery of the Christian life, is the symbol of the seeming contradictions that make up life. Its vertical bar, pointing to the heavens, represents God and eternity. The horizontal beam stands for the things of this world, time and humanity. Some of the opposites symbolized by the crossing of the two bars are the following:

- *Death is the door to life.*
- *Victory comes in defeat.*
- *Love is born of hate.*
- *Greatest joy comes through deepest suffering.*

Sometimes when Christians are thinking over what they should do for Lent, they consider only penances that seem negative: giving up fighting at home, giving up shows or games, giving up desserts or snacks. These things seem worthwhile because people concentrate on the difficulty of the penance. Yet all these negative things have a positive value: they express one's love of Christ.

If negative penances have a plus value, positive penances are helpful in a different way. In doing a positive penance, we concentrate on how it will affect the other person, rather than on how much it costs. Here are some positive penances to try for Lent:

- *Read Scripture every day (alone or with someone).*
- *Visit a sick person.*
- *Do something helpful around the house.*
- *Attend church services more frequently.*
- *Make donations of money or possessions to help the poor.*

There are many positive things you can do to help you grow as a Christian during Lent.

Chapter 11 Cycles of Time in the Worship of the Church

Two Lenten Traditions: Prayer and Fasting

A Lenten Prayer (The *Ecce Homo*, "Behold the Man"):

> *A ragged cloak on his shoulders, a crown of thorns on his head—*
> "Here is the Man!"
>
> *Whipped and mocked and falsely charged—*
> "Here is the Man!"
>
> *Abandoned by his friends cast off by his people—*
> "Here is the Man!"
>
> *Look at the loser, the victim, the scapegoat, He has no armies, no advocates, scarcely a friend.*
> "Here is the Man!"
>
> *Alone, but not lonely. Beaten, but undefeated. Crushed, but calm.*
> "Here is the Man!"
>
> *And in that one Man, see all of us. In his defeat, see our victory.*
> "Here is the Man!"

The Tradition of Fasting: The tradition of a "strict life" involving fast, abstinence, and solitude goes back to John the Baptizer, who lived in the desert, wore rough clothes, and subsisted on locusts in order to be a better instrument for preparing the way for the Savior. Jesus himself spent forty days in the desert fasting and praying before he began his life work. As a human being, he needed to strengthen his purposes and unite himself completely with God.

During Lent, the Church reminds Christians of the age-old importance of fasting. On Ash Wednesday and Good Friday, all Christians over twenty-one and under sixty years of age are required to fast—eat only one full meal a day. During these forty penitential days, all persons over fourteen are bound by the law of abstinence, which forbids the eating of meat on all Fridays of Lent.

Each year during Lent (Holy Week), people around the world reenact the story of Jesus' crucifixion.

Worship and Sacraments: We Celebrate, We Praise

14. *Think of some duties you do on the job, in school, or in your family that are not pleasant. Why do you accept the discomfort involved in doing them?*

15. *What were the values that made Jesus accept his passion and death?*

16. *Why do you think Sundays are not counted in the forty days of Lent?*

The Easter Vigil

The Easter season officially begins with the Easter Vigil on Holy Saturday. The glorious alleluias of the Easter Sunday Mass ring throughout the fifty days of the festive Easter season. During this time the risen Lord is kept before the minds of the faithful through the Gospel readings of Christ's appearances after the resurrection.

Although Christ was glorified at the instant of his death, the feast of the Ascension commemorates that glorification. At the same time, it launches ten days of prayer in preparation for the coming of the Holy Spirit.

Christ the Light

The Easter Vigil, which is held late Holy Saturday evening, is the most glorious celebration of the Church year. It opens with the beautiful light service at which new fire (the symbol of Christ in his transformed state) is blessed and the Paschal Candle (which represents the dazzling appearance of the risen Lord) is carried into the darkened church building. This first portion of the four-part service climaxes in the joyful singing of the *exsultet,* an ancient hymn proclaiming Christ's resurrection.

Light was a symbol of God's presence for the Hebrews. Similarly, fire is a symbol of Christ the Light and of one's response to him. This symbolism is expressed in the prayer over the fire: "Let us be so inflamed with desire for heaven that we may attain with pure souls to the feast of everlasting brightness."

The Easter candle is a sign of Jesus' resurrection and a reminder of our baptism. Through the candle, we proclaim Jesus as the "Light of the World."

Chapter 11 Cycles of Time in the Worship of the Church

Touching the Sacred

Alleluia: A Single-Word Prayer

The experience of meeting the risen Lord can never be put into words, but the word that comes closest to expressing the wonder for the early Christians was the Hebrew word *alleluia.*

This exclamation of joy is really a combination of two words: *hallelu* (a cry of praise) and *Yah* (Yahweh). By means of this expressive word, the Israelites poured themselves out in admiration, adoration, and awe before their God in return for all that had been done for them.

The Easter alleluia is our response to the greatest saving action God has performed: raising Jesus from the dead. For in the resurrection, those who are joined with Christ know that they, too, will rise.

Saint Augustine said, "Christians must be an alleluia from head to toe." He meant that Christians are people of profound adoration to God who has given them reason for gladness. The Easter liturgy rightly repeats again and again, Alleluia!

In the Easter Vigil service, the Paschal Candle is carried forth in solemn procession to be enthroned on the altar. The procession itself reminds Christians of the Hebrews who were led by a pillar of fire through the Red Sea toward the Promised Land. In the Easter Vigil liturgy, the pillar of light represents Christ, who leads the new Chosen People through the waters of baptism to the promised land of the kingdom.

All present bear candles enkindled from the light of the Paschal Candle as they stand to hear the Easter message in the thrilling words of the *exsultet.* In this moving song of joy, they hear of the Christian mysteries first enacted by Christ long ago but ever renewed among them in the paschal celebrations.

Reflecting on God's Word

In the second part of the service, the Liturgy of the Word, the Church meditates on the saving actions of God in the world since the creation. Christians reflect on the mystery of God's salvation of the Hebrews: the rescue of the Hebrews from Egypt, the long journey through the desert, and, finally, the entrance into the Promised Land. Christians recall on this night that they, too, are the People of God, and on this night are called to share even more completely in the divine action of God.

Baptismal Service

In the third part of this liturgy, the Baptismal service, all who have been instructed in the faith are sacramentally joined with Christ in baptism. It is in baptism that Christians are made members of Christ and sharers in his death and resurrection. In baptism, Christ rescues us from the kingdom of darkness and raises us into his own kingdom of light. Therefore, it is on this great night, looking forward to the dawn of resurrection, that the Church welcomes new members and invites Christians to renew their baptismal promises.

Baptism is both an individual and a social affair. For the individual, baptism is a new birth, a dying and rising with Christ. But it is also an initiation into the Church. In the new Passover from death to life, baptism makes Christians the new People of God. Thus the Easter Vigil is a celebration of

The celebration of Baptism is a high point of the Easter Vigil.

the Christian community. In the renewal of baptismal promises, Christians testify to each other that they explicitly and corporately undertake the obligation of these promises. They then join in the Christian prayer, the Our Father.

Conclusion to the Drama

The fourth part of the liturgy, the Eucharistic service, is a perfect conclusion to the drama of the night. Emulating Mary Magdalene in the Gospel of the Vigil Mass, Christians seek Jesus, who was crucified and who has risen, and find him in their Easter Communion.

In the prayers after Communion, Christians pray that all who have taken part in this night will be filled with the Spirit and may live together in love and peace. The service closes with the glad chanting of the alleluia.

---

17. The Easter Vigil is celebrated at night and it uses the symbols of fire and light to begin the service. What religious significance do you see in these details?

Forty Days After Easter: The Ascension

The word **ascension** means "a going up." The feast seems to celebrate Jesus' being "lifted off the earth," as Luke puts it in the Acts of the Apostles. See Acts of the Apostles 1:9; Mark 16:19; Luke 24:51 for more details. Painters throughout the centuries have depicted Jesus ascending into a cloud.

Since you know that heaven is not up or out there beyond the farthest star, what are the evangelists and artists saying about this feast? To human beings, going up (an action that defies the pull of gravity and suggests heavenly ascent) is different from what people are naturally used to. Ordinarily, things fall down. Walking down steps is an experience of one's own heaviness. The ability to rise overcomes that obstacle which binds us to the earth.

In Mark's Gospel we are told that "the Lord Jesus, after he spoke to them, was taken up into heaven and took his seat at the right hand of God" (Mark 16:19). The evangelist is trying to express in human terms what is really inexpressible: that Jesus, the very man whom the Apostles knew and loved and lived with, was glorified, that he was somehow equal with God.

What is the meaning of the Ascension?

Pentecost: Feast of the Holy Spirit

Pentecost means "fiftieth day," or the feast day which we celebrate fifty days after Easter. Actually, Pentecost was a Jewish celebration *(Shabuoth)* which commemorated God's Covenant with the people given to Moses in the Ten Commandments on Mt. Sinai. The Christian liturgy of Pentecost praises God for the new Covenant, offered to us by Jesus and sealed by the sending of the Holy Spirit.

The third person of the Trinity, the Holy Spirit, may seem less a person than the Father and the Son. Christians tend to think of the Spirit as a rushing wind, a burning flame, or a dove. The Bible does not say the Holy Spirit is these things, but that he is like them. Some of the qualities of the Spirit include power (the strength of the mighty wind); spirit (the gentleness and peace of a dove); and fire (the brightness and cheerfulness of a cozy fireplace drawing all to its warmth).

Beneath all of these symbols arises one single quality that is more personal than anything known: the very heart of God, love. The Holy Spirit is love as a person. As God's gift to the world, the Spirit lives in the midst of believers to bring out in them their potential to love.

In the letter of Saint Paul, the Holy Spirit teaches the characteristics of genuine Christian love of neighbor: "Love is patient, love is kind. It is not jealous, [love] is not pompous, it is not inflated, it is not rude, it does not seek its own interests, it is not quick-tempered, it does not brood over injury" (Corinthians 13:4-5).

In the letter to the Ephesians, Saint Paul says that what binds people to one another is not their love, but actually God's own love—the Holy Spirit: "[Strive] to preserve the unity of the Spirit through the bond of peace: one body and one Spirit" (Ephesians 4:3-4).

Pentecost (the celebration of the presence of the Holy Spirit in the followers of Jesus) teaches that unless we love with God's love (that is, in the Spirit), it will be hard, even impossible, to love truly and consistently.

Pentecost is celebrated as the birth of the Church.

Chapter 11 Cycles of Time in the Worship of the Church

18. List five things you associate with the Holy Spirit.

19. The feast of Pentecost is called "the birthday of the Church." In what sense is that true?

Ordinary Time

On the day after Pentecost, Ordinary Time begins again and extends until the Saturday before the first Sunday of Advent. This is a period of deepening one's life in the Gospel spirit by prayer and service to others. The Sunday readings of this time bring out many themes that serve as an instruction on God's plan of salvation.

Three feasts are prominent in the period of Ordinary Time after Easter. Trinity Sunday, the first Sunday after Pentecost, celebrates the mysterious revelation Christ made of the Father's mercy. It points out his own divine Sonship and the Holy Spirit's presence in the Church as well as in the hearts of all people who love God. Corpus Christi (Body of Christ), celebrated on the following Sunday, worships the real presence of Christ in the Eucharist. On the last Sunday before the beginning of Advent, the feast of Christ the King commemorates the coming reign of Christ over the entire universe and in all hearts.

Many people celebrate the feast of Corpus Christi by marching and praying in a procession.

Summary

- Lent is a time of self-denial. It is also an opportunity to express our willingness to grow closer to Christ and his ultimate sacrifice of self through positive activities of love.

- Easter is the feast of the Paschal Mystery. Jesus, who was crucified, was raised up to new life, a life we too will enjoy with him forever.

- Pentecost celebrates the sending of God's Holy Spirit, the Spirit of love and truth, who guides the Church on its way to the fullness of Christ.

Worship and Sacraments: We Celebrate, We Praise

SECTION 3
Checkpoint!

■ Review

1. How can self-denial be a positive thing?

2. Why is Lent a time for giving more freely of ourselves?

3. Why is Easter the climax of the Liturgical Year?

4. How does the "Alleluia" prayer express the spirit of this season?

5. What is the meaning of the Ascension?

6. What does the feast of Pentecost celebrate?

7. Words to Know: Lent, Ash Wednesday, Easter, Pentecost, Ascension, Easter Vigil Service, Paschal Candle, alleluia, fasting, abstinence, Ordinary Time.

■ In Your World

1. What are some positive things you can do as a class to increase individual motivation to persevere in a penance throughout Lent?

2. In your own words, describe the faith that we celebrate in the Easter liturgy. How can this faith help us be more helpful as we confront difficulties and suffering in our daily lives?

■ Scripture Search

1. Study the stories of Jesus' appearances after his resurrection. How is the risen Lord Jesus **both** like and unlike Jesus as the disciples knew him before his death? Read Luke 24:13-49 and John 20:11-29 for answers.

2. Read the story of Pentecost in the Acts of the Apostles (2:1-41). How does this story describe the descent of the Holy Spirit?

CHAPTER 11 Review

■ Study

1. What is the purpose of the liturgical year?
2. What is the special importance of Sundays in the liturgical cycle?
3. What is meant by the term "liturgical seasons"?
4. Explain the liturgical seasons and what they celebrate.
5. How do celebrations help us to experience the **effect** of events that are recalled? (Hint: Think of birthday celebrations or anniversaries.)
6. Describe the importance of Advent in Christian worship.
7. How does the Incarnation affect our relationship with God and our salvation?
8. Did Christians always celebrate Christmas? Give a brief history of this liturgical feast.
9. What is the spirit and three purposes of Lent?
10. What do Christians celebrate at Easter?
11. Why do we say that every Sunday is a mini-celebration of the Paschal Mystery (Good Friday and Easter Sunday)?
12. Describe the religious significance of the Ascension and Pentecost.
13. What is Ordinary Time in the liturgical calendar?

■ Action

1. Research the meaning of the various colors of the vestments worn by the priest at Mass. What do the colors signify and which colors are used for which liturgical seasons?
2. Find out the next major feast or solemnity coming up on the liturgical calendar. Discuss the meaning of this "sacred time," the readings used at Mass, and how this celebration fits into the liturgical cycle.
3. Study the liturgy of Good Friday. What are the parts of this service? How many readings are there? Why do people venerate the cross? What groups of people are prayed for on this day? Why do you think the Church prays for them at this time?

■ Prayer

This class prayer is modeled after the Liturgy of the Hours described in the "Ways of Worship" feature on page 282. To celebrate this public prayer, select a leader and a reader. Separate the class into two parts (e.g., right and left sides or men and women). Light a candle to symbolize Christ's presence among you. Then begin your prayer. (Remain seated until the Gospel reading. Then remain standing until the end of the prayer.)

Leader: O God, come to my assistance. **All:** Lord, make haste to help me.

Leader: Glory be to the Father, the Son, and the Holy Spirit. **All:** As it was in the beginning, is now and ever shall be, world without end. Amen.

Leader: Praise the Lord, O my soul. **All:** I will praise the Lord all my life.

Side 1:	**Side 2:**
Sing joyfully to the Lord all your lands.	Break into songs, sing praise.
Sing praise to the Lord with the harp.	With the harp and melodious song.
With trumpets and the sound of the horn.	Sing joyfully before the King, the Lord.

Leader: Praise the Lord, O my soul. **All:** I will praise the Lord all my life.

Reader: Let us stand as we hear a reading from the Gospel according to Luke, chapter 1, verses 39-56. (All are silent for the reading of Scripture.)

Reader: This is the Gospel of the Lord. **All:** Praise to you, Lord Jesus Christ.

Leader: Let us offer our praise and petitions to God. The response to our prayers is: "Lord, hear us."

Class: (Volunteers offer prayers as in the "Prayers of the Faithful" at Mass. At the end of each prayer, the volunteer says, "We pray to the Lord.")

All: (After each petition) Lord, hear us.

Leader: (After all class prayers have been offered) Let us pray now as Jesus has taught us.

All: (Recite the "Our Father" together holding hands uplifted.)

—Psalm 146:1-20 and 98:4-6.

CHAPTER

12

Taking Time to Praise God

OBJECTIVES

In this Chapter you will

- Understand the meaning of spirituality and gain an appreciation for Catholic spirituality.

- Discover ways of deepening your spiritual life through prayer and discernment.

- See how Catholics praise God by the way they live their lives in the world.

For everything created by God is good and nothing is to be rejected when received with thanksgiving, for it is made holy by the invocation of God in prayer.
—1 Timothy 4:4-5

SECTION 1
Understanding Spirituality

The seniors at Central Catholic High School were finishing a unit on religious traditions which differ from the Catholic tradition when they let it be known that they wanted to study a more "practical" topic. When the teacher asked what that topic might be, they said, "our spiritual life."

The term "spiritual life" can be misleading because it seems to separate the "life of the spirit" from "real life." Many people identify the "life of the spirit" with God and the Church and "real life" with day-to-day realities like school, work, recreation, family life, and interactions with others. Actually, there is no separation between your spirit and your life. What goes on in your spirit (psyche) shapes your everyday activities, and your day-to-day actions influence your spirit. Instead, you are what you long for, what you value, and what you have faith in, as revealed uniquely through your bodily activities.

Spirituality and Becoming More Human

To be a human being is to be spirit, and to be spirit is to be God-like. Of all creation, only we can center our lives on spiritual matters like values, hopes, and goals. Only human beings have spirituality or a spiritual life. We don't just live; we live with a perspective that looks beyond the present moment and our own welfare. We can freely decide what we want to live for and what we want to care about; that is our spirituality. It develops moment by moment out of our past experiences, our present values, and our vision of the future. Even if we choose not to care, then that is what we stand for and what we want to care about, and that is our spirituality. This means that everyone has a spiritual life.

For Example

The idea of "truth" may be a strong value in your life, and your spirituality may center on your quest for truth and right and justice. If you are a nature lover, your approach to God, the world, and the People of God will usually reflect your love affair with nature.

The question, then, is not **whether** you will have a spirituality, but **which** spirituality is worthy of you as a human being. Some spiritualities are humanly destructive. Under their tyranny, people barely survive, become dehumanized, and possibly enslaved by the false promises of drugs, alcohol, wealth, power, fame, and sex. Some non-Christian spiritualities may uphold noble ideals, such as respect for life and nonviolence. Some may be inconsistent or off target in their pursuit of true life, liberty, and happiness.

Catholic Christians believe that of all the spiritualities that have evolved in human history, none measures up to the way of life given to us by Jesus.

Spirituality, then, in its widest meaning, is the entire framework out of which you live. It concerns your past and your future. It is your total approach to life: all that you cherish and dream, and all that you do to make your dreams come true. It is the rudder of your ship.

If the term "spiritual life" refers to a person's entire framework of values, "spirituality" is the unique expressions of your spiritual life. It has a flavor all its own (yours), but it may reflect certain qualities in common with others.

---

1. *How can an action such as surprising someone with a gift affect your attitude toward the person? Toward yourself?*

2. *Although we all possess values and goals, we are not always fully aware of them. Insofar as you can, write down the three things that hold **top** priority in your life. How do you foster them?*

3. *Name some non-Christians who have achieved a high quality of life. What elements of Christ's values did they hold?*

The Foundation of Catholic Spirituality

It is said that the genius of the great Renaissance man, Leonardo da Vinci, consisted in his insight that all creation exists in a beautiful harmony of relationships. By noting interconnections, he was able to open new worlds of meaning and power in the arts and sciences.

Despite the incredible technological progress of our century, many people throughout the world experience their lives as fragmented, powerless, alienated, and meaningless—in a word, out of harmony. They search in vain for inner peace. They find their interpersonal relationships, whether in the family, at school, on the job, or other social situations torn apart by competition, jealousy, selfishness, and violence. On the world level, excessive nationalism, greed, and lust for power create tension, hunger, and war. "What's it all about?" sums up the question on everyone's lips.

Worship and Sacraments: We Celebrate, We Praise

Seeking Ultimate Meaning: The Spiritual Quest

One commentator on the spiritual life writes that true Christian lives have **purpose** as well as **meaning.** Each of these characteristics is accompanied by different attitudes and has different effects.

When you do something for a **purpose**, your aim is achievement; you control the circumstances to reach a desired outcome. When the action is over, the purpose is achieved. If your purpose is to mow a lawn, you start the mower, climb on or push the mower, and cut the grass. All the while you are looking to the moment when the lawn will be cut. When the job is done, you can keep riding or pushing the mower, but the purpose has already been achieved.

Life is full of purpose. People keep going, keep smiling, keep busy—all to get things done. But getting at the meaning of what is being done is a different matter. It invites risks. And to seek the ultimate meaning is the basis of the spiritual life; it is the quest for God.

When something has **meaning** for you, you use expressions like, "It really touched me," "It blew my mind," or "Something just hit me." You become the passive recipient instead of the active agent. In contrast to fulfilling a purpose in which you **take** things in hand, you have to **give** yourself to the meaning. You must have a certain disposition of readiness or openness, and leave some "slack in the line."

♦

Catholic spirituality is founded on faith in God's love as revealed in his divine Son, Jesus Christ (2 Corinthians 5:17–18). In being joined to Jesus, we are restored to a gifted relationship with God and learn what all our other relationships are to be if our lives are to have meaning and our society is to be healed.

Being in love affects how we think and feel, how we relate to others, and how we perceive the world.

Chapter 12   Taking Time to Praise God

On the Record

Three Spiritual Giants

1. Saint Francis Assisi (1181-1226) was the founder of the Franciscan Order. Leaving his life as a rich merchant's son, he became poor for the Lord. Saint Francis glorified God in the beauties of creation, speaking of Brother Sun and Sister Moon. His life was characterized by joyful simplicity.

2. Saint Ignatius of Loyola (1492-1556), founder of the Society of Jesus (the Jesuits), was a soldier of God. Converted to a spiritual life while recovering from a wound suffered in battle, Ignatius saw life as a battlefield on which one fights evil. His spirituality is characterized by discipline, obedience, and heroism.

3. Saint Therese of Lisieux (1873-1897) entered a Carmelite convent at the age of fifteen and spent her short life doing ordinary things extraordinarily well. The depth of Saint Therese's love for God allowed the ordinary things she did to take on great value because of her motive for doing them.

Anyone who has been in love understands that any deep relationship has an impact on how we think and feel about everything, how we relate to others, and how we perceive the world. Friendship with God provides a new view of ourselves, links us at a deeper level with all God's children, and gives us a more meaningful perspective on evil and suffering.

Unlike the love of a possessive spouse, God's love does not smother our personality or demand that we abandon our identity or our humanness. God does not require us to turn from the world. In fact, the more we open ourselves to reality, the more like God we become, the more God-like we grow, and the more our true self emerges.

4. How does faith in God's love affect our worth? Our relationship with others? Our relationship with the nonhuman world? Our attitudes toward evil and suffering? What disorders of modern society could it heal?

The Secret of Catholic Spirituality

The impact of Catholic spirituality will be apparent in everything you do. Perhaps you know a mechanic or cook who can turn a humble job into a work of art. These experts make you realize that a thing done with care and love becomes greater than the work itself. Their sense of high purpose turns it into an act of worship, accomplished with God's help. At a time when magnanimity has become rare, these people who excel stand out for their magnanimity, that fullness of life that lifts the soul. We are surprised when a gas station attendant or a clerk in a store goes beyond the usual duty in a generous gesture. We take note of people who show devotion to a disabled person, forgive the murderer of their child, or go out of their way to protect an endangered species. These devoted people's sense of mission and inner peace intrigue us. What is their secret?

The secret of Christian spirituality is to make all of life a prayer, a continuous act of adoration of our Father. We try to find God in everything and live always in God's presence. True Christians don't do work for the sake of work or live for the sake of life, just to get it over with. They're called to live in a spirit of leisure. Leisure does not imply slow motion or laziness. It is a quality of mind that keeps you open to what God has to say to you in the grain of wood you're finishing, in the softness of the towel you're drying with, in the harmony of the numbers you're computing, in the uniqueness of the child you're babysitting—it's listening to what God has to say to you.

Catholic Christians take for their model Mary, who burst into song while visiting and serving Elizabeth. When we are aware of God's presence with us in all that we do, we want to sing, whether we work or whether we play. Joy is the result of a life that includes its divine dimensions. As Elizabeth recognized Christ in Mary, the world gets a glimpse of God when Christians pass by.

5. Can you think of some people you know who demonstrate magnanimity? What characteristics of theirs do you most admire?

6. How can "leisure" be an important part of a person's spiritual development? Give some examples.

Summary

- Spirituality is living life in the image and likeness of God. The spiritual person recognizes the importance of having a religious perspective and of making room in life for the action of God's Spirit.

- Catholic spirituality is founded on faith in God's love as revealed in Jesus Christ and lived out in the Christian community.

- The "secret" of Catholic spirituality is to make all of life a prayer and to find God in everything we do.

Simple things you do, such as helping at home, can be part of your spirituality.

Magnanimity: "being great-souled," or extremely generous.

SECTION 1
Checkpoint!

■ Review

1. Make a list of three attitudes or actions which cannot be defined as "spiritual" and three that can. Give reasons for your choice of examples.

2. What does "magnanimity" have to do with living a spiritual life?

3. Who were Saint Francis, Saint Ignatius, and Saint Therese? How are these three people good examples of Catholic spirituality?

4. What is the difference between purpose and meaning? How does this distinction help us to understand the quest for spiritual insight better?

5. Words to Know: spirituality, spiritual life, magnanimity, purpose, meaning.

■ In Your World

1. Suppose you have been asked to write a spiritual autobiography. Survey your life and compose a list of chapter titles that summarize your spiritual journey so far.

2. What changes would you expect to occur in a person's spirituality as he or she passes from childhood, to adolescence, to adulthood, and finally to old age?

■ Scripture Search

1. Read Luke 1:26-56. How does Mary's visit to Elizabeth demonstrate Mary's spirituality?

2. It is said that genius consists of never forgetting first principles. Jesus gave us the key to genius in the art of Christian spirituality when he said, "Seek first the kingdom of God and his righteousness, and all these things will be given you besides" (Matthew 6:33). What does this mean to you?

SECTION 2
Growing in the Spiritual Life

No relationship can remain static. It must either develop dynamically toward greater intensity and fuller union or it will begin to disintegrate. Our relationship with God raises questions applicable to other relationships: Is our relationship going anywhere? What am I doing to hold it together? Am I allowing other preoccupations to get in the way? How does this relationship enhance the total quality of life?

More Than Keeping the Law

For Catholics, just keeping the commandments is not enough to support a growing relationship with God. We are called to be sensitive to much more demanding unwritten laws: the voices within that alert us to the slightest promptings of the Holy Spirit. Spirituality becomes a story of the instinctive union of hearts that grounds our lives and affects our very destiny.

Christians are not the only ones who have recognized this voice within which calls us to go beyond ourselves. Socrates referred to "a kind of inner voice" that he noticed as a child. He called it his "inner oracle," which was more than "head knowledge" or reason. The ancient Chinese had an awareness of the need to unite with a large plan to find fulfillment. They used the word *yi* to mean the "oughtness of life" (the things we ought to do) and *ming* to express one's fate or destiny, which Kung Fu-tzu (Confucius, in Latin) believed was the will of heaven.

Socrates (469-399 B.C.): a Greek philosopher unafraid to speak out for what he believed to be true and right.

Chapter 12 Taking Time to Praise God

Touching the Sacred

How can friends be a source of inspiration for you?

Taking Advantage of Prayer

Knowing the purpose of prayer and the kinds of prayer available to you will help you to take advantage of all the benefits that can be derived when you lift your mind and heart to God.

- *Kinds of Prayer*

Private: our own individual prayers.

Public: prayers with the community, including liturgy.

Formal: set prayer forms, like the "Our Father."

Informal: prayers we offer in our own words.

- *Purpose of Prayer*

Adoration: praising God.

Contrition: prayers seeking God's forgiveness.

Thanksgiving: prayers of gratitude.

Supplication: begging God's help.

Such obedience can be very challenging because our inner nudges often lack the sureness of scientific precision and clear-cut logic. We're not concerned with rightness and wrongness only, but with the appropriateness of the action as well. We ask ourselves, "What kind of person does this sort of thing? Is that the kind of person I am or want to become?" But for such questions we see "indistinctly, as in a mirror" (1 Corinthians 13:12). And if we neglect our inspirations, they can weaken, and we will find ourselves traveling without the guidance of the only One who knows where we ought to be headed.

Therefore, a sound spirituality must be grounded in **humility** a basic self-respect that allows us to honestly face our limitations. We acknowledge the mystery of life and our need of assistance by earnest prayer and by consulting others when in doubt. To keep the inner voices of our fallen selves from drowning out the gentler voices, we need regular periods of communication with God in prayer and the study of Scripture. We must also constantly work to identify and eliminate false values, such as too much concern for money, excessive desire for popularity, too great a love of convenience, food, drink, and pleasure, as well as laziness, which can drown out God's will and lead to self-destruction. These values require discernment.

Faith needs constantly to be nourished by the support of our church community and by active participation in the sacraments, especially the Eucharist and Reconciliation. Having a person to help us on our Christian journey is helpful, but God is the spiritual director par excellence and the most faithful "survival partner" we can have. Keeping the channels of communication with God open through prayer is one of the surest avenues to a maturing spiritual life.

8. Why are periods of reflection and silence important for becoming the person God destines us to be? When do you encounter such periods?

9. Why is the sacrament of Penance especially important to taking the right direction in life?

10. How do Church teaching, the Mass, devotion to Mary and the saints, and the liturgical year affect a Catholic's discernment?

Christian Prayer

Because relationships cannot exist, much less grow, without communication, prayer is the lifeblood of the spiritual life. So essential is prayer to our relationship with God that Saint Paul exhorts us, "Pray without ceasing" (1 Thessalonians 5:17). Through prayer we attain God-awareness and self-awareness and draw closer to God.

There are many forms of prayer and techniques for praying. Not all of them appeal to everyone. You must experiment and find the prayer style that is right for you. The only way to learn to pray is by praying. You can pray in highly intensive ways or in secondary, peripheral ways.

For some practical ideas on growing to prayer, consider how the following real people responded when they were asked, "What is your favorite way to pray? Why?"

- **A grandmother who cleans office buildings—**
  "I pray while I work. As I mop floors and wash dishes, I talk to God in my own words. There is always

Obedience: from a Latin root meaning "to listen" or "to hear."

Discernment: the process of sifting through all our experiences in the light of faith to identify what is authentic.

Spiritual director: a person experienced in prayer and spiritual living who directs others on their journeys.

Prayer: raising the mind and heart to God.

Chapter 12 Taking Time to Praise God

something to thank him for. If I am burdened with something, I discuss it with him and I know he hears. Talking with God brings me close to him and lifts my spirits."

- **A construction worker**—"I begin each day with the Sign of the Cross, and I thank and praise the Lord for a new day. Before leaving for work, I bless my wife and each of my nine children. Then I go to church to read the Bible for about a half hour and think about God's words. The Mass is my greatest source of strength and has carried me through many difficulties. On my way to work, I remember the Lord's presence with me and try to bring his blessing to everyone I meet."

- **A secretary and mother of four grown children**—"My best-loved prayers are the novena to Our Lady of Perpetual Help and prayers to the Infant of Prague, Saint Jude, and the Holy Spirit. These ready-made prayers express my innermost thoughts and feelings. They lead me to meditate on my requests, to thank God for her blessings, and to search for ways to improve myself."

- **A diocesan priest**—"I need the dimension of community prayer in the Mass to relate to God along with my believing and worshiping brothers and sisters. I also need private prayer when I listen to God in different ways. In a quiet setting, preferably a church or chapel, I read, pray the rosary, or walk slowly, realizing the all-present God. Sometimes I kneel or sit and focus on the source of all life, love, and truth."

- **A high school senior**—"I pray best in the woods, in my backyard, or while riding my bike."

Catholics are called to constant prayer: on the job, at school, at play, or in church.

11. Saint Jerome said that ignorance of Scripture is ignorance of Christ. Why must all prayer ultimately be rooted in Scripture?

12. How do Christians come to know the Word of God? Why do Christians have different degrees of familiarity with it?

13. Which methods of praying described in this section have you used? What is your favorite way of praying now? What are some ways you want to experiment with?

Discernment: Knowing What to Do

We are constantly called to make decisions that alter the courses of our lives, and every day brings its share of minor decisions to be made, too.

Like Jesus, whose entire life was a fulfillment of his Father's will, we pray, "Thy will be done." However, to know God's will sometimes presents a real dilemma. The process of arriving at a right decision through prayer and the guidance of the Holy Spirit is called discernment. To determine if an impulse to act is from God, follow these suggestions:

- ■ ***Evaluate*** the proposed action by means of objective norms found in God's Word (in Scripture and in tradition). An act or its consequences which are incompatible with God's Word are suspect.

- ■ ***Evaluate*** the proposed action by means of subjective norms (subtle interior feelings). Peace of mind indicates a correct decision; there is a comfortableness in relating to God regarding the decision. An experience of joy, love, and peace may indicate union with God. On the other hand, discontent, tears, or sorrow are not necessarily signals that the Lord wants a particular decision.

- ■ ***Gather facts*** by consulting books and helpful people. List the pros and cons of the action. Use logic.

- ■ ***Discuss*** the decision with the Lord. Consider how the action will affect your relationship with God and ask for divine help.

- ■ ***Take*** plenty of time to make a major decision.

You will know if you have made the right decision. However, a choice contrary to God's Will will cause turmoil, anger, diminished love, and cynicism.

Learning to make good decisions may be one of the most difficult challenges you face. The guidance of the Holy Spirit can help you discern the truth.

Fostering Your Spiritual Life

Because the spiritual life is basically your way of relating to God, yourself, others, and the world, there is no standing still. You are always either forging ahead or backsliding. There are several time-tested ways to ensure continual growth in your ability to love. One way is to insert periods for silence and solitude into your schedule. Every day you can nurture your inner self and foster your relationship with God through quiet prayer and reflection. Occasionally, you will need longer stretches of time for renewal, which involves reviewing, refocusing, and recharging. For this purpose, you can participate in days of recollection, renewal, and retreat. It is also helpful to have a guide or spiritual director to help nurture your spirituality.

In addition to depending on a particular spiritual guide for assistance in the spiritual life, belonging to a support system of loving Christian friends is a real advantage. Through the experience of praying together and sharing insights, mutual concern, and love, members of a Christian community advance together toward their shared vision: union with God. Recognizing the strength that comes from corporate faith, believers have always helped one another by the support of their example at public worship, usually once a week. However, many people today, besides establishing Christian households, are forming prayer or Bible study groups. Becoming involved with others in your parish community can open up a whole new world. Nothing will strengthen your faith more than sharing your spirituality with others.

The sincere effort to live out your personal covenant with Christ in persevering service to others prevents your spirituality from degenerating into mere privatism, the kind of religion exemplified by the woman who thought herself a good Christian because she read the Bible every day but would never lift a finger to help anyone. Service to others that is inspired by loyalty to Christ can strengthen and support the emotional stimulation of conversion, a renewal, or a spiritual retreat. Warm and human love, based on the realization of God's personal call to everyone, keeps us from cold institutionalism. And our zeal causes us to reach out to broader horizons as we help others or as we participate in Church ministry.

If you are serious about developing a prayer life, select someone to serve as a Spiritual Guide.

Another source of nurturing the spiritual life is reading. Ideas on spirituality are as close as the nearest bookstore. There are books on methods of prayer, living a good life, suffering, the life of Christ, the Church in the world, and other topics. However, the Bible remains the most influential book in shaping our spiritual lives. Prayerfully reading the Word of God makes us more perceptive to God's actions, more desirous of the Will of God in our lives, and more open to divine grace.

How do you know if you are growing in your spiritual life? Spirituality is not determined by the number of times you attend church or by the number of religious books you have read. The most reliable indicators of righteous living are the absence of selfishness in your life and the presence of love, joy, peace, and the other gifts of the Holy Spirit (Galatians 5:22).

14. *Which of the ways of fostering spiritual life described above appeals to you? Have you been involved in any of them? If so, share your experience.*

Summary

- God calls us to grow in our spiritual lives and to deepen our relationship.

- Our spirituality is nourished by a life of prayer. When we pray, we allow God to work in us more effectively and intensely.

- We can progress in the spiritual life by making retreats, having a spiritual director, forming support groups, and being faithful to our spiritual reading.

Chapter 12 Taking Time to Praise God

SECTION 2
Checkpoint!

■ Review

1. Why is humility necessary for the spiritual life?
2. What are the four kinds of prayer? Give examples of each.
3. List as many ways as you can to grow in spirituality.
4. What is discernment? How does this practice help us to make right decisions?
5. What are the four purposes of prayer?
6. Words to Know: humility, discernment, spiritual director, private prayer, public prayer, formal prayer, informal prayer.

■ In Your World

1. Interview one or two people about their favorite way of praying. Draw conclusions and then write a report.
2. Discuss the "Lord's Prayer" in class. Study this beautiful prayer together line by line. Identify the "purposes" evident in this prayer and discuss the spirituality that Jesus was calling us to when he gave this prayer to us.

■ Scripture Search

1. Saint Paul experienced the same "tug" of sin that we do. Read Philippians 3:10-16. What advice does he give to other participants in the race?
2. What are some of the important ingredients for a good spiritual life which Saint Paul suggests in 1 Thessalonians 5:12-19?

SECTION 3
Praising God in the World

Everyone has his or her own *Weltanschauung*, that is, a comprehension of the world or world outlook. To discover your *Weltanschauung*, decide whether or not you would approve of each of the following actions:

- *Disgusted with the world, Peggy decides to join a cloistered community of nuns.*
- *Seeking a simple life, Tim moves his family to the country where they raise their own food without the electrical gadgets that complicate modern life.*
- *Theresa is very talented in art. Out of humility, when she draws or makes things, she lets others get the credit.*
- *Instead of just praying and trusting in God, Larry spends considerable money going to a psychiatrist for help with his problems.*
- *Margie enjoys life. She always finds time for dances, concerts, movies, swimming, horseback riding, and camping trips.*
- *In discussing birth control, Lucy says, "If you ask me, I think the Church should stay out of my bedroom."*

In certain eras of the past, Christians considered the world evil. You have probably heard of men and women who took up residence in the desert in order to avoid the world. A person's holiness was considered in proportion to how much he or she refrained from earthly pleasures and showed contempt for the world. Saints supposedly did not enjoy such adventures as a dip in the lake, a glass of choice wine, an exquisite ballet, and certainly not sex. The body, thought of as the lesser part of their being, had to be

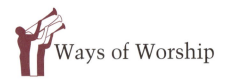
Ways of Worship

The Worship of Christian Witness

Dr. Martin Luther King, Jr. was a young African-American Baptist minister in Montgomery, Alabama who had a charismatic personality and a gift for delivering masterful sermons. It was Dr. King who was the leading proponent in abolishing the humiliating practices of the South that denied African-Americans their rights as human beings and as American citizens.

Dr. King was awarded the Nobel Peace Prize in 1964 for his nonviolent resistance to social injustice. To combat discrimination on buses ("colored" people had to sit in the rear of buses and relinquish their seats to white people), King engineered a massive boycott. African-Americans walked, taxied, or formed car pools rather than ride the buses. To induce restaurants and businesses that refused to serve African-Americans to change their policies, he staged sit-ins and demonstrations. On April 6, 1968, Dr. King was assassinated for his beliefs and works.

subdued for the soul to be saved. The secret of a good life was to deal with this world as little as possible and to await the rewards of the next.

Taking a Positive Approach

Vatican II turned that thinking completely around. At the opening of the Second Session, Pope Paul VI said: "May the world know that the Church looks at it with profound understanding, with a sincere admiration, sincerely disposed, not to subjugate it, but to serve it, not to depreciate it, but to appreciate it, not to condemn it, but to sustain and serve it."

This positive approach to the world goes back to Genesis. After each phase of the earth's creation, God saw that it was good. And on the sixth day, "God looked at everything he had made, and he found it very good" (Genesis 1:31).

Dr. Martin Luther King, Jr. chose to be a force of love in the world, even though his action led to his untimely death.

Even after sin entered the world, spoiling its pristine beauty, God "so **loved** the world that he gave his only Son" (John 3:16a). Jesus explained, "He has anointed me to bring glad tidings to the poor. He has sent me to proclaim liberty to captives and recovery of sight to the blind, [and] to let the oppressed go free" (Luke 4:18). By dwelling among us, delighting in the things of the earth, and working as a healer on the road as well as on the cross, Jesus, the God-man, redeemed the world. He saved us, body and soul and spirit, and won for us the resurrection of the flesh. On the evening of the resurrection, Jesus said to his followers, "As the Father has sent me, so I send you" (John 20:21b). Faith does not remove us from the world, but leads us deeper into it.

Christians continue the redemptive work of Christ. Acting as light and leaven, they live in the world as saving agents. Baptism commits Christians to be apostolic, that is, to be a divine force of love in the world, perfecting it until that day when Christ keeps his promise and returns. On that day, the time for building the kingdom on earth will be over, and all creation will shine forth the glory of God.

At times of violent outbursts of evil, along with other features of our day and time, we may long to cry out the words of an old play, **Stop the World, I Want to Get Off!** Among these features are excessive materialism, exploitation, bureaucracy, accelerated change, imperialism, loneliness, tension, burnout, and boredom. People are confused, starving for the Absolute, but uncertain of how to find it.

Perhaps more than ever, the world needs the presence of the Savior with his offer of hope. The salvation he brings, which is the "great gift of God," is "liberation from everything that oppresses man or woman but is, above all, liberation from sin and the Evil One" (Paul VI, *"On Evangelization in the Modern World,"* #9).

Vatican II links the Church with humankind: "The joys and the hopes, the griefs and the anxieties of the [people] of this age, especially those who are poor or in any way afflicted, these too are the joys and hopes, the griefs and anxieties of the followers of Christ" (Vatican II, *"The Church in the Modern World,"* #1). Since they are a community of people who have welcomed the news of

God's salvation brings joy, such as that experienced by a former hostage reunited with his family.

salvation that is meant for all people, Christians are intimately joined to humankind and its history. With all people, they are on a pilgrimage toward the possession of the Truth.

15. Soap operas and sitcoms portray one view of contemporary life. How have recent shows reflected the problems, unChristian attitudes, and warped values of society?

16. What groups are making an effort to counteract specific evils in the world?

17. What are some good features of the modern world?

Christians as Light

Concentrating on the woes of the world can be discouraging or depressing, but we should not look at the world through rose-colored glasses. Christians should strive for a balanced, realistic view of the world. Aided by revelation, we must be sources of light and hope for this planet.

It is up to us to humanize and spiritualize the world, to work for a better world and a better spirit, and to bridge heaven and earth, time and eternity. According to the Christian mentality, since salvation is attained here, this world cannot be divorced from the next, nor life from religion; the secular and the sacred merge.

We share the light of Christ by certain attitudes toward life that we demonstrate. Here are a few examples of Christian attitudes that can spiritualize the world. We might call these attitudes the "Christian facts of life."

- **The environment** is entrusted to us for our use, but also for our care and protection. As stewards of the world, we maintain the balance of nature through environmental and ecological control, and regulate the consumption of natural resources.

Worship and Sacraments: We Celebrate, We Praise

- ***Human acts*** *are meaningful. Christ is found acting in daily events. The love of God is usually pursued in ordinary circumstances and routine actions. Because in this light even the most ordinary acts are related to the kingdom, human enterprises and efforts are worthwhile.*

- ***Other people*** *are fellow members of the human family, the Family of God. Therefore, we are responsible for the world community and bound to work for the spread of peace and justice. Because each person has God-given dignity and destiny, we believe in the equality of all, respect differences, and stand for human rights, especially freedom and the right to life.*

- ***Progress*** *is God's leading us to unfold the mysteries of time and space in order to improve society. Conquests in space, communications, environment, and technology reveal the riches of the earth. There is much to be learned from the world. For instance, the findings of psychology and sociology tell us more about ourselves. When illumined by the light of faith, progress is good, not frightening.*

- ***Pain and struggle*** *play a role in the perfection of the world, though they remain a mystery. Through the cross, Jesus redeemed the world. In union with his suffering, our suffering somehow furthers the fulfillment of God's plan for the world. In this hope, we find strength.*

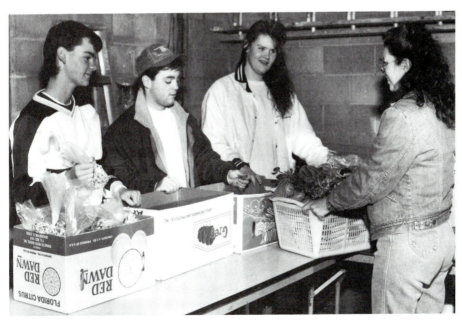

For Christians, human acts are meaningful. They are a way of witnessing Christ's love for others.

Chapter 12   Taking Time to Praise God

When we share with others the mystery of the Father's love and vision of the world as God has revealed it, then we are a light for the world, shining like a city set on a hill (Matthew 5:14-16).

---

18. *How could the Christian understanding of each of the "Christian facts of life" discussed here be conveyed to others by word or by deed? Be specific.*

19. *Sometimes Catholics find that their faith-life is divorced from their everyday life. Why is this? Why shouldn't it be this way?*

Christians as Leaven

What can be more delicious than homemade bread, baked to a golden brown, soft, warm, fragrant, and fresh from the oven? Bread would not be so tempting if it weren't for the one ingredient that makes it rise: yeast (or leaven). A bit of yeast expands a sticky mass of dough and transforms it into a loaf. In a homely comparison, Jesus says that the reign of God is like yeast (Matthew 13:33). More than

There is no other way to love God except through your neighbor.

Worship and Sacraments: We Celebrate, We Praise

History of the Relationship Between Church and State

In the year A.D. 800, Pope Leo III crowned Charlemagne emperor of the Holy Roman Empire, and, in turn, Charlemagne became the special protector of the Church. It was the era of a Christian Europe when Church and State were closely knit. A new barbarian onslaught splintered the Empire and gave rise to feudalism, in which bishops and abbots were involved in wars and politics. Because the pope governed the Papal States, the papacy, too, was a political power.

Beginning with Leo IX (1049), the reform popes reversed the situation. The papacy became a centralized government and the Church came to be ruled by Rome. The popes also engaged in a power struggle with secular rulers. The Church was involved in wars, treaties, and boundary disputes. By the sixteenth century, the papal court was more worldly (in the negative sense of the word) than religious. The Rome-dominated Church's preoccupation with politics was one reason for the formation of different Christian traditions like the Lutherans, Calvinists, and Anglicans.

In the sixteenth century, responding to the Reformation Movement, the Council of Trent initiated a religious reform movement that put the focus of the Church on doctrine, liturgy, and Catholic life. This Council and the multiplication of religious communities removed from the Roman Church the control of civil governments. Liberated from secular politics, it was better able to foster the kingdom of God. For the most part, the Church and the State each went their separate ways. Science, the rise of humanism, and political revolutions further divorced religion from direct involvement in national politics.

◆

anyone else, the laity, filled with the Holy Spirit, have the potential to penetrate the whole world with the Christian spirit. The role of the Christian unfolds in several directions: (1) by *kerygma,* the proclamation of the spoken word; (2) by *koinonia,* the witness of friendship in Christian community; (3) by *diakonia,* the witness of loving, personal service; and (4) by *leitourgia,* public celebration and thanksgiving for God's goodness in saving us. The reign of God will be established when enough people unleash the power of love in their spheres of influence: family, neighborhood, city, parish, school, factory, and office. They do this by assuming the threefold rules of prophets, healers, and humble servants, and by ministering to the needs of their sisters and brothers in the Lord.

Practically speaking, how can a Christian be leaven in today's world? Jesus revealed that our love for God and neighbor are not two loves, but one. He tells us that we love God by loving our neighbor. "I was hungry and you gave me food" (Matthew 25:35-40). There is no other way to love God except **through** your neighbor.

20. *How can young people be God's spokespersons? Healers? Servants?*

21. *What are some practical ways for teenagers to fulfill their spiritual lives by becoming leaven in the world?*

22. *What reasons can you give for putting social justice concerns high on your list of spiritual values as you live your life in the world?*

Summary

- It is the vocation of Christians to praise God by living their spiritual lives as witnesses for the world.

- As a light of the world, Christians show the way to God's kingdom by their attitudes and activities.

- As a leaven in the world, Christians are agents of change and hope in society.

SECTION 3
Checkpoint!

■ Review

1. Why is it not appropriate for Christians to hate the world?

2. What do we mean when we say that followers of Christ should "humanize and spiritualize" the world? What Christian attitudes ("facts of life") can help us do this?

3. What are *kerygma, koinonia, diakonia,* and *leitourgia* and what do these actions have to do with Christian life in the world?

4. How was Dr. Martin Luther King, Jr. light and leaven in the world?

5. Words to Know: *Weltanschauung, kerygma, koinonia, diakonia, leitourgia,* light of the world, leaven.

■ In Your World

1. Christians are called to be peacemakers, to work for reconciliation and harmony. Discuss how one becomes a peacemaker: the personal qualities that are necessary, the steps in bringing about reconciliation between you and another person or between two parties, and opportunities for being a peacemaker. Peace is not easily achieved. Sometimes risks are necessary. What might these risks be?

2. Many people feel a sense of powerlessness in the face of government and big business. Can the "little people" change the world? If so, how?

■ Scripture Search

1. Read Genesis 1:31, John 3:16, Luke 4:18, John 20:21, and 1 Timothy 4:4-5. What do these passages suggest about the world God created and God's attitude toward creatures and creation?

2. Discuss the teaching of Jesus in Matthew 5:14-16. How can this teaching help us to understand our relationship to the world?

CHAPTER 12 Review

■ Study

1. Why is "spiritual life" actually **human** life as God intended us to live it?

2. Write your own definition of spirituality.

3. What is the foundation of Christian spirituality? Explain.

4. If someone were to ask you the "secret" of Catholic spirituality, what would you answer? Explain.

5. In what sense is spirituality a relationship? With whom?

6. Since spirituality does indeed involve a relationship, why can't spiritual development ever reach a plateau and remain constant?

7. What is a spiritual director? Describe his or her role in the lives of Christians.

8. Give some examples of how we can tell that we are growing in our spiritual lives.

9. List the four purposes of prayer, and write your own two- or three-sentence prayers as examples of each of these four purposes. Are the four prayers you wrote formal or informal? Why? Are they public or private?

10. How is the Church's attitude toward the world today different than that of the past?

11. What does it mean to say that we should be "light" and "leaven" for the world? Give some examples of how we can become light and leaven.

12. What should our attitude as Christians be toward the environment, technological progress, and pain?

■ Action

1. Investigate ways in which you can relieve the suffering of another person. Carry out at least one idea.

2. Write a skit in which someone receives a "nudge" from the Spirit and either follows it or doesn't. Portray the consequences.

3. Exercise the power of the pen by writing to your representative in Congress, a newspaper editor, or some other authority who can help effect a needed change in society.

4. Collect five newspaper clippings portraying someone being a Christian in action. Explain each one.

5. Christ likened his followers to light, salt, and sheep among wolves. Complete this statement with an original metaphor: "A Christian is . . ." Write a poem or short essay based on your image.

■ Prayer

Day One: Pay special attention to the readings of the weekend liturgy. Spend a few minutes after Mass thinking about these readings and asking God to speak to you through them.

Days Two, Three, and Four: On Day Two, carefully read the first Scripture reading of last Sunday's Mass. (On Day Three, read the second reading; on Day Four, read the third.) You are now familiar with the texts, but in this part of the prayer, ask God to help you see one thing you can **do** each day in response to the reading you are focusing on. Make your response simple and be sure to carry it out.

Day Five: Consider how the Scriptures you have been working with can help you overcome sin in your life. Make a list of some personal faults that you hear God calling you to overcome. Ask for God's help to overcome it.

Day Six: Go back to the list of faults you made yesterday. Next to each shortcoming, write yourself a few suggestions that will help you overcome it. Try to give yourself advice you can take! Keep it simple.

Day Seven: Write a short prayer that expresses praise of God, thanksgiving for the gifts God has given you, sorrow for your sins, and a request for guidance to live your life more faithfully. Keep this prayer and, if possible, celebrate the sacrament of Penance the next weekend. Use your prayer as your "act of contrition" in the sacrament.

CHAPTER

13

Mary and the Saints: Roadsigns from the Past

OBJECTIVES

In this Chapter you will

- Review the Church's practice of honoring saints and experience the liturgical cycle that helps us to remember these holy women and men.

- Become more familiar with the feasts and solemnities that honor Mary, our Blessed Mother.

- Examine the lives of several saints in greater detail and learn how their lives are examples for us today.

The Mother of Jesus, in the glory which she possesses in body and soul in heaven, is the image and the beginning of the Church as it is to be perfected...a sign of certain hope and comfort to the pilgrim People of God.
— "Dogmatic Constitution on the Church," Paragraph 68.1

Worship and Sacraments: We Celebrate, We Praise

SECTION 1
Honoring the Saints

You can't drive through any city without encountering at least one statue of a founding father or some hero or heroine from mythology. One of the most famous statues of the twentieth century commemorates the raising of the American flag at Iwo Jima during World War II.

Likewise, families often have certain pictures of relatives on display somewhere in the home. It seems to be a human need to put up images and symbols of those who are admired.

Saints: Models of Christian Life

In the lives of the saints, the Church offers us other human models of the Christian life. Honoring the saints began with the practice of venerating the martyrs who had given their lives for the Faith. When persecution ended, the Christian community began to celebrate the holiness of outstanding persons. Feasts and special devotions grew and revealed the riches and multiplicity of gifts bestowed by the Spirit on God's people.

In the rosary, the classic Catholic devotion to Mary, we contemplate the mysteries of Christ and his mother as we repeat the praise offered by the angel of the Annunciation. In the feasts of the saints, we consider that other, ordinary people like ourselves were divinely empowered to fulfill Christ's Law of Love in their lives. As Catholics, we believe that Mary and the saints not only show us the way, but they are interested and helpful companions in our journey to our heavenly homeland. By honoring them, we glorify God and grow in holiness.

Martyr: "witness" for Christ, especially someone who dies for his or her faith.

Annunciation: the event in which the angel Gabriel announced to Mary that she was going to be the Mother of God (Luke 1:26-38).

Chapter 13 Mary and the Saints: Roadsigns from the Past

1. Why do you think people erect statues of their heroes? How do teens honor their heroes?
2. Which heroes does your city or town honor with a statue?
3. What pictures of people do you have on display in your home? Why?
4. What help have you received from the saints? Which saints are especially appealing to you? Why?

On the Record

Becoming a Saint

The word "saint" in English comes from the Latin word *sanctus,* which means "holy." We are called by God to be saints, and we can presume that there are literally millions of holy people who now live with God forever in heaven. In fact, we celebrate the lives of these unnamed saints on November 1, All Saints Day.

But those who are officially **named** saints by the Church must go through a rigorous process of investigation after their deaths. This process is called "canonization."

When a saint is canonized, she or he is declared by the Church to be in heaven. Therefore, the Church teaches, it is fitting for us to honor the saints at Mass and offer prayer and devotion to them.

The Sanctoral Cycle

Although the liturgical year focuses on the Paschal Mystery and the life and teachings of Jesus, it includes many feasts of the saints. These saints are honored because, although they were human, they were able, with and in Christ, to become free of the slavery of sin and become the free people God intends all to be. They exemplify the power of the Paschal Mystery.

There are more than 150 saints honored in the present liturgical calendar. The cycle in which they are honored is sometimes called the **sanctoral cycle**. There are many more saints who are no longer honored on this calendar. This does not mean that these persons are not saints, only that the scant knowledge we have of their lives makes it impossible for them to serve as models for modern Christians.

The saints were not people set apart from their own times. Each one was a unique individual and became a saint in his or her own way. Like all of us, they had their heroes and heroines, found good in people around them, and struggled with day-to-day problems.

The feasts of saints are celebrated on weekdays. In most cases, they may not replace Sunday celebrations or other proper feasts of Christ.

Among the greatest saints are the Apostles, who were closely associated with Christ during his public life and who had privileged roles in God's plan of salvation.

Worship and Sacraments: We Celebrate, We Praise

The feasts of the Apostles are as follows: May 3: Saints Philip and James; May 14: Saint Matthias; July 3: Saint Thomas; July 25: Saint James; August 24: Saint Bartholomew; September 21: Saint Matthew; October 28: Saints Simon and Jude; November 30: Saint Andrew; and December 27: Saint John. Saints Peter and Paul have two feasts each: June 29 commemorates their martyrdom; the Conversion of Saint Paul is celebrated on January 25; and February 22 is the feast of the Chair of Saint Peter, which honors Peter as the head of the Church and first bishop of Rome.

The two feasts of Saint Joseph occur on May 1 and March 19. On the latter feast, Saint Joseph is honored as the husband of Mary. On May 1, Joseph is honored as "The Worker." He is held up as an ideal for Christians because of his prompt obedience to God's Will, his loving care and concern for Mary and her child, his observance of the Mosaic law, and the faithful fulfillment of his religious duties.

John the Baptizer ranks high in the Church's liturgy because of his important role as Christ's precursor. His two feasts are on June 24 and August 29. They celebrate his birth and his martyrdom.

The Feast of All Saints, November 1, celebrates all who have died and are now enjoying the vision of God. All Souls, November 2, honors those dead who still need healing before experiencing the joy of heaven. November, the season of falling leaves and the coming of winter, is a good month for these two celebrations because nature "goes to rest." The saints and all other members of the Church who have died can no longer work on earth: the Church speaks of them as having gone "to their eternal rest."

Feasts that are celebrated only in the United States are

- *January 4: Saint Elizabeth Ann Seton;*
- *January 5: Saint John Neumann;*
- *May 15: Saint Isidore;*
- *September 9: Saint Peter Claver;*
- *October 19: Saints Isaac Jogues and John de Brebeuf, companions and martyrs;*
- *November 13: Saint Francis Xavier Cabrini.*

Saints Peter and Paul are honored with two feast days.

Chapter 13   Mary and the Saints: Roadsigns from the Past

Honoring the Saints: The Teaching of Vatican II

The Fathers of Vatican II offered this reflection on honoring saints:

"It is not merely by the title of example that we cherish the memory of those in heaven; we seek, rather, that by this devotion to the exercise of fraternal charity the union of the whole Church in the Spirit may be strengthened (see Ephesians 4:1-6). Exactly as Christian communion between men on their earthly pilgrimage brings us closer to Christ, so our community with the saints joins us to Christ, from whom as from its fountain and head issues all grace and the life of the People of God itself. It is most fitting, therefore, that we love those friends and co-heirs of Jesus Christ who are also our brothers and outstanding benefactors, and that we give due thanks to God for them, 'humbly invoking them, and having recourse to their prayers, their aid and help in obtaining from God through his Son, Jesus Christ, our Lord, our only Redeemer and Savior, the benefits we need.' Every authentic witness of love, indeed, offered by us to those who are in heaven tends to and terminates in Christ, 'the crown of all the saints,' and through him in God who is wonderful in his saints and is glorified in them.

"It is especially in the sacred liturgy that our union with the heavenly Church is best realized; in the liturgy, through the sacramental signs, the power of the Holy Spirit acts on us, and with community rejoicing we celebrate together the praise of the divine majesty, when all those of every tribe and tongue and people and nation who have been redeemed by the blood of Christ and gathered together into one Church glorify, in one common song of praise, the one and triune God. When, then, we celebrate the eucharistic sacrifice we are most closely united to the worship of the heavenly Church; when in the fellowship of communion we honor and remember the glorious Mary ever virgin, Saint Joseph, the holy apostles and martyrs and all the saints" (*"Dogmatic Constitution on the Church,"* Paragraph 50).

The feast of Saint Joseph on March 19 celebrates his marriage to Mary. On May 1, Joseph is honored as the patron of all workers.

Saint Peter Claver is honored as the "Apostle to the Slaves."

5. Spend some time thinking about what you would like to do with your life. Think big, remembering that with God all things are possible.

6. Saint Joseph is also included in the Feast of the Holy Family on the Sunday after Christmas. Why do you think that he is honored on that day?

7. What is the significance of celebrating All Saints Day in the fall of the year?

Summary

- Saints are holy women and men whose lives provide us with examples of how to follow Christ more faithfully.

- The Church honors the saints by promoting devotion to them and by setting aside special days for liturgical celebration of their memory.

- The process by which someone is officially named a saint of the Church is called canonization.

Chapter 13   Mary and the Saints: Roadsigns from the Past

SECTION 1
Checkpoint!

■ Review

1. Why do we honor saints in the Catholic Church?
2. What is the Sanctoral Cycle and the Calendar of Saints?
3. What did Vatican II teach about the practice of honoring the saints?
4. What does the word "saint" literally mean?
5. Explain the process of officially naming someone a saint of the Church.
6. Words to Know: Canonization, Sanctoral Cycle, martyrs, Annunciation, All Saints.

■ In Your World

1. Organize a class discussion on the Church's practice of venerating saints. Talk about reasons why this is a good practice these days and why every group (especially the Church) needs to honor its ancestors.
2. A saint may be called a hero or heroine of Christ. Look up the words "hero" and "heroine" in the dictionary and write a brief explanation of why these are appropriate terms to describe holy men and women.

■ Scripture Search

1. Read Matthew 14:1-12. How did John the Baptizer die? Why? What is it about John's life and death that makes him a saint?
2. Read Matthew 1:18-25 and 2:13-23. List some of the qualities in the life of Saint Joseph which demonstrate his holiness.

SECTION 2
Saint Mary: Our Blessed Mother

Veneration of Mary, the Mother of Jesus, is characteristically Catholic. It goes back to the very early Church, which recognized Mary as the first and best disciple of Christ and, as such, a model for all Christ's followers. It has been shaped by centuries of meditation on Mary's identity and role. In her perfect discipleship and special cooperation in the redemption won by her Son, Mary is hailed as Mother of the Church.

Mary in Scripture

When Jesus was twelve, his parents took him to Jerusalem for the festival. As happens with all adolescents, Jesus was curious and wandered away from his parents. Apparently Mary and Joseph thought that Jesus had returned home with his cousins because it was a day before they realized he was missing from the caravan. Returning to Jerusalem, they found Jesus teaching in the Temple. "When his parents saw him, they were astonished, and his mother said to him, 'Son, why have you done this to us? Your father and I have been looking for you with great anxiety.' And he said to them, 'Why were you looking for me? Did you not know that I must be in my Father's house?' " Mary took Jesus home, but kept in her heart all that had happened concerning this special child of hers (see Luke 2:41-52).

What little is found in Scripture about Mary comes mainly from the infancy narratives and Saint John's accounts of

Chapter 13 Mary and the Saints: Roadsigns from the Past

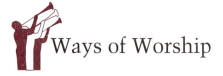

Ways of Worship

The Marian Calendar

December 8* Immaculate Conception

December 12 Our Lady of Guadalupe

January 1* Solemnity of Mary, Mother of God

February 11 Our Lady of Lourdes

March 25 The Annunciation

May 31 The Visitation

June— Immaculate Heart (first Saturday after the feast of Sacred Heart)

July 16 Our Lady of Mount Carmel

August 15* The Assumption

August 22 The Queenship of Mary

September 8 Birthday of Mary

September 15 Our Lady of Sorrows

October 7 Our Lady of the Rosary

November 21 The Presentation of Mary

* Holy Days of Obligation (obliged to celebrate Mass)

Mary's "yes" to God at the Annunciation is celebrated by the Church on March 25.

Mary at the wedding feast in Cana and under the cross, where she is symbolically portrayed as the Mother of the Church. In these recollections, Mary is presented as submitting to God's plan of salvation, regardless of its demands on her (see Luke 1:26-38, 2:1-20; John 2:1-13, 19:25-27).

The mystery of God's dealings with Mary is the same as that of God's dealings with us in the design of salvation: God waits for our cooperation. In contrast to the disobedience of Eve, Mary's humble openness to God's Will makes her an example for all. "Behold, I am the handmaid of the Lord. May it be done to me according to your word" (Luke 1:38).

Although Mary is mentioned in passing by "the synoptics" (Matthew, Mark, Luke) during Jesus' ministry, the Acts of the Apostles show her as a vital part of the young community gathering after the Ascension. With the Apostles, she prayed for and shared in the fruits of her Son's victory: the fullness and joy of the Spirit bestowed on the Church, to be shared with the world. In recognition of her powerful intercession, the Church has accorded Mary special devotion and feasts from earliest times (Acts 1:14).

Mary's virginity is proclaimed in Matthew and Luke in order to point out the special character of the one to be born of her. Reference to Jesus' brothers and sisters in the Gospels have been interpreted in the Catholic tradition as allusions to cousins and other kin of Jesus, as is allowed by the Hebrew idiom (see Mark 3:31-35, 6:3). The Church teaches that Mary remained a virgin before, during, and after Jesus' birth, having been overshadowed by the Holy Spirit in the conception of Jesus (Matthew 1:25).

---

8. What is it about Mary's life that prompts us to speak of her as the Mother of the Church?

9. In what ways is Mary a good example for modern women? Explain your answer.

Mary is recognized as the first disciple of Jesus, with him even to his death on the cross.

The Church's Reflection on Mary

In early Church councils, as the Fathers reflected on the mystery of Christ, Mary was declared Mother of God, since she is the mother of the divine person who possesses both a human and a divine nature. Through reflection, theologians down the ages came to recognize other privileges of Mary besides those of her divine maternity and perpetual virginity. Two that not only show Mary's God-given dignity but also give us insight into our own gifts as Christians are the Immaculate Conception and the Assumption.

By the gift of her Immaculate Conception, Mary alone, of all human beings, possessed the effects of Christ's redemption from the moment of her conception: freedom from Original Sin and full union with God. This grace, afforded her in anticipation of Christ's merits, reveals the state to which all people are called by God's plan and that Christians celebrate and receive in the sacrament of

Celebrating the Birth of an Extraordinary "Ordinary" Woman

With three exceptions, the Church never celebrates the birthday of the saints. The reason is that before their baptism, saints lacked the full union with God that Christ came to restore. The three exceptions are Christ, who is, always was, and always will be the Son of God; John the Baptizer, who would announce Jesus to the world; and Mary, Christ's Mother.

The birth of every child is a source of wonder, but the birth of the holiest human being ever to live is something to celebrate until the end of the world. Although Mary's birthday was not celebrated until the eighth century, her birthplace has been venerated in Jerusalem since the sixth century. In Hebrew, Mary's name was pronounced *Meer Yahm*.

Nine months after the celebration of the Immaculate Conception, the feast of Mary's birthday is celebrated and the Church praises God for choosing her, out of all the women on earth, to be the Mother of Jesus. She probably did not stand out as different from people of her day. Like the other Galilean women, she probably wore colorful clothes and perhaps even earrings, gold rings, bracelets, and ankle chains. Mary drew water from the common well and shared a common oven, exchanging news with the villagers. But she was different. Free from the least sin, she nursed deep within her a flame of love that would one day become the Light of the World. Her birthday is celebrated on September 8.

Baptism. Mary was not exempted from the **consequences** of humankind's sinful condition: sickness, suffering, and death.

A Marian privilege that complements the Immaculate Conception is Mary's Assumption. In this mystery, Catholics affirm that when Mary's close union with God was brought to perfect fulfillment at the end of her earthly journey, she entered body and soul into God's eternal presence.

A result of Christ's resurrection, Mary's Assumption reinforces our faith in bodily resurrection as professed in our creeds. Like Mary, we are all destined to share eternal life in our total, body-spirit nature. From beginning to end, then, Mary's life shows what it means to live as people created, redeemed, and gifted by God.

In these days of greater awareness of the dignity of women, Mary's call and response offer us a feminine model that is instructive for men as well as women. The veneration we give Mary cannot compare with the adoration we give to God: there is only one God and one Son, but as Catholics we hold his Mother and ours as someone special.

The Assumption celebrates Mary's close union with God.

Understanding Mary Through Her Special Feasts

No other saint has as many feast days yearly as Mary. And that is appropriate, for no other saint has played such an important role in God's plan for our salvation. You can grow in appreciation for the importance of our Blessed Mother by reviewing some of her "special days" in the liturgical life of the Church.

Immaculate Conception

During Advent (on December 8), the Church celebrates Mary's freedom from Original Sin and all its effects from the first moment of her conception. Under this title, Mary is the patroness of the United States.

This feast is not to be confused with the Annunciation, which celebrates Christ's conception in the womb of Mary nine months before his birth.

Solemnity of Mary

During the Christmas season (on January 1), the Church solemnly honors Mary as the Mother of God. She has the greatest privilege possible to a human being. The readings of the day focus on the birth of Jesus and on Mary, who "kept all these things, reflecting on them in her heart" (Luke 2:16-21).

Annunciation

In this feast, the Church rejoices that Mary pronounced her great act of consent, which brought the Son of God to earth (Luke 1:38). This feast shows God's reliance on human cooperation for carrying out the divine plan of redemption. It is celebrated nine months before Christmas: March 25.

Mary's Month

From the earliest days of the Church, people have created paintings, mosaics, and statues honoring the greatest people and events connected with the redemption. Perhaps no one besides Christ has been more honored by artists than Mary, his Mother.

For centuries, people of the Eastern Church have had Marian shrines in their homes. Lighting candles before icons, they pray there alone or gather as a family to offer prayers. People of wealth sometimes expanded these shrines into churches where the local villagers could join them in their devotions.

In the United States, the custom developed of placing flowers before a statue or picture of Mary in homes and schools during May. The May altar, as it is called, may be a simple statue placed on the window ledge, a larger shrine backed with drapes and adorned with candles and flowers, or a full-grown grotto in the garden or backyard.

The purpose of the Marian shrine is to cultivate a habit of turning to Mary, the woman whose response of perfect obedience to God's proposal to the human race allowed God's entire plan of redemption to come about.

Catholic tradition holds that Mary is crowned "Queen of Heaven and Earth."

Worship and Sacraments: We Celebrate, We Praise

The Assumption

This most recently established Marian feast (1950) honors Mary for experiencing what all who die in God's favor will experience: the transformation of the whole person, body and soul, in the glorious life of eternity. Because of her privileged role in God's plan, Mary's glory is most apparent in this mystery of faith. Artists picture this event by showing Mary's body being taken up (assumed) into heaven.

10. How would sinlessness free you?

11. How does your family honor Mary in your home?

12. In what ways can your class foster devotion to Mary?

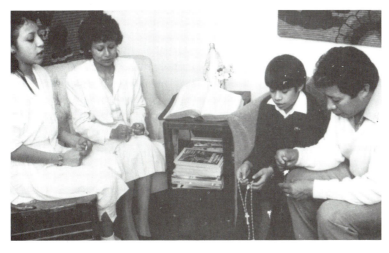

One way that Catholics honor Mary is through praying the Rosary.

Summary

- Mary is honored as the first and best disciple of Christ. That is why we call her Mother of the Church, our Blessed Mother.

- The Mother of Jesus is also called the Mother of God because she gave birth to the Son of God.

- Catholics believe that Mary was conceived without sin (Immaculate Conception) and that her body was taken up to heaven after she died (Assumption).

SECTION 2
Checkpoint!

■ Review

1. Why do we say that Mary was free from sin?

2. What do we celebrate on the feasts of the Immaculate Conception and Assumption? Why do we believe the things about Mary that these two feasts celebrate?

3. What month is referred to as "Mary's Month" and what sort of activities are common during this month?

4. Which three feasts of Mary are Holy Days of Obligation? What is required of Catholics on Holy Days?

5. Words to Know: Immaculate Conception, Assumption, Mary's Month, Annunciation, Mother of God.

■ In Your World

1. Write an essay in which you describe the importance of Mary for Christians today. Use ample Scripture references and some of Mary's feasts to develop your essay.

2. Protestants sometimes object to the devotion of Catholics to Mary since many of the things we say about her are not quoted literally in Scripture. How would you answer that objection? Are there other Church positions that cannot be established by a literal reading of Scripture? Why is the Catholic approach legitimate?

■ Scripture Search

1. The Church teaches that Mary was a virgin and that she never had intimate relations with Joseph. How do we explain, therefore, reference to Jesus' "sisters and brothers" in Mark 3:31-35 and 6:3?

2. Read Numbers 6:22-27. How does this text apply to the feast of the Solemnity of Mary?

3. Read Luke 1:26-38. What are some things in your own life where God is asking your consent?

SECTION 3
Examples of Well-Lived Lives

Practically any group of saints could exemplify the life of holiness that you are called to live, but the group discussed here may be especially helpful to you as you develop your own saintly qualities.

The Traveler

Francis Xavier wasn't interested in studies, but he liked school because he was very sports-minded. He put his natural temperament to work by being super-aggressive and determined in the contests he engaged in.

At nineteen, at the University of Paris where he had begun college, Francis met a man much older than himself who was to have an immense influence in his life. It took some time for Ignatius of Loyola to win Francis over from his original goals and get him to join the Society of Jesus (the Jesuits). But in 1534, Francis Xavier was one of the first six, including Ignatius, to take vows in the new order.

Once "converted," Francis gave himself to winning the world for Christ. By the time of his death in 1552, he had traveled the greater part of the Far East. He died on a lonely island, waiting to obtain entrance to China, where he had visions of spreading the Gospel message.

Considering the conditions of travel, the means of transport, and the delays and difficulties Francis Xavier encountered, his adventures seem like epics. But the flourishing Christian communities he left behind are the real

Saint Francis Xavier was co-founder of the Jesuits.

miracles of his life. It is said he had the power of prophecy and healing.

Saint Francis Xavier, co-founder of the Society of Jesus with Saint Ignatius of Loyola, is co-patron, with Saint Therese of Lisieux, of all missions. His feast is December 3.

13. Who is your favorite saint? Do a little homework on his or her life and write a one page report on what you have learned.

14. What qualities of temperament do you see in Francis Xavier's life?

15. Ask someone who knows you what qualities you have that might be used in God's service.

Riches to Rags

Elizabeth Ann Bayley was a most courageous woman. She was born into wealth and position in a prominent family of New York two years before the Declaration of Independence was signed. Related to the Gothams, Barclays, Delanceys, and Roosevelts, she was reared by her mother and stepmother as a member of the Episcopal Church. From them, Elizabeth learned to pray and to love the Scriptures. Her father, the respected Dr. Richard Bayley, was not a regular churchgoer, even though he was genuinely involved in humanitarian efforts.

At nineteen, Elizabeth married the handsome and wealthy New York merchant William Magee Seton and later bore him five children. Nine years after they married, her husband became gravely ill with tuberculosis. Elizabeth nursed him faithfully, sailing with him to Italy where he died.

After his death, Elizabeth was taken in by a Catholic family in Italy whose kindness and devotion to Catholicism attracted her to the Church. But it was the real presence of Jesus in the Blessed Sacrament, the central love of her life, that led Elizabeth, against the opposition of her minister and friends, to enter the Catholic Church on her return to New York.

It was the turning point in her life. As Elizabeth's spiritual life grew deeper and more intense, external circumstances caused her more and more suffering. Her former wealthy friends sneered at her for joining an "immigrant" church. Her family abandoned her, and she lacked even the necessities of life. Because of sexual prejudice, she could not get a job to support her family.

At the invitation of her friend Father Dubourg, Elizabeth left New York to live in Maryland, where she formed a school for Catholic girls. Later, gathering other young women around her, she founded the first religious congregation of women in the United States, the Sisters of Charity of Emmitsburg. She is credited with founding the American Catholic school system. Elizabeth suffered for her courage. Her own serious illness, the deaths of two daughters, a wayward son, and misunderstandings within the community of sisters she founded all weighed heavily on her mind.

Elizabeth's journey was not one of rags to riches, but the opposite. Yet her diary shows her great inner happiness even as she suffered. In 1975, Pope Paul VI canonized her as the first American-born saint of the Roman Catholic Church. Her feastday is January 4.

Elizabeth Bayley Seton is the first American-born saint.

16. *What advantages have come to Catholics in America through the Catholic school system?*

Chapter 13   Mary and the Saints: Roadsigns from the Past

Determined Lovers of Christ

A teenager once acquired a medal with Saint Agnes on one side and Saint Thomas Aquinas on the other. The craftsman who struck the medal saw in the virginal purity of the two saints a common bond. Agnes was once approached by a man who wanted her to have sexual intercourse with him. She resisted, despite his threats, and insisted on her desire to remain a virgin for the sake of Christ. Insulted, the man reported Agnes as a Christian to the Roman prefect. The prefect, in turn, had her placed in a house of prostitution and then killed.

Saint Thomas displayed a similar determination to remain celibate. When he decided to become a Dominican friar, his wealthy family, shocked that Thomas was joining a beggar order, sent a beautiful woman to seduce him. Legend has it that, seizing a red-hot poker from the fire, Thomas drove the woman from the room, insisting on his right to remain unmarried for the love of God.

Saint Agnes is honored on January 21. January 26 is the feastday of Saint Thomas Aquinas.

Saint Agnes is honored for her virginal purity.

17. *What is the difference between the decision of a priest, a religious brother, or a sister to remain celibate for the sake of Christ and that of a person choosing to remain single for the sake of a career or to care for parents? Or is there a difference?*

A simple man of faith, Thomas Aquinas was a great teacher and scholar.

Patron Saints

Did you know that many occupations and countries have their own special patron saints? A "patron saint" is a saint of the Church who protects countries and people in certain professions in a special way. They also serve as inspirations for people in these groups. The saint you are named after may also be called a patron saint, yours!

Sometimes people of other religious traditions misunderstand the Catholic emphasis on the saints. But contrary to what some people believe, we do not worship the saints. We simply honor them and ask them to pray to God on our behalf. When we have statues of the saints in our churches or wear medals depicting our patron saints, we are simply reminding ourselves that we are not alone on our journey towards God's kingdom. We are part of a great company of holy women and men that extends back in time over 2,000 years.

Here are a few patron saints:

Patrons of Occupations
Actors:	Saint Genesius
Athletes:	Saint Sebastian
Booksellers:	Saint John of God
Cooks:	Saint Martha
Ecologists:	Saint Francis of Assisi
Lawyers:	Saint Thomas More
Scientists:	Saint Albert
Teachers:	Saint John Baptist de la Salle

Patrons of Countries
Ireland:	Saint Patrick
Mexico:	Our Lady of Guadalupe
Philippines:	Sacred Heart of Mary
United States:	Immaculate Conception

There are even patron saints of young people. They are Saint Aloysius Gonzaga, Saint Maria Goretti, Saint Kateri Tekakwitha. Research the life of one of these saints to see why he or she is a saint for teenagers.

Saint Kateri Tekakwitha is the first native American to be proclaimed a saint.

Chapter 13 Mary and the Saints: Roadsigns from the Past

Touching the Sacred

Saint Augustine's Prayer

Saint Augustine (396-430) was bishop of Hippo in Africa. But before becoming a Christian, Augustine lived a pretty "care-free" life. To put it mildly, he was no saint!

After his conversion, however, he dedicated his life to Christ. Later, he wrote one of the greatest spiritual autobiographies ever published, called simply *The Confessions.*

Saint Augustine's *Confessions* begins with a prayer.

"You are great, O Lord, and greatly to be praised. Great is your power and to your wisdom there is no limit. And people, who are part of your creation, wish to praise you, people who bear about within themselves mortality, who bear about within themselves testimony of their sin and testimony that you resist the proud. Yet this part of your creation wishes to praise you. You arouse us to take joy in praising you, for you have made us for yourself, and our hearts are restless until they rest in you."

The Simple Life

Oriental philosophers say that you can get to the heart of humanity by reaching into your own heart. In other words, deep understanding of yourself will give you hints about what makes everyone else tick.

Saint Patrick, the Apostle of Ireland who lived from 389 to 461, discovered a similar secret. He found that by getting to the heart of things, he could reach the heart of God. In the middle of his sermons explaining the doctrine of the Trinity, he would reach down to the beautiful green clover that carpets most of the Emerald Isle and hold up a shamrock as a symbol of three persons in one God.

A wealthy Roman in his youth, Patrick and some of his father's servants were captured by pirates and transported as slaves to Ireland, where he herded swine. Holding to his Christian faith, he learned humility. He wrote in his *Confessions* that he changed from a person who was "as stone lying in the deep mud" to "a stone placed by God's mercy on the very top of the wall." His experience taught

The patron saint of Ireland, Patrick was once a slave. His faith and determination led him to convert all of Ireland to belief in Jesus.

Worship and Sacraments: We Celebrate, We Praise

him wisdom. Patrick escaped, returned to his homeland for his education, and became a priest. At age forty-three, after a dream calling him to return to Ireland, Patrick did indeed return to convert the pagans. He often preached the gospel at the risk of his life.

Like Christ, this bishop used the things all around him to explain the love of God to the people he served for thirty years. When he died, the Church in Ireland flourished with its own native clergy. No one loves Saint Patrick today more than the Irish, many of whom emigrated to America and became leaders of the Church during the last century. Saint Patrick's Day is March 17.

18. *Use a concrete object to explain some doctrine to a child you know, such as the presence of Christ in the Blessed Sacrament, Mary's freedom from sin, or Jesus' being both divine and human.*

19. *Saint Patrick came from a wealthy family, but he gave up his wealth to become a missionary. What responsibilities do wealthy people today have? Assuming that they don't give away all their money, what things might they do to be "poor in spirit" (Matthew 5:3)?*

The Monk with a Temper

Although many saints have been held up for public veneration, there are many more saints whom people either don't know or whose cause has not come up for canonization.

One example of an uncanonized holy man is Brother Joachim, a saintly monk who spent only a little more than ten years at the Abbey of Gethsemani in Kentucky. During his last years there, it is said he worked miracles. Once, it seems, he walked calmly for ten minutes through a torrential downpour carrying his infant nephew who had just recovered from pneumonia. Both remained bone dry. Since his death, Brother Joachim has answered many people's prayers.

But Brother Joachim wasn't always close to God. As a teenager, before running away from home in Lebanon, Kentucky, he burned down the family tobacco barn in a fit of anger at his father. He stayed away from home for nine years, never letting his family know whether he was dead or alive. During this time, he lost his faith and became known in the West as the cowboy "Kentucky Jack." Because of his vicious temper, he was also nicknamed "The Quick One."

After his mother's death, he experienced a change of heart. He delayed his wedding a year. Then he broke off the engagement completely after visiting the Trappist monastery. He felt drawn to the monastic life.

Inside the monastery, his hot temper was not put off as quickly as his secular clothes. Several times, he lashed out against other monks who annoyed him, and, because of his impatience, he frequently broke things.

Eventually, however, the monk with the temper became one of the holiest men of the order. Maybe it was because he redirected his excess energy into loving God.

20. *If Jesus was alive today, what kinds of things do you think would make him angry? Why did he become angry one day when he was in the Temple (John 2:13-17)?*

21. *Tell how the following faults could be converted to virtues: a tendency to worry; the habit of bossing others around; constant complaining.*

Stained glass windows often tell the life of a saint. This window tells of Saint Peter in Rome.

Summary

- Saints come from all walks of life, and even though they are all examples of well-lived lives, they had to struggle for holiness just as we do.

- All the saints had two things in common: their dedication to Christ and their willingness to follow him without reservation.

- Patron saints are saints who inspire people in certain occupations or those who live in countries placed under their special protection.

SECTION 3
Checkpoint!

■ Review

1. How would you describe the Catholic understanding of saints to a non-Catholic?

2. Who are patron saints and why are they honored? Who is the patron saint of the United States?

3. What is it about Saint Augustine's early life that prompted him years later to pray, "Our hearts are restless until they rest in you"?

4. When did Saint Augustine live and what position did he hold in the Church?

5. For what are Saint Francis Xavier and Saint Patrick known?

6. Words to Know: *Confessions* of Saint Augustine, patron saints.

■ In Your World

1. Who is someone (living or dead, famous or not) that you think is a saint, even though she or he has not been canonized? Give reasons for your choice.

2. The year is 2101 and you have just been canonized by the Pope. (Congratulations!) Write the proclamation of your canonization that Pope John XXV is going to read at Mass this Sunday telling the world about the great things you have done and about your Christ-like characteristics. (Think of things you would like to do and like to be remembered for as well as those Christ-like characteristics you already possess.)

■ Scripture Search

1. Recall that the word "saint" comes from the Latin word for "holy," *sanctus*. Read the following greetings that Saint Paul used to address the various Christian communities to whom he was writing. What do these kinds of greetings suggest about the true meaning of "saint": Romans 1:7; 1 Corinthians 1:1-2; 2 Corinthians 1:1; Ephesians 1:1; Colosians 1:1?

2. How does Sirach (Ecclesiasticus), chapter 44 set a Biblical foundation for the practice of venerating the saints?

CHAPTER 13 Review

■ Study

1. A friend asks why Catholics rely on the intercession of Mary and the saints since Christ is more than adequate as a mediator. How would you respond?

2. What are the two feasts of Saint Joseph and when are they celebrated each year?

3. What is meant by the "process of canonization" and what is involved in that process?

4. The word "saint" comes from the Latin word for "holy," *sanctus*. Why are these people considered saints: Saint John the Baptist; the Blessed Mother; Saint Joseph; Saint Agnes; Saint Thomas Aquinas?

5. There are far more saints in heaven than the people listed in the Calendar of Saints. Explain. What is the official feast day of these unnamed saints?

6. Why do we call Mary the Mother of God? The Mother of the Church?

7. How many feasts are set aside to honor Mary in the "Marian Calendar"? What does this suggest about the Church's attitude toward Mary?

8. Briefly explain the Annunciation, the Immaculate Conception, and the Assumption.

9. What specific events in Mary's life demonstrate her holiness?

10. Explain the practice of naming patron saints.

11. Who is the patron saint of everyone who cares deeply for the environment?

12. List five qualities that you think a modern saint should possess.

13. Who was Saint Augustine and what famous book did he write?

■ Action

1. Research the life of the saint whose name you took at Confirmation (or, if you are not yet confirmed, a name you might want to take). What qualities in her or his life do you find attractive? Why do you think we have the custom of choosing a saint's name at Confirmation and, frequently, at Baptism?

2. Find out when the Church celebrates the next important feast day of a saint. Plan to go to Mass that day as a class. See if the priest will allow your class to help prepare the liturgy with special songs, petitions, art, and a brief written reflection on the life of the saint to be read or acted out at Mass.

3. On February 14th, people still like to exchange Valentine's Day cards. Saint Valentine has been dropped from the Calendar of the Saints, but as we saw in the text, this does not mean that he is not a saint! Find out what you can about this man's life and make a Valentine's card that truly reflects the religious significance of this day.

■ Prayer

This prayer, called **The Angelus,** dates from the first century. Its name comes from the first word of the Latin text of the prayer, "*angelus*" (angel). Traditionally, **The Angelus** is prayed in honor of Mary and Jesus three times a day: at 6:00 a.m., at Noon, and at 6:00 p.m. It can, however, be offered at any time, especially as a morning prayer or a prayer to begin class.

1. The angel of the Lord declared unto Mary,
2. And she conceived of the Holy Spirit.
All: Hail Mary, ...

1. Behold the handmaid of the Lord,
2. Be it done unto me according to your word.
All: Hail Mary, ...

1. And the Word of God was made flesh,
2. And dwelt among us.
All: Hail Mary, ...

1. Pray for us, O holy Mother of God,
2. That we may be made worthy of the promises of Christ.
Leader: Let us pray.
Leader (or All): Pour forth, we ask you, O Lord, your grace into our hearts, that we to whom the Incarnation of Christ, your Son, was made known by the message of an angel, may by his passion and cross be brought to the glory of his resurrection, through the same Christ, our Lord.
All: Amen (see Luke 1:26-38).

CHAPTER

14

Our Passage from Time to Eternity

OBJECTIVES

In this Chapter you will

- Explore various attitudes people have toward death and recognize the process of facing death with courage and dignity.

- Understand death and its related problems for survivors.

- Examine how grieving and the celebration of Christian burial help the living experience healing when a loved one has died.

And when this which is corruptible clothes itself with incorruptibility, and this which is mortal clothes itself with immortality, then the word that is written shall come about: "Death is swallowed up in victory. Where, O death, is your victory? Where, O death, is your sting?"
—1 Corinthians 15:54-55

Worship and Sacraments: We Celebrate, We Praise

SECTION 1
Viewing Death

"I remember the first time I saw a dead person. My grandfather, who had been a big man, was laid out in a funeral home. I was about nine years old, and I was frightened. He looked so small and fragile. As I sat watching him in the coffin, I would jump, sure that I had seen him blink an eye or move a lip. But, of course, nothing of the sort happened. So this was death. What surprised me the most were all the people who would go up to 'Poppa' and say, 'He looks so good.' I wanted to scream, 'No he doesn't, he looks like he's dead.'"

Death is a difficult issue to discuss in our culture. Over three hundred years ago the French philosopher Pascal stated the idea this way: "Since men [and women] have not succeeded in curing death, they have decided not to think about it at all." When death is considered, it is often personified as the grim reaper, a skeleton wielding a scythe. Similarly, in Greek mythology, life was controlled by women called the Fates. Clotho spun out the thread of one's life, and Atropos ended it with a snip of her "abhorred shears." Death is also sometimes depicted as a handsome youth. It is hoped that you will find this unit a good preparation for dealing with death when it enters your life or the lives of people you care about.

The Faith View of Death

From our limited perspective, death can look like the end of everything. Without faith, death can seem final. But with faith, it is only the end that marks the beginning of another phase of the journey. For the Christian, death means only the loss of life in this world. Family, friends, accomplishments, possessions, and pleasures are left behind. There's

Grim Reaper: a mythic image of death. The reaper "cuts down" the life of a person like a harvester cuts fruit from a vine.

Scythe: a tool with a long, curved blade used for cutting tall grass.

no denying that death is dreaded by those who have the instinct of self-preservation and who treasure the gift of life.

But because of the promises of Jesus, we know that our journey really extends beyond this world's horizon. Jesus, a human being like us, experienced death. He suffered on the cross in pain and in thirst; then, with an agonized cry, he died. However, he arose to life in a new, glorified form. The Apostles found the state of glory impossible to describe. It was a new and different life. In his appearances, Jesus was not immediately recognizable. And yet, somehow, he was connected with his earthly experience. They found him to be the same person they had loved so well, yet full of serene joy.

It is this risen Jesus who has gone before us through the door of death, and who is still with us as we follow in his footsteps to the fullness of eternal life (the quality existence that he promised and attained for us). In light of the resurrection, we can exclaim with Saint Paul, "Where, O death, is your victory? Where, O death, is your sting?" (1 Corinthians 15:55)!

After his resurrection, Jesus appeared in a new form. The story of Emmaus (Luke 24:13–35) tells us that Jesus was only recognized in the breaking of bread.

1. When was the last time you thought of death? Your death? The death of your parents? What emotions did you feel at the time?

2. Which teachings of Christ and the Church give Christians hope when facing death?

Contemporary Attitudes

We tend to push death out of our lives; it is fled from, fought against, and feared. Because death makes us uncomfortable, we avoid it, talk about it in whispers, or awkwardly rush through any unavoidable encounters with it. We even use figures of speech like "passed away" to shield us from the reality of death.

In the past, dying people orchestrated their own deaths. They called their friends and relatives together, delivered final speeches, and imparted blessings. In tribal culture, death is often simply accepted as a fact of life. But, in our society, we act as if death does not exist. Acceptable behavior for dying patients is to pretend that they are not going to die.

People have negative feelings toward death mainly because they fear the unknown, though, actually, dying is as natural as being born. Every year about ten percent of the population of the United States is directly affected by the death of someone close to them. More than five thousand Americans die every day. However, except for "actor" deaths on television and in movies, you probably have witnessed few, if any, deaths.

Long ago, most people died in their homes and were attended to and buried by their families. Death was a familiar event. Now more people live to an old age and many are put into institutions where death occurs. Professionals now care for the dying and the dead, while relatives are merely "visitors," paying their last respects. This lack of personal contact with death makes it difficult to cope with when it occurs in our families.

Researchers have gathered evidence that shows we need to face death, understand it, and accept it as a fact of life. Just one benefit of pondering death is that it forces us to acknowledge who we are, what our lives are all about, and how fragile life is. As the world grows in realizing the importance of dealing with death, it is bringing death out into the open. Currently, death education courses and workshops are flourishing. Books on death sometimes appear on the best-seller lists. **Hospices,** facilities or programs where terminally ill people are supported as they die a natural, dignified death, are becoming more common. Cicely Saunders popularized hospices in London during the 1950s. The concept has spread to the United States. As long ago as the Middle Ages, though, Catholic Sisters cared for the dying in special homes.

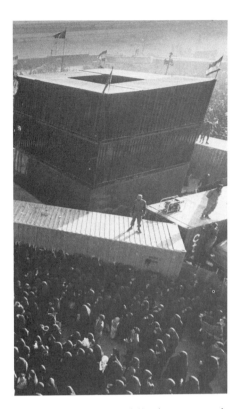

Funeral celebrations differ between cultures. The funeral of a beloved leader can produce a mass outpouring of public grief in some cultures, while in others, emotions are controlled.

3. In what ways do you think that "orchestrating" one's own death was therapeutic (healing) for the dying person's loved ones?

4. Why do you think that the terminally ill choose to die in a hospice rather than in a hospital?

Chapter 14   Our Passage from Time to Eternity

The Christian Approach to Death

King Henry VIII declared death for anyone who refused to take an oath supporting the Act of Supremacy that made him Supreme Head of the Church of England. When in conscience Saint Thomas More, the Chancellor (the highest ranking government official) of England, chose to remain a Catholic loyal to the pope, he was sentenced to be beheaded.

During his last moments on earth he joked with the executioner, telling him to aim well because his neck was short. Then he said, "Let me lay my beard over the block lest you strike it, it has never offended his highness."

How could this man face death so lightheartedly? The answer lies in his last words: "I die the King's good servant, but God's first." Jonathan Swift (1667-1745), a writer with an acid pen, called him, "the person of greatest virtue this kingdom ever produced." Thomas More was a good husband, a loving father, a shrewd chancellor, but most importantly, a holy Christian. Because he had always had a deep and personal relationship with God, and had lived in faith, trust, and love, death held no fear for him. He was prepared to meet his God and be greeted with, "Well done, my good and faithful servant" (Matthew 25:23).

No one who lives according to his or her conscience needs to fear death. In the words of Franklin D. Roosevelt, "The only thing we have to fear is fear itself." Death is just a translation from one form of life to another, even better, form. It is going home to our Father.

Saint Thomas More, according to tradition, faced death bravely. More is the patron saint of lawyers.

Facing Death

"I've got the world by the tail," Rita thinks. "I've just been accepted by the college I've always wanted to attend. David, the love of my life, has asked me to the prom. And my parents are giving me a brand new car for graduation. What could be better? Now if I could just figure out what's causing these strange stomach pains. At first I thought they were 'just nerves,' but now the pain is getting worse, so first thing Monday I've got to get that check-up."

Rita's check-up does not go well. The doctor schedules her for emergency surgery for a tumor that she thinks looks benign. After the test results from the operation are in, Rita learns that she has cancer. Her doctor says she has six months to live. How does Rita react to the news? What will she do?

The time, the place, the cause, and the circumstances of your death are all unknowns. Furthermore, no one who has been dead for any length of time has returned to tell us about the experience. The only certain thing we know about our own death is that it is inevitable: "We've all got to go sometime." But Sigmund Freud, the founder of modern psychiatry (1856-1939), said that we unconsciously deny our limitations. Each of us thinks that we're different: I won't die; I will be like the people on television who reappear in movie after movie after I've seen them die on the screen.

For this reason, a person confronted with the truth that he or she is dying has to make a traumatic, psychological adjustment. Researchers have been able to identify emotions that dying people might have in common, though they might not experience them in the same order or to the same degree. The most notable study is that of psychiatrist Elisabeth Kubler-Ross, who describes five stages people pass through in reconciling themselves to death. Knowledge of these stages helps toward understanding, comforting, and dealing openly with the dying person. Let's see how Rita responded to the news of her illness. Following a brief explanation of each stage listed there is a suggestion for helping someone like Rita pass through that stage.

1. **Denial:** "No, not me." This was Rita's first response. This is the normal response to the news of one's impending death. Denial helps cushion

The natural response to tragic news is denial: "No, not me," "That can't be true," or "You must have the records confused."

the reality of death so that it can gradually be accepted. The strength and duration of the denial vary. Fortunately, Rita moved through this stage rather quickly. Unfortunately, some people never proceed from this stage.

- ■ ***Supportive response:*** *Give physical, emotional, and spiritual comfort. Her friends allowed Rita to talk about her fears, discomforts, and fantasies surrounding death. Her friends were free to cry and laugh with Rita.*

2. **Anger:** "Why me?" Rita's anger was typical as she struggled to blame herself or someone else for her illness. Her anger was directed at God for allowing this to happen, at the doctors for their neglect or lack of knowledge, at the nurses, at her family for not being around when she needed them, or at anyone who was healthy. It's okay for Rita to be angry with God. As Kubler-Ross says, "God can take it. He understands."

- ■ ***Supportive response:*** *Rita's friends admitted that they didn't have the answer as to why she had cancer. They reminded her that knowing when the end will come enables her to live her life more intensely now. She could make plans and act upon them.*

When someone you know or love is facing death, your supportive friendship and understanding is important.

Worship and Sacraments: We Celebrate, We Praise

3. **Bargaining:** "Yes, me, but..." Rita tried to make deals with God and with her doctors. She promised to be good. She would become a missionary sister to Africa if only she could live until after basketball season and graduation were over. She had thoughts like "If I could just get well, I know I'd be a much better person."

   ■ *Supportive response:* Rita was encouraged to accept the inevitable fact of her coming death. She was not encouraged to think that bargaining would help.

4. **Depression:** "Oh, me." People who came to visit Rita saw that she seemed to withdraw from them as if she were in mourning. This is a state of preparatory grief as death approaches. Visitors were not wanted because Rita was trying to let go of all the significant people in her life. She especially didn't want to see David. "Everyone else seemed so happy. Well, they were only losing me, but I'm losing everyone," Rita said.

   ■ *Supportive response:* All Rita's friends and family could do was show care and concern for her. No false cheerfulness here, but they did hold her hand, pray with her, and simply sit quietly with her until she needed to talk. Rita enjoyed having one person visit at a time.

5. **Acceptance:** "Yes, me." In this phase, Rita gained a sense of peace. She reached a point

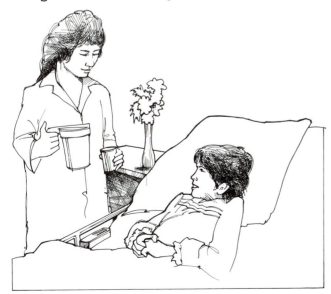

When Rita was able to accept her illness, she experienced a sense of peace.

On the Record

Preparing for Death

One secret of coping with the reality of death is always to be prepared. The quality of our lives should be such that we are not speechless when God asks us what we have done to show our love (see Colossians 3:1-4). Someone said that most people's lives are like a jewelry store where the price tags are mixed up: diamonds are marked low; worthless trinkets are set at thousands of dollars. We must make the effort, take the time to get our priorities in order, set the right values, and live according to them.

Although Christians are not spared physical death, in the experience there is an undercurrent of joy and peace made possible by faith in Jesus. By dying, he gave death meaning. Our own death has the value of worship, the worship of the cross. Death for Catholics is a mystery of triumph. "Whether we live or die, we are the Lord's" (Romans 14:8).

where she felt that there was a certain dignity about dying. Rita felt that now she could offer her strength to her family and friends who would soon have to go on living without her.

■ **Supportive response:** *By accepting her death, Rita was able to comfort many of her friends, especially those who were willing to accept her death. Some of her friends, however, refused to accept Rita's death. They tried to convince her that she was mistaken. But Rita was ready now; she knew the truth.*

(See *On Death and Dying*, Elisabeth Kubler-Ross, Macmillan, 1969.)

5. How would you respond to a child who asks you: "What is death?"

6. Describe your first experience with death. Which feelings do you recall? How did you deal with them?

7. What do you think of Rita's struggle to accept death? Discuss how you think you might respond in a similar situation where a friend of yours was dying.

A Personal Testimony

Ted Rosenthal, who wrote a book after he discovered that he would die within a short time, identified seven fears he experienced before death came.

1. Fear of the process of dying: the pain, the fright, the peace.

2. Fear of losing control: inability to provide for my family, my dependence on others for health care.

3. Fear for loved ones: the uncertainty of their futures without the breadwinner, the added burden to them.

4. Fear of the aloneness of dying: the pain of separation, isolation, decreased frequency of visits, the inability to speak at the end, the fake cheerfulness.

5. Fear of fear: as reflected in the eyes of those who care.

6. Fear of life's meaninglessness: that the world will be no better for my having been born, wonder at the reason for my creation and whether I fulfilled it.

7. Fear of the unknown: the constant shifting of the emotions from hope of a cure and extended life, to enjoyment of small things like a flower, a birth, or a holiday, to thoughts about eternal life.

(See *How Could I Not Be Among You?*, © 1973 by Ted Rosenthal, used by permission of Persea Books.)

At the hour of death, it is urgent for Catholics to be present with their loved ones to support and encourage them in their faith. Not only is it consoling for the dying ones, but the witnesses are helped to come to terms with their own deaths.

---

8. With which of Mr. Rosenthal's fears can you already identify? What comfort is there for the pain of any of them?

9. Name three specific things that Catholics can do to support and encourage their friends and families who are facing death soon.

Summary

- For Christians, the ultimate understanding of death comes from their faith in Jesus Christ—the resurrection and the life.

- Many people in contemporary society avoid the topic of death probably because they fear it and don't know how to respond to those who are terminally ill.

- A person who learns that he or she will die soon goes through several stages until finally accepting the situation. At every step along the way, Christians are obliged to make supportive responses.

SECTION 1
Checkpoint!

■ Review

1. List as many contemporary attitudes toward death as you can. How can Christian faith help a person have a healthier attitude toward death?

2. What five stages of dying did Dr. Elisabeth Kubler-Ross identify?

3. How can we prepare for death, even though it may be many years in the future?

4. How is Saint Thomas More an example of facing death with Christian courage and dignity?

5. Words to Know: hospice, denial, anger, bargaining, depression, acceptance.

■ In Your World

1. What are the responsibilities of the family and friends toward the sick and dying? What good can serious illness or sudden death bring to a family?

2. Write a short composition or prayer that expresses your personal attitudes toward sickness, pain, aging, and death.

■ Scripture Search

1. What does Saint Paul tell us about a healthy Christian attitude toward death in 2 Corinthians 4:1-18?

2. How did Jesus respond to the death of his friend Lazarus in John 11:1-43, especially 11:33? How did he prepare for his own death (Matthew 26:36-46)?

SECTION 2
The Meaning of Death

To accept death means to understand the significance of dying. In order for a new life to unfold, something has to die. Our Lord illustrated this with the parable of a seed. "Unless the grain of wheat falls to the earth and dies, it remains just a grain of wheat. But if it dies, it produces much fruit" (John 12:24). Only when hydrogen and oxygen molecules surrender their identity as hydrogen and oxygen can they become water. And only when we experience a physical death, can we come into the glorious existence of eternal life with the Lord.

Journey of Life

Death is closely related to love, the mysterious force that binds two people to each other so that they desire to share their lives together. Someone who loves another person longs to be with that loved one as much as possible. On earth, no love is perfect or complete. The love between human beings is only a hint of a larger answer to the heart's desire: an infinite love—God is love. Love in the human heart is the beating of the infinite. It is death that is the way to the complete and permanent experience of God's love, for it is death that unites us with God forever.

Actually, our death is the culmination of a series of death experiences beginning with Baptism. The baptismal vows bind us to die to our old ways and put on Christ. In every Eucharist we unite ourselves with the dying Jesus. Every act of Gospel charity is a kind of death to self. The Gospels repeatedly tell us that only if we lose our life for Christ's sake (by loving our neighbor) will we find it.

The last Communion, or Viaticum, which is brought to the dying, literally translates, "on the way." Just as Jesus has been with us on our journey through life, he is with us during the last stage of our earthly journey. We pass through death hand in hand with Christ. Christ's resurrection is our pledge that life is changed, not ended. Someone has said that death is not the period that ends the sentence of life, but a comma punctuating it for better things.

One practical value of death is that it renders life in this world more precious by making it temporary. Sunsets, dandelions, waterfalls, kittens, baseball games, pizzas, parents, and friends become more wonderful when we realize that our enjoyment of them will someday end. According to Saint Catherine of Siena, "All the way to heaven is heaven." The entire journey of life can be a marvelous adventure for those who make it a pilgrimage with Christ, who is "the way and the truth and the life" (John 14:6).

Determining Death

What does it mean to be "dead"? Theology and philosophy define death as the separation of the soul—the life-giving principle—from the body. Exactly when this occurs is a mystery. Science defines death as the disappearance of all signs of life in the organism as a whole. This death is sometimes called "somatic death."

The Moment of Death

The definition of death is still evolving. The absence of breath and heartbeat is no longer the sole criterion for determining the moment of death. Often, respiratory failure can be remedied by artificial respiration. Heart failure (cardiac arrest) does not always result in loss of consciousness, and treatment by chest massage, called cardiopulmonary resuscitation (CPR), and electrical stimulation can bring about reanimation, or reactivation.

Certain organs can die before **somatic** or complete death occurs. **Necrosis** is the death of individual body parts. On the other hand, some organs can remain alive a few hours after somatic death. This means that they can be donated to other people.

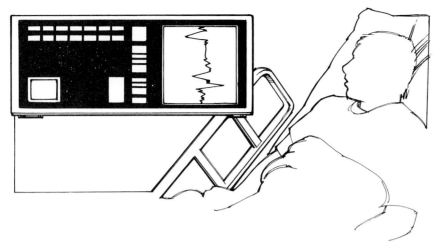

Modern medical science keeps changing the definition of death. One sign of death is zero brain activity as measured by the EEG.

The death of the total brain has been proposed as the determiner of death. Fed continuously by oxygen carried in the blood, brain cells stop functioning after three or four minutes without oxygen.

Even if breathing and circulation are restored after three or four minutes, the human personality can be lost. The brain stem continues to maintain vital functions and there is response to painful stimuli, but the cerebral cortex (the brain's outer layer largely responsible for higher nervous functions) no longer works.

After eight to ten minutes, these parts also die and, unlike body cells, cannot be replaced. After this point, if oxygen is applied and the heart is reactivated, the brain shows no signs of functioning, no reactions at all. This state is called "death of the brain." The death of the brain is defined as the irreversible loss of all brain functions. It is signaled by a zero-line EEG (electroencephalograph, the graphs of the electrical currents in the brain show no activity) and by changes in the brain's blood vessels. However, there may be brain activity to which the EEG is not sensitive.

In 1968, a Harvard University Committee under the direction of Dr. Henry Beecher proposed four criteria for determining the irreversible coma that is brain death:

1. no response to external stimuli or internal needs;
2. no spontaneous muscular movements or breathing;

Touching the Sacred

A Prayer for Mourners

While the Church teaches that it is "a holy and pious thought" to pray for the dead, and thus make "atonement" for them (2 Maccabees 12:45-46), the Church also encourages us to pray for those who mourn the loss of family and friends.

Here is one such prayer:

"Father, God of all consolation, in your unending love and mercy for us, you turn the darkness of death into the dawn of new life. Show compassion to your people in their sorrow. Your Son, our Lord Jesus Christ, by dying for us, conquered death, and by rising again, restored life. May we then go forward eagerly to meet him, and after our life on earth, be reunited with our brothers and sisters where every tear will be wiped away. (We ask this) through Christ our Lord. Amen" (prayer for mourners from the Liturgy of the Catholic Burial Rite from *The Rites of the Catholic Church*, Pueblo Publishing Co.).

3. no brain flexes; and
4. a flat EEG.

Twenty-four hours after the tests are made they must be repeated before the doctor pronounces death. Unmistakable signs that death has occurred are general decay, loss of body heat by three or four degrees each hour, and stiffening **(rigor mortis),** which sets in four to ten hours after death.

The Process of Dying

The actual process of dying can occur instantaneously and painlessly, or it can last for days in what is known as the death agony. Through medication, the suffering that death entails can be alleviated. The 1980 *"Declaration on Euthanasia,"* issued by the Vatican Congregation for the Doctrine of the Faith, permits the use of narcotics at the approach of death, even if it will shorten life, on the condition that no other means of suppressing pain and consciousness exist, and if it does not prevent the carrying

Mourning for a loved one is a natural reaction to death. There is no reason to feel embarrassed about a public expression of grief.

out of religious and moral duties as well as family obligations. Dying people have a right to prepare to meet Christ.

In the conviction that psychological pain can sometimes be worse than physical suffering surrounding death, a ministry known as the Hospice Movement provides means for terminally-ill patients to die with dignity. Hospice programs have been developed in many communities of the United States, through the efforts of concerned laity and professional people. They are supported by community donations.

A hospice team consists of a medical director who works with the family physician, nurses, social workers, lawyers, ministers, and care volunteers whose services enable families to provide quality home care for terminally-ill members. The team also advises and assists the survivors of the deceased. In Catholic hospice programs, through pain management and loving attention and care, the sick people are freed and encouraged to concentrate on the spiritual task of uniting themselves with Christ for the final segment of their journey.

Experience of People Who Have "Died"

Recently, people who claim to have died and then were brought back to life have related their experiences in encouraging terms. Many of them speak of leaving their body and going at great speed through a dark tunnel toward a brilliant light that is perceived as a Being. Often they enjoy flashbacks of their past life. Sometimes they are welcomed by friends and relatives who have died. Upon returning to life they remember being at peace and filled with joy. After his experience, one "dead" man said, "I am no longer afraid to die."

Cryonics is a modern attempt to cheat death. In Berkeley, California, some corpses are in cold storage, waiting until the causes of their deaths can be treated. Their bodies are frozen to -186 degrees Celsius in stainless-steel containers that are filled with liquid nitrogen. Advocates of cryonics speak hopefully of a time when eighty percent of the people who die now from certain diseases will be frozen just before death, then thawed out after cures have been discovered.

Chapter 14   Our Passage from Time to Eternity

10. *If you were able to select your own death, what kind of death would you choose?*

11. *What is your opinion of cryonics? Would you volunteer to be a living "frozen" person? Why or why not?*

12. *In what sense is death like love?*

13. *What rights do you think that dying people have?*

Death-Related Problems

Scientific advances have given rise to a host of moral problems concerning life and death. The Church's stand on any life issue is based on the belief that life is sacred and that no one can dispose of it at will. It is a gift of God's love to preserve and make fruitful.

Organ Transplants

Because the moment of death is debatable, the practice of transplants always involves risks. After the death of a whole organism, but when some organs are still alive, eye, heart, kidney, and liver transplants are possible. However, at least one doctor, who removed organs early enough to be used for transplant, has been accused of murder because another physician disagreed with his pronouncement of death.

One way in which death can bring new life is through an organ donation program.

Using Extraordinary Means

Through modern technology, a body can be kept functioning while the person is in a coma. This twilight state is the subject of the "pull the plug" controversy exemplified in the Karen Ann Quinlan case of 1975. Karen, a twenty-one-year-old woman in New Jersey, was kept alive through a respirator and intravenous feeding. With no hope for her recovery, her parents appealed to the courts to withdraw artificial life-support systems, which was done. Karen remained alive in a coma until June 11, 1985.

Helping Children Understand Death

Often, parents say nothing about death to their offspring because they wish to shield them or are themselves upset by it, or because they assume death is beyond a child's comprehension. Sooner or later, though, parents have to answer questions like "Why do people die?" and "Where do you go when you die?"

If parents impart the facts of death honestly and within a child's comprehension, they can prevent emotional harm to the child. Usually at the ages of seven and eight children learn to accept the inevitability and universality of death. Though admitting that they do not know everything about death, parents should awaken both an awareness of God's Providence and a corresponding trust in God. They can also share their Christian hope of eternal life based on the promises of Jesus: "Everyone who lives and believes in me will never die" (John 11:26). This hope enables us to live with the unanswered questions of life and death.

Adults can help children after the death of a loved one by allowing, but not forcing, them to attend the wake and funeral services. If the children are not at the burial, they can visit the cemetery later, after an explanation to prepare them for the experience. Children should be permitted healthy expressions of grief. To say "Be brave" or "Don't cry" is unrealistic and inhuman.

Children's symptoms of grief are similar to adult symptoms. Children sometimes seek a replacement for the love of the deceased, and may imitate or idealize him or her. It is not uncommon for them to blame themselves for a death in the family and to imagine that their wishes or bad deeds caused the death. To alleviate these symptoms, listen to a grieving child with patience, understanding, and sympathy, and emphasize the happy experiences shared with the deceased.

You can help others deal with the loss of a loved one by understanding about death yourself.

A major ethical question is, "Do we have an obligation to use life-supporting equipment to maintain life even when there is no hope of the person recovering consciousness?"

The Church's position is that when a person is manipulated by costly machines and measures that only serve to prolong dying and not to heal, that person is entitled to be allowed to die. *"The Declaration on Euthanasia"* affirmed a pronouncement of Pope Pius XII in 1957: "Normally one is held only to use ordinary means according to the circumstances of persons, places, times, and cultures, that is to say, means that do not involve any great burden for one's self or another." Extraordinary or disproportionate means would be those that are exceptionally 1. costly, 2. unusual, 3. painful, or 4. dangerous. The document encourages the use of means of **due proportion.** In other words, the judgment whether or not to use certain life-supporting systems must take into consideration: the conscience of the sick person; those who speak for him or her; the doctors who have studied the degree of complexity or risk, the cost, the feasibility of use, and the hope of results; and the state of the sick person. The patient has the "right to die" peacefully and with human and Christian dignity.

On the other hand, the document allows the use of advanced medical technology, even procedures that involve risk, if the patient consents. By this, the patient can be doing a service to humanity.

Euthanasia

Euthanasia is "mercy killing," an action or an omission that causes death in order to eliminate suffering. **Euthanasia** comes from the Greek *eu* (easy) and *thanatos* (death). Although euthanasia at first may sound like an act of mercy, a little thought reveals that besides violating a divine law, it is directly opposed to freedom and human dignity. It ignores the fact that suffering can have a purifying effect on the sufferer and those who come in contact with that person. Furthermore, euthanasia has dangerous consequences. Elderly or sick people may be pressured into asking to be killed. Handicapped babies might well be "mercifully" killed, too. But who determines which life should be ended? Does the value of human life vary with intelligence, facial characteristics, or physical defects? It was amoral answers to just these questions that spawned Hitler's Holocaust in which six million people not of the "master race" were put to death.

Obviously, there are no pat answers to these serious problems. For any rule that is proposed, there are bound to be exceptions. There is still too much we do not know about life and death. The general guideline is to treat each dying person with love and concern and to act according to conscience and with the advice of physicians.

14. How is removing a person from machines different than euthanasia?

15. What obligations do you think loved ones have to keep a dying person on life-support systems?

16. As terrible as it is to think about, what would you say to your family about sustaining your life if you were ever in Karen Ann Quinlan's situation?

17. What reasons would you give for either becoming an organ donor or refusing to become one?

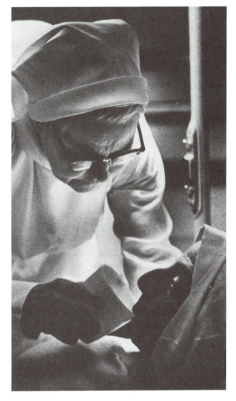

As a Christian you are called to care for the sick, treating each person with love and respect.

Summary

- Passing from life to death is really passing from one kind of life to another, more complete kind of life. In this, dying completes our love union with God.

- There are still a lot of questions about the exact moment of death. Everyone agrees, however, that dying is a process which the person involved must be allowed to face with dignity.

- The Catholic Church allows the use of extraordinary means to keep a terminally-ill person alive if that is the wish of the dying person or the family or guardian. It also allows loved ones to cease using these means when there is no hope of recovery. Euthanasia, however, is never permitted.

Chapter 14 Our Passage from Time to Eternity

SECTION 2
Checkpoint!

■ Review

1. What is the meaning of the terms "somatic death" and "necrosis"?

2. Which four criteria have been proposed for determining the irreversible coma that is brain death?

3. What is the Church's position on using extraordinary means to keep someone alive? On euthanasia?

4. While it is important for Catholics to be well-informed about medical questions regarding death and dying, what important religious issues must they also consider when facing their own deaths or that of family members or friends?

5. Words to Know: brain death, somatic death, necrosis, "extraordinary means" of life support, euthanasia.

■ In Your World

1. Discuss this situation: Mrs. Michaels thinks she has a bad case of pneumonia. Her doctor, however, just confirmed that her patient has lung cancer. Afraid that this news might crush her, the doctor chooses not to inform Mrs. Michaels of her condition. Besides, the doctor reasons, she will probably die peacefully in her sleep within a few days. So the doctor just tells Mrs. Michaels' family and advises them to decide for themselves whether to keep the secret or not.

2. A person who had a "death" experience and later lived to tell the story said, "I am no longer afraid to die." He spoke of experiencing peace and joy. Which teachings of Jesus seem to support the truth of this person's report?

■ Scripture Search

1. Discuss Jesus' image of the seed in John 12:24-25 as it pertains to the meaning of death for Christians.

2. What important message of hope does Jesus proclaim in John 11:25-26?

SECTION 3
Saying Good-Bye

When a loved one dies, survivors experience the natural and healthy reaction of profound sorrow and loss called grief. The symptoms of grieving vary. Although the acute grief process normally takes from six to twelve weeks, total readjustment can require from two to seven years. The stages of the grief process parallel Dr. Kubler-Ross's stages of dying. After all, dying people are grieving for all that they will soon be losing.

The Process of Grieving

The first reaction to the death of a loved one is **shock and denial.** Realization of the tragedy may take a few days. This is a time of numbness and disbelief. The survivors feel as if they are experiencing a nightmare or a fantasy trip. A type of **emotional release** is needed. Crying, a normal reaction to death, releases feelings. It is not uncommon for family fights to break out at funerals because of the tension. The emotional **pain** of grief and anxiety may cause **physical distress:** upset stomach, insomnia, headache, faintness, diarrhea, and sweating. Survivors might even develop the same symptoms the deceased had. Adding to the grief are the worry of being a burden to others and the sensitivity to comments that others make.

Two feelings that accompany grief are **guilt** and **anger.** Guilt, real or imagined, almost always occurs at the thought of things that should have been done for the person who died. Friends and families are haunted by regrets. Planning the funeral may alleviate some of these feelings. Anger arises at the feeling of being cheated. Blame is cast on those who might have prevented the death. Survivors feel that they do not know the whole truth about the death. One relief for these feelings is to vent them to a sympathetic listener.

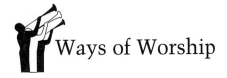
Ways of Worship

A Catholic Funeral

The actual funeral service begins with a ceremony recalling the person's baptism when he or she first experienced the death and resurrection of Christ. Then a white pall is placed on the coffin as a reminder of the baptismal robe. Just as at baptism the person received the Light of Christ, during the funeral Mass, the Paschal Candle burns. The Eucharist is the heart of the funeral rites. The mood is one of joy reflected in the white vestments of the priest. The reason for the celebration in the midst of sorrow is given in the prayers and readings of the Mass: the Church's faith in resurrection. At the end of Mass, a final commendation is a last farewell on the part of the community. Finally, the priest and the people unite in prayer at the cemetery. Many families gather after the funeral to share in a meal where the bereaved can experience further community support.

After the funeral, **loneliness** becomes more intense. Those who grieve feel incomplete; there is a vacancy in their lives. The grief-stricken can't express the loss they experience when the deceased is no longer present. They are restless and disorganized and find little peace, no matter what they do. An intense preoccupation with the deceased might cause the survivors to think something is wrong with them. They are tormented by questions, guilts, doubts, and mental replays of the death. Not understanding that this feeling of loss can last as long as six or twelve weeks can result in **panic.** Several weeks after the death, it is normal to experience **depression.** The bereaved feel weary and wish to withdraw and to suffer in silence. They doubt whether they can go on living, and they feel abandoned and useless. Deep, lonely feelings can be relieved by speaking about them with someone and by getting involved in activities.

Healing takes place when the survivors enter into activities; life begins to look brighter and more meaningful again. **Readjustment** has occurred when recalling the deceased is no longer a painful experience for them.

If you wonder how you will cope with death, consider this. If you had a very close friend who stopped being a friend for no reason that you could understand, you would probably experience some of the symptoms of the grief process. Also, how you react to other painful losses in your life might be a good indication of how you will react to death.

Managing Grief

The grief process is probably the most painful experience life offers. Yet it is unavoidable for anyone who has ever chosen to love another person. People are gifts who are given to us only for a time. We have to be ready to let go someday, and it hurts. The only way around grief is to experience it. However, there are measures that the bereaved can take to make the process more bearable.

In times of grief, your greatest reservoir of strength is God. You can also accept the sympathy of friends and relatives and let them support you. It is a mistake to play the role of a controlled, "model" sufferer. There is no need to try to live up to what you imagine are other people's expectations. The best therapy is to talk about your memories, fears, doubts, anger, guilt, depression, and loneliness. Also, feel free to consult professionals such as priests, physicians, psychologists, or funeral directors, all of whom understand the grief process.

Other Approaches to Grief

Other strategies for managing grief are

- *Face the fact of death to promote the passage of grief. Although viewing the body and discussing the deceased are painful, these things help you to accept the loss.*
- *Recall good memories and the time you spent together.*
- *Don't be afraid to cry. Although some consider tears a sign of weakness, tears heal. Jesus wept at the death of his friend Lazarus (John 11:35).*
- *Accept that what you're going through is normal.*
- *Realize that people grieve differently.*
- *Reach out to serve others to relieve your loneliness and to give new meaning to your life.*
- *Take the initiative in developing a new life with new interests, new choices, and new friendships.*
- *Don't try to avoid unpleasantness by making hasty decisions.*
- *Rely on faith and prayer. God will supply the amount of comfort and strength you need.*

One positive way to handle grief is to discuss your feelings freely with a person you trust.

18. How can you assist a friend or relative who is going through the healing process of grieving?

19. Why do you think that some families find themselves fighting after the death of a loved one? Why is this normal?

20. Some people believe that it is never "manly" for men to cry. What reasons can you give for saying that it's not only "manly," but it's also healthy?

21. If you had a friend who was depressed over the death of her father, what kinds of things can you think of doing to help her through the depression?

Chapter 14 Our Passage from Time to Eternity

The Funeral: Expressing Grief

Funeral customs of different cultures vary. Many of them are linked to belief in an afterlife. The Egyptians, for instance, constructed elaborate pyramids and underground tombs, well-equipped for life after death. The Greeks put a coin in the mouth of their corpses as payment for Charon, the ferryman who took the dead across the river Styx to the world of the dead. Funerals have a two-fold function: besides disposing of the dead person's body, they provide the framework for the expression of grief in a social context.

Arranging the Funeral

The closest relatives are usually responsible for arranging the funeral. At death, three professionals are prepared to offer assistance: a physician should be contacted to pronounce the person dead; the funeral director should be called immediately, at any time of the day or night, to assist with the practical and legal requirements of the funeral; and the parish priest should be notified, if he is not already on the scene, to minister to the survivors. Relatives and friends should be informed personally of the death. In consultation with the funeral director and the priest, the relatives make the necessary arrangements: write the obituary (a public notice of a person's death); file for financial benefits from insurance or service in the armed forces; decide on disposition of the body; plan the visitation, wake, funeral Mass (Mass of Christian Burial), cemetery arrangement, and burial.

Of the three methods of disposing of the remains of the deceased person, burial is the most common in the Western Church. The body may also be entombed in a mausoleum crypt (a vault above the ground—other crypts are underground) or it may be cremated. In the past, cremation was forbidden to Catholics, unless it was necessary (as in times of plagues), because frequently it was used as an act of defiance against belief in the resurrection of the dead. Few, if any, people today desire to be cremated for the sake of a theological argument; therefore, the Church now permits cremation. Because the body is a sacrament, the conditions for cremation are that no disrespect be intended for the body, and the ashes are not to be scattered.

Making funeral arrangements is a concrete way to say goodbye to the person you loved.

The "Farewell Process"

A funeral service is a sign of love and caring in a society that values life and respects the dignity of men and women even after death. When the body is buried and a typical religious funeral is celebrated, six elements of the "farewell process" are usually evident.

This process is really more for the survivors than for the deceased, since it helps mourners to deal with their grief in a psychologically healthy manner.

Catholic funeral practices normally incorporate all six of these elements:

Social support provides comfort during visitation, the funeral service, and committal to the grave.

Viewing the body is a step toward accepting the death and resolving grief. It erases denial and often initiates the emotional response. For all, it illustrates the reality of death.

The **religious ritual** allows for an expression of feelings and faith. It focuses the attention on ultimate realities and lets the bereaved assist the dead by prayers.

The **funeral procession** (cortege) draws people together, shows the community that a member has died, and honors the memory of the deceased.

Committal service demonstrates vividly that the earthly relationship between the mourners and the deceased is ended. It helps in coping with the finality of death.

Post-funeral service activities show mourners that people care.

◆

The Funeral Liturgy

The funeral liturgy meets the psychological and social needs of the family and friends. The contemporary Catholic funeral celebrates the resurrection and allows the mourners to participate in a final tribute to the dead person. Therefore, it strengthens faith and consoles the mourners.

Wake: a prayer service usually celebrated at the funeral home the evening before the funeral Mass.

Family members may choose from a variety of options in planning a beautiful and uplifting Eucharistic Liturgy. They may select the theme, the Scripture readings, and the music. Their participation might include being a lector, server, or pallbearer, composing the General Intercessions, being in the offertory procession, or distributing Communion. They might have individualized memorial cards and liturgy programs printed.

The Catholic funeral service is designed to allow as much family participation as possible in a final tribute to the dead person. The funeral expresses a belief in the Communion of Saints.

22. What personal touches have you witnessed at a funeral Mass that made it meaningful?

23. What is the proper funeral etiquette to console and support the bereaved? For instance, what can you say to the family at the wake? What can you do for them to show your concern?

24. Some people spend thousands of dollars for a funeral. They purchase a very expensive casket and order costly arrangements of flowers. While the sentiments of respect for the deceased are understandable in cases like this, what reasons can you give for a Christian funeral that is less extravagant? (Recall the funeral of Jesus.)

25. Why do you think that more and more Catholics today are choosing cremation? Why did the Church prohibit this practice in the past? Would you permit cremation of your body? What about organ donation? Give reasons for your answers.

Summary

- Grieving is a normal and healthy response to the loss of someone we love. Grief often involves the release of several emotions including guilt, anger, and depression.

- Grief is managed by a gradual process of healing which, for the Christian, always includes the courage that comes from faith and prayer.

- The funeral Mass is the most important prayer of healing for mourners that Christians can celebrate. At this liturgy, we express our hope in the life to come and we pray that God will strengthen our resolve to live in this hope.

SECTION 3
Checkpoint!

■ Review

1. What are some of the symptoms of grief? Why is it necessary for mourners to express (not repress) them?
2. How can survivors manage their grief?
3. What three methods of respectfully disposing of the body does the Church approve?
4. Name the six elements of the "farewell process."
5. Words to Know: grief, the "farewell process," cremation, wake.

■ In Your World

1. Write an essay to convince people that funerals are necessary.
2. In California's Forest Lawn Memorial Parks, the deceased are laid to rest in magnificent surroundings. Some funeral parlors arrange the bodies in natural settings and lifelike postures. What does this say about American attitudes toward death?

■ Scripture Search

1. Sirach had high praise for the physicians of his day, but he also realized the inevitability of death. Discuss Sirach (Ecclesiasticus) 38:1-23 and his thoughts on sickness and death.
2. Describe Paul's teaching about the resurrection in 1 Corinthians 15:12-44.

CHAPTER 14 Review

■ Study

1. How is death both an ending and a beginning?
2. How is ours a death-denying culture? Give examples.
3. What is brain death? How is it determined?
4. What is the role of the Hospice Movement?
5. Name some complex, current moral problems related to life and death.
6. Why is it important to express grief?
7. What are some typical symptoms of grief?
8. How can the process of grief be made less painful?
9. What is the two-fold purpose of funerals?
10. How does each assist at death: doctor, funeral director, priest?
11. How does the funeral liturgy strengthen faith? Console mourners?
12. How does our faith give a positive value to death?
13. How is death related to life? To love?
14. In what ways does a Christian die during life?

■ Action

1. Work out a multimedia presentation on death, incorporating music, art, and literature with death themes.

2. Visit a funeral home and note (a) features planned for the comfort of the bereaved; (b) ways the funeral director helps the family; (c) how the body is prepared; and (d) the qualities needed by a good funeral director. Write a report on your findings.

3. Collect articles on a crucial issue related to death and dying ("pulling the plug," living wills, cryonics, euthanasia, and so on). Write your reaction to them or organize a debate around them.

4. Plan your own obituary, funeral arrangements, and Mass. Compose your epitaph (a brief statement or verse that reveals the values or characteristics of the deceased) and design your tombstone.

■ Prayer

This prayer, adapted from traditional prayers for the dead and from Psalm 23, helps us to remember our loved ones who now live with the Lord. It also speaks God's Word of comfort and hope to us especially if someone we love has recently died.

The Lord is my shepherd; I shall not want.
In green pastures he gives me repose.
Besides restful waters he leads me; he refreshes my soul.
Even though I walk in the dark valley,
I fear no evil, for you are at my side.
O God, creator and salvation of all your people,
Hear my prayer for (Name/s).
Welcome all the departed into your kingdom.
Forgive their sins. Eternal rest grant unto them, O Lord.
And let perpetual light shine upon them.
(Pause to remember those for whom you are praying. Thank God for the gift of their lives. Then, continue your prayer.)
You spread a banquet for me in the sight of my foes.
You anoint my head with oil, My cup of blessing overflows.
Only goodness and kindness shall follow me,
All the days of my life. And I shall live in the house of the Lord forever.
May the souls of all the faithful departed rest in peace. Amen.

CHAPTER

15

Our Final Destiny

OBJECTIVES

In this Chapter you will

- Understand the Catholic belief that new life comes through death.

- Consider the Church's teaching about heaven and hell.

- Examine the doctrines of purgatory, the Last Judgment, and the end of the world.

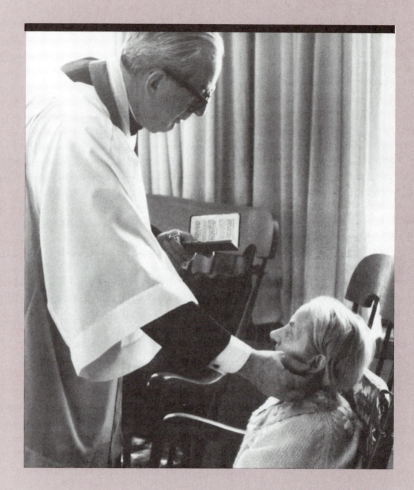

At present we see indistinctly, as in a mirror, but then face to face. At present I know partially; then I shall know fully as I am fully known. So faith, hope, love remain, these three; but the greatest of these is love.
—1 Corinthians 13:12-13

SECTION 1
Where to from Here?

One afternoon a father decided to take his family with him to a talk he was to give. His six-year-old daughter had not been informed of their destination. As they drove along, she suddenly piped up, "Daddy, when we get to where we're going, where will we be?"

That same question has intrigued people for centuries. We feel in our bones that when the journey of our earthly life is ended, a future awaits us on the other side of the grave. But what this future is remains a mystery.

In this chapter, the last things are analyzed according to popular notions, what the Church teaches, scriptural references, and theological speculation. For full knowledge of your final destination, you will have to wait until you cross the threshold.

The Last Things

Death, judgment, heaven, and hell are referred to as **the last things. Eschatology** is the study of these things, the ultimate fate of humanity and creation. The root of **eschatology** is the Greek word, *eschatos,* which means "last, farthest, extreme." The Church has defined very little concerning the afterlife, and the Bible's revelation about it often is packaged in obscure, symbolic language. Down through the years, though, Christian imagination has filled in answers to eschatological questions. Many of these conjectures, some highly questionable, became entrenched in people's minds as firmly as dogma. They continue to shape popular concepts of the last things today.

A major difficulty in pondering the afterlife is that our language and concepts are based on what we have experienced in this world, but they are inadequate to describe what must be the utterly different world of the future. At best we can only be sensitive to the hints of eternal life in this world, study God's revelation, pray, and then use our common sense to speculate on what the next world will be like.

---

1. *The eschatological image that Jesus most often used was "kingdom of God." What are some of the images for the kingdom that have been discussed in this book so far? How do they describe "the last things"?*

Death and Resurrection

Humanity has always hoped to live forever. Ponce de Leon and his men weren't the only ones ever to search for the fountain of youth. None of us wants to think of ourselves as no longer in existence. The Christian hope in eternal life is that it gives meaning to the present life. The crucial question we face is not, "Why do we die?" but, "How can we best live?" This question is satisfactorily answered only in terms of a future.

Prehistoric peoples concluded there must be an afterlife. So did advanced civilizations like that of the Egyptians, who equipped their tombs with food, models of servants *(ushabtis),* and even restrooms for the convenience of the deceased in the next life. The Jews believed in Sheol, a land of the dead in the deepest regions of the earth. There, they believed, people lived like shadows in a dark, sad, and meaningless existence.

In the face of death, which looks so final, Christianity confidently offers hope for immortality to those who believe in and live for Jesus.

Because of its significance for the whole human race, the resurrection of Jesus Christ is the key event in history, revealing, as it did, our future. Scripture promises, "If the Spirit of the one who raised Jesus from the dead dwells in you, the one who raised Christ from the dead will give life to your mortal bodies also, through his Spirit that dwells in you" (Romans 8:11). Jesus' resurrection heralded the coming of a new age and was the beginning of the last days.

Through the ages, artists have pictured the afterlife in many ways.

Hope in the Kingdom of God

The Israelites of the Hebrew Scriptures longed for the reign of God where peace and justice would rule the land. Today we still hope for this type of existence.

We believe that the last day will bring the kingdom of God to its completion. Our union with the communion of saints that we believed in on earth will be manifested, and all our hopes will be fulfilled. We echo the prayer of those Christians who closed the last book of the Bible with "Come, Lord Jesus!" (Revelation 22:20). While we wait, we celebrate Eucharist because "For as often as you eat this bread and drink the cup, you proclaim the death of the Lord until he comes" (1 Corinthians 11:26). This sacred banquet anticipates the heavenly banquet won for us by Christ, the "Alpha and the Omega, the first and the last, the beginning and the end" (Revelation 22:13).

At the end of our earthly journey, if we are real pilgrims, we will begin another journey, one that promises to be more exciting than the one we travel now. The journey of eternity consists of penetrating evermore deeply into the mystery of God. United with God, and with one another in God, we will walk the streets of the heavenly Jerusalem where the Lord will be our Light and "night will be no more" (Revelation 22:50).

Beginning to Experience the Kingdom Now

We don't have to wait until after death to experience the power and the glory of Christ's resurrection and the peace and joy of his kingdom (Philippians 3:10). Although eschatology belongs to the realm of "not yet," there is what is called "realized eschatology." Because the fate of humankind has been sealed by the firstborn (Revelation 1:5), who is seated at the right hand of the Father, we already can experience union with God through the sacraments, especially Baptism and Eucharist. The kingdom

Touching the Sacred

A Prayer of Preparation for the Life to Come

There are many beautiful prayers in the liturgy that refer to everlasting life, for union with God is the goal of all Christians and the hope that we proclaim to the world.

This prayer comes from the liturgy of the Seventh Sunday of Easter:

"Eternal Father, reaching from end to end of the universe, and ordering all things with your mighty arm; for you, time is the unfolding of truth that already is, the unveiling of beauty that is yet to be. Your Son has saved us in history by rising from the dead, so that transcending time he might free us from death. May his presence among us lead us to the vision of unlimited truth and unfold the beauty of your love. We ask this in the name of Jesus the Lord. Amen."

has already come (see Luke 17:21). The reign of God is in our midst, and we are progressing into God's future. We "are being transformed into the same image from glory to glory, as from the Lord who is the Spirit" (2 Corinthians 3:18).

The *"Document on the Church"* from Vatican II stressed that the restoration of all things has begun. Christians, transformed by God's grace, work to bring creation to the ultimate glory for which it was made. However, our longing for perfection, fulfillment, and transcendence will not be completely satisfied until the *Parousia,* the worldwide manifestation of the glory of Jesus at the end of time. *Parousia* (a Greek word) refers to Christ's (second) coming in glory. Until then, as Saint Paul says, "I consider that the sufferings of this present time are nothing compared with the glory to be revealed for us... We know that all creation is groaning in labor pains even until now; and not only that, but we ourselves, who have the firstfruits of the Spirit, we also groan within ourselves as we wait for adoption, the redemption of our bodies" (Romans 8:18-23).

We don't know what we will be like in eternity. Saint Paul speaks in a parable, "And what you sow is not the body that is to be but a kernel of wheat, perhaps, or of some other kind... It is sown corruptible; it is raised incorruptible. It is sown dishonorable; it is raised glorious. It is sown weak; it is raised powerful. It is sown a natural body; it is raised a spiritual body" (1 Corinthians 15:37-44).

A New Mode of Existence

Obviously, in eternity we will have a new mode of existence and live in another dimension. But we will not be just a depersonalized life force or a shadowy soul separated from the body. Jesus "will change our lowly body to conform with his glorified body" (Philippians 3:21). In his risen body, Jesus walked, talked, and ate. He was identifiable as himself and even bore the sacred wounds (of the crucifixion) in his body. Yet something was different because people did not recognize him immediately.

That we will be ourselves but different in eternity should not be too upsetting considering that, of the sixty trillion cells in our bodies, five hundred million are renewed every day. Our genetic structure ensures our identity despite the change. Similarly, we will still be ourselves in eternity but in a glorified body.

The body of Christ in the Transfiguration and after Easter provides clues as to what our bodies will be like after our resurrection. Since the Council of Trent (sixteenth century), the traditional characteristics of the glorified body are believed to be **agility,** the ability to move instantly from one place to another; **subtlety** or **spirituality,** the ability to pass through matter; **impassibility,** freedom from death and pain; and **clarity,** beauty and brightness of soul manifested in the body.

In the Apostles' Creed, Christians profess, "I believe in the resurrection of the body." Because of this belief, Christians hold the body in great reverence, and, to their last breaths, never know a purposeless moment. Whatever we do affects our existence forever; therefore, belief in the afterlife increases our responsibility for ourselves and for others.

2. What are some consequences of the mystery of the resurrection in your life? How does it affect your attitudes? Your actions?

3. What are some of the things non-believers do that express a desire to live forever?

4. What are some of the characteristics of the "glorified body"?

Jesus' body was glorified after the Resurrection. Your body will experience a new mode of existence after your death as well.

Summary

- Death, judgment, heaven, and hell are called "the last things," sometimes referred to as the topic, "eschatology."

- As Christians, we believe that we are destined to live with God forever in a new kind of existence, the kingdom of heaven.

- Though the fullness of new life awaits us after death, we can begin to experience the joys of God's kingdom now by following Christ faithfully and by celebrating the sacraments.

Chapter 15 Our Final Destiny

SECTION 1
Checkpoint!

■ Review

1. Define "eschatology" and relate this term to our belief in the things to come.

2. How is the "glorified body" different than the body as we now experience it?

3. Describe Paul's comparison of the life to come with the seed that is planted and grows.

4. What is the *Parousia*?

5. Words to Know: eschatology, *Parousia*, glorified body.

■ In Your World

1. Complete these two statements:
   Heaven is ...   Hell is ...
   Describe why you ended your statements as you did.

2. How do the following natural phenomena suggest resurrection?
   ■ A caterpillar spins a cocoon and emerges from it as a butterfly.
   ■ A winter landscape bursts into green in the spring.
   ■ A sleeping person wakes up at dawn.
   ■ An inconspicuous seed produces a beautiful flower.

■ Scripture Search

1. Our Lord's description of the Second Coming is found in Matthew 24:25-35. As you read these verses, make a list of the symbols Christ uses to emphasize the suddenness of this event and the need to be ready for it at all times.

2. Read Luke 14:16-24 and Matthew 22:1-14. What do these parables reveal about who participates in the heavenly feast of the kingdom?

SECTION 2
Heaven and Hell

Not many people are eager to reach heaven as our ancestors conceived it. Imagine typical TV "bad guys" or "jet setters" trying to lead good lives so that they can live forever on puffy pink clouds and play harps. Even Catholics who like the latest fashions and plenty of activity probably wouldn't look forward to wearing a long white robe and spending forever in the state of "eternal rest." But do not fear. About the only fact we know about heaven is that it exists.

The New Vision of Heaven

Saint Paul, who had a vision of heaven, could only say, "What eye has not seen, and ear has not heard, and what has not entered the human heart, what God has prepared for those who love him" (1 Corinthians 2:9). We can be sure that whatever heaven is like, we will enjoy it. God who made us knows best what makes us happy, and sometimes he gives us a foretaste of eternal bliss on earth.

Seeing the beauty of a sunset or of sunlight reflecting on a waterfall, receiving an unexpected gift from a friend, experiencing creative inspiration, or spending time with someone you love are all occasions when you might experience a foretaste of heaven.

The main source of joy in heaven will be the face-to-face encounter with God, creator of all the wonderful things in this world and whose presence is more than our limited imaginations can fathom. **Beatific Vision** is the term for the clear "sight" of God that produces exalted joy and blessedness in those who attain heaven. We will be with the Father, Son, and Holy Spirit forever. On earth we sometimes feel far from God, from others, and even from

Dore illustration from Dante's Paradiso
This is one person's attempt to imagine heaven. What would your picture of heaven look like? Draw it.

Ways of Worship

In Thanksgiving

"Father of mercy, you always answer your people in their sufferings. We thank you for your kindness and ask you to free us from all evil, that we may serve you in happiness all our days. We ask this through our Lord Jesus Christ, your Son, who lives and reigns with you and the Holy Spirit, one God, for ever and ever. Amen" (Opening Prayer, Votive Mass of Thanksgiving).

ourselves. In heaven we will be fully integrated individuals, free to respond completely to the love of God and of others. Another advantage of heaven is that we will be in the company and mutual love of Mary, the angels, the saints, and our loved ones. Also, the ties of blood and friendship will somehow continue in eternity. Saint Paul wrote, "At present we see indistinctly, as in a mirror, but then face to face. At present I know partially; then I shall know fully as I am fully known" (1 Corinthians 13:12). By knowledge he meant not only book knowledge, but intimate knowledge of people and things.

To express the communion and fellowship of heaven, we often speak of it in terms of a meal. Our Lord in his parables frequently speaks of heaven as a great supper or wedding feast. In Marc Connelley's play *Green Pastures,* heaven is an everlasting fish fry!

Worship and Sacraments: We Celebrate, We Praise

Scripture implies that heaven will be different for each person. There are degrees of happiness according to how much God was known and loved on earth. John 14:2; 1 Corinthians 3:8, 15:14-44; and 2 Corinthians 9:6 refer to the different degrees of happiness in heaven. Saint Therese of Lisieux explains these degrees by speaking of different-sized glasses. Each glass holds a different amount of water, yet each glass is full. In heaven we will be perfectly happy, but not equally happy.

5. What experiences have you had that make you sense what it means to be perfectly happy?

6. A modern parable describes both heaven and hell as banquets where the tables are laden with food, but chopsticks three feet long are at every place. In Hell, the people sit staring at the food, helplessly starving. In heaven, the guests joyfully feed one another. What is the point of this parable?

7. Write a description of heaven as you would wish it to be.

8. What does speaking of heaven as a "face-to-face" encounter with God suggest about the life we are destined to live forever?

Hell

The Church declares that, like heaven, hell does exist. Moreover, it teaches that hell is eternal. What it doesn't explain is the nature of hell.

An element common to most people's view of hell is fire because, in speaking of hell, Christ mentions fire many times. Most Scripure commentators today think that this fire, along with the gnashing of teeth and the worms that never die, is symbolic language characteristic of apocalyptic writing. **Apocalyptic writing** is a form of writing that flourished between 200 B.C. and A.D. 200. It focuses on the last things and relies heavily on spectacular imagery. Those who wrote about the eternal place of punishment chose imagery that conveyed the ideas of pain and horror.

The traditional image of hell shows people suffering in fire, punished by the devil. What is your image of hell?

Hell in Literature

Feodor Dostoevski (1821-1881) was a Russian novelist; Jean Paul Sartre (1905-1980), a French philosopher, playwright, and novelist; T. S. Eliot (1888-1965), an English poet, critic, and playwright; Dante Alighieri (1265-1321), an Italian poet.

These four writers have given us some of the most enduring images of hell in Western literature. After reading their descriptions of eternal damnation, decide which one you think is closest to the reality of eternal loss that we call hell.

In Dostoevski's *Brothers Karamazov,* a holy priest states, "Hell...is the suffering of being unable to love." In Sartre's play, *No Exit,* a character says, "Hell, it's other people." And, according to T.S. Eliot's play *The Cocktail Party,* "Hell is oneself." Probably the most creative hell is detailed in the *Divine Comedy* by Dante. Modeled on the Middle Age's conception of perfection in nine degrees, Dante's hell and heaven have nine levels each. Sinners in his hell are punished in a manner that matches their outstanding sin. Lustful sinners, for example, are attacked by violent winds that represent their unleashed passions. Hypocrites are burdened by heavy, gorgeous robes. And traitors are frozen in a block of ice because they could feel no loyalty.

The one thing that all these descriptions have in common is that they are consequences of attitudes and behaviors that people exhibited in life. To put it another way, these writers seemed to be suggesting that we make our own hell. If they are correct, maybe wicked people don't have to wait until the next life before they begin to experience hell. Maybe they start "going to hell" in **this** life. What do you think?

The agony of hell is complete separation from God and so the complete absence of love. This pain of loss, this powerlessness to love is forever. You can imagine the anger, frustration, regret, solitude, and emptiness of those who are in hell. Through the centuries, theologians of several persuasions have proposed three possibilities for those who choose evil: (1) eternal damnation, which means continued existence and frustration of all that it means to be human; (2) annihilation, or total cessation of existence; and (3) *apokatastasis*, a complete restoration by which eventually no one will be either destroyed or eternally frustrated.

Eternal damnation acknowledges the seriousness of human decisions, but for some it raises questions about God's plan for universal salvation. Annihilation implies that moral decisions are serious, but it makes evil triumph over good. Complete restoration undercuts the seriousness of human choice because, even if the punishment period lasts "two or three million years," what is that compared to an eternity of happiness with God?

Some theologians, reflecting on the great mercy of God, question whether anyone is damned. However, considering God's justice and the price Jesus paid for sin, it would seem a mockery of God's plan and a diminishment of human responsibility to discount the existence of eternal punishment. Christianity has consistently rejected annihilation as well as *apokatastasis* (ultimate restoration) and, instead, has spoken of eternal frustration (hell) for those who opt against God.

Summary

- Catholics believe that God wills the salvation of all people and that our destiny is to live with him forever in the life we call heaven.

- The Church also recognizes the existence of hell, an eternal separation from God.

- While both heaven and hell are modes (ways) of life **after** death, there's a sense in which we begin to experience either eternal bliss or eternal separation from God by how we conduct our lives in this world.

SECTION 2
Checkpoint!

■ Review

1. What is the Beatific Vision?

2. In the kingdom of heaven, whose company do we enjoy, besides that of God?

3. Name and explain the three theological theories that propose possibilities for those who lived and died as genuinely evil people.

4. What are some of the literary attempts to image hell? How do these images portray the effects of sins?

5. Words to Know: Beatific Vision, *apokatastasis*.

■ In Your World

1. Which is more effective: to live in fear of hell or to live in hope while seeking heaven? Why?

2. When are people apt to think about heaven and hell? Why is it good to consider the afterlife from time to time?

■ Scripture Search

1. Read the parable about the rich man and Lazarus in Luke 16:19-31. Why is the rich man in hell? How does this parable describe hell?

2. What do these verses tell you about heaven: Matthew 5:12, 6:9; John 14:1-2; Hebrews 8:1-2; 1 Peter 1:3-5; Revelation 4:1-11?

SECTION 3
Purgatory and the Last Judgment

The Church teaches that the life of each person is evaluated by God at the moment of death in what is called "the particular judgment." Those whose journeys toward union with God have led them to the Beatific Vision, continue their life after death in the kingdom of heaven. Those who have completely cast God out of their lives on earth, live on in an eternity of separation from God.

But as we well know, our lives are often not lived clearly for or against God. We can be oriented toward God and be moderately successful in our efforts to remain faithful, but still not be prepared for final union with the Trinity when we die. In that case, the Church teaches, we enter a period of final cleansing before the "general judgment" at the end of time. We continue our journey toward heaven after death in the state of purgatory.

The Interim Period

On November 2, after the Feast of All Saints, the Church celebrates the Feast of All Souls when we remember the people who have died but who have not yet entered into God's presence. We believe that they are in purgatory. Purgatory, a symbolic way of speaking of a mystery we do not fully understand, takes its name from the word **purge.** The Church teaches that through some kind of suffering during an interim period, the guilty acts of a person's life can be atoned for and purged. In this final transformation of love, we are enabled to endure the gaze of God.

Chapter 15   Our Final Destiny

On the Record

Indulgences

An indulgence is a partial or complete ("plenary") remission or cancellation of the punishment that we might otherwise receive for our sins after death.

This belief is closely related to belief in purgatory. In about the eleventh century, Catholics began to see that even though our sins have been forgiven, it is still necessary for us to "cleanse" ourselves in purgatory from the effects of sin.

This "cleansing," of course, is accomplished by prayer and good works in this life, too. Therefore, the Church began assigning special significance to certain acts of prayer, fasting, and almsgiving. These acts were called "indulgences."

When a particular prayer, for example, is said to gain an indulgence of three hundred days, the Church is telling us that it has the same helpful effect as praying, fasting, or giving alms over the course of an entire year. It does not mean that we get out of purgatory three hundred days sooner!

The Book of Revelation says of heaven, "nothing unclean will enter it" (Revelation 21:27). Those who die in a state of friendship with God, but unworthy yet of union with God, need purification. Unlike hell, the so-called "fire" of this state is a fire of joy, the pain of love, because it leads to everlasting bliss in heaven. For an idea of this joyful agony, recall when you have waited to see someone you love. Remember how the days dragged by and how your longing to see the person became so intense that it was painful. And yet, you were happy because you knew that eventually he or she would be with you.

Since there is no measurement of time in eternity, we can't speak of how long any state beyond earthly bounds lasts. Some theologians propose that purgatory is the suffering that people experience when they directly encounter the holiness of God and realize their wretchedness. Some suggest that it is the process of knowing God better than God was known on earth, so as to be better prepared to share the divine love in heaven.

A beautiful point of the uniquely Catholic doctrine of purgatory is that we on earth can assist the people in purgatory by our prayers and actions. We can offer Masses for the Dead. On the other hand, those in purgatory can pray for us. This is partially what is meant by "the communion of saints." Traditionally, this has also been phrased as the Church Suffering assisting the Church Militant. The concept of purgatory is based on a long-standing Church tradition as well as a Hebrew Scriptures text. Scripture comments on the sacrifice that Judas Maccabees offered: "He made atonement for the dead that they might be freed from this sin" (2 Maccabees 12:46).

9. Some religious groups believe in "predestination," that is, God has already decided (destined) ahead of time (pre) who will be condemned. Why do you think that the Catholic Church rejects predestination?

10. Some people who do not want to spend any part of eternity separated from God hope to bypass final purification altogether. What could they do on earth to avoid it?

Detail in The Last Judgment, **Michelangelo, Sistine Chapel ceiling, Rome**
Purgatory is not a place of punishment as this picture might indicate. Rather, Purgatory is understood to be a period of preparation before facing God.

The General Judgment

In 2 Corinthians 5:10, we read, "We must all appear before the judgment seat of Christ, so that each one may receive recompense, according to what he did in the body, whether good or evil."

Although there is no definite dogma on specifics of the judgment, it is generally held that at the end of time God will judge all people. One source of this belief is the Biblical description of such a judgment in which Christ separates people according to the way they treated one another (see Matthew 25:31-46). Those who loved will be rewarded with eternal life, whereas those who refused to love will be consigned to hell. This is the general judgment, a social judgment.

We shall be judged as members of the human race to reveal to all God's justice and mercy (see Hebrews 9:27).

Chapter 15   Our Final Destiny

Immediately after death, we shall be judged on our service of God and our moral conduct. As we have already seen, this is called the particular judgment.

Vatican II focused on the communal aspect of the general judgment. Humanity as a whole will be judged as fulfilled or not. It is the responsibility of each member to work for the perfection of the human race.

---

11. *Why do you think that the general judgment is sometimes called a "social judgment"?*

12. *Scripture has been called a "two-edged sword." It's God's Word of mercy **and** judgment. In what sense does the Word of God "judge" us even before we face the Lord in the particular and general judgments?*

The End of Time

Chances are that, as you read this, someone somewhere is predicting that the end of the world is near. But Jesus declared, "But of that day and hour no one knows, neither the angels of heaven, nor the Son, but the Father alone" (Matthew 24:36). That means no one knows if the last day of life in this world will be in thirty thousand years or today.

Scripture paints the scene of the last day in vivid and terrifying technicolor. Its symbols convey the awe and grandeur of the atmosphere of that day. The theologians of previous centuries portrayed the end of the world as a black day when "even saints shall comfort need." However, our thinking is more like the first Christians who looked forward to the Second Coming of Christ. The Day of the Lord brings all creation and all people to fulfillment. It will come like the blossoms that appear overnight in the springtime and renew the earth. It will be a great day of rejoicing, for we will be transformed and enter into eternal life with the Lord. Saint John describes this day in the book of Revelation: "I also saw the holy city, a new Jerusalem, coming down out of heaven from God, prepared as a bride adorned for her husband. I heard a loud voice from the throne saying,

The Apocalypse, *drawn by Albrecht Dürer*
When the end of the world will occur only God knows. Read the Book of Revelation to see how the writer envisioned that time.

Dreaming the Possibilities

Key truths of religion have often been described in abstract terms, but today, television, print, radio, and high technology are helping us to visualize new horizons as we see our world in images never even considered by the abstract thinkers of the past.

On television, you watch a play in a football game from hundreds of miles away. Then you see a replay in slow motion, again close up, and then from another angle. Time and space collapse into each other before your very eyes. Different kinds of ships now take us over water, into air, and to the ocean floor. In some ways, the space shuttle is a ship that can carry humans into space. Telescopes, microscopes, X-ray, and ultrasound images reveal new worlds.

What will your world, transformed according to Gospel expectations, be like? Have you ever tried to imagine the possibilities? It is sometimes helpful to put our imaginations to work when trying to understand the future God has in store for us.

Theologians tell us that the world, transformed into the kingdom of God as it will come to us in its fullness at the end of time, is not just a **better** kind of world. Rather, it will be a **brand new** kind of world. What God is preparing for us after the Second Coming of Christ is impossible to predict in detail. Expressions like the "Beatific Vision" and "Paradise" can only approximate the joy and peace that is to come.

But dreaming the possibilities for transformation and new life in the final age may help us strive for ways to cooperate with God's divine plan more faithfully now. What kind of brand new world can you imagine?

Your dreams for the future are important: career, vocation, special trips. Your dreams about life with God are very important, too.

'Behold, God's dwelling is with the human race. He will dwell with them and they will be his people and God himself will always be with them [as their God]. He will wipe every tear from their eyes, and there shall be no more death or

Chapter 15 Our Final Destiny

mourning, wailing or pain, [for] the old order has passed away' " (Revelation 21:2-4).

Besides thinking of the "end" of time exclusively in terms of the **destruction** of the world, as some Christians do, we can also speak of the "end" as the word is sometimes used in English: that is, the **final purpose.** (As in the expression: "Toward what **end** do we work day after day?")

The end of time, the *Parousia* and the final judgment, will indeed involve the transformation of God's people. It will also be the moment in time when God's purpose for us is fulfilled. All creation, destined to be God's own likeness from the first moment of creation (Genesis 1:26) will finally become what God made us to be.

Sin will be conquered. People will live at peace. All things will be reconciled to God (2 Corinthians 5:19). This is our faith, and because it is, we joyfully respond to God's great gift of divine grace in the "Glory to God" prayer at Mass when we say "We worship you, We praise you!"

---

13. *What are some practical ways that we can worship and praise God in preparation for the end of time?*

Summary

- Purgatory is the period of transition and atonement for those who will eventually be one with God in heaven.

- The general judgment, sometimes called the last judgment, is God's final evaluation of how well we lived our lives. After this time, the fullness of God's reign will be expressed by all who are saved.

- The end of time is the achievement of God's final purpose for all creation. Though Scripture uses images of destruction to describe the end of the world as we know it, the "Good News" of revelation is that God will **transform** creation at that time into a brand new kind of life.

SECTION 3
Checkpoint!

■ Review

1. Summarize the meaning of the Church's teaching on purgatory.

2. Describe the particular judgment and the general (last) judgment.

3. How does the doctrine of the end of time help us to understand God's ultimate purpose for creation?

4. What are indulgences and how are they helpful reminders of our need for reconciliation with God?

5. Words to Know: purgatory, general judgment, particular judgment, communion of saints, indulgences.

■ In Your World

1. How is one's afterlife the outgrowth of a creative or destructive lifestyle?

2. How would you explain heaven, hell, and purgatory to a child?

■ Scripture Search

1. What reasons can you give for God's evaluating (judging) our lives when we die and at the end of time? (See Luke 19:11-27.)

2. What images does Jesus use in Mark 13:32-37 for the day of his return? What other images can you think of?

Chapter 15   Our Final Destiny

CHAPTER 15 Review

■ Study

1. Why do we believe in our resurrection?
2. How is eschatology concerned with the present as well as with the future?
3. In what sense is the Eucharist a "taste" of God's kingdom even now?
4. What is a glorified body like?
5. What are the joys of heaven?
6. What is known about hell? What is unknown?
7. What are some of the images that are frequently used to depict hell?
8. What determines the fate of a person in eternal life?
9. How is the general judgment different from the particular judgment?
10. Why can we anticipate the end of the world more in hope than in fear?
11. How does our belief in indulgences help us to be more aware of the importance of reconciliation in our lives?
12. Why is it not exactly correct to say that the kingdom of God is a **better** world yet to come?

■ Action

1. Ask some people what they believe about heaven and hell. Report on their answers.
2. Research what people of other religions believe about the afterlife.
3. Write a poem or essay on heaven or hell using images from today's world.
4. Collect quotes or poems on death, heaven, or hell, or write one of your own.
5. Examine the funeral liturgy for references to: (a) resurrection; (b) judgment; (c) heaven; and (d) hell. What truths are they based on?
6. Find a book that discusses Egyptian religion. How did the ancient Egyptian view immortality?

■ Prayer

As we prepare for our final destiny by living good Christian lives, this prayer (attributed to Pope Clement XI) can help us recall the things that really matter for Christians. Clement XI was pope from 1700 to 1721, but the words of his "Universal Prayer," quoted in part below, speak encouragement and hope for all of us today.

"Lord, I believe in you: increase my faith. I trust in you: strengthen my trust. I love you: let me love you more and more. I am sorry for my sins: deepen my sorrow.

"I worship you as my first beginning, I long for you as my last end, I praise you as my constant helper, and call on you as my loving protector.

"Guide me by your wisdom, correct me with your justice, comfort me with your mercy, protect me with your power.

"I want to do what you ask of me: in the way you ask, for as long as you ask, because you ask it.

"Lord, enlighten my understanding, strengthen my will, purify my heart, and make me holy.

"Help me to repent of my past sins and to resist temptation in the future. Help me to rise above my human weaknesses and to grow stronger as a Christian.

"Help me to conquer anger with gentleness, greed by generosity, apathy by fervor. Help me to forget myself and to reach out toward others.

"Teach me to realize that this world is passing, that my true future is the happiness of heaven, that life on earth is short, and the life to come eternal.

"Help me to prepare for death with a proper fear of judgment, but a greater trust in your goodness. Lead me safely through death to the endless joy of heaven.

"Grant this through Christ our Lord. Amen" (from *The Sacramentary,* 1974, pages 1012-1013).

Index

Abortion, 231
Abraham, 23, 24, 25, 28, 37, 63, 252
Abstinence, 254, 298
Absolution, 260
Acts of the Apostles, 82, 102, 122, 212, 213, 302, 342, 343
Adam and Eve, 112, 235, 251
Advent, 282, 283, 287, 289, 290, 345
Agnes, Saint, 352
Alleluia, 174, 175, 300
All Saints, 84, 336, 403
All Souls, 403
Alpha and Omega, 393
Altars, 17, 23, 186
Ambo (lectern), 186
Amen, the Great, 82, 172, 178
Anglicans, 329
Anointing of the Sick, 114, 121, 269, 270, 272–276
Annunciation, 290, 342, 345
Antioch, 204
Apocalyptic writing, 399
Apostles, 39, 45–48, 52, 64–66, 71–77, 97, 117, 148, 164, 168, 212, 213, 336, 337
Aquinas, Saint Thomas, 114, 152
Ark of the Covenant, the, 28–30
Armstrong, Neil, 35
Ascension, feast of the, 84, 299, 302, 342
Ash Wednesday, 296, 298
Assumption, 84, 342–347
Atonement, 265, 374, 404
Augustine, Saint, 114, 300, 354

Baptism, 113, 114, 121
　anointing with oil, 145
　blessing of water, 145
　covenant of friendship, 144
　a death experience, 371
　Easter Vigil service of, 138
　Holy Spirit given, 148
　infant, 133, 145, 147
　infusion of virtues, 198
　immersion, 145
　initiation, 137, 143
　of Jesus, 143
　of John the Baptist, 143
　into life of Spirit, 29
　parents' role, 145
　prayer, 145
　reception of, 82
　sacrament of vocation, 193
　Rite of, 143, 145
Beatitudes, 39
Beecher, Dr. Henry, 373
Berakah, 166, 168, 178

Bible, the, 38, 320, 321 (*see also* God's Word, Gospels, Good News)
Bishops, 39, 66, 75, 147, 150, 213, 215
Blessed Sacrament, the, 103
Body of Christ, 72, 133, 153, 163, 178, 211, 240
Bread, 114, 154, 164, 168, 184
Brother Joachim, 355, 356
Buddhist worship, 103, 104

Cain and Abel, 235
Calendar, 336, 337, 342
Calvary, 188
Calvinists, 329
Candidates, 137, 139
Cardinal Virtues, 196
Catechesis, 137
Catechist, 139, 140
Catechumen, 138, 161
Catechumenate, 135–138
Catherine of Siena, Saint, 372
Catholic Faith, 42, 135, 138, 309–313
Catholics, 35, 38, 163
Celebrant's chair, 187
Celebration(s), 12, 80, 81, 114, 164, 172, 189, 283–286, 289
Character, 144
Charism, 149
Charity, 196
Charlemagne, 329
Choices, making, 319
Chosen People, 23, 28, 63, 97, 98, 150, 154, 167
Chrism, 145, 150
Christ
　appearances of, 362
　as eternal high priest, 188
　"Law of Love," 335
　mysteries of, in the liturgical year, 283, 284
　mystery of, 144, 148
　Paschal candle, symbolism of the, 299
　presence of, 52
　　the Eucharist, 103, 177, 183, 184
　　the Christian assembly, 173
　　the priest, 173
　redeeming sacrifice of, 177
　revelation in, 26
　risen life of, 144
　as sacrament of God, 124
　sacrifice of, 181, 284
　union with, 71, 292
　(*see also* Jesus)
Christians
　definition of, 125

　as leaven, 328
　life experiences of, 27, 311
　mentality of, 325
　role of, 56
　vocation, 192, 194
　Weltanschauung, 325
　worship, 82
　witnessing, 325
Christian Scriptures, 65
Christmas, 84, 281, 282, 289, 291–293
Church
　community of believers, 29, 71, 138
　definition of, 125
　founded by Christ, 72
　as guide, 38
　guided by Holy Spirit, 65, 72, 74
　hierarchy, 75
　images of, 72
　indefectibility, 76
　infallibility of, 76, 77
　mark of membership in, 144
　marks of, 73
　mission of, 72
　Mother of, 341
　mystery of, 71
　People of God, 74, 75
　a Pilgrim People, 74, 127
　and the power to forgive sin, 259, 260
　as Sacrament, 123, 124
　social teaching of, 48, 56
　and State, 329
　the teaching, 184
　visible sign of God, 72, 77, 125
　year, 281–304
Clement XI, Pope, 411
Cleopas, 40
Colossians, Letter to the, 59, 125, 357, 368
Columbus, Christopher, 35
Commandments, 29, 54, 64, 138
Communion, Eucharistic, 184, 292 (*see also* Eucharist)
Communion of saints, 335–339
Community, need for, 48
Confession, 262, 263 (*see also* Penance, sacrament of; Reconciliation)
Confirmation, 114, 121, 137, 143, 148–151, 193
Confucious, 315
Connelly, Mark, 398
Conscience, 11, 249
Contrition, 20, 261
Corinthians, First Letter to the, 52, 54, 72, 78, 85, 102, 116, 139, 149,

153, 154, 159, 168, 204, 316, 357, 360, 362, 387, 390, 394, 397–399, 404
Corinthians, Second Letter to the, 70, 102, 119, 311, 357, 370, 399
Council of Trent, 68, 395
Conversion, 135, 144, 254, 255, 296
Covenant, 52, 72, 81, 98, 167, 168, 202, 203
Counsel, 150
Creation, 28, 111, 112, 233, 310, 324
Creator, 7, 11, 235
Creed, 66, 67, 74, 171, 395
Cross, the, 52, 297
Cyronics, 375

Dante, 400
David, King, 30
  and Bathsheba, 256
Da Vinci, Leonardo, 310
Deacon, 76, 147, 212
Death, 361–368, 371, 372, 376, 377, 380, 392
Diakonia, 330
Dignity of individual, 51, 74
Discernment, 319
Disciples, 38, 42, 45, 53, 72, 73
Divine Love, Providence, Wisdom, 36
Dostoevski, 400

Easter, 40, 138, 143, 281–283, 299–301
Ecclesiasticus, 357, 387
Election, 137, 283
Elliot, T.S., 400
Emmanual, 45
Emmaus, 40, 42
Encounters with God, 11, 15–19, 23–27, 46, 126
Ephesians, Letter to, 132, 204, 211, 303, 357
Eschatology, 57, 391, 393
Eternal life, 36, 126
Eucharist, the, 121, 143, 153–159
  celebration of community, 153
  chief sacrament of reconciliation, 153
  in the early Church, 175
  as forgiveness of sin, 54
  healing and life, 187
  institution of, 168
  Jesus' presence in, 169, 183
  last sacrament for dying, 275, 372
  Liturgy of, 171, 382
  memorial of the Last Supper, 169
  names for, 166
  offering of, 156, 166
  as part of initiation, 137
  as Passover fulfillment, 165, 168
  people uniting in, 29
  as praise, 82
  purpose of, 169
  a reminder of reconciliation, 181

rite of, 156, 171–174, 177–179
sacrament of unity, 162
as sacrifice, 177
as source of unity, 164
as thanksgiving, 176
union with God, 154, 393
(*see also* Mass, the; Real Presence; Transubstantiation)
Eucharistic participation, 42, 82
Eucharistic prayers, the, 82, 156, 192
Euthanasia, 374, 378
Evil, 66, 226, 240
Ex cathedra, 76, 77
Exodus, Book of, 27, 63, 66, 81, 82, 85, 144, 152

Faith, 6, 10, 12, 29, 42, 66, 103, 196, 317
Fall, the, 233, 235
False Worship, 113
Family of God (*see* People of God)
Fast, 254
  days of, 298
  Lent, season of, 298
Fear, 368
Fear of the Lord, 150
Fellowship, table, 164 (*see also* Eucharist; Mass)
Forgiveness, 251–276
Fortitude, 150, 198
Francis of Assisi, Saint, 312
Freud, Sigmund, 365

Galatians, Letter to, 321
Genesis, Book of, 7, 24, 37, 44, 94, 144, 152, 204, 226, 233, 235, 238, 247, 251, 252, 324, 331
Gifts, 38, 149, 150, 176, 195
Glorified bodies, 118, 362, 394, 395
Gnostics, 65
God
  alienation from, 235, 240
  communication with, 28, 100
  Creator, 7, 36, 111, 235
  Giver and Gift, 48
  goodness of, 24
  in Hebrew Scriptures, 27, 100, 252
  mystery of, 10, 15, 20
  our Reconciliation, 252
  relationship with, 163, 241
  sharing life, 47
God's
  accessibility, 20
  blessing, 123, 153
  call, 37, 73, 320
  challenge, 112
  grace, 73, 92
  living word, 39, 45
  love, 38, 117, 154, 181, 312
  plan, 23, 24, 28, 51, 181
  priestly people, 144
  road map, 38

Self-communication, 28, 195
Self-revelation, 23, 25, 26, 63, 65, 66, 171
union with Mary, 342
will, 47, 74
Word, 48, 63, 100, 114, 174, 284
God's People (*see* People of God)
Godparents, 140, 147, 150
Good Friday, 296
Good News, 46, 65, 72
Gospel, 46
Gospels, the, 40, 119 (*see also* Matthew, Mark, Luke, John)
Grace, 47, 73, 92, 194–196, 198
Grief, 381–384
Guilt, 226

Hamartia, 234
Heart, 54
Heaven, 391, 397–399
Heidegger, Martin, 226
Hebrews, Letter to, 37, 65, 70, 402, 405
Hebrew Scriptures, 27, 39, 100, 111, 150, 155, 174, 233, 256
Hell, 391, 397, 399–401
Henry VIII, King, 364
High Priest, 155
Holy Days, 84
Holy of Holies, 155
Holy Orders, 76, 114, 121, 194, 214–218
Holy Spirit, the, 115
  Apostles dependent on, 66
  bestowed in Baptism, 148
  endowed Church with gifts, 76
  equal to Father and Son, 48
  gifts of, 82, 148, 149
  guides the Church, 47, 66, 72, 194
  laying on of hands, 148, 150
  Pentecost, 52, 81, 124
  as Person, 48
  power of, 52, 76, 77, 148, 183
  presence of, 65, 117, 148, 182, 183
  promise of, 72, 148
  role of, 48, 148
  transforming action of, 183
  universality of, 39
  work of sanctification, 123
Holy Saturday, 299
Holy Thursday, 296
Holy Trinity, 124
Holy Week, 296
Hope, 9, 16, 196
Hosea, 250
Hospices, 363, 375
Hours, Liturgy of the, 282, 287
Human condition, 227, 233

Idolatry, 26
Immaculate Conception, 84, 342, 343
Incarnation, 38, 67, 292

Indefectibility, 76, 77
Indulgences, 404
Infallibility, 76
Initiation, 133–137, 163
Isaac, 23
Isaiah, 100, 149, 150, 197
Israel, 29, 72, 227
Israelites, 24, 28, 30, 77, 81, 98, 167

James, Letter of, 273
James, Saint, 337
Jesus
   ascension of, 72
   birth of, 47, 281
   as companion, 40, 45
   death, 47, 48, 64
   excluded no one, 57
   faith of, 29
   fidelity, 46
   as forgiving Savior, 182
   founder of New Law, 52, 53
   as guide, 38, 45
   as High Priest, 155
   as human, 47
   identified with sinners, 253
   and the Incarnation, 38, 47, 64
   is present, 40
   as Lamb of God, 82
   at the Last Supper, 164, 182
   made God's Word visible, 45, 64
   as the meeting place of God, 45
   presence, 42, 45, 79, 183
   as sacrament of God, 46, 115–119
   and his sacrifice of worship, 183, 187
   saves from sin, 47
   taught God's love, 38, 325
   took on sin of world, 325
   "the way," 65
   and women, 55, 57
Jesus'
   baptism, 143
   healing ministry, 118, 187, 253
   intimacy with God, 181
   moral teaching, 39, 52
   passion for justice, 51, 57
   perfect offering, 276
   redemptive love, 181
   resurrection, 36, 46, 47, 52, 117
   social morality, 52
Jewish
   Berakah, 165, 168, 178
   Feast of Weeks, 81
   Festival of Tents, 81
   Passover, 81, 165, 168
   primitive revelation, 65
   sacred places, 29
   Seder, 165, 167
   symbols, 29, 95
   understanding of sin, 253
John, Gospel of Saint, 38, 46, 48–51, 66, 70, 74, 76, 102, 116, 119, 122, 129, 146, 159, 182, 253, 281, 325, 331, 342, 370, 371, 377, 380, 399
John the Baptist, 112, 143
Joseph, Saint, 337
Journey, 35–42, 226, 362, 371, 393
Judgment, 391, 403, 405
Jung, Carl, 229
Justice, 56, 198
Justin Martyr, Saint, 175

Kerygma, 330
Kierkegaard, Soren, 241
King Jr., Martin Luther, 324
Kingdom of God, 37, 42–46, 51, 54, 57, 72, 118, 326, 329, 393
Knowledge, 150
Koinonia, 330
Kübler-Ross, Elisabeth, 365–368, 381

Laity, 75, 330
Lamech, 235
Last Supper, the, 82, 115, 148, 166–169, 182
Lazarus, 272
Law of Love, 54
Leitourgia, 330
Lent, 282, 295–298
Leo III, Pope, 329
Leo IX, Pope, 329
Life
   bright side, 223, 224
   Christian *Weltanschauung,* 323
   dark side, 225
   through death, 227
   growing in spiritual, 310–312
   imperfection in, 227
   mystery of, 9
   purpose and meaning of, 36
   realities of, 223–229
   spiritual, 310–312
Lindbergh, Charles, 35
Liturgy
   of the Chosen People, 97
   in the Christian community, 176
   definition of, 97
   Eucharistic, 171–179
   of the Hours, 282, 287, 307
   names for Eucharistic, 166
   of the Word, 171, 174
Liturgical
   calendars, 336, 337, 342
   cycle of readings, 174
   dress, 176
   furnishings, 186
   hierarchy of feasts, 286
   readings, cycles of, 174
   seasons and feasts, 282, 283, 286, 289
   year, chart of the, 286
   year, the, 281–283, 336
Liturgical furnishings, 186
Liturgical hierarchy, 286
Liturgical Year, the, 281–283, 336
Liturgy of the Word, 171
   cycle of readings, 174
Liturgy of the Eucharist, 156, 171
   Communion Rite, 172, 176
   Concluding Rite, 172
   Eucharistic Prayer, the, 156, 172, 177, 178, 192
   Preparation of Gifts, 176
Lord's Day, the, 284 (*see also* Sabbath; Sunday)
Lord's Prayer, 179
Love, 38, 42, 72, 196
Loyola, Saint Ignatius, 312, 349
Luke, Gospel of, 40, 44, 46, 49, 54, 57, 59, 70, 115, 116–119, 142, 168, 182, 222, 246, 271, 282, 290, 302, 325, 331, 341, 342, 348, 394, 396, 402, 409
Lutherans, 329

Maccabees, 404
Magellan, Ferdinand, 35
Magisterium, 66, 76
Mandela, Nelson, 35
Mark, Gospel of, 45, 46, 48, 49, 54, 57, 116, 118, 119, 143, 273, 302, 343, 348, 409
Mark, Saint, 337
Martha and Mary, 117
Mary, 198, 334, 335, 341–345
Mass, the, 114
   the Eucharistic Prayer in the, 156, 177
   names for the, 166
   Liturgy of the Eucharist, 176, 177
   Penitential Rite, 242
   (*see also* Eucharist, the)
Matrimony, sacrament of, 121, 194, 201, 205–209
Matthew, Gospel of, 34, 37, 39, 41, 46, 49, 53, 54, 57, 58, 61, 64, 70, 72, 115–119, 123, 125, 142, 143, 148, 163, 178, 182, 184, 197, 204, 21, 253, 273, 282, 290, 302, 328, 330, 331, 340, 343, 364, 370, 396, 402, 405, 406
Matthew, Saint, 337
Meal Celebrations (*see* Eucharist; Passover; Seder)
Messiah, 40, 45, 143
Metanoia, 53, 259
Ministry, 71, 73, 82, 211
Mission, 72, 164
Monarchy, 30
More, Saint Thomas, 364
Moses, 27, 28, 167, 168
Muslim prayer postures, 99
Mystagogia, 137

Mystery, 7–10, 15, 20, 27, 37, 64, 70, 283
(see also *Paschal Mystery*)
Myths, 17

New Covenant, 72
New Testament, 65, 150, 174, 227
Newman, Cardinal, 233
Noah, 24, 252
Numbers, Book of, 282, 348

Old Testament, 54, 174
Ordinary Time, 282, 304
Original sin, 54, 147, 232–235, 242, 270, 343, 345

Palestine, 46
Parousia, 394, 408
Pascal, Blaise, 361
Paschal Mystery, the, 92, 117, 153
   celebration of, in the liturgical year, 82, 284
   Easter Vigil celebration of, 300
   and elements of time, 336
   as the fulfillment of the Passover, 82
   the Last Supper and, 82, 168
Passover
   definition of the, 165, 166
   as different from the Eucharist, 168, 169
   the first, 28, 165, 167
   Jewish ritual of the, 81, 165, 168
   (see also Seder)
Patriarch, 17
Patrick, Saint, 38, 353, 354
Paul, Letters of, 46
Paul, Saint, 66, 203–204
Paul VI, Pope, 324, 325
Peace, 56
Penance
   as atonement, 265
   Lent, the season of, 297
   negative, 297
   positive, 296, 297
Penance, the sacrament of, 114, 121, 259, 260
Pentecost, 52, 81, 82, 124, 282, 302
Penitential Rite, 242
People(s)
   ancient, 281
   Chosen, the, 23, 24, 28, 63, 72, 97, 98, 150, 154
People of faith, 114
People of God, 20, 36, 72, 74, 76, 150, 173, 174, 338
Peter, First Letter of, 72, 402
Peter, Saint, 45, 66, 72, 75, 77
Philippians, Letter to, 322, 393, 394
Philip, Saint, 337
Piaget, Jean, 229
Piety, 150
"Pilgrim Church," 35–39

Pilgrimage, qualities needed for, 36, 37, 42
Polarity, 226
Poles, sacred, 17
Pope
   Bishop of Rome, 39, 75, 76
   infallibility of, 76
Prayer
   contemplative, 333
   of faith, 317
   funeral, 374, 382
   groups, 320
   growing in, 42, 316
   kinds of, 316
   lifeblood of Christian life, 317
   Lord's, 179
   methods of, 109, 316
   personal, 316
   purpose of, 316
   rooted in Scripture, 333
Prayer of Christians (see Hours, Liturgy of the)
Prayer Services, 33, 61
Prayers, short
   Act of Contrition, 279
   Agape Service, 191
   Angelus, 359
   anointing, prayer of, 274
   Augustine's, 354
   Beatitudes prayer service, 61
   Breastplate, Saint Patrick's, 38
   Creator of the day and night, 87
   daily, 87
   Hail Mary, 198
   John 17:11–13, 76
   Liturgy of the Hours, 307
   Native American, 20
   Preface for Ordinary Time IV, 156
   Psalm 23, 106, 389
   Psalm 24, 30
   Psalm 80, 30
   Saint Francis of Assisi's Prayer for Peace, 236
   Seventh Sunday of Easter, 394
   Universal, 411
   Votive Mass of Thanksgiving, 398
Precatechumenate, 137
Prefaces, 156
Presbyters, 212, 213
Presence of God
   in the Ark of the Covenant, 28, 29
   in certain places, 17, 18, 23, 25
   in the Eucharist, 168
   in nature, 111
   revealed to Abraham, 23–25
   (see also God)
Priest, 79, 214, 215
   call to service, 217
   minister of Baptism, 147
   in Rite of Anointing, 272
   as traveling companion, 39, 139

Profession of Faith, 171
Promised Land, 28
Prophets, 63, 65, 97
Prudence, 196
Psalms
   23, 106, 389
   24, 30
   84, 30
   119, 39, 44
   139, 40
   148, 94
Punishment for sin, 399–401
Purgatory, 403, 404
Purification and enlightenment, 404

Quinlan, Karen Ann, 376

Rahner, Karl, 92
Real Presence, 103, 183, 351
Reconciliation, 153, 233, 235, 261
Reconciliation, revised rites of, 266
Redemption, 67, 82, 251
Reformation, 329
Religious orders, 194
Repentance, 260, 295 (see also Atonement; Contrition; Conversion)
Resurrection, 36, 38, 46, 64, 161, 362, 392
Revelation
   authentic, 65
   in daily life, 11
   direct, 63
   of God, 48, 65, 111
   in Jesus, 45, 64
   natural, 11, 63, 111
   to Moses and the Chosen People, 27, 28
   private, 68
   public, 15, 67
Revelation, Book of, 107, 393, 402–406
Rite of Christian Initiation, 134–138, 145
Rites, 374
   definition of, 101
   of the Eucharist, 171
   initiation, 138
   revised
      of communal celebration of the Rite of Reconciliation, 266
      of general confession and absolution, 266
      of individual confession, 266
      of marriage, 206
Rituals, 98, 281
Romans, Letter to, 74, 78, 234, 247, 251, 276, 392, 394
Rosary, the, 131
Rosenthal, Ted, 368

Sabbath, the, 55, 81
Sacrament(s)
  as actions of Christ, 29, 51, 110
  acts of worship, 110, 123
  Church as, 71
  definition of the, 111, 114, 115, 126
  of the dying, 275, 276
  explained, 110–129
  of forgiveness, 259, 260
  gestures of God's love, 111
  of initiation, 133, 143, 152, 193
  institution of the, 113
  Jesus as, of God, 46
  number of the, 97, 113
  as sources of life, 38
  symbols of the, 96, 113
  three last, 275
  time elements of the, 128, 283
  union with God, 71, 393
  of vocation, 194, 201, 269
  (see also Baptism; Eucharist; Holy Orders; Matrimony, sacrament of; Penance, sacrament of; Symbolism)
Sacramentality, 111, 183
Sacramental actions, 114
Sacramental grace, 120
Sacramental people, 112
Sacramental signs, 114, 118
Sacramentals, 120
Sacramentary, the (Missal of Paul VI), 411
Sacred poles, 17
Sacred, the
  ancient people and, 15, 26
  Chosen People and, 24–26
  the Christian community and the presence of, 72
  in the history of the Chosen People, 63–65
  Jesus and, 29
  the monarchy and, 30
  Moses and, 27
  places and, 17–25
  sense of, in nature, 15, 16, 20
Sacrifice
  animal, 183
  of Jesus, 72, 181
  as liberating, 25
Saint(s)
  calendar of, 337
  as companions on journey, 335
  of the United States, 337, 351
  as models of faith, 335
  patron, 353
Salvation, 23, 25, 46, 67, 75, 401
Sanctification, 197
Sanctoral cycle, the, 336
  calendar of saints, 337
Sarah, 37
Savior, 56, 98, 181, 235, 253, 270

Scrutinies, 136
Scripture, 65, 69, 72, 113, 233, 174
  (see also Bible, the)
Second Coming, 406
Seder, Jewish, 165, 167
  (see also Passover; Meal)
Sermon on the Mount, 53
Seton, Elizabeth Bayley, Saint, 337, 350, 351
Shema, 48, 49
Sign(s), 90
  complex, 92
  of healing, 118
  sacramental, 95, 97, 201
  simple, 91, 92
  visible, 23, 28
Sin
  among Apostles, 253
  biblical understanding of, 232, 234
  conditions for, 241, 243, 244
  confession of, 262
  deadly, 54
  definition of, 227, 232, 334
  effects of, 237
  forgiveness of, 259–262
  free to, 54
  insights into, 54, 235–237
  mortal, 54, 240, 263
  original, 54, 147, 232–235, 242
  personal, 237, 240
  problem of, 45
  satisfaction for, 265
  serious, 262–264
  venial, 54, 264
Sirach, Book of, 97, 100, 102
Social Justice, 56
Sodom and Gomorrah, 252
Socrates, 315
Solomon, 30
Son of God, 115
Spiritual
  director, 317
  growth exercises, 320
  living defined, 309, 310
Spirituality
  Catholic, 310–312
  defining, 309, 310
  grounded in humility, 316
  indicators of, 316
  model for, 313
  non-Christian, 315
  sharing with others, 320
Sponsor
  as traveling companion, 140
  in Confirmation, 150
Suffering, 269–276, 378
Suicide, 240
Sunday, 92, 174, 284, 285
Swift, Jonathon, 364
Symbol(s)
  ark as, 95

  of the brazen serpent, 95
  bread as, 96
  definition of, 92
  development of the meaning of, 88
  Easter, 299
  how to encounter, 103
  meaning of, 92
  sacramental, 95
Symbolic
  action, 95, 97, 186
  posture, 99
  words, 98
Symbolism
  of actions, 95
  of the Christmas crib, 292
  of the Easter fire, 299
  of the Easter season, 299
  of Muslim prayer postures, 99
  of the Paschal candle, 95, 299
  of words, 92

Tabernacle, 103
Temperance, 198
Temple of Jerusalem, 30, 177
Ten Commandments, 39, 52–54, 64
Teresa of Avila, Saint, 240
Thanksgiving, 82
Theological virtues, 196
Therese of Lisieux, Saint, 312, 399
Thessalonians, 276, 317, 322
Timothy, First Letter to, 308, 331
Tradition, 71
Transcendence, 9, 11, 25
Transfiguration, 395
Transubstantiation, 184, 185
Trent, the Council of, 329, 395
Triduum, Easter, 282, 283
Trinity, 46, 48
Truth, 17, 23

Union with Christ, 71
Union with God, 36, 171
Unleavened Bread, 168

Vestments, liturgical, 382
Viaticum, 275, 372
Virtues, 195
Vocation, 193, 194, 201, 269

Water, 144, 145
Weltanschauung, 323
Wisdom, 42, 150
Witness, 71
Worldview, 64
Worship, 15, 26, 48, 72, 96, 280

Xavier, Saint Francis, 349

Yahweh, 28, 64
Yurts, 21